P9-CKW-146

# Computer Systems Performance Evaluation and Prediction

L.C.C. SOUTH CAMPUS LIBRARY

# Computer Systems Performance Evaluation and Prediction

Paul J. Fortier
Howard E. Michel

**Digital Press**
**An imprint of Elsevier Science**

Amsterdam • Boston • Heidelberg • London • New York • Oxford • Paris • San Diego
San Francisco • Singapore • Sydney • Tokyo

L.C.C. SOUTH CAMPUS LIBRARY

Digital Press is an imprint of Elsevier Science.

Copyright © 2003, Elsevier Science (USA). All rights reserved.

No part of this publication may be reproduced, stored in a retrieval system, or transmitted in any form or by any means, electronic, mechanical, photocopying, recording, or otherwise, without the prior written permission of the publisher.

 Recognizing the importance of preserving what has been written, Elsevier Science prints its books on acid-free paper whenever possible.

**Library of Congress Cataloging-in-Publication Data**

Fortier, Paul J.
  Computer systems performance evaluation / Paul J. Fortier, Howard E. Michel.
    p. cm.
  ISBN 1-55558-260-5 (pbk. : alk. paper)
    1. Computer systems—Evaluation. 2. Computer systems—Reliability.   I. Michel, Howard. II. Title.

QA76.9.E94 F67 2003
004.2'4—dc21                                                                       2002034389

**British Library Cataloguing-in-Publication Data**

A catalogue record for this book is available from the British Library.

QA
76.9
.E94
F67
2003

The publisher offers special discounts on bulk orders of this book.
For information, please contact:

Manager of Special Sales
Elsevier Science
200 Wheeler Road
Burlington, MA 01803
Tel: 781-313-4700
Fax: 781-313-4882

For information on all Digital Press publications available, contact our World Wide Web home page at: http://www.digitalpress.com or http://www.bh.com/digitalpress

10 9 8 7 6 5 4 3 2 1

Printed in the United States of America

NOV 1 0 2005

This book is dedicated to my wife, Kathleen, and my children, Daniel, Brian, and Nicole, for the encouragement, patience, and support they provided during the development and writing of this book.

—P. J. F.

This book is dedicated to my wife, Linnea, and my daughters, Kristin and Megan, without whose love and understanding this work would not have been possible, and to my parents, Howard and Christine, who gave me a thirst for knowledge and skills to pursue it.

—H. E. M.

# Contents

# *Preface*

This book provides an up-to-date treatment of the concepts and techniques applied to the performance evaluation of computer systems. Computer systems in this context include computer systems hardware and software components, computer architecture, computer networks, operating systems, database systems, and middleware. The motivation in writing this book comes from the inability to find one book that adequately covers analytical, simulation, and empirical testbed techniques applied to the evaluation of systems software and the computer systems that support them. The book can be used as a single- or multiple-semester book about computer systems performance evaluation or as a reference text for researchers and practitioners in the computer systems engineering and performance evaluation fields.

Over the last 10 to 25 years a vast body of knowledge has accumulated dealing with the performance evaluation of computer systems. Specialized measurement tools, both hardware and software, have become available to aid in the testing and monitoring of a computer system's performance, as have numerous simulation languages and tools aimed at specific components of a computer system or for generalized modeling studies. Analytical techniques and tools can be readily acquired and easily applied to the high-level analysis of computer systems and their applications. However, many of these efforts have resulted in disparate solutions whose results are difficult, if not impossible, for the computer engineer or analyst to easily apply to new problems. In addition, most realistic problems require the application of all of these techniques at some level to ascertain the performance of a system and all of its component elements to support rapid product design, development, and fielding.

To consider performance in the design and development stages of a system's inception, modeling must be used, since the intended product system is not yet available for instrumentation and empirical testing. Modeling is relatively well understood by practitioners in the field with the appropriate background; however, these techniques are not as easily transferred to the other members of a design team who could also benefit from such knowledge. The purpose of this book is to make analytical-, simulation-, and instrumentation-based modeling and performance evaluation of computer systems components possible and understandable to a wider audience of computer systems designers, developers, administrators, managers, and users. The book assumes the reader has a familiarity with concepts in computer systems architecture, computer systems software, computer networks, and elementary mathematics including calculus and linear algebra.

The thrust of this book is to investigate the tools for performance evaluation of computer systems and their components and provide an overview of some tools used in practice.

Chapter 1 discusses computer systems performance evaluation and prediction and why these techniques are necessary in today's world of ever decreasing computer systems cost.

In Chapter 2 the components making up computer systems are examined in further detail regarding their architectures, basic hardware elements construction, networks and topologies, operating systems control protocols and architecture, database management systems components and technologies, distributed systems, client/server systems, and other computer systems configurations.

Chapter 3 readdresses the modeling issue from the slant of modeling computer systems, how the various tools have been useful in past systems, and how they can be applied to future endeavors. The basic concepts of time, events, measurements, intervals, response, and independence as they pertain to computer systems are discussed.

Chapter 4 expands on the basic definitions outlined in Chapter 3. Concepts in general measurement processes, service time distributions, scheduling, and response time related to computer systems applications are presented.

Chapter 5 introduces the concepts of probability of events. The concept of sample space and its application to computing basic probability of event occurrence within a sample space are investigated. This is followed by discussions of randomness of events and the relation of this phenomenon to probability. Conditional and joint probability concepts are then presented, as is the concept of random variables and probability distributions.

Chapter 6 builds on the fundamentals of probability into stochastic processes. The basic definition of a stochastic process is provided and then its relationship to the Poisson process is presented. With these definitions, the concept of a pure birth and death process is developed, as are analysis techniques. The chapter then delves into the Markov process and Markov chains as they relate to the analysis of computer systems and their elements.

In Chapter 7, we introduce the concept of a queue and the analysis techniques required to evaluate single queues and networks of queues. These techniques are then developed into modeling techniques applied to computer systems evaluation.

Chapter 8 introduces the concept of simulation modeling. The methods for constructing simulation models from a description of an intended modeled system are presented. The concepts of simulation events and timekeeping are addressed, followed by the application of techniques to computer systems analysis.

Chapter 9 introduces another analysis technique: Petri nets. The basic elements comprising Petri nets are developed and then applied to modeling aspects of computer systems. Fundamental Petri nets are described, as are timed and general Petri nets.

Chapter 10 shows prospective designers or architects how to model future systems configurations using present systems information. The chapter shows how to instrument a system in order to extract and measure systems performance numbers. These measurements and data are then used in development of analysis processes for defining present performance and predicting future performance of computer systems and their components.

Chapter 11 aids the reader in determining what specific analysis tool is best used to evaluate a computer system or component of interest. The modeler is presented material to aid in determining when to use analytical techniques, which technique to use, and when to use it. If analytical techniques are not the best to use, the reader is advised how to select a simulation modeling tool and when to apply it in analyzing a computer system. Finally, the reader is given information regarding when and how to select the appropriate operational analysis tool for measuring and modeling existing computer systems and components.

Chapters 12 through 15 provide analysis examples for specific computer systems components. Computer architecture and component evaluation are provided, as are operating systems, database systems, and network systems modeling and analysis.

# *Introduction*

What is computer systems performance evaluation and prediction and why are these techniques necessary in today's world of ever decreasing computer systems cost? To answer these questions requires the computer engineer to understand how all elements of a computer system come into play in realizing a user's application and its implementation, fielding, and maintenance. All aspects of a computer system's lifetime are important when trying to understand issues of performance. It is not sufficient to simply buy the "best" general-purpose computing machine one can find today and then implement the intended application on it. One must consider how the system will fit into an existing computing facility and what the requirements on the computer system are today and what these requirements will be during the computer system's lifetime.

The most important driving factors when designing, building, and fielding a computer system are that it performs the intended function correctly, performs the intended function efficiently, and does so in a cost-effective manner. Therefore, initial design for correctness may often outweigh performance and cost as the driving force. Having said this, it is often the case that computer systems designers think of performance, cost, and correctness interchangeably. They are, however, different. A correct design may not imply one that performs blazingly fast or is very cost effective. This may be due to other considerations—for example, we may need to trade off performance or perfect correctness to save cost per unit. This is more typical of engineering designs. We do not always (if ever) have the luxury of infinite time and budget, allowing one to design, build, and field the most elegant and optimal-performing computer system. Therefore, we need methods to aid us in developing systems where we can trade off these conflicting items in some logical manner. That is what computer systems performance evaluation is and what this book is all about.

The objective of this book is to describe a variety of performance analysis methods that can be applied to the various stages of a computer system's design, construction, fielding, and life-cycle maintenance. The goal is to provide the reader with an understanding of what tools or techniques are best applied within a computer system's life cycle so that the designer can analyze alternatives and select near optimal solutions for each stage of this process. We cannot hope to be exhaustive in our coverage of all aspects of a computer system's design, nor can we do so for each analysis technique available. Our goal is to provide sufficient detail, examples, and references so that an interested reader can know what performance evaluation technique is best to apply, how to apply this technique to some level of sophistication, and where to look for further detailed information on a topic if it is needed. Our intention is to provide more of an in-depth survey so that the reader can understand how all the various concepts and techniques apply to computer systems tradeoff analysis.

# 1.1    Evolution of computer systems architectures

Computers came into being with the development of the ENIAC computer system in the late 1940s. The early ENIAC and subsequent computers were constructed of vacuum tubes and filled a large room. These early computer systems were dedicated to a single task and had no operating system. The power of these early computers was less than that of the handheld calculators in use today. These computers were used mainly for ballistic missile trajectory projections and military research. The architecture of these early computers was based on the von Neumann stored program, single-stream instruction flow architecture (Figure 1.1). This basic architecture and philosophy is still in use today in most computer systems.

These early computer systems had no sophisticated operating systems, databases, networks, or high-level programming languages to simplify their operations. They stored program instructions and data needed for computation in the same place. Instructions were read from memory one at a time and were mostly associated with the loading and storage of program data from memory to registers where the data were to be operated on. Data in these early systems were not shared by programs. If a program needed data produced by another program, these data items were typically copied into a region near the end of a program's space, and the end addresses were hard-coded for use by the application program in which they were embedded.

A user application resides on a computer system. The computer system provides the physical medium on which the data and programs are stored

**Figure 1.1**
*Basic computer system.*

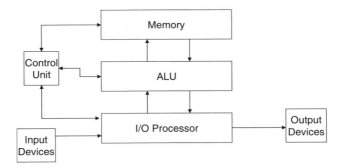

and the processing capacity to manipulate the stored data. A processing unit of a computer system consists of five main elements: the memory, an arithmetic logic unit, an input unit, an output unit, and a control element. The memory unit stores both the data for programs and the instructions of a program that manipulates stored data.

The program's individual elements or instructions are fetched from the memory one at a time and are interpreted by the control unit. The control unit, depending on the interpretation of the instruction, determines what computer operation to perform next. If the instruction requires no additional data, the control indicates to the arithmetic logic unit what operation to perform and with what registers. (See Figure 1.1.)

If the instruction requires additional data, the control unit passes the appropriate command to the memory (MAR, memory address register) to fetch a data item from memory (MDR, memory data register) and to place it in an appropriate register in the ALU (data register bank) (Figure 1.2).

**Figure 1.2**
*Low-level memory access.*

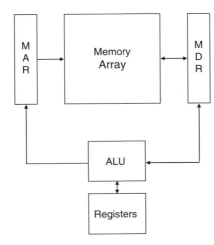

This continues until all required operands are in the appropriate registers of the ALU. Once all operands are in place, the control unit commands the ALU to perform the appropriate instruction—for example, multiplication, addition, or subtraction. If the instruction indicated that an input or output were required, the control element would transmit a word from the input unit to the memory or ALU, depending on the instruction. If an output instruction were decoded, the control unit would command the transmission of the appropriate memory word or register to the output channel indicated. These five elements comprise the fundamental building blocks used in the original von Neumann computer system and are found in most contemporary systems in some form or another.

A computer system is comprised of the five building blocks previously described, as well as additional peripheral support devices, which aid in data movement and processing. These basic building blocks are used to form the general processing, control, storage, and input and output units that make up modern computer systems. Devices typically are organized in a manner that supports the application processing for which the computer system is intended—for example, if massive amounts of data need to be stored, then additional peripheral storage devices such as disks or tape units are required, along with their required controllers or data channels.

To better describe the variations within architectures we will discuss some details briefly—for example, the arithmetic logic unit (ALU) and the control unit are merged together into a central processing unit, or CPU. The CPU controls the flow of instructions and data in the computer system. Memories can be broken down into hierarchies based on nearness to the CPU and speed of access—for example, cache memory is small, extremely fast memory used for instructions and data actively executing and being used by the CPU. The primary memory is slower, but it is also cheaper and contains more memory locations. It is used to store data and instructions that will be used during the execution of applications presently running on the CPU—for example, if you boot up your word processing program on your personal computer, the operating system will attempt to place the entire word processing program in primary memory. If there is insufficient space, the operating system will partition the program into segments and pull them in as needed.

The portion of the program that cannot be stored in memory is maintained on a secondary storage device, typically a disk drive. This device has a much greater storage capacity than the primary memory, typically costs much less per unit of storage, and has data access times that are much slower than the primary memory. An additional secondary storage device is the tape drive unit. A tape drive is a simple storage device that can store massive amounts of data—again, at less cost than the disk units but at a reduced access speed. Other components of a computer system are input and output units. These are used to extract data from the computer and provide these data to external devices or to input data from the external device. The external devices could be end-user terminals, sensors, information network ports, video, voice, or other computers.

A computer system's architecture is constructed using basic building blocks, such as CPUs, memories, disks, I/O, and other devices as needed.

In the following sections we will examine each of the components of a computer system in more detail, as we examine how these devices can be interconnected to support data processing applications.

## 1.1.1   CPU architectures

The central processing unit (CPU) is the core of a computer system and consists of the arithmetic logic unit (ALU) and the control unit. The ALU can come in a variety of configurations—from a single simple unit, up to extremely complex units that perform complex operations. The primary operation of the ALU is to take zero or more operands and perform the function called for in the instruction. In addition to the ALU, the CPU consists of a set of registers to store operands and intermediate results of computations and to maintain information used by the CPU to determine the state of its computations. For example, there are registers for the status of the ALU's operation, for keeping count of the instruction to be performed next, to keep data flowing in from memory or out to memory, to maintain the instruction being executed, and for the location of operands being operated on by the CPU. Each of these registers has a unique function within the CPU, and each is necessary for various classes of computer architectures. A typical minimal architecture for a CPU and its registers is shown in Figure 1.3 and consists of a primary memory connected to the CPU via buses. There are registers in the CPU for holding instructions, instruction operands, and results of operations; a program location counter, containing either the location in memory for instructions or operands, depending on the decoding of instructions; and a program counter containing the location of the next instruction to perform.

The CPU also contains the control unit. The control unit uses the status registers and instructions in the instruction register to determine what functions the CPU must perform on the registers, ALU, and data paths that make up the CPU. The basic operation of the CPU follows a simple loop,

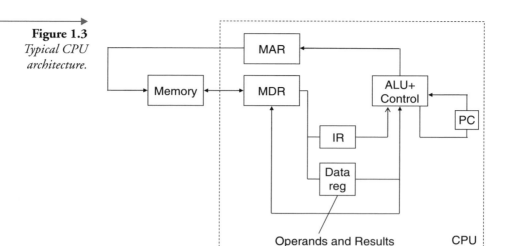

**Figure 1.3**
*Typical CPU
architecture.*

called the instruction execution cycle (Figure 1.4). There are six basic functions performed in the instruction loop: instruction fetch, instruction decode, operand effective address calculation, operand fetch, operation execution, and next address calculation. This execution sequence represents the basic functions found in all computer systems. Variations in the number of steps are found based on the type and length of the instruction.

## 1.1.2   Instruction architectures

There are numerous ideas about how to organize computer systems around the instruction set. One form, which has come of age with the new powerful workstations, is the reduced instruction set computer (RISC), where each instruction is simple, but highly optimized. On the far spectrum of architectures is the very long word instruction architecture, where each

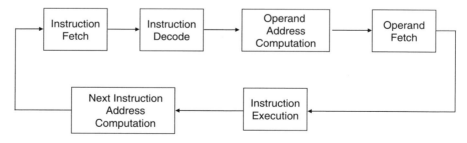

**Figure 1.4**    *Instruction cycle execution.*

instruction may represent an enormous processing function. A middle
ground is the complex instruction set computer (CISC).

### Memory-addressing schemes

There are also numerous ways in which to determine the address of an oper-
and from an instruction. Each address computation method has its benefits
in terms of instruction design flexibility. There are six major types of
addressing computation schemes found in computers: immediate, direct,
index, base, indirect, and two-operand. We will examine these further in
Chapter 2.

## 1.1.3   Memory architectures

Generally, a computer system's memory is organized as a regular structure,
addressed using the contents of a memory address register and with data
transferred through a memory data register (Figure 1.5). Memory architectures are based on the organization of the memory words. The simplest
form is a linear two-dimensional structure. A second organization is the
two-and-a-half-dimensional architecture.

## 1.1.4   I/O architectures

Input and output architectures are used by computer systems to move
information into or out of the computer's main memory and have evolved
into many forms. I/O architectures typically rely on the use of one element
of the computer as the router of I/O transfers. This router can be the CPU,
the memory, or a specialized controller. Chapter 2 discusses these architectures in greater detail.

**Figure 1.5**
*CPU memory*
*access.*

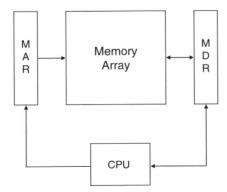

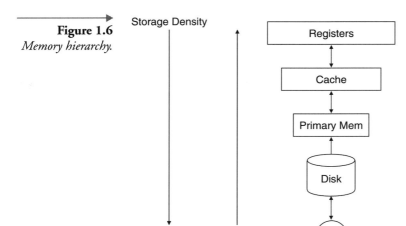

**Figure 1.6**
*Memory hierarchy.*

## 1.1.5 Secondary storage and peripheral device architectures

I/O devices connect to and control secondary storage devices. Primary memory has grown over the years to a fairly high volume, but still not to the point where additional data and program storage is not needed. The storage hierarchy (Figure 1.6) consists of a variety of data storage types. From the highest-speed memory element, cache, to the slowest-speed elements, such as tape drives, the tradeoff the systems architect must make is the cost and speed of the storage medium per unit of memory. Typical secondary storage devices include magnetic tape drives, magnetic disk drives, compact optical disk drives, and archival storage devices such as disk jukeboxes.

Magnetic tape information storage provides a low-cost, high-density storage medium for low-access or slow-access data. An improvement over tape storage is the random access disk units, which can have either removable or internal fixed storage media. Archival storage devices typically are composed of removable media configured into some array of devices.

## 1.1.6 Network architectures

Networks evolved from the needs of applications and organizations to share information and processing capacity in real time. Computer networks provide yet another input and output path for the computer to receive or send information. Networks are architected in many ways: They could have a central switching element, share a central storage repository, or could be connected using intelligent interface units over a communications medium such as telephone wires or digital cables. The configuration used depends on the degree of synchronization and control required, as well as the physical distribution between computers. Chapter 2 will examine some architectures and topology configurations for networked computer systems.

## 1.1.7    Computer architectures

Computer architectures represent the means of interconnectivity for a computer's hardware components as well as the mode of data transfer and processing exhibited. Different computer architecture configurations have been developed to speed up the movement of data, allowing for increased data processing. The basic architecture has the CPU at the core with a main memory and input/output system on either side of the CPU (see Figure 1.7). A second computer configuration is the central input/output controller (see Figure 1.8). A third computer architecture uses the main memory as the location in the computer system from which all data and instructions flow in and out. A fourth computer architecture uses a common data and control bus to interconnect all devices making up a computer system (see

**Figure 1.7**
*Basic computer architecture.*

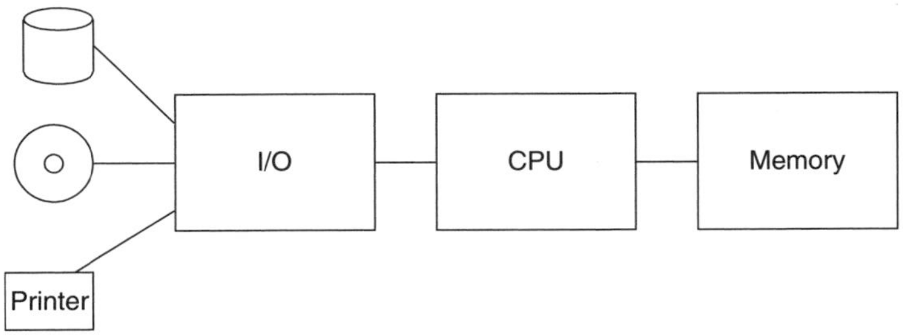

**Figure 1.8**
*Alternative computer architecture.*

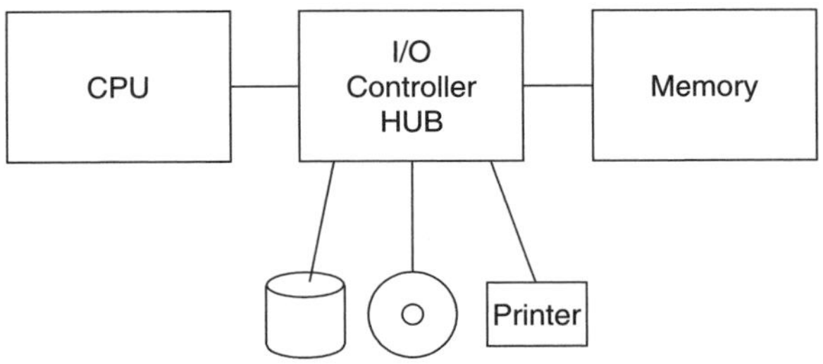

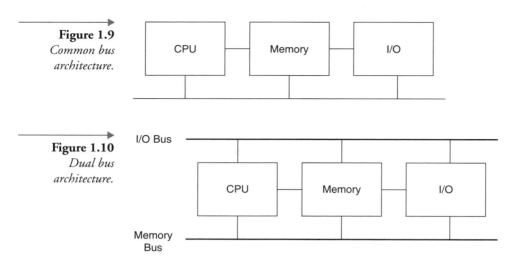

**Figure 1.9**
*Common bus
architecture.*

**Figure 1.10**
*Dual bus
architecture.*

Figure 1.9). An improvement on the single shared central bus architecture is the dual bus architecture. This architecture either separates data and control over the two buses or shares them to increase overall performance (see Figure 1.10).

We will see how these architectures and elements of the computer system are used as we continue with our discussion of system architectures and operations.

## 1.2    Evolution of database systems

Database systems have been with us since the 1960s as research vehicles (first-generation products wrapped around the hierarchical and network data models) and since the mid 1980s as fully functional products using the relational data model. Since these early beginnings, database systems have evolved from simple repositories for persistent information to very powerful tools for information management and use.

Database systems have been of interest to the computer systems performance analyst and to computer systems applications developers since the earliest days of commercial computers. Early computer systems lacked extensive on-line data storage (primary memory as well as secondary disk storage), forcing systems architects and developers to rely heavily on externally archived information (typically stored in tape drives). Initial data storage repositories were constructed using simple direct addressing schemes that linked specific storage to a specific device and specific location on that device. For example, to extract a piece of information an application needed to know what device a specific piece of information was stored on (e.g., disk 01) and the exact address on that device (e.g., sector 05, track 22, offset 255, length 1,024). Each device had its own unique way of storing, accessing, and retrieving information, making it very difficult to port applications from one place to another.

These initial repositories evolved to more robust file management systems, driven by a move toward simplifying the application/system interface. The drive to simplification was motivated by application developers and operating systems evolutions to remove the complexity of the typical storage hierarchy from the user/developer side and place it in the operating system's side. The motivation was to do the interface at the operating system level to simplify the interface. The initial file systems offered a simple interface, where applications could access persistently stored information logically by file name instead of physically by specific address paths. These initial file management systems offered the means for an application to logically persistently store information for future retrieval and use. Initial file systems offered a simple interface and implementation to store and retrieve information using coarse semantic means. One could open a file, read the record-oriented contents of a file, write a record or entire file, and close the file. Information within the file had no meaning to the control software of the operating system or to the database system. The file management software knew about entry points to a file, or subset of a file, but nothing concerning details of information content within the file. These early file systems and their crude access schemes served the needs of early mainframe machines, where jobs were run in a sequence and no sharing between jobs was explicitly required at run time.

The advent of multiuser operating systems, and multiuser applications' evolving needs for concurrent access to information stored in file systems, spawned the need for database systems to evolve from single user persistent stores into multiuser concurrent database systems. Multiuser and multiprocessing computer systems demanded that stored information within the application's computer system's file system be available for sharing. In addition, this information was not only to be shared, but was to be done so in a dynamic manner. Information storage, access, and retrieval—within such evolving systems—needed more controls in order that information could be shared, yet remain correct and consistent from the perspective of all applications using it.

One problem with information sharing within the context of these new systems was security—how do you allow only the owner, or group of users, to access or alter a file while still providing for access by others? In concert with this issue was access integrity—how to keep data intact and correct while multiple users access, modify, add, or delete information. Initially, file systems addressed most of these concerns by adding access controls, such as locks, and access lists to file managers to control such access, but these did not accomplish the intended goals. Though these were admirable enhancements, they were far too crude to allow applications true sharing of on-line data. Files needed to be further decomposed into finer-grained elements if finer concurrency of access were to be achieved. Simple file-level locking resulted in longer waits and reduced availability of data for use by other applications.

To alleviate these problems, file systems added finer-grained definitions of stored information. For example, files evolved from unstructured data to structured, record-oriented collections of information, where each record had a specific head and tail, as well as semantic meaning for the file system and its organization. At first, semantic meanings may have simply represented the order of occurrence in a file system. Semantics of data dealing with structure led to added organization of files by using records as the fundamental units of organization for applications-required information and for environmental storage. Records provided a mechanism from which to construct more complex storage structures. Records became the granularity of storage used to construct file organization as well as access schemes. It became easy to find a record within a file, since files became composed of collections of records. Through such means, access controls such as record-locking techniques evolved to control how access was to be allowed to these files and encased records.

It was only a matter of time before records, grouped into files, took on further semantic meaning and became the focal point for organizing information. For example, to define a group of students, a set of records could be defined so that each record holds the information needed to define a single student. To organize the students in a way that the application can use them, a file system could allocate one region of a file for storage of these records or could provide a means to link related records in a chain using some control strategy.

This structural concept for information focused around records led to one of the first database system storage concepts and access schemes, referred to as the network database model. The network database model organizes data as linked lists or chains of related information. In the network data model, any information that has a relationship to some other piece of stored information must have a physical link to the related pieces of information. The network database structuring model was formalized into the CODASYL database language standard and was widely implemented but never found acceptance as a true standard. Network database systems became the mainstay of most early information systems until the advent of the relational database system in the 1970s. The network database systems began to lose their luster in the mid to late 1970s into the early 1980s due to their inherent complexity and limitations. The network model requires information to be physically linked if a logical relationship between information is required. This implied that as the number of logical relationships between information items increased so did the required number of physical links to capture these logical relationships.

This added metadata requirement caused the complexity of applications to increase exponentially in size, making this model a poor choice for any system that would grow and change over time. The loss of a single link could result in the database becoming useless to the original application it was developed for. The complexity of the chains constructed within an application over time made the maintenance of such systems very expensive. Another detriment to this database model is encountered when one attempts to access stored information within this data model. To access information, the database must be entered at a specific entry point, followed by the traversal of data chains (paths) defined by the encoded relationships between the data items. This does not mean that the needed information will be found; the paths could be traversed and end in the end of the path being encountered with no data being found. There are no ways to bypass paths. To find specific data items one must traverse the path leading to this item and no other, if the information is to be located.

These and other limitations with the network database model led to the gradual demise of the model. An issue to consider with the network model is its legacy. Even though this model has not been the prevalent model of new applications over the last 20 years, there are still many databases constructed from this model due to its early entrance and long use in the information community. It is highly unlikely that all or even a majority of this information will be rehosted in a newer data model such as the relational model. Due to this large volume of legacy information, this model must be understood from its impact on the past, present, and future of information management systems. New systems, if they have a reach beyond their local system, will possibly be required to interact with such legacy systems, necessitating the understanding of their impact on performance.

The network database system's demise began with the development and publication of Codd's relational database model and seminal paper published in the early 1970s. The fundamental premise of the paper was that all information in the database system can be formed into tables called relations. These relations have a regular structure, where each row of the table has the same format. Relationships between tables are defined using concepts of referential integrity and constraints. The fundamental way one operates on these tables is through relational algebra and calculus techniques. This paper's publication was followed by an experimental system built by IBM called system R and another developed by university research called Ingress. These early developments had as their goal the proof of the relational database's theories. The relational model on paper showed much promise, but constructing software to make it real was a daunting task. A fundamental major difference in the two models is found in their model for data acquisition. The network model is a procedural model, where a user tells the system how to find the needed information, whereas the relational model is nonprocedural, where one states what one wants and lets the "system" find the information.

This shift in the fundamental way the database finds information was a very significant one—the ramifications of which the industry still improves upon. A fundamental need in the new model was system services to find information. This system service is called "query processing." The fundamental function of query processing is to determine, given a user's query, how to go about getting the requested piece of information from the relations stored in the database. Query processing led to further improvements in accessing information from the database. One primary improvement was in query optimization. The goal of query optimization is to find ways to improve on the cost of extracting information from the database and do this in real time.

These early relational database systems were instrumental in the development of many concepts wrapped around improving concurrency of access in database systems. The concept of concurrent access was not present in early network-based databases. The theory of serializability as a correctness criterion evolved from the relational model and its fundamental theories, motivated by a need to have correct and concurrent access to stored information. The serializability theory and concurrency control led to further improvements in database technology. In particular, concepts for transactions followed next—along with theories and concepts for recovery. The fundamental tenet of transactions and transaction processing is that they execute under the control of the "ACID" properties. These properties dictate that transactions execute "atomically" (all or nothing), "consistently" (all constraints on data correctness are valid), "isolated" (transactions execute as if done in isolation), and "durable" (effects of transaction execution are not alterable except by another transaction's execution). To guarantee these properties requires concurrency control and recovery.

The relational model and relational databases led the way during the 1980s in innovations and growth within the database industry. Most of the 1980s was spent refining the theories of correctness for databases and for their fundamental operation: the transaction. In addition to these fundamental improvements, the 1980s saw the improvement of the modeling capability of the model.

This period was followed by another, which we'll call the object-oriented period. During this period of time, the late 1980s and early 1990s, the need of applications developers to more closely match the data types of their applications with those provided by the database drove the need for more semantic richness of data specification and operations on these data. The object-oriented databases of this period met this need. The problem with these early object-oriented databases was that they did not possess some of the fundamental concepts developed during the evolution and growth of the relational database systems.

The late 1990s and the beginning of the twenty-first century saw the merger of the relational model with the object-oriented database model—forming the object relational database model. This model was embraced by the U.S. and international standards bodies as one worth refining and supporting for growth. The major national and international vendors have embraced this model as the next great database evolution and are all presently building products around the newly adopted standard with some of their own extensions.

It appears after this revolution that the next major change in the database arena will probably come in the area of transactions and transaction processing. The conventional model wrapped around the concept of a flat or single-tiered transaction execution segment controlled strictly by the ACID properties may be altered. There is much research and development looking at a variety of alternative execution models and theories of correctness that may lead us into the next decade of database improvements.

## 1.3   Evolution of operating systems

A modern operating system is computer software, firmware, and possibly hardware that interact at a low level with the computer system's hardware components to manage the sharing of the computer's resources among various software applications. The goal of this piece of systems software is to allow for the fair sharing of these resources among any and all active jobs within the system. An operating system runs as the most privileged of software elements on the system and requires basic hardware support for interrupts and timers to effect control over executing programs.

Operating systems evolved over a long period of time, driven as much by the hardware available as the needs of the applications running on the machines. In the beginning, there were few tools available to enhance the usefulness of a computer to the general populace, and they were relegated to be used by a select few who could trudge through the translation of real problems into sequences of simple machine instructions. These machine instructions were at first in microcode (the lowest form of software) or assembly code. In either case there were no controls over what the coder did with the computer system. These early coders required great talent to be able to master the art of changing a problem such as missile guidance into the software required to carry it out. These early coders simply loaded the software into the machine at a specific memory location and indicated to the hardware to begin processing the job. The machine would continue processing this same job until the machine detected an error (such as an overflow) or there was a stop command issued to the machine. There were no automated means to switch from one job to another.

The first operating system problem tackled by systems programmers to change this situation was to develop a means to transition from one job to another processing job without the need to stop the machine, enter the new program, and start it up again, as was the case in the past. The monitor or batch operating system concept provided the solution to this early defined problem. These early systems offered means for operators to load several jobs at one time; the computer system then performed them in a sequential manner. As one job completed, the operating systems software would take over control of the machine's hardware, set it up for the next job, and then release control back to the new job, which then ran to completion. Although this was a step in the right direction, the expensive computer systems of the day were not being efficiently utilized. New devices were being developed to aid in input and output (early terminals) and storage (improved disk drives, tape units), but the control mechanisms to use them efficiently still were not there.

These new computer peripheral devices, which were coming into place in the 1970s, provided the impetus for systems designers to find ways to make them more fully utilized within the system. One of the biggest drivers was the input/output terminal. These demanded that the system provide mechanisms for the operators to input code and data and to request compilation, linking, loading, and running of their jobs as if they were running alone on the machine, when in reality there would be many users on the machine concurrently. The system management service developed to meet these demands was called the executive program.

The executive program provided policies and mechanisms for programs and devices such as terminals to run concurrently under control of the executive's watchful eye. The function was to control interaction so that devices did not interfere with each other in running their jobs on the machine. They still, however, pretty much ran one at a time on the machine. This crude operating system provided many of the rudimentary services expected from an operating system and became the vehicle upon which many innovations were developed.

Research carried out on these early executive programs led to supervisor programs, which took on more functions from the systems operators and coders. The supervisor programs provided rudimentary services for "swapping" of programs from primary memory and control over the CPU based on the concept of time slices. Following the success of these developments came the first true operating systems in the 1960s. Many of the services found in modern operating systems today have their roots in this early system.

Generically, an operating system provides the following services:

1.    Hardware management (interrupt handling, timer management)

2.    Interprocess synchronization and communications

3.    Process management

4.    Resource allocation (scheduling, dispatching)

5.    Storage management and access (I/O)

6.    Memory management

7.    File management

8.    Protection of system and user resources

An operating system begins with the management of a computer system's hardware. Hardware management requires the ability to set limits on the holding of resources and the ability to transfer control from an executing program back to the operating system. These functions are realized through the use of hardware timers and interrupt services. A hardware timer is a counter that can be set to a specific count (time period). When the time expires, an interrupt signal is released, which stops the processor, saves the processor's state (saves all active register contents, ALU registers, status registers, stack pointers, program counters, instruction registers, etc.), and turns control over to an interrupt service routine. The interrupt service routine examines the contents of predefined registers (e.g., the CPU status register or a predefined interrupt register) or sets memory locations and determines what operations are to be performed next. Typically, control is immediately turned over to the operating system's kernel for servicing of the interrupt.

The goals of these services and developments had one common thread: to make more efficient use of computing facilities. They were meant to provide convenient interfaces to users while hiding the details of the bare machine from them. The operating system provides for transparent use of computing resources, relieving users and operators from the burden of needing to know the particular system's configuration. The operating system also provided users and systems programmers protection from accidental or malicious destruction, theft, or unauthorized disclosure.

The most obvious accomplishment of an operating system is the hiding of the computing platform's details and the optimal use of resources. Users need not know what particular device they are using, only that they need one of a certain class of device (e.g., a tape or disk). This shields users from the problems of down components. If it were necessary to specify a particular device that was not available, work might not be able to go on. If the user can specify a class of device, any one of that type can meet the need, increasing the ability of the user to get the job done.

The systems programmers and the hardware and software researchers did not end their quest for perfection at this point. There were more areas to be looked at, and system problem areas needed to have solutions developed for them. Sharing of resources introduced its own set of problems. As systems became more usable, more uses were envisioned and implemented. Systems began to meet the raw processing capacity of the machines. Designers needed to find ways to get additional resources to improve processing cycles for user applications. Software developers looked to streamline computational complexity of the operating system, providing some relief. Hardware designers improved the computational capacity of the systems through improved architectures and instruction execution schemes. All such improvements, however, were only temporary.

The research and development community began to look at ways to improve performance within fixed or marginally improving processor performance. The problem is that no matter how much we improve the performance of a processor, it will still have a limited amount of available cycles for applications and required systems services. The initial concept looked at was not to grow single processing power, which is limited, but to instead add entire new processors. This concept was initially examined as part of architecture improvements in the 1980s. The multiple processors could each be set up to run their local operating systems, with added services to allow remote systems to request services (resources) from another machine that was not busy or not fully utilized. By using these systems calls, multiple processors running separate operating systems could be synchronized to perform a single, larger processing task in much less time. The effective improvement in performance, however, is not simply the multiplicative factor of the number of machines but some fraction of this computation. This is due to the added overhead to synchronize the operations of the loosely coupled systems.

These systems led to further research and experimentation. If loosely coupled machines could be collected and grouped together to perform larger functions, why couldn't they be grouped in a tightly bound fashion to perform large computational applications that could not be done on a single machine? These new systems were called "distributed processors." What distinguishes these classes of systems from their loosely coupled multiprocessor counterparts is the degree of cohesiveness the processors exhibit. The processor's operating system is a single global operating system, which is spread across the machines in a variety of ways. In one case the entire operating system can be replicated on each site, with individual processors only needing additional state information to indicate what their function is and what their state presently is in relation to the entire distributed systems state. The second configuration uses the concept of partitioning the operating systems components across the various sites of the distributed computer system. Each processor then has a specific function—for example, process scheduling or device access.

These new operating systems concepts are still being examined in the realm of research and have not as yet found their way into the mainstream systems. On the other hand, we have client/server processing, which uses a form of the multiprocessing operating systems to provide for remote access to resources. They differ, however, in not enforcing strict synchronization requirements on client/server processing. Many additional protocols have been developed to provide this form of processing, which is prevalent in most products one uses today for computing remotely over the Web.

## 1.4   Evolution of computer networks

The term *network* can mean many different things. It can imply an interconnection of railway tracks for the rail network; highways and streets for transportation networks; telephone lines and switching centers for the phone network; coaxial lines for the cable television network; fiber lines for cable communications networks; or the interconnection of service centers, businesses, and so on to form a network. All of these configurations refer to the means to tie together various resources so that they may operate as a group, realizing the benefits of numbers, sharing, and communications in such a group.

In computer systems terminology of a network is a combination of interconnected computing equipment and programs used for moving information (and computations) between points (nodes) in the network where it may be generated, processed, stored, or used in whatever manner is deemed appropriate. The interconnection may take on many forms, such as dedicated links, shared links, telephone lines, microwave links, and satellite links. Networks in this sense form a loose coalition of devices that share information. This was one of the first uses of a network, although it was not the last. Users found that the network could offer more than just information sharing; it could offer other services for remote job execution and ultimately distributed computing.

The earliest concept of a network was of a loose binding together of devices or resources for sharing. An early computer communications network that exhibited these traits was the ARPANET. ARPANET was first brought on-line in 1969 as a research tool to investigate long-haul network issues and to provide a tool for research and development solutions. It has evolved into the Internet, connecting millions of computers over local area networks, metropolitan area networks, and other wide area networks. ARPANET provided the vehicle for early research into communications protocols dealing with congestion, control, routing, addressing, remote invocation, distributed computing, distributed operating systems and services, and many other areas.

The reasons for using networks such as ARPANET were to provide greater availability and access to a wider range of devices. Early applications of computers dealt with performing engineering tasks and major data processing functions. As the technology of computers changed, and as researchers and users alike added more and more applications, information access and manipulation took on greater emphasis.

Earlier networks provided the necessary information exchange services but were limited to basically just this service. The information availability stimulated more imaginative uses of this information. As this occurred and the technology of networks improved, new applications arose. These new applications not only used information exchange but also remote job execution. It began simply as sending a batch job down the link to a less busy host, having the job completed there, and then shipping the results back to the originator.

This sufficed for awhile, but it still did not provide the real-time or interactive environments that users were beginning to become accustomed to, including more advanced protocols and network operating systems to provide further services for remote job invocation and synchronization. The era of the local area network was coming. The wide area networks' biggest shortfall was in throughput or turnaround time for jobs and interprocessor communications. Because of the wide distances, delays of seconds were commonplace and caused added overhead in performing otherwise simple tasks. Network designers saw the need to provide another link in the network: the local area network.

Local area networks began showing up on the networking landscape in the early to mid 1970s as mostly research activities in universities and government laboratories. It was not until Ethernet was released in the mid 1970s that LANs became more widely available. Since that time, numerous LAN designs have been produced to fit an extremely wide spectrum of user requirements—for example, the fiber ring. Additionally, standards have evolved, providing basic LAN topologies and their services to a greater number of users.

Local area networks are finding their way into all aspects of modern society. We find them in our homes through cable modems and phone modems, automobiles via wireless technologies, banking (e.g., ATMs), schools via Internet connections, businesses, government, and industry. There are not too many aspects of information exchange and data processing in which a LAN cannot be found. Local area networks and their associated technologies represent one of the great growth areas of the 1990s and early 2000s. As more and more LANs become available, so will new products and uses for them. LANs are used to connect all personal computers in offices, classrooms, factory floors, retail establishments, and now even many homes. They are used in these environments to send memoranda, issue directives, schedule meetings, transmit documents, send e-mail, discover new information, and process large volumes of data concurrently at many sites.

LANs are used to link factory robots together with area and factory controllers. They provide sensor data, control data, and feedback to the control centers, while at the same time providing a vehicle to issue production changes and notices to users and robots alike. A fine example of a local area network providing diverse services to the users is seen in Walt Disney World. Disney uses LANs and computers to monitor all aspects of services, including fire protection, scheduling, ride management, on-line information, security, personnel services, and a plethora of other park management functions. Large banks, such as the World Bank, have adopted LANs as the means to interconnect their various local sites into smaller networks linked together by wide area networks. However, the LAN is not for everyone.

Network evolution has not stopped there. As wireless technology has improved, so has the interest in networking vendors to provide their services to users of these domains. Wireless networks began fairly quietly in the 1970s with the Aloha net as the foundation. Since then, wireless phone network development has opened the door for computer networks. Today one of the great growth areas in networking will be in further developing wireless networks and integrating these into existing LAN and WAN networks to provide an even wider array of applications to the wireless cell phone community.

## 1.5    Need for performance evaluation

Selecting a specific computer architecture for an application, an operating system, a database system, or a wide area or local area network system that will provide the optimum service to users requires up-front analysis and knowledge. As indicated, a specific computer architecture, operating system, database, and/or LAN are productivity-enhancing tools, but, as with other tools, if they are not used properly, they can actually decrease productivity. An operating system can provide a means to increase concurrency of access and to improve overall system resource utilization or it can become a bottleneck by blocking access. A database system can provide the means to more efficiently share information among many applications in a correct and concurrent manner or it can cause extensive blocking of information by dropping data availability. A LAN can provide a means to streamline information processing and eliminate redundancies, but it may also deter users from logging on because of link or protocol problems. To the common user, operating systems resource management, data processing, data extraction, data communications, and local area networks are a black hole of protocols, access schemes, routing algorithms, cabling and topology issues, and service problems. To alleviate these problems, the users should be educated about the basics of computer architecture, operating systems, database systems, and local area network technology and be provided with metrics and tools with which they can adequately wade through the myriad issues and select a computer system mapped to their needs.

When you look at the many options available for prospective computer systems purchasers to evaluate, you can see the reasons for their distress. A computer system can be very simple, providing just a single central processing unit, single primary memory bank, a single I/O channel for peripheral device access, and a single network link to interconnect to another machine. Conversely, the computer system can be highly elaborate, with multiple processors; cache memory; a high-tech associative memory system; SCSI controlled disk banks; specialized graphics engines; and possibly its own distributed operating system, protocols, and services. The prospective computer system purchaser must decide what type of motherboard(s) is required and how many of these; what type of memory and its architecture; what form of operating system, database system, and network cabling is necessary; and the types of electrical characteristics, signaling scheme, protocol for controlling transfers, routing schemes, topology of interconnection, reliability requirements, system and component fault tolerance if necessary, services, interface characteristics and requirements, and numerous other aspects. The extent of control, understanding, and compatibility with other equipment a user requires will decide which of these and other issues need to be addressed before a computer system is purchased.

## 1.6    Role of performance evaluation in computer engineering

Presently there is a great deal of interest and activity in the design and use of computer systems, such as centralized, vector, parallel, distributed, and client/server architectures. These computer systems are being researched, developed, produced, and marketed by individuals and organizations from government, industry, and academia. These research and development activities are motivated by the rapidly changing technologies of devices, software and systems, increased performance requirements, increasing complexity and sophistication of basic building blocks, peripherals, interconnections and control, the constant demand for improved reliability and availability, and the increasing reliance of organizations on the use of computer facilities in all aspects of business.

Present desktop computer systems provide more features than were previously available in a single, large time-sharing system. Specifically, some features include the sharing of resources on a much more global scale, as well as the fulfillment of system requirements such as expandability, flexibility, availability, reliability, reconfigurability, fault tolerance, graceful degradation, responsiveness, speed, throughput capacity, logical complexity, and ease of development (modularity). Another appealing feature of contemporary computer systems is their ability to bring the computing power to the user without sacrificing the ability to get at all the available information assets from the business.

The optimal design and/or selection of a computer system is, therefore, of the utmost importance if the target computing facility is to provide new and improved services over what is presently available to the target domain application. But how does one go about doing this? What techniques and tools are available for this purpose? These are among the questions that this book will address for the computer systems architect, researcher, designer, purchaser, or student. It is set up to cover the essentials of modeling and analysis of computer systems hardware and software environments. Covered topics include the basic technologies associated with computer systems hardware, software, and networking; details of modeling techniques used to study computer hardware and software configurations; and the description of software tools that have been used to model such systems.

# 1.7   Overview of performance evaluation methods

Models provide a tool for users to define a system and its problems in a concise fashion; they provide vehicles to ascertain critical elements, components, and issues; they provide a means to assess designs or to synthesize and evaluate proposed solutions; and they can be used as predictions to forecast and aid in planning future enhancements or developments. In short, they provide a laboratory environment in which to study a system even before it exists or without actually effecting an actual implementation. In this light models are descriptions of systems. Models typically are developed based on theoretical laws and principles. They may be physical models (scaled replicas), mathematical equations and relations (abstractions), or graphical representations. Models are only as good as the information put into them. That is, modeling of a system is easier and typically better if:

- Physical laws are available that can be used to describe it.

- Pictorial (graphical) representations can be made to provide better understanding of the model.

- The system's inputs, elements, and outputs are of manageable magnitude.

These all provide a means to construct and realize models, but the problem typically is that we do not have clear physical laws to go by; interactions can be very difficult to describe; randomness of the system, environment, or users causes problems; and policies that drive processes are hard to quantify. What typically transpires is that a "faithful" model of a system is constructed: one that provides insight into a critical aspect of a system, not all of its components. That is, we typically model a slice of the real-world system. What this implies is that the model is an abstraction of the real-world system under study. With all abstractions, one must decide what elements of the real world to include in the abstraction—that is, which ones are important to realize as a "faithful" model. What we are talking about here is intuition—that is, how well a modeler can select the significant elements; how well these elements can be defined; and how well the interaction of these significant elements is within themselves, among themselves, and with the outside world.

## 1.7.1    Models

As stated previously, a model is an abstraction of a system. (See Figure 1.11.) The realism of the model is based on the level of abstraction applied. That is, if we know all there is about a system and are willing to pay for the complexity of building a true model, the abstraction is near nil. On the other hand, in most cases we wish to abstract the view we take of a system to simplify the complexities. We wish to build a model that focuses on some element(s) of interest and leave the rest of the system as only an interface with no detail beyond proper inputs and outputs.

**Figure 1.11**
*Modeling process.*

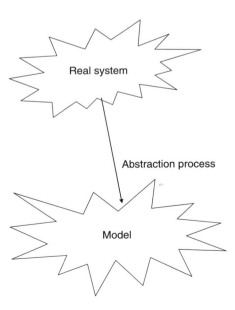

**Figure 1.12**
*Abstraction of a system.*

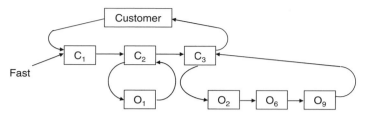

The "system," as we have been calling it, is the real world that we wish to model (e.g., a bank teller machine, a car wash, or some other tangible item or process). In Figure 1.12 a system is considered to be a unified group of objects united to perform some set function or process, whereas a model is an abstraction of the system that extracts the important items and their interactions.

The basic concept of this discussion is that a model is a modeler's subjective view of the system. This view defines what is important, what the purpose is, detail, boundaries, and so on. The modeler must understand the system in order to provide a faithful perspective of its important features and to make the model useful.

## 1.7.2    Model construction

In order to construct a model, we as modelers must follow predictable methodologies in order to derive correct representations. The methodology typically used consists of top-down decomposition and is pertinent to the goal of being able to define the purpose of the model or its component at each step and, based on this purpose, to derive the boundaries of the system or component and develop the level of modeling detail. This iterative method of developing purpose, boundaries, and modeling level smooths out the rough or undefinable edges of the actual system or component, thereby focusing on the critical elements of it.

The model's inputs are derived from the system under study as well as from the performance measures we wish to extract. That is, the type of inputs are detailed not only from the physical system but through the model's intended use (this provides the experimental nature of the model). For instance, in an automated teller machine, we wish to study the usefulness of fast service features, such as providing cash or set amounts of funds quickly after the amount has been typed in. We may decide to ignore details of the ATM's internal operations or user changes.

The model would be the bank teller machine, its interface, and a model (analytical, simulation) of the internal process. The experiment would be to have users (experimenters) use the model as they would a real system and measure its effectiveness. The measures would deal with the intent of the design. That is, we would monitor which type of cash access feature was used over another, which performed at a higher level, or which features were not highly utilized.

The definition of the required performance measures drive the design and/or redesign of the model. In reality, the entire process of formulating and building a model of a real system occurs interactively. As insight is gained about the real system through studying it for modeling purposes, new design approaches and better models and components are derived. This process of iteration continues until the modeler has achieved a level of detail consistent with the view of the real system intended in the model-purpose development phase. The level of detail indicates the importance of each component in the modeler's eye as points that are to be evaluated.

To reiterate, the methodology for developing and using a model of a system is as follows:

1. Define the problem to be studied as well as the criteria for analysis.

2. Define and/or refine the model of the system (includes development of abstractions of the system into mathematical, logical, and procedural relationships).

3. Collect data for input to the model (define the outside would and what must be fed to or taken from the model to "simulate" that world).

4. Select a modeling tool and prepare and augment the model for tool implementation.

5. Verify that the tool implementation is an accurate reflection of the model.

6. Validate that the tool implementation provides the desired accuracy or correspondence with the real-world system being modeled.

7. Experiment with the model to obtain performance measures.

8. Analyze the tool results.

9. Use these findings to derive designs and improvements for the real-world system.

Although some of these steps were defined previously, they will be readdressed here in the context of the methodology.

The first task in the methodology is to determine what the scope of the problem is and if this real-world system is amenable to modeling. This task consists of clearly defining the problem and explicitly delineating the objectives of the investigation. This task may need to be reevaluated during the entire model construction phase because of the nature of modeling. That is, as more insight comes into the process, a better model, albeit a different one, may be developed. This involves a redefinition of questions and the evolution of a new problem definition.

Once a problem definition has been formulated, the task of defining and refining a model of this real-world problem space can ensue. The model typically is made up of multiple sections that are both static and dynamic. They define elements of the system (static), their characteristics, and the ways in which these elements interact over time to adjust or reflect the state of the real system over time. As indicated earlier, this process of formulating a model is largely dependent on the modeler's knowledge, understanding, and expertise (art versus science). The modeler extracts the essence of the real-world system without encasing superfluous detail. This concept involves capturing the crucial (most important) aspects of the system without undue complexity but with enough to realistically reflect the germane aspects of the real system. The amount of detail to include in a model is based mainly on its purpose. For example, if we wish to study the user transaction ratio and types on an automated teller machine, we only need model the machine as a consumer of all transaction times and their types. We need not model the machine and its interactions with a parent database in any detail but only from a gross exterior user level.

The process of developing the model from the problem statement is iterative and time consuming. However, a fallout of this phase is the definition of input data requirements. Added work typically will be required to gather the defined data values to drive the model. Many times in model development data inputs must be hypothesized or be based on preliminary analysis, or the data may not require exact values for good modeling. The sensitivity of the model is turned into some executable or analytical form and the data can be analyzed as to their effects.

Once the planning and development of a model and data inputs have been performed, the next task is to turn it into an analytical or executable form. The modeling tool selected drives much of the remainder of the work. Available tools include simulation, analytical modeling, testbeds, and operational analysis. Each of these modeling tools has its pros and cons. Simulation allows for a wide range of examinations based on the modeler's expertise; analytical analysis provides best, worst, and average analysis but only to the extent of the modeler's ability to define the system under study mathematically. Testbeds provide a means to test the model on real hardware components of a system, but they are very expensive and cumbersome. Operational analysis requires that we have the real system available and that we can get it to perform the desired study. This is not always an available alternative in complex systems. In any case, the tool selected will determine how the modeler develops the model, its inputs, and its experimental payoff.

Once a model and a modeling tool to implement it have been developed, the modeler develops the executable model. Once developed, this model must be verified to determine if it accurately reflects the intended real-world system under study. Verification typically is done by manually checking that the model's computational results match those of the implementation. That is, do the abstract model and implemented model do the same thing and provide consistent results?

Akin to verification is validation. Validation deals with determining if the model's implementation provides an accurate depiction of the real-world system being modeled. Testing for accuracy typically consists of a comparison of the model and system structures against each other and a comparison of model tool inputs, outputs, and processes versus the real system for some known boundaries. If they meet some experimental or modeling variance criteria, we deem the model an accurate representation of the system. If not, the deficiencies must be found, corrected, and the model revalidated until concurrence is achieved.

Once the tool implementation of the model has been verified and validated, the modelers can perform the project's intended experiments. This phase is the one in which the model's original limitations can be stretched and new insights into the real system's intricacies can be gained. The limitations on experimentation are directly related to the tool chosen: Simulation is most flexible followed by testbeds, analytical analysis, and operational analysis.

Once experimentation is complete, an ongoing analysis of results is actively performed. This phase deals with collecting and analyzing experimentally generated data to gain further insight into the system under study. Based on the results generated, the modeler feeds these results into the decision-making process for the real-world system, potentially changing its structure and operations based on the model's findings. A study is deemed successful when the modeling effort provides some useful data to drive the end product. The outputs can solidify a concept about the system, define a deficiency, provide insight into improvements, or corroborate other information about the system. Modeling is a useful tool with which to analyze complex environments.

## 1.7.3   Modeling tools

As was briefly indicated in the previous section, there are major classes of modeling tools in use today: analytical, simulation, testbed, and operational analysis. Each has its niche in the modeler's repertoire of tools and is used for varying reasons, as will be discussed later in the book.

### Analytical modeling tools

Analytical modeling tools have been used as an implementation technique for models for quite some time, the main reason being that they work. Analytical implementations of models rely on the ability of the modeler to describe a model in mathematical terms. Typically, if a system can be viewed as a collection of queues with service, wait, and analytical times defined analytically, queuing analysis can be applied to solve the problem. Other analytical tools such as Petri nets can also be applied to the solution of such problems.

Some of the reasons why analytical models are chosen as a modeling tool are as follows:

1.    Analytical models capture more salient features of systems—that is, most systems can be represented as queuing delays, service times, arrival times, and so on, and, therefore, we can model from this perspective, leaving out details.

2.    Assumptions or analysis is realistic.

3.    Algorithms to solve queuing equations are available in machine form to speed analysis.

What is implied by this is that queuing models provide an easy and concise means to develop analysis of queue-based systems. Queues are waiting lines, and queuing theory is the study of waiting line dynamics.

In queuing analysis at the simplest level (one queue), there is a queue (waiting line) that is being fed by incoming customers (arrival rate); the queue is operated by a server, which extracts customers out of the queue according to some service rate (see Figure 1.13).

The queue operates as follows: An arrival comes into the queue, and, if the server is busy, the customer is put in a waiting facility (the queue) unless

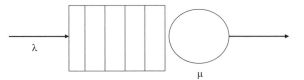

**Figure 1.13**
*Single server queue.*

the queue is full, in which case the customer is rejected (no room to wait). On the other hand, if the queue is empty, the customer is brought into the service location and is delayed the service rate time. The customer then departs the queue.

In order to analyze this phenomenon we need to have notational and analytical means (theories) with which to manipulate the notation. Additionally, to determine the usefulness of the technique, we need to know what can be analyzed and what type of measure is derived from the queue.

The notation used (see Figure 1.13) to describe the queue phenomenon is as follows: The arrival distribution defines the arrival patterns of customers into the queue. These are defined by a random variable that defines the interarrival time. A typically used measure is the Poisson arrival process, defined as:

$$P(\text{arrival time}) = 1 - e^{-\lambda} \tag{1.1}$$

where the average arrival rate is $\lambda$. The queue is defined as a storage reservoir for customers. Additionally, the policy it uses for accepting and removing customers is also defined. Examples of queuing disciplines typically used are first-in first-out (FIFO) and last-in first-out (LIFO). The last main component of the queue description is the service policy, which is the method by which customers are accepted for service and the length of the service. This service time is described by a distribution, a random variable. A typical service time distribution is the random service given by:

$$W_s(t) = 1 - e^{-\mu t} \tag{1.2}$$

where $t \gg 0$, and the symbol $\mu$ is reserved to describe this common distribution for its average service rate. The distributions used to describe the arrival rate and service ratios are many and variable; for example, the exponential, general, Erlang, deterministic, or hyperexponential can be used. The Kendall notation was developed to describe what type of queue is being examined. The form of this notation is as follows:

$$A/B/c/K/m/Z \tag{1.3}$$

where $A$ specifies the interarrival time distribution, $B$ the service time distribution, $c$ the number of servers, $K$ the system capacity, $m$ the number in the source, and $Z$ the queue discipline.

This type of analysis can be used to generate statistics on average wait time, average length of the queue, average service time, traffic intensity, server utilization, mean time in system, and various probability of wait times and expected service and wait times. More details on this modeling and analysis technique will be presented in Chapter 7.

### Simulation modeling tools

Simulation as a modeler's tool has been used for a long time and has been applied to the modeling and analysis of many systems—for example, business, economics, marketing, education, politics, social sciences, behavioral sciences, international relations, transportation, law enforcement, urban studies, global systems, computers, factories, and many more. Simulation lends itself to such a variety of problems because of its flexibility. It is a dynamic tool that provides the modeler with the ability to define models of systems and put them into action. It provides a laboratory in which to study myriad issues associated with a system without disturbing the actual system. A wide range of experiments can be performed in a very controlled environment; time can be compressed, allowing the study of otherwise unobservable phenomena, and sensitivity analysis can be done on all components.

However, simulation modeling can have its drawbacks. Model development can become expensive and require extensive time to perform, assumptions made may become critical and cause a bias on the model or even make it leave the bounds of reality, and, finally, the model may become too cumbersome to use and initialize effectively if it is allowed to grow unconstrained. To prevent many of these ill effects, the modeler must follow strict policies of formulation, construction, and use. These will minimize the bad effects while maximizing the benefits of simulation.

There are many simulation forms available based on the system being studied. Basically there are four classes of simulation models: continuous, discrete, queuing, and hybrid. These four techniques provide the necessary robustness of methods to model most systems of interest. A continuous model is one whose processing state changes in time based on time-varying signals or variables. Discrete simulation relies instead on event conditions and event transitions to change state. Queue-based simulations provide dynamic means to construct and analyze queue-based systems. They dynamically model the mathematical occurrences analyzed in analytical techniques.

Simulation models are constructed and utilized in the analysis of a system based on the system's fit to simulation. That is, before we simulate a real-world entity we must determine that the problem requires or is amenable to simulation. The important factors to consider are the cost, the feasibility of conducting useful experimentations, and the possibility of mathematical or other forms of analysis. Once simulation is deemed a viable candidate for model implementation, a formal model tuned to the form of available simulation tools must be performed. Upon completion of a model specification, the computer program that converts this model into executable form must be developed. Finally, once the computer model is verified and validated, the modeler can experiment with the simulation to aid in the study of the real-world system.

Many languages are available to the modeler for use in developing the computer-executable version of a model—for example, GPSS, Q-gert, Simscript, Slam, AWSIM, and Network 2.5. The choice of simulation language is based on the users' needs and preferences, since any of these will provide a usable modeling tool for implementing a simulation. Details of these and the advantages of other aspects of simulation are addressed in Chapter 8.

### Testbeds as modeling tools

Testbeds, as indicated previously, are composite abstractions of systems and are used to study system components and interactions to gain further insight into the essence of the real system. They are built of prototypes and pieces of real system components and are used to provide insight into the workings of an element(s) of a system. The important feature of a testbed is that it only focuses on a subset of the total system. That is, the important aspect that we wish to study, refine, or develop is the aspect implemented in the testbed. All other aspects have stubs that provide their stimulus or extract their load but are not themselves complete components, just simulated pieces. The testbed provides a realistic hardware-software environment with which to test components without having the ultimate system. The testbed provides a means to improve the understanding of the functional requirements and operational behavior of the system. It supplies measurements from which quantitative results about the system can be derived. It provides an integrated environment in which the interrelationships of solutions to system problems can be evaluated. Finally, it provides an environment in which design decisions can be based on both theoretical and empirical studies.

What all this discussion indicates, again, is that, as with simulation and analytical tools, the testbed provides a laboratory environment in which the modeled real-world system components can be experimented with, studied, and evaluated from many angles. However, testbeds have their limitations in that they cost more to develop and are limited in application to only modeling systems and components amenable to such environments. For example, we probably would not model a complex distributed computing system in a testbed. We would instead consider analytical or simulation models as a first pass and use a testbed between the initial concept and final design. This will be more evident as we continue our discussion here and in Chapter 8, where testbeds are discussed in much greater detail.

A testbed is made up of three components: an experimental subsystem, a monitoring subsystem, and a simulation-stimulation subsystem. The experimental subsystem is the collection of real-world system components and/or prototypes that we wish to model and experiment with. The monitoring subsystem consists of interfaces to the experimental system to extract raw data and a support component to collate and analyze the collected information. The simulation-stimulation subsystem provides the hooks and handles necessary to provide the experimenter with real-world system inputs and outputs to provide a realistic experimentation environment.

With these elements a testbed can provide a flexible and modular vehicle with which to experiment with a wide range of different system stimuli, configurations, and applications. The testbed approach provides a method to investigate system aspects that are complementary to simulation and analytical methods.

Decisions about using a testbed over the other methods are driven mainly by the cost associated with development and the actual benefits that can be realized by such implementations. Additionally, the testbed results are only as good as the monitor's ability to extract and analyze the occurring real-world phenomena and the simulation-stimulation component's ability to reflect a realistic interface with the environment.

Testbeds in the context of local area networks can and have been used to analyze a wide range of components. The limitation to flexibility in analyzing very diverse structures and implementations has and will continue to be the cost associated with constructing a testbed. In the context of a computer system, the testbed must implement a large portion of the computer system's computing hardware, data storage hardware, data transfer hardware, and possibly network hardware and software to be useful. By doing this, however, the modeler is limited to studying this single configuration. It will be seen in later sections what these modeling limitations and benefits are and how they affect our approach to studying a system.

### Operational analysis as a modeling tool

The final tool from a modeler's perspective is operational analysis, also sometimes referred to as empirical analysis. In this technique, the modeler is not concerned as much with an abstraction of the system, but with how to extract from the real system information upon which to develop the same analysis of potential solutions that is provided with the other models.

Operational analysis is concerned with extracting information from a working system that is used to develop projections about the system's future operations. Additionally, this modeling method can be used by the other three modeling techniques to derive meaningful information that can be fed into their analysis processes or used to verify or validate their analysis operations.

Operational analysis deals with the measurement and evaluation of an actual system in operation. Measurement is concerned with instrumenting the system to extract the information. The means to perform this uses hardware and/or software monitors.

Hardware monitors consist of a set of probes or sensors, a logic-sensing device, a set of counters, and a display or recording unit. The probes monitor the state of the chosen system points. Typically, probes can be programmed to trigger on a specific event, thereby providing the ability to trace specific occurrences within a system.

The logic-sensing subsystem is used to interpret the raw input data being probed into meaningful information items. The counters are used to set sampling rates on other activities requiring timed intervals. The last component records and displays the information as it is sensed and reduced. Further assistance could be added to analyze the information further. The ability to perform effective operational analysis is directly dependent on the hardware and software monitors' ability to extract information. The hardware monitor is only as effective as its ability to be hooked into the system without causing undue disturbance.

The problem is that the hardware-based monitor cannot, in a computer system, sense software-related events effectively. The interaction of software and system hardware together will provide much more effective data for operational analysis to be performed. Software monitors typically provide event tracing or sampling styles. Event trace monitors are composed of a set of system routines that is evoked on specific software occurrences, such as CPU interrupts, scheduling phases, dispatching, lockouts, I/O access, and so on. The software monitor is triggered on these events and records pertinent information on system status. The information can include the event triggered at the time, what process had control of the CPU prior to the event, and the state of the CPU (registers, conditions, etc.). These data can reveal much insight as to which programs have the most access to the CPU, how much time is spent in system service overhead, device queue lengths, and many other significant events.

The combination of the hardware and software monitors provides the analyst with a rich set of data on which to perform analysis. Typical computations deal with computing various means and variances of uses of devices and software and plotting relative frequencies of access and use.

The measurements and computations performed at this level only model present system performance. The operational analyst must use these measures to extend performance and to postulate new boundaries based on extending the data into unknown regions and performing computations based on the projected data. Using these techniques, the analyst can suggest changes and improvements and predict their impact based on real information.

# 1.8  Performance metrics and evaluation criteria

Selecting a computer system architecture and system support software requires performance metrics and evaluation criteria. In order to generate such information, a user must follow a methodology of selection that defines the user needs, the motivations, and the environmental and technological boundaries. As with the purchase of any product, the purchaser should identify how the product (in this case a computer system) will be used. This first element of the selection process is the most important, since if we don't define the needs and uses properly, the remaining tasks will have a predefined built-in error. Therefore, the prospective buyer should compile a wish list of all potential uses. For example, the list may include the following:

- Multiple processors
- Distributed file server
- Redundant disk drives
- Word processing
- Spreadsheet analysis
- Electronic mail
- Remote job entry
- Real-time control

- Interactive log on and execution or results

- Physical installation layouts

- Maximum node count and types

- Reliability considerations

- Network management

- Factory automation

- Computer types

- Video, audio, or both

- Interconnection to existing MANs or WANs

- Resource sharing

- Distributed computing

- Very large database

From this wish list the user must generate processing requirements, communications transfer, and management requirements. For example, given that we have $N$ computers, which must be able to simultaneously transfer data to other sites, we have given a requirement for bandwidth (or an I/O rate maximum) and concurrency of access, both of which affect protocols, topology, and media requirements, to name a few. This set of processing requirements, communications transfer, and management requirements can now be used to aid us in the other phases. The second portion of the methodology is to develop a motivational purpose for the computer system: to define why we want one in the first place. For example, we may want to compete with our competitors, who are offering better or extended service to their customers by the use of an enhanced backplane, to have an edge in information availability to enhance the corporation's decision-making ability, or to provide better control or use of the company's computing resources. The motivation for computing system selection will also provide our prospective buyer or designer with more performance and evaluation criteria upon which to base a decision.

The next phase within the computer systems evaluation methodology is to assess the environmental and technological aspects in which the computer system must fit. For example, is the computer system and its interconnection subsystem intended for implementation in a dirty, hot, cold, or varying environment? Will the computer system or some of its components be subjected to stress and strain from natural elements such as wind, rain, snow, or lightning? Will the computer system or its components be put in an air-conditioned computer room or be spread out throughout a building? Is the building new construction or old construction? Will computer systems interconnects need to penetrate floors and go up risers? If so, what is the prevailing fire code? Will the computer system link many buildings together? If so, will interconnections be strung overhead or be poled from building to building? Will wiring be buried? Will it go under water or within water-carrying pipes?

From a technological viewpoint, the computer system may need to interconnect to a diverse set of present company assets and also be able to link planned new resources. These resources have their own peculiarities in terms of electrical specifications, pin count, and makeup. These peculiarities will also map into requirements on the interface equipment and software. The computer system's interconnect components must be able to interface these devices directly or via an intermediate device, which should be an off-the-shelf component if possible.

Once all these initial analyses have been completed and their data compiled, the prospective purchasers or designers should have a large volume of data from which to drive the computer systems requirements.

The next question is: How to use these data to assist in the selection? Do you compile these data into a model of a prospective computer system and use this information to derive analytical and qualitative analysis of the prospective computing system and then compare these results to other known product parameters? Or is a simulation model more in line? In any case, a means of evaluating these data must be provided and must be able to use data that have been collected.

The collected data can be divided into quantitative and qualitative classes. That is, there is one set of data from which specific performance measures can be derived and another from which only subjective measures can be derived. The quantitative data sets should be used to build a model of the proposed system and derive composite measures to evaluate given prospective computer systems architectures and configurations. The methods used for this analysis are analytical and simulation models. The testbed and operational analysis methods may not be viable to test alternatives early on in systems analysis.

# 2

# *Computer Data Processing Hardware Architecture*

This chapter defines the hardware and software components used in computer-based applications. Included here is the fundamental composition of computers (CPU, memory, I/O), secondary storage devices, other peripheral input and output devices, multiprocessing architectures, and networks. Our discussions are tailored to focus on the architecture and use of these components as they relate to computer management of persistent data.

## 2.1    Introduction

A computer-based application resides on a computer system. The computer system provides the physical medium on which the application data are stored and the processing capacity to manipulate stored data. A processing unit of a computer system consists of five main elements: the memory, an arithmetic logic unit, an input unit, an output unit, and a control element. The memory unit stores both the data for programs and the instructions of a program that manipulates stored data.

The program's individual elements or instructions are fetched from the memory one at a time and are interpreted by the control unit. The control unit, depending on the interpretation of the instruction, determines what computer operation to perform next. If the instruction requires no additional data, the control indicates to the arithmetic logic unit what operation to perform and with what registers. (See Figure 2.1.)

If the instruction requires additional data, the control unit passes the appropriate command to the memory (MAR, memory address register) to fetch a data item from memory (MDR, memory data register) and to place it in an appropriate register in the ALU (data register bank) (Figure 2.2). This continues until all required operands are in the appropriate

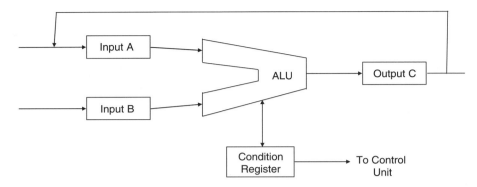

**Figure 2.1**     *Basic processing unit of a computer.*

registers of the ALU. Once all operands are in place, the control unit commands the ALU to perform the appropriate instruction—for example, multiplication, addition, or subtraction. If the instruction indicated that an input or output were required, the control element would transmit a word from the input unit to the memory or ALU, depending on the instruction. If an output instruction were decoded, the control unit would command the transmission of the appropriate memory word or register to the output channel indicated. These five elements comprise the fundamental building blocks used in the original von Neumann computer system and are found in most contemporary computer systems in some form or another.

In this chapter we will examine these fundamental building blocks and see how they are used to form a variety of computer architectures.

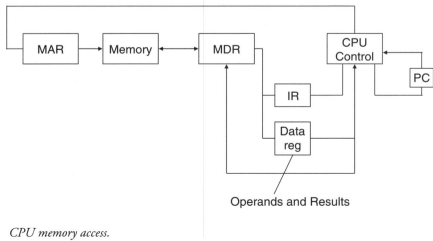

**Figure 2.2**     *CPU memory access.*

## 2.2    Computer hardware architecture

A computer system is comprised of the five building blocks previously described, as well as additional peripheral support devices, which aid in data movement and processing. These basic building blocks are used to form the general processing, control, storage, and input and output units that make up modern computer systems. Devices typically are organized in a manner that supports the application processing for which the computer system is intended—for example, if massive amounts of data need to be stored, then additional peripheral storage devices such as disks or tape units are required, along with their required controllers or data channels.

A computer system's architecture is constructed using basic building blocks, such as CPUs, memories, disks, I/O, and other devices as needed.

To better describe the variations within architectures we will discuss some details briefly—for example, the arithmetic logic unit (ALU) and the control unit are merged together into a central processing unit or CPU. The CPU controls the flow of instructions and data in the computer system. Memories can be broken down into hierarchies based on nearness to the CPU and speed of access—for example, cache memory is small, extremely fast memory used for instructions and data actively executing and being used by the CPU and usually resides on the same board or chip as the CPU. The primary memory is slower, but it is also cheaper and contains more memory locations. It is used to store data and instructions that will be used during the execution of applications presently running on the CPU—for example, if you boot up your word processing program on your personal computer, the operating system will attempt to place the entire word processing program in primary memory. If there is insufficient space, the operating system will partition the program into segments and pull them in as needed.

The portion of the program that cannot be stored in memory is maintained on a secondary storage device, typically a disk drive. This device has a much greater storage capacity than the primary memory, typically costs much less per unit of storage, and has data access times that are much slower than the primary memory. A more recent external storage device is the CD-ROM drive. This device, in its read-only mode (ROM), allows users only to extract information from the drive. In the more recent read/write variety the device can be used somewhat like the traditional tape drive. An additional secondary storage device is the tape drive unit. A tape drive is a simple storage device that can store massive amounts of data—again, at less cost than the disk units but at a reduced access speed. Other components of a computer system are input and output units. These are used to extract data from the computer and provide these data to external devices or to input data from the external device. The external devices could be end-user terminals, sensors, information network ports, video, voice, or other computers.

In the following sections we will examine each of the components of a computer system in more detail, as we examine how these devices can be interconnected to support data processing applications.

## 2.3   CPU architectures

The central processing unit (CPU) is the brains of a computer system. The CPU consists of the arithmetic logic unit (ALU) and the control unit, as indicated previously. The ALU can come in a variety of configurations— from a single simple unit, shown in Figure 2.1, that performs simple adds, subtracts, increments, decrements, load, and store, up to extremely complex units that perform operations such as multiply, divide, exponentiation, sine, cosine, and so on. The primary operation of the ALU is to take zero or more operands and perform the function called for in the instruction. In addition to the ALU, the CPU consists of a set of registers to store operands and intermediate results and to maintain information used by the CPU to determine the state of its computations. There are registers for the status of the ALU's operation, for keeping count of the instruction to be performed next, to keep data flowing in from memory or out to memory, to maintain the instruction being executed, and for the location of operands being operated on by the CPU.

Each of these registers has a unique function within the CPU, and each is necessary for various classes of computer architectures. A typical minimal architecture for a CPU and its registers is shown in Figure 2.3. This architecture consists of a primary memory connected to the CPU via buses that use a memory address register and memory data register to address a location in memory and transfer the contents of the location from the memory into the memory data register or to transfer the contents of the memory data register into memory. There are registers in the CPU for instructions (the instruction or IR register), instruction operands, and results of operations; a location counter (which contains either the location in memory for instructions or operands, depending on the decoding of instructions); a program counter or PC (which maintains the location of the next instruction to perform); and status registers.

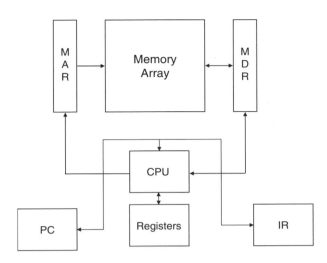

**Figure 2.3**
*The CPU and its associated registers.*

The CPU also contains the control unit. The control unit uses the status registers and instructions in the instruction register to determine what functions the CPU must perform on the registers, ALU, and data paths that make up the CPU. The basic operation of the CPU follows a simple loop (unless interrupts occur that alter the flow of execution). This loop is called the instruction execution cycle (Figure 2.4). There are six basic functions performed in the instruction loop: instruction fetch, instruction decode, operand effective address calculation, operand fetch, operation execution, and next address calculation.

Instruction fetch uses the program counter register to point to the next instruction stored in memory. The address is placed in the memory address register and the instruction is then gated (electronically signaled by the CPU control element to transfer the data) from the data memory into the memory data register. The instruction then flows into the instruction register under the direction of the control unit.

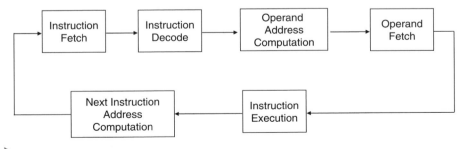

**Figure 2.4**    *Instrumentation execution cycle.*

Once an instruction is in the instruction register, the second cycle in instruction execution can be performed—decode. To decode the instruction the control unit must recognize what type of instruction is being requested—for example, does the instruction require additional data from memory to perform its intended function, or does the instruction involve only ALU resident registers?

The third cycle within instruction execution is the operand effective address calculation. This phase of instruction execution operates by extracting operand address information from the instruction and then performing some form of calculation (e.g., base plus offset) with this information to form a physical address in memory. We will discuss the various types of addressing in later sections of this chapter. Once the type and number of operands are determined, the ALU can acquire the operands and then set up to perform the decoded instruction.

Once we have a physical address, we can fetch the operand (the fourth function of the instruction execution cycle). To fetch the operand the effective address is placed in the memory address register, and the control gates the contents pointed to by the memory address register into the memory data register. The extracted operand is then gated from the memory data register into an ALU register. If an additional operand is needed, the two cycle steps for operand fetch would be repeated to get the remaining operand. With all required operands in ALU registers the instruction requested can now be performed. The instruction execution is controlled by the CPU control unit. The control unit signals to the ALU to perform the instruction—for example, if an add is requested the ALU would add the A and B registers and place the result in the C register. After the instruction is completed the last step in the instruction execution cycle can proceed.

The next address calculation uses the program counter and/or any pertinent computation result (such as a go to–type instruction) to determine where in the memory the next instruction is to be found. The normal mode of address calculation is to increment the contents of the program counter. With the new address the instruction cycle begins once more.

This execution sequence represents the basic functions found in all computer systems. Variations in the number of steps are found based on the type and length of the instruction.

## 2.3.1   Instruction types

Based on the number of registers available and the configuration of these registers several types of instruction are possible—for example, if many registers are available, as would be the case in a stack computer, no address computations are needed and the instruction, therefore, can be much shorter both in format and execution time required. On the other hand, if there are no general registers and all computations are performed by memory movements of data, then instructions will be longer and require more time due to operand fetching and storage. The following are representative of instruction types:

0-address instructions—This type of instruction is found in machines where many general-purpose registers are available. This is the case in stack machines and in some reduced instruction set machines. Instructions of this type perform their function totally using registers. If we have three general registers, $A$, $B$, and $C$, a typical format would have the form:

$$R[A] <-- R[B] \text{ operator } R[C] \qquad (2.1)$$

which indicates that the contents of registers $B$ and $C$ have the operator (such as add, subtract, multiply, etc.) performed on them, with the result stored in general register $C$. Similarly, we could describe instructions that use just one or two registers as follows:

$$R[B] <-- R[B] \text{ operator } R[C] \qquad (2.2)$$

or

$$\text{operator } R[C] \qquad (2.3)$$

which represents two-register and one-register instructions, respectively. In the two-register case one of the operand registers is also used as the result register. In the single-register case the operand register is also the result register. The increment instruction is an example of one-register instruction. This type of instruction is found in all machines.

1-address instructions—In this type of instruction a single memory address is found in the instruction. If another operand is used, it is typically an accumulator or the top of a stack in a stack computer. The typical format of these instructions has the form:

$$\text{operator } M[\text{address}] \qquad (2.4)$$

where the contents of the named memory address have the named operator performed on them in conjunction with an implied special register. An example of such an instruction could be as follows:

Move $M[100]$ (2.5)

or

Add $M[100]$ (2.6)

which moves the contents of memory location 100 into the ALU's accumulator or adds the contents of memory address 100 with the accumulator and stores the result in the accumulator. If the result must be stored in memory, we would need a store instruction:

Store $M[100]$ (2.7)

1-and-1/2-address instructions—Once we have an architecture that has some general-purpose registers, we can provide more advanced operations combining memory contents and the general registers. The typical instruction performs an operation on a memory location's contents with that of a general register—for example, we could add the contents of a memory location with the contents of a general register, $A$, as shown:

Add $R[A], M[100]$ (2.8)

This instruction typically stores the result in the first named location or register in the instruction. In this example it is register $A$.

2-address instructions—Two address instructions utilize two memory locations to perform an instruction—for example, a block move of $N$ words from one location in memory to another, or a block add. The move may appear as follows:

Move $N, M[100], M[1000]$ (2.9)

2-and-1/2-address instructions—This format uses two memory locations and a general register in the instruction. Typical of this type of instruction is an operation involving two memory locations storing the result in a register or an operation with a general register and a memory location storing the result on another memory location, as shown:

$$R[A] - - >> M[100] \text{operator} M[1000]$$
$$M[1000] - - >> M[100] \text{operator} R[A]$$ (2.10)

3-address instructions—Another less common form of instruction format is the three-address instruction. These instructions involve three memory locations—two used for operands and one as the results location. A typical format is shown:

$$M[200] --\!\!> M[100] \, \text{operator} \, M[300] \qquad\qquad (2.11)$$

## 2.3.2   Instruction architectures

There are numerous ideas about how to organize computer systems around the instruction set. One form, which has come of age with the new powerful workstations, is the reduced instruction set computer (RISC). These machines typically have a small number of instructions that are simple and that take a relatively short equal number of clock cycles per instruction. Each of the instructions is highly optimized and operates efficiently. Machine-coded programs are typically longer, but the actual code may run faster due to the highly optimized and regular code.

On the other side of the spectrum are architectures built around complex instructions. These computers are referred to as complex instruction set computers, or CISC. These machines use instructions that each perform some complex function—for example, a matrix multiply or a complex number manipulation trigonometric function. Each instruction may take numerous machine cycles to perform and may itself be coded in lower-level microcode. Programs written in this type of architecture may be shorter, but may not take any less time and in some cases may even take more time due to their complexity.

## 2.3.3   Memory-addressing schemes

Just as there are a variety of instruction formats, there are also numerous ways in which to determine the address of an operand from an instruction. Each form of address computation has its benefits in terms of instruction design flexibility. There are six major types of addressing computation schemes found in computers: immediate, direct, index, base, indirect, and two-operand. We will briefly examine these.

Immediate—Immediate addressing is not really an addressing mode into memory; rather, it is an instruction format that directly includes the data to be acted on as part of the instruction. This form of operand access simplifies the instruction execution cycle since no additional fetches are required.

Direct—For direct addressing there is no operand address decoding required. The instruction operand address field contains the physical address of the operand. The control simply places the operand address field into the memory address field and the operand is fetched from memory.

Index—A refinement of direct addressing is indexed addressing. In this form of operand address decoding, the operand address field is added to the contents of a designated register to compute the effective physical address.

Base—Base addressing expands on this concept. A base register contains an address base, which is added to the indexed address to form an effective physical address. This scheme is used in computer systems for addressing and partitioning the memory into segments. When more than one base register is available in an architecture, we can more easily manage partitioned memory for multiple users and systems control software.

Indirect—For this address computation scheme we use the contents of a specified memory location as the effective address. The control fetches the contents of the named memory location and uses this as the memory address register pointer to extract the actual operand.

Two-operand addressing—In two-operand addressing any combination of the above schemes could be used together to access multiple operands for an instruction.

## 2.3.4    Memory architectures

Memory storage can also have an architecture (configuration) that can aid in the storing and fetching of memory contents. Generally a memory is organized as a regular structure, which can be addressed using the memory address register and have data transferred through the memory data register (Figure 2.5). The memory is accessed through the combination of addressing and either drivers or sensors to write or read data from or to the memory data register. Memory structures are built based on the organization of the memory words. The simplest form is a linear two-dimensional structure. Each memory location has a unique word line, which, when energized, gates the $N$-bit lines' (where $N$ is the size of a data word in the computer) contents into the memory data register.

A second organization is the two-and-a-half-dimension architecture. In this memory structure the memory words are broken up into separate data planes, each consisting of one bit for all memory locations. To access a word the $n$ planes must be energized with the composite $X$ and $Y$ coordinates,

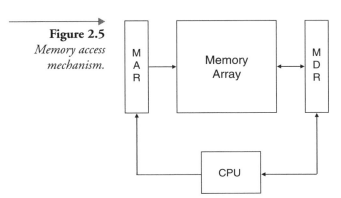

**Figure 2.5**
*Memory access mechanism.*

which correspond to the wanted memory word. The individual plane drivers gate the proper bit into the memory data register for the addressed memory word. Other data organizations have been derived and we leave it to the interested reader to investigate these.

## 2.4    I/O architectures

Input and output mechanisms are used by computer systems to move information into or out of the computer's main memory. A typical sequence for performing this movement of information from or to an input and output device is as follows:

1.     Select an I/O device.

2.     Busy—wait until the device is ready.

3.     Transfer a word from the device I/O buffer into the CPU accumulator.

4.     Transfer the contents of the accumulator into a memory location.

5.     Compute the next memory location for I/O data.

6.     Go back to step 2 and repeat until all data are transferred.

The above sequence assumes that all data must pass through the CPU to control the flow.

If, instead, we have the ability to place or extract data directly to or from memory without passing through the CPU, we can get further improvements in performance and a refined architecture. To allow for the CPU to be taken out of the I/O loop we need an additional control element. For I/O to be controlled directly and bypass the CPU en route to memory requires added control; this controller is referred to as a direct memory access (DMA) device. The DMA device allows us to alter what the CPU must do. The CPU issues a begin I/O command to the DMA control unit with the address of the data block to be transferred. The CPU is now free from added input and output overhead and can be relieved to do some other processing or simply wait until the DMA responds that the transfer is complete. To effectively provide this notification an added capability is required of the CPU: an interrupt capability. The interrupts can be of several types, as follows:

- Interrupts can be immediate, causing the CPU to halt and service the interrupt.

- Interrupts can be deferred, allowing the CPU to service them when it is ready.

- Interrupts can be prioritized, allowing for prompt service to critical actions occurring in the system.

## 2.5   Secondary storage and peripheral devices and architectures

Memory storage volume is always looked at as an important feature when one thinks about acquiring a computer system. Whether the system is a desktop personal computer, a workstation, or a large special-purpose processor, data storage has always been a major selling point and a requested feature. As the price of memory has come down, the size of memory purchased for all classes of computers has gone up. One nonchanging feature is the general structure of the memory hierarchy. No matter how sophisticated or how simple the systems are, we will find that they all have something in common. The designers of the systems have organized data storage to maximize performance and provide adequate information volume storage.

The storage hierarchy (Figure 2.6) consists of a variety of data storage types that respond to the information needs of the system. From the highest-speed element (a cache) to the slowest-speed elements (archival devices), the tradeoff is the cost and speed of the storage medium per unit of memory. What is being attempted is to match the speed of the computer processor with the highest-speed devices within a reasonable cost curve. In the following sections we will examine the information storage devices outside of the central processing unit realm. This leaves out the high-speed expensive cache memories and primary memory. We will begin our review by looking at tape devices, magnetic disks, and archival devices.

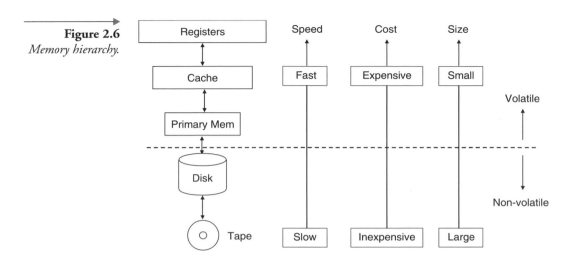

**Figure 2.6**
*Memory hierarchy.*

## 2.5.1   **Tape storage devices**

Magnetic tape information storage provides a low-cost, high-density storage medium for low-access or slow-access data. A tape unit consists of the storage medium (a spool of magnetic material formed into a tape), access electronics, and mechanical components (see Figure 2.7). A tape unit operates in a simple manner. Data on a tape can only be accessed in sequential form. Data must be located on the tape and then removed from the tape. A tape drive mechanically can rewind a tape, sequentially search the tape, and stop the tape. To access data stored on a tape an I/O program would have to command the tape unit to rewind the tape and then sequentially search the tape from the beginning until a match is found. Once found the addressed data can be removed.

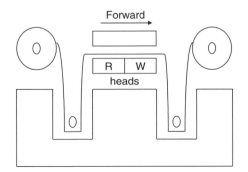

**Figure 2.7**
*Schematic diagram of a magnetic tape storage system.*

To improve the performance of tape units, additional storage semantic access schemes have been devised. The beginning of the tape is reserved to maintain pointers to the start points of files stored on the tape. Instead of sequentially searching the entire tape, the controller searches the tape's directory, finds out where on the tape (e.g., how many feet from the directory region) the data are stored, and then uses this information to fast forward to the general location where linear search can resume. This allows for a speedup in the access and transfer of the data stored on the device—an important feature when a database management system is involved.

## 2.5.2   Magnetic and optical disk storage devices

An improvement over tape storage is the random access disk units, which most users of computers are aware of. The disks can be removable or internal fixed forms. A disk unit is typically comprised of one or more of the following: a controller, a movable access arm, and a magnetic storage medium in the form of a rotating platter (see Figure 2.8). The platter(s) is mounted on a spindle, which rotates at some given speed. The platter is organized into a set of rings called tracks and a partitioning of these tracks called sectors.

The movable arm contains the sensing and driving hardware to allow for the reading and writing of the magnetic or optical data stored on the platter. The controller orchestrates the access of the stored data based on a variety of access algorithms, only the simplest of which we will discuss here. The simplest form of disk access is that found in the sequential search paradigm. The disk controller knows on what sector and track a data file is stored and using this information the disk controller must perform some simple functions, such as moving the access arm out to the track the data are stored on (this is called seeking and the time it takes is called the seek time).

Once on the proper track, the controller must find the proper sector where the data are stored. This requires the controller to recognize the start of the sector markers on the track and to find the appropriate sector as it

**Figure 2.8**
*Schematic diagram of a magnetic or optical disk system.*

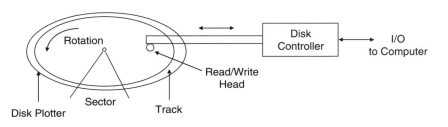

passes under the access arm's sensors. The time required for this is called the rotation time. Once the arm is over the proper sector and track, the data can be transferred from the medium to the controller. This time is called the transfer time.

So, for the average access of a data file on a disk we must take the following time:

$$T = t\{\text{seek}\} + t\{\text{rotate}\} + t\{\text{transfer}\} \qquad (2.12)$$

One can readily see from this that the time to access data on a disk unit is greater than that of the primary memory and would typically be less than the time to extract a similar amount of data from a tape unit.

The density of the disk is based on the medium used to store the data. Disk units built on a magnetic medium are getting fairly dense, but they are approaching their limits. In addition, the medium is susceptible to failures due to airborne pollutants and magnetic fields. To improve this the industry has developed optical disk technology. This technology replaces the magnetic medium with an optical medium where data are stored as reflective optical media. The medium is similar to what is seen in television optical disk players.

### 2.5.3   Archival storage devices

Even with all of the disk and tape technology available, not all required data for a computer system can be kept on line. To keep data that are only occasionally needed we require archival storage devices. Archival storage devices typically have removable media. If you have access to the new multimedia systems or have a personal computer or workstation for use, you have interacted with a form of archival device: the removable disk, compact disk, or tape cartridge. This represents the most visible form of archival storage device. Data are loaded into the system as needed and removed when completed. The most recent archival storage device developed, the CD read/write drive, has begun to blur the distinction between archival and on-line storage. Many systems use CD drives as enhanced storage for long-term applications memory. Some systems have even gone to the length where these represent the primary on-line storage.

Other, more elaborate, archival systems have been developed that use a combination of mechanical and electrical systems to port media on line and off line. These are similar to compact disk magazines and resemble jukeboxes. When a particular data item is needed, its physical storage location is found, and the medium is placed into the active storage hierarchy on line where the archived data can now be accessed. Again, this is a useful feature when we are talking about a very large database.

## 2.6    Distributed and network architectures

Not all systems consist of one computer. Modern systems used in academia, business, and government are more frequently being interconnected to form information-sharing systems or multiprocessing systems. These networks and computer interconnects are constructed by providing yet another input and output path for the computer to receive or send information. The input and output unit and controller for the network peripheral device are called a network interface unit (NIU) or processor bus. The function of these interface units and buses is to provide a seamless (typically) way for one computer to interact with another as if they were located in the same machine. Networks come in a variety of configurations—for example, the NIUs can be configured as a single global bus topology, as a central star or hub topology, as a ring topology, or as some hybrid. When interconnected in such ways over a relatively small distance (a single floor, building, or small organization), we have what is referred to as a local area network, or LAN. A LAN is used to interconnect a subunit of some larger organization or to interconnect a small number of users who need to share information. Beyond a LAN we have wide area networks and the Internet. Multiprocessor systems are interconnected using similar concepts. They are combined using shared buses or shared memory.

### 2.6.1    Computer to network interface elements

The network can be formed in many ways: It could have a central switching element, which could be a stand-alone computer acting as a router (see Figure 2.9a); it could share a central storage repository; or it could be connected using intelligent interface units into a communications medium.

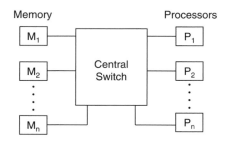

**Figure 2.9a**
*Multiprocessor computer system with distributed memory.*

**Figure 2.9b**
*Multiprocessor
computer system
with Simms
memory.*

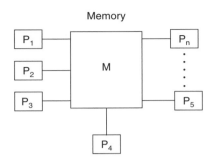

The configuration used depends on the degree of synchronization and control required, as well as the distribution between computers.

The tightly coupled multiprocessor uses a shared central memory as the interconnection device (see Figure 2.9b). All processors on the network use the central memory to access and pass data among the interconnected processors. This distributed architecture provides an easy means to coordinate actions between processors. A distinction is that each processor does not have any local memory; all instructions and data are acquired from the shared memory bank. An improvement over this architecture is the loosely coupled multiprocessor. In this architecture each processor has some primary local memory and is interconnected via a shared secondary storage system. Each processor has its own operating system and local storage for programs and local data. Coordination occurs through the passing of data from one computer system to another through the shared storage device. The data exchange and signaling of transfers are handled through mechanisms such as messages or coordination of shared storage regions in the secondary storage medium.

**Figure 2.9c**
*Multiprocessor
computer system
with private local
memory.*

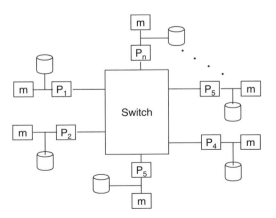

**Figure 2.9d**
*Multiprocessor computer system with a communications subsystem.*

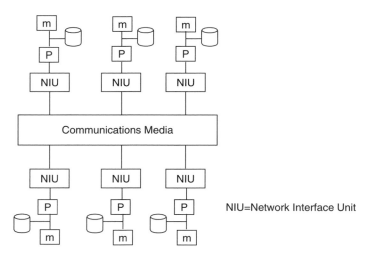

NIU=Network Interface Unit

A further refinement removes the shared secondary storage device and replaces this with a communications switching element. The switch allows each of the disjoint computer systems to address and send information among themselves. Each computer system has its own local memory and can have additional secondary storage devices (see Figure 2.9c). Each computer communicates with interconnected systems by addressing the called system, forming a connection, and then initiating a conversation. This is analogous to how we converse over a phone system. The switching-based distributed system requires additional software at each site to coordinate access.

A further enhancement is to remove the central switch and replace it with a shared communications path (see Figure 2.9d). The path could be a shared bus, a ring, or a star medium. The interconnected computers are each required to have a medium interconnect unit, which controls the access to the medium. This architecture requires further control software and policies to allow for control over the shared medium. Only one computer at a time can be accessing the medium and sending information. We will see in subsequent sections how this software operates.

## 2.6.2  Network bridges

We can further expand on the local area network or multiprocessing systems by introducing another networking control unit. To interconnect multiple networks or multiprocessing systems requires a bridge. (See Figure 2.10.) A bridge can be viewed as a speed-matching device to synchronize

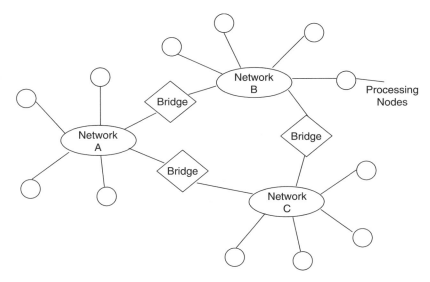

**Figure 2.10**
*Connecting networks through a bridge.*

the traffic between networks. Bridges typically contain software and hardware to buffer incoming messages, to determine and rectify variances in addresses on interconnected networks, and to forward messages to the addressed unit. Routers and switches found in most medium to large network configurations fall into this category of device.

## 2.7   Network topologies

As mentioned earlier, there are a variety of interconnection topologies used in local area networks. They are the global bus, the ring, and the star topologies.

### 2.7.1   Global bus topology

A global bus is a single shared medium, which can only be used by one device at a time. The global bus is controlled by a variety of schemes. One of the simplest is the carrier sense multiple access scheme. This protocol works by using two principles: first, the delay taken to send a bit from one end of the bus to the other and, second, the ability to send and then listen to the medium. The protocol in its simplest form operates as follows:

- Listen to the bus—if busy, wait; if clear, send data.

- Once data have been sent, continue to listen and compare what is heard against what was sent.

- If what was sent matches what is heard for the entire end-to-end communications time, then I control the bus and can continue sending a message (the assumption here is that if I wait for an end-to-end transfer time, then all other nodes must have heard my message and will now delay if they wish to transmit).

- When complete, go back into listen mode.

- If I do not hear the same message that I sent, then a collision occurred on the bus. I immediately stop transmission and delay before trying to send again.

By using this simple protocol, devices on the network can send and receive messages fairly efficiently. The problem with this protocol is that it inherently wastes media bandwidth in the sending and sensing process.

A different approach to control access to a global bus is based on a reservation scheme. In a reservation scheme the available bandwidth is broken up into chunks, which are then allocated to various devices on the network. To access the medium to transmit data a device must first wait until its reservation slot becomes available. There are numerous schemes through which the slots can be allocated and controlled. The problem with this approach is that it is inherently static. The slots cannot be reallocated easily from one system to another. Numerous variations on this protocol have been developed and implemented in systems with varying degrees of success.

## 2.7.2   Ring topology

The ring topology links the computer systems in the network in a continuous ring. Messages flow around the network from one computer system to another until they return to the sender. (See Figure 2.11.) This topology allows for better utilization of the medium. The medium can be broken into slots that flow around the network. The slots are marked as either empty or full depending on whether or not a message is present in the slot. To send a message a computer senses the slot beginning and checks whether it is full or empty. If the slot is full, the sender waits for the next slot. If the slot is empty, the sender inserts its message. The problem with this scheme is that the slot size limits the size of messages that can be sent in a single slot. Variations on this protocol have alleviated this problem, but have their own set of problems. A different protocol, which allows for variable-size messages, is the insertion ring protocol. This protocol requires hardware support to buffer incoming messages that would interfere with a sender's message. A computer that wants to send a message on the network can

**Figure 2.11**
*Ring topology.*

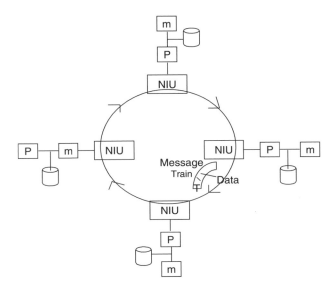

simply send the message if no other message traffic is sensed by the sender. If another message should then arrive at the sender's input during the transmission of its own message, the sender simply queues up the arriving message and appends it to the sending message when it has completed.

### 2.7.3  Star topology

The star topology has the physical layout of a star. It has a central network processor at its center, with nodes arranged around and connected to the central point. Wiring costs can be considerably higher with this topology.

## 2.8  Computer architectures

To continue our earlier discussion of computer configurations we will examine how the various components can be interconnected to form a computer system. The basic premise of these architectures is to speed up the movement of data to allow for increased processing. The basic architecture has the CPU at the core with a main memory and input/output system on either side of the CPU (see Figure 2.12). In this architecture all data flows into, out of, and through the CPU under the control of the CPU. This represents the basic von Neumann architecture described earlier. Refinements of this architecture have been designed to remove the CPU from the burden of controlling all data movement.

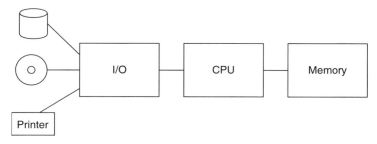

**Figure 2.12**
*Basic computer architecture.*

## 2.8.1 Central I/O controller architectures

To remove the CPU from the central function of coordinating all data flow the central input/output controller architecture was developed (see Figure 2.13). This architecture has the IOC at the core of the system with the CPU, main memory, and I/O devices connected to the IOC hub. To transfer data from the main memory to an I/O device the CPU would command the IOC to initiate the transfer. The data would flow under control of the IOC from the main memory through the IOC to the named output device. The problem with this architecture is that the CPU must also use the IOC to transfer data from the main memory to the CPU. This results in potential reduction in CPU performance. Variations of this architecture have a secondary path to the main memory for better service to the CPU.

## 2.8.2 Memory-mapped architectures

The main memory is the location in the computer system where all data and instructions flow in and out. As a consequence of this, an architecture was proposed that had the main memory as the central element (see Figure 2.14). The main memory sits between the CPU and I/O. All data flow between the I/O and CPU goes through the memory. A variety of control schemes have been devised to control the access to the shared memory. One

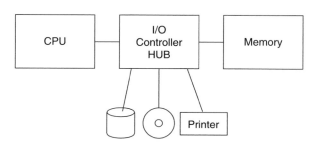

**Figure 2.13**
*Computer architecture utilizing an I/O controller.*

**Figure 2.14**
*A computer system
organized around
memory.*

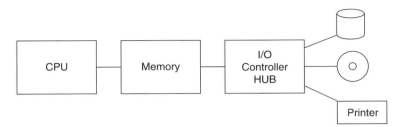

**Figure 2.14**
*A computer system
organized around
memory.*

is to partition the memory into regions: one region for the CPU to use and one for each of the I/O devices on the system. To send data to an I/O device the CPU simply addresses the memory location for the device. By doing this the device's input register is directly loaded with the data. To the CPU the I/O transfer is the same as a write to main memory.

### 2.8.3    Common bus architecture

An architecture that is similar to the global network architecture previously described is the unibus architecture. The unibus or global bus architecture uses a single communications bus to interconnect memory, CPU, and I/O devices (see Figure 2.15). These elements are connected to the bus and communicate with each other using addresses over the bus. As in the network case, this design will result in reduced utilization if conflicts between bus accesses are frequent. This architecture was successfully used in numerous early digital equipment computers and is still in use in many systems.

### 2.8.4    Dual bus architecture

A refinement on the single bus architecture is the dual bus architecture (Figure 2.16). In this architecture the central hub of the computer is a dual bus configuration: one bus for memory traffic and one for I/O traffic. All devices, CPU, main memory, disks, tapes, terminals, and direct memory access devices are connected to both buses. This architecture removed some of the contention between the CPU memory accesses and I/O transfers. The CPU and memory were free to actively move data to and from mem-

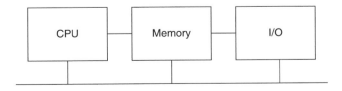

**Figure 2.15**
*Unibus
architecture.*

**Figure 2.16**
*Dual bus
architecture.*

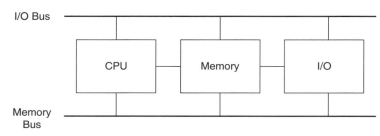

ory, as were the I/O devices, without conflict. An I/O device could be writing into one region of memory while the CPU was concurrently accessing another section. Architectures that have derived from this philosophy are more common in modern computer systems. We will see how these architectures and elements of the computer system are used by database management systems as we continue with our discussion of database management system architectures and operations.

## 2.9   Computer systems support software architecture

A computer systems–based application requires services and cooperative support from a collection of computer hardware and software to perform its designated function. The application requires a computational platform consisting of a CPU, memory, and secondary data storage, as well as a supporting operational infrastructure consisting of an operating system, database management system, network management, and additional process and resource management components. To understand how a computer-based application utilizes these components we must first understand the operation of these software infrastructure elements.

The central processing unit (CPU) and the main memory make up the basic computational engine and support the execution of all software within this computer. The CPU is composed of a collection of registers, computational subunits, data paths, and status registers that are used to move data about and to perform basic manipulations on these data (Figure 2.17). For example, a CPU can add, subtract, multiply, divide, and compare values or simply move them from one location to another. These are basic operations, which the remainder of the system's infrastructure is built upon and where it resides. The CPU also includes some additional support hardware, such as timers, interrupt registers and latches, input and output registers, and interconnections. For additional details on these elements refer to previous sections in this chapter.

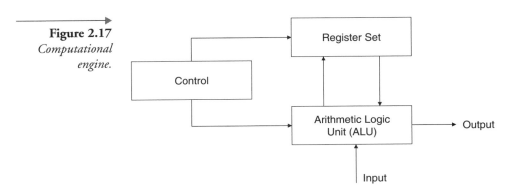

**Figure 2.17**
*Computational engine.*

In addition to the CPU, the other primary element within the basic system is the memory. A memory hierarchy is typically comprised of high-speed data registers, fast cache memory, primary memory, and secondary storage (Figure 2.18). The memory hierarchy at the closest point to the CPU hardware is populated with very expensive and limited high-speed registers. These registers are used to move a very limited number of data items into and out of the CPU for actual processing. The second level of the hierarchy is the cache memory. A cache memory is a bank of high-speed memory organized in a manner that allows for rapid retrieval of data; it executes at nearly the speed of on-chip or CPU registers. A cache memory is used to keep data most likely to be used next in close proximity to the CPU and in fast storage. The problem with cache memory and registers is that they are very expensive, thereby limiting the amount of either that may be found in an architecture. This type of storage hardware requires additional infrastruc-

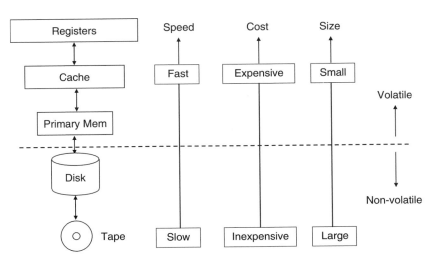

**Figure 2.18**
*Memory hierarchy.*

ture support from the operating system and hardware to maintain the most appropriate piece of data in the most appropriate level of the hierarchy.

This control has typically been performed by a memory management hardware and software combination that uses locality of reference and locality of use principles to determine what information to place into the appropriate storage level and what information to remove.

The third element of the memory hierarchy is the primary memory. The primary memory in most machines today is sized in the hundreds of megabytes of storage range. This volume of storage allows for large portions of a data processing task to be memory resident during processing for small data processing applications. This is not to say that there is no swapping of information between the primary memory and the bulk secondary storage disk units. The volume of storage on such units is now in the order of tens of gigabytes range. The main emphasis in a computer system is on how and what performs the management of this hierarchy. The system's memory manager could do the best job for the typical application, but at a cost to all other high-performance applications of the operating system.

For the collection of computer hardware elements described previously, a working computer system requires policies and mechanisms for control of these resources and coordination between them to exist. This has typically been the function of a computer's operating system. An operating system consists of specialized software with hardware support to manage the interaction of the CPU and all other hardware elements supporting applications software running on the computer system.

## 2.9.1   Operating systems architecture

An operating system is computer software that interacts at a low level with the computer system's hardware to manage the sharing of the computer's resources among various software applications. An operating system runs as the most privileged of software elements on the system and requires basic hardware support for interrupts and timers to effect control over executing programs. An operating system typically provides the following services:

1.   Hardware management (interrupt handling, timer management)

2.   Interprocess synchronization and communications

3.   Process management

4.   Resource allocation (scheduling, dispatching)

5.   Storage management and access (I/O)

6.      Memory management

7.      File management

8.      Protection of system and user resources

9.      Interprocess communications management

10.     Network management

An operating system begins with the management of a computer system's hardware. Hardware management requires the ability to set limits on the holding of resources and the ability to transfer control from an executing program back to the operating system. These functions are realized through the use of hardware timers and interrupt services. A hardware timer is a counter that can be set to a specific count (time period). When the time expires, an interrupt signal is released, which stops the processor, saves the processor's state (saves all active register contents, ALU registers, status registers, stack pointers, program counters, instruction registers, etc.), and turns control over to an interrupt service routine. The interrupt service routine examines the contents of predefined registers (e.g., the CPU status register or a predefined interrupt register) or set memory locations and determines what operations are to be performed next. Typically, control is immediately turned over to the operating system's kernel for servicing of the interrupt.

### Interrupt management and semaphores

The use of interrupts is one means for an operating system to effect control over the hardware of the system. Another means is through the use of cooperative software and control actions or instructions. The concept described here is mutual exclusion. An operating system, to guarantee singular, noninterfering access to a resource, must have a means to limit the access to a resource or a resource allocation mechanism via some mutually exclusive operator. A mutual exclusion primitive must possess the ability to limit access to a region or resource by only one element at a time, even when concurrent access is being attempted (atomic action). The all-or-nothing operation of an atomic function is required for the guaranteed, nonconflicting access and control over system resources by the operating system. A specific hardware instruction called test and set is provided in many computer systems to support this mutual exclusion primitive. The instruction in a single atomic instruction cycle reads a variable specified, tests its value against some basic value, and sets the variable to a new value if the condition tested for is valid.

The test-and-set instruction forms the basis for constructing sema-phores. A semaphore is a system variable that can exist in only one of two states, either true or false, with no other valid states holding for the variable. The semaphore variables have atomic operations that can be performed on them, with no other operations outside of these being valid operations. The valid operations are of two types. The first operation is a request to set the variable, sometimes referred to as $P(S)$. The second operation is a request to reset the variable and is sometimes referred to as $V(S)$. These act much like a flip-flop in a logic circuit. The flip-flop can be set or reset, holding a zero or one value only. The set and reset operations of a semaphore variable are used to construct lock and unlock operations on resources or to hold and release operations on the resources. Semaphores are used to construct monitors, which encase the control of an operating system's controlled resource. For example, a monitor could be used as a means to limit the access to a tape unit to one process at a time by constructing a queue of waiting processes and one service routine. The operation would be to build an outside shell around the tape service routine to allow only one process access to it at a time. The $P$ and $V$ operators can be used for this function.

$$P(S) \text{ If } S = 0 \text{ THEN } S := 1 \text{ ELSE  Enqueue requester}$$

$$\text{Tape Service Routine} \qquad\qquad (2.13)$$

$$V(S) S := 0, \text{ If Queue} <> \text{null then Dequeue}$$

The processes that wish to use the tape service routine request service by first requesting the set function $P(S)$. If no process is presently using the tape, then the $S$ variable is zero. If it is free, the variable gets set, and the process is allowed to enter the critical section of code reserved for the tape service routine and use the routine. If the tape routine is already being used (indicated by the $S$ semaphore variable being set to one), the request is enqueued, awaiting the release of the resource. Once a process finishes with the tape service routine, the $V(S)$ or reset operation is requested. The reset operator resets the value of the semaphore back to zero and tests the queue of waiting processes to see if any processes still require service. If there are waiting processes, the top of the queue is removed and a $P(S)$ request is issued for the process, starting over the entire process.

In this manner, using semaphores, complex monitors can be constructed to control access to a variety of system hardware and software resources. Monitors and semaphores have been used as a means to construct synchronization mechanisms to coordinate the actions of cooperating resources. For example, using the simple $P$ and $V$ semaphores described, one could con-

struct two cooperative resource management routines by using three semaphore variables and the $P$ and $V$ operators, as follows:

$$P(S) \text{ If } S = 0 \text{ THEN } S := 1 \qquad P(S1) \text{ If } S1 = 0 \text{ THEN } S1 := 1$$
$$P(M) \text{ If } M = 0 \text{ THEN } M := 1 \qquad P(M) \text{ If } M = 0 \text{ THEN } M := 1$$

Resource $A$ Service Routine          Resource $B$ Service Routine          (2.14)

$$V(M) M := 0 \qquad\qquad\qquad V(M) M := 0$$
$$V(S1) S1 := 0 \qquad\qquad\qquad V(S) S := 0$$

The two semaphores ($S$ and $S1$) would provide for the synchronous
operation of the two resources in such a way that they would toggle back
and forth—either the resource $A$ service routine first followed by the
resource $B$ service routine or the resource $B$ service routine followed by the
resource $A$ routine. They could not, however, be executed concurrently due
to the use of the $M$ semaphore. One can see from this example some of the
rudimentary needs of the database management system's functions being
implemented using similar concepts to guarantee mutual restricted access to
database-stored information and management routines.

### Process management

A process is typically viewed as the lowest executable level of software recognized by the operating system. Processes can have additional internal management layers that are outside the domain of the operating system. The
process does not, however, equate to a user program. A user program may
be partitioned into multiple processes, or it could be a single process. The
process does not have to be a fixed-size image in the system. It can take a
variety of shapes and forms. The important aspect of a process is that there
is a measurable entity that the operating system knows about and has information about, at least in terms of how this process interacts with and fits
into the resources being managed.

Process management performs the task of managing software processes
on a computer system. The operating system provides the services to create
a process (build and populate a process control block for a new process), to
kill a process (remove its process control block), to fork a process into tasks,
to join tasks, and to dispatch processes. A process is described in the operating system using a process control block, or PCB. The PCB is created for a
process upon its initial instantiation in the system. A typical process control
block contains information such as a process identifier; a process type (user,
system, database, network, etc.); process priority; process state information;
process resource requirements (memory, disks, peripherals, other processes,

etc.); and the state of required resources, process size, and present process memory load location. This is only a representative set of information and is by no means complete.

The operating system uses the process control block information from all processes within the system to coordinate the execution of all of the processes in order to meet some operating system's goal, such as fair execution, equal execution times, or some minimum average execution time. Processes run at a variety of levels within the operating system. Some processes are privileged and can, therefore, access protected regions of memory or hidden routines. Application processes may have no outside access other than the programmer's immediate load image. Others, such as the database management system, have some form of access rights in-between these two extremes. Processes exist within the system in many different degrees of completion, called states. A process within the system can be in one of these four states: ready to run, running, suspended or blocked, and terminated or dead (Figure 2.19).

The ready state refers to the state a process is in when it is prepared to run on the hardware but is awaiting the go-ahead from the operating system. To be in this state the process must have all the resources it requires to run allocated or at least fully specified, and it must have a known state for the resources stored in the PCB. Transitions from the ready state include terminate, dispatch, or block.

Terminating the process can be the result of a user action to kill the process or a command from another process, such as an operating system command, due to resource removal or an error condition (e.g., a bad control word for a printer). Dispatching a process moves a process from the

**Figure 2.19**
*Process states.*

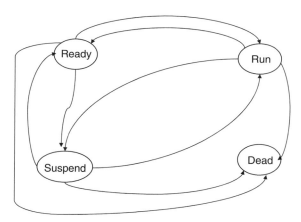

ready state to the running state due to a scheduling action. The block transition moves a process from the ready state to the waiting state and is due to the removal of an acquired resource by the operating system or to some other deficiency that will not allow the process to go forward.

The running state refers to the point when the process has control of the CPU and is executing its instructions on the bare machine. The process has control of the hardware at this level and is only removed from execution by an interrupt from the operating system or an error condition. Transitions to this state only occur under control of the operating system and are due to scheduling actions. Transitions out of this state are due to a variety of conditions. A process can go from the running state to the termination state upon completion of execution, or a process can go back to the waiting state due to an input/output request (which is serviced by another process) or to the ready state due to an interrupt from the operating system for some other condition.

The waiting or suspended state for a process is used to hold processes that have not acquired the needed resources to execute or that have been removed from active execution due to some blocking action. A waiting action could be due to the transfer of data from the disk into memory or the completion of a cooperating process. Transitions to the waiting state are typically caused by requests for added resources, the removal or reallocation of some needed resources waiting for a cooperating process to finish its service, or waiting for resources to be freed up for other requests.

The termination or dead state is the state from which all processes originate and finally return to for exiting the system. This state is where a process is originally given basic assets, such as a process control block, initial memory load space, and so forth. In addition, this is the state where processes that have been terminated for whatever reason are returned. The functions here deallocate held resources and remove the process from the system.

Processes are moved from state to state based on the actions of various operating system support routines, such as the scheduler, dispatcher, and allocation routines. These routines have the job of determining when to move a process from one state to another, which process to move from one state to another, how to move the process, and where to move it. All these decisions are based on the interpretation of the operating system's managed process control block and the state of the system resources.

To determine which one of a set of ready processes to move from the ready state to the running state requires a scheduling policy and supporting

**Figure 2.20**
*Process flow in a
round-robin
scheduler.*

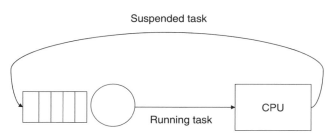

mechanism to implement this policy. Originally computer systems used simple FIFO scheduling, where the next process in a list (queue, linked list, or some other data structure of PCBs) is the process scheduled for transition from the ready state to the running state. Other scheduling techniques try to be more fair and break up running processes into chunks of time called quantums. One such scheduler is the round-robin technique, where processes are moved from running to blocked or suspended states once they exceed their allotted quantum of time (a time slice or period). Suspended processes are placed on the circular queue, where they wait until they move around to the front of the queue to once again receive service. In this manner the CPU time is shared equally among all active processes (Figure 2.20). This type of scheduling is typical of a time-share system.

There are other techniques where the quantum time is not equal and where the selection process does not simply choose the next in line. The time slices are broken up into varying levels with the top level being short, small time slices; the intermediate being longer slices, but with also a longer wait time between getting service; and, finally, a long-term scheduler, where there is a greater time slice allocated but where the time between service intervals is even greater (Figure 2.21).

A variety of other schedulers have been constructed for almost every conceivable measurable system quantity. For example, schedulers have been constructed that use priority (from a few levels to thousands of levels), execution time remaining, fixed deadline time scheduling, priority ceiling, and other techniques to select which process will get serviced next.

Once a process has been scheduled for service, it still must be moved from the inactive process control block state to a state where it is being prepared to execute upon the hardware. The task of preparing the process for actual execution falls on the operating system dispatcher. The dispatcher accepts the given process control block from the scheduler and proceeds to perform tasks required to ready the CPU for execution of the provided process. The dispatcher loads the stored CPU register values for the process

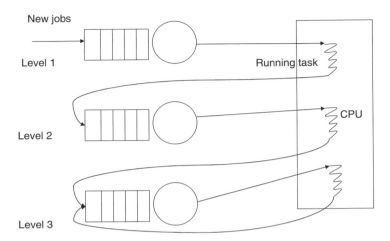

**Figure 2.21**
*Multilevel time-slice scheduling.*

New jobs

Level 1

Running task

CPU

Level 2

Level 3

into the appropriate registers and restores the CPU status registers. The stored program counter for the process is loaded into the CPU's program counter register, and the proper physical addressing information for the process is loaded into the appropriate memory-addressing registers and data structures. Once all of the parameters are in place, the dispatcher turns over control to the process by making the program counter for the process the next jump address from which to acquire the following instruction. The dispatcher may also have the task of resetting timers and interrupt flags before it turns over execution control of the CPU. The setting of interrupt timers is essential if the operating system is to reacquire control of the CPU at a later time.

Another operating system function responsible for the movement of processes from one state to another state is the memory allocation service. This will be discussed in more detail later in this chapter. Additional features that the operating system must provide for process management include error management and deadlock detection, both of which are also important to a database management system but not in the form used in an operating system. The error management services provide functions to detect, correct, avoid, and prevent errors, depending on the class of service required and the price the operating system and serviced applications are willing to pay.

Deadlock detection is performed for the processes and for the resources required by the processes running in the system. Deadlock occurs when one process is holding a resource another requires and a resource this process needs is held by the other (Figure 2.22). Deadlock management can take

**Figure 2.22**
*A deadlock.*

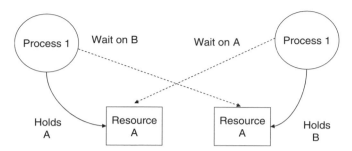

many forms. We may wish to detect deadlock and correct it by removing some of the offenders. We may wish to prevent deadlock from occurring by guaranteeing ahead of time that the allocation of requested resources cannot result in a deadlock. One way to realize this is to preallocate all of the resources needed for an executing process before it is allowed to begin. This is a safe algorithm but one that has an enormous amount of built-in holding time on resources and one that will directly result in longer waiting time by processes, resulting in longer overall execution times and lower system process throughput. Another means to deadlock management is to avoid deadlock altogether. Avoidance can be achieved by setting up resources in a specific order of access, which must be followed by all processes. In this way processes can only access resources in order and cannot hold a resource held by another that you are waiting for. The circular wait is removed in this approach.

### Resource management

Resource management requires that the operating system coordinate the access and transmission of information from resources connected to the computer. Typical of functions handled by the resource management function of the operating system are memory management, peripheral device initialization, device setup, control over the data transfer, and closing of the peripheral device. In early systems the operating system controlled these devices down to a low level. In more modern systems the operating system sets up the parameters of a transfer and leaves the details of the data transfer to the device controllers and to direct memory transfer control devices. This leaves the operating system and CPU free to do other required resource management tasks.

### Memory management

An operating system's storage manager manages the memory hierarchy of the computer. The operating system in particular must coordinate the movement of information into and out of the computer's primary memory, as well as the maintenance of the memory's free space. To perform these functions an operating system typically uses a scheme where the primary memory is broken up into fixed-size pieces called pages or variable-sized pieces called segments. The operating system then manages the movement of pages or segments in memory based on policies in use. The memory manager must allocate space for processes upon initiation, deallocate space when a process completes, and periodically clean up the memory space when the memory becomes fragmented due to allocation and deallocation of uneven partitions. The memory allocation problem is directly tied to the memory map. (See Figure 2.23.)

The memory map indicates which areas in memory are allocated to a process and which areas are free to be allocated to a new process. This memory map can be managed in a variety of ways to help the allocation manager. The list of free areas can be organized into a free list, where the blocks are structured as a tree of increasing block size, or as a heap, with the largest block always toward the top of the heap. Memory allocation then becomes a function of selecting a block of appropriate size based on the selection policy in place. Some policies include first fit, where the first block encountered that fits this process is selected. Another policy is best fit, where the blocks are scanned until one is found that best fits the size of the process to be loaded into the memory. There are numerous other schemes, but they are beyond the scope of this chapter.

**Figure 2.23**
*Memory map.*

Program
Address
Space

Physical Address Space

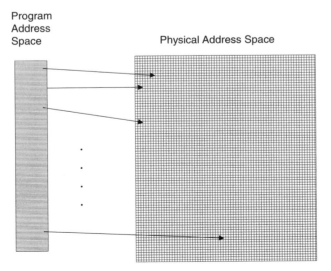

Hand in hand with allocation is deallocation of memory. As pages or segments are released by processes leaving the running state, they must be removed from the allocated list and replaced into the free list of free pages or segments. The deallocated segments are restored to the list in a block equal to the size of the allocated process that held them. These free segments are then placed into the free list in a location appropriate to the size of the free segments being restored.

However, not all replacements are done in such a nice manner on process execution boundaries. Most are performed on a full or near-full primary memory. In order to still allow processes to move forward in their execution, we must reorder the active pages by some policy that will allow us to remove some active pages and let them be reallocated to other more demanding or starved-out processes. The most common page replacement algorithm and deallocation policy is based on the least recently used (LRU) principle. This principle indicates that the least recently used page is most likely to stay that way for the foreseeable future and, therefore, is a prime candidate to be removed and replaced by a waiting process. Other schemes used for page replacement include most recently used, least frequently used, and random removal. All of these policies have been examined in detail in the past and have merits for certain process activities, although for database systems some of these are downright disastrous. The database process acts in a way that is not typical of most applications and, therefore, will not react the same to a certain policy.

Another job for memory management is to maintain a map of free memory areas and to periodically clean up memory to free up larger contiguous chunks to make allocation easier. This process is called garbage collection and reallocation. The allocation and deallocation policies discussed

**Figure 2.24**
*Fragmented memory.*

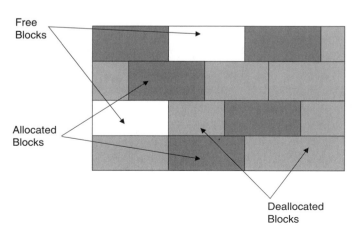

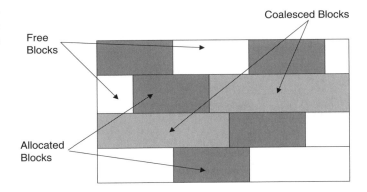

**Figure 2.25**
*Marking free blocks
in memory.*

previously result in memory becoming periodically fragmented. When memory is fragmented into very fine fragments, it may become impossible to find contiguous blocks of free memory to allocate to incoming processes (Figure 2.24). To rectify this problem, memory management services periodically check the map of memory to determine if cleaning up the loose fragmented free blocks into larger segments will result in significant increases in free contiguous blocks of sufficient size.

One technique scans all marked free blocks and coalesces adjacent holes into marked, larger free segments. These are then added to the free list with the coalesced disjoint holes removed from the free list (Figure 2.25).

This in itself may not result in sufficient free space of adequate size. To get larger free blocks it may be necessary to periodically scan the entire memory and reallocate where processes are stored to clean up the memory allocation map into two areas—one a contiguous area consisting of all allocated memory blocks and the other all free memory blocks. The process by which all allocated blocks are moved and reallocated to one end of memory is called compaction, and the process for reallocating all of the newly freed space into the free list is referred to as garbage collection (Figure 2.26). As

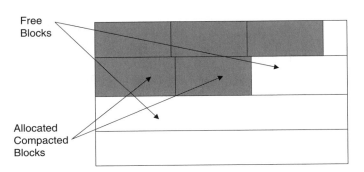

**Figure 2.26**
*Memory after
garbage collection.*

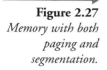

**Figure 2.27**
*Memory with both
paging and
segmentation.*

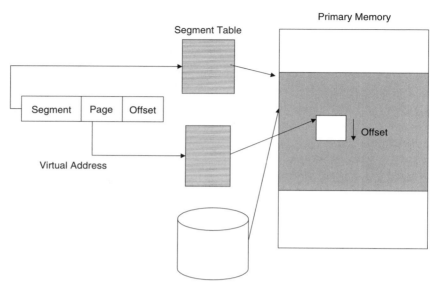

with a garbage truck, compaction strives to compress the contents into one end of the container, freeing up the remainder of the space for more garbage. The process requires the reallocation and movement of processes and their addresses (all references must be changed in PCB and physical load segments).

Beyond these basic memory management schemes some operating systems, along with support hardware and software, support both paging and segmentation. In this scheme the memory is decomposed into segments. A segment has some number of pages, and a page is of a fixed size. The segments are mapped into and out of memory as pages were in the first scheme (see Figure 2.27).

### File management

File management is a function of the operating system that controls the structure and storage of information on nonprimary storage resources. A typical application of file management is the files stored on a disk drive or tape drive. Files are collections of data and/or programs that are moved to or from memory. To perform this movement requires that the file's structure, format, and location be known to the operating system. The file manager uses this information to request memory space from the memory manager to move a file from storage into the memory. When ready to move back into storage, the file system uses information from the memory manager to determine if any changes have been made to the file. If no changes have been made, then the file can simply be discarded. If changes have been made, the file manager needs to determine if more space than the file originally occupied is required. If it is, the file is possibly stored in a different location or requires fragmentation on the device. Similar to the memory manager, the file manager may periodically be required to reallocate storage space and move files to free up larger contiguous areas.

The file manager provides additional services to the applications. File management provides functions to create, delete, and insert information into files; append information to the end of a file; and alter the contents of a file. File control mechanisms support the sharing of files among users in order to control the form of access allowed, to structure files for optimal space and time use, to name or rename files, and to copy and replicate files as needed for system support.

Management of the location and contents of a file system is controlled by the use of a file directory service. A file directory can be used as the means to facilitate access to files and to limit the use of a file as specified by the owner or the operating system. Some file managers organize files by type, such as .EXE for executables, .TXT for text files, .FOR for FORTRAN files, .PAS for Pascal files, and .C for C files. To aid in the management of files the file manager maintains a file control block with information about the files under its control. This information can facilitate the maintenance and use of the files.

### Protection

Protection is an operating system function that manages access to controlled resources. Protection typically consists of access authorization, access authentication, and access restrictions. The operating system checks the authorization rights of a service requester before the service is performed. If the proper rights exist, the access is allowed; if not, the requester is blocked from access.

Access authorization is a process through which the operating system determines that a process has the right to execute on this system. The most common form of this control is the user name, which we are all familiar with when we log on to a computer. The second form of operating system protection is authentication. Authentication deals with the problem of a user being verified as to who he or she claims to be. The most common form of authentication is the password. The combination of user authorization through a stored user name and user authentication through a password has proven adequate for most noncritical computer systems' access restriction management. If necessary, these two methods can be applied to the access of any resource to limit access to it. The problem to be addressed is the degree of protection required and the amount of overhead we are willing to pay for it.

Access control is a more involved issue and deals with how to control the use of information and programs by users who have authorization to be on a system. To control who uses software on the system and how it is used, an operating system must provide mechanisms to limit the execution rights of controlled software. To do this operating systems use some form of access control. The most common are access control lists, access control matrixes, and capabilities. Access control lists provide a means to list all software elements to be controlled in the system and provide a list of users or processes that have the right to use these software elements. The control can also limit the type of execution rights the process or user may have. For example, we may only allow for the invocation of a process, not the freeing of the CPU to the calling process. We may allow only read access to a region of a software process or insert rights, or we may give unrestricted rights. The main mechanism (the comparison of a user identifier against a list of rights) for an access control list is performed in a centralized site, possibly within a separate operating system service or within the controlled software itself. Capabilities perform a similar function but do it in a distributed fashion. Capabilities are created for each controlled element and are requested by processes that wish to use the controlled element. If the capability is appropriate for a process, it is given to the process. The process can then use the capability like a ticket to access and use the controlled element.

### Peripheral device management

Input/output and peripheral device management services were created to remove the physical details of use from user processes and to provide for more seamless and fair management of the resources. The goal of peripheral device management services is to make access clear, clean, and transparent to users. Management should remove all physical dependencies from users' access requirements and replace these with logical mechanisms that are already common in programming environments. The control is to make access device independent. The user should not have to know what type of device or where the device is located to access data or service software.

Management for peripheral devices is bound into two classes of operating systems service routines: I/O and device managers. The operating system strives to make all accesses appear the same. The typical method is to make all accesses have the look and feel of a file access. The I/O management process has the function to set up and maintain the logical channels or paths between CPU-resident processes and the outside world. The functions provided by this element include channel allocation and deallocation, channel setup, channel coordination, and remote data transfer and control. Included in this may be error detection and correction over the channel. In concert with this function is the device management function. Device management services provide mechanisms to perform device-dependent setup, allocation, control, synchronization, deallocation, and data transfer.

I/O and device management create the physical link and control the transfer. Included in this function is the request for buffer assets for the channel to utilize in transferring information from the secondary storage to the internal computer's memory. The buffers are used as the intermediary between the devices and the CPU. They allow for the concurrent operation of the I/O with applications processing within the system. The I/O channel control and device control are typically handled in an operating system as an independent process. The operating system initiates the I/O or device operation and departs, allowing the device and I/O managers to perform the task and, when completed, interrupt the operating system to indicate the completion of the task. The interrupt can be active, where it stops the operating system for immediate service, or it can be message oriented, where it sets some status indicator, which the operating system will check at its leisure.

When integrated with the operating system's file manager, these routines form a seamless link between the stored programs, data, and the run-time system. The file manager is used for the direct access of logical storage elements by the operating system and controlled processes. The file manager provides services to name files, address files, control access, select and coordinate access paths, perform background copying and backup for recovery, coordinate the allocation and deallocation of resources where file information is located, and manage the placement (logical) of stored information. An important function of the file management system is lock management. File managers create, issue, and control the locking and unlocking of files and records within files. This service is extremely important for concurrency control.

## 2.9.2   Network control software

Network management software manages the sending and receiving of information over a communications medium. Typical functions include message routing, naming, addressing, protection, media access, error detection and correction, communications setup, and management.

Routing is a system network management function needed to coordinate the movement of information over a network(s). In a local area network this function is not needed in all cases. Routing may simply require sending the data in a certain direction over the medium, or it may require more elaborate policies for selecting a channel or wire to send the message, based on the sender's location and network traffic. Routing is a required function in wide area networks such as the Internet.

Naming is required to facilitate the transparent access to all system resources, local or remote. A naming scheme should have the following features: provide for sharing of objects, provide access to replicants, and provide fully transparent access. The naming function must support two types of names for each item managed: an internal (systems) name and en external (user) name. The naming function must manage the translation and management of the external names with internal (unique) names.

Addressing is the means through which the system determines where a named item is located. Addressing schemes may be broken up into hierarchies, where local computers have their own set of names, which may not be unique between systems. The combination of the system's address (a node on the network) and the local name is sufficient to provide a system's unique name. Likewise, we could have a unique name and address for each network in a collection of interconnected networks.

Access control over a network deals with policies and mechanisms to limit the mode of access given to network users. Access limitations could be as simple as login privilege or more complex, such as limiting the type of connections one can acquire or the type of access to remote information. The mechanism for limiting access may be embedded in software accessing the network or may be explicitly provided by the user of the software accessing the network.

Protection is a function of the operating system that deals with the management of resources from malicious or accidental access that may deadlock the system. There are two major classes of protection schemes: The first tries to avoid the problem by preallocating resources; the second allows deadlock to occur but provides means to detect and correct problems. Avoidance builds access to resources in a methodical fashion. One scheme requires a process to acquire all resources it will need ahead of time and hold them for the duration of its access. This is highly restrictive and may cause excessive delays for other resources that may need the held resources. Deadlock detection allows for more concurrent access of resources but at the cost of potential deadlocks. One scheme requires the construction of waits-for graphs, which allow for the detection of potential and actual deadlocks and provides mechanisms to remove deadlock by aborting conflicting processes.

One can see from this simple description the possible problems from a database's perspective. The operating system may limit the sharing of resources between processes, even if the database would allow it. Media access software controls the interaction of users and software processes with the network. Typical mechanisms deal with the recognition and login interaction with a network node. Media access software deals with the connection to the communications medium and the setup of communications sessions. Access allows a process to log in with the network and be recognized by others over the network.

Communications setup and management act in conjunction with media access software to interact with remote nodes and set up a link. Typically, one node requests a linkup with a remote node. If the remote node can support an additional session, it creates a control block to hold information about the setup. The requesting node is signaled that a session was successfully created. Once created the interacting processes can send and receive information using their preallocated parameters.

### Client/server policies and mechanisms

The client/server mode of remote resource access and control is commonplace. One just has to open up a trade magazine to find advertisements for systems claiming client/server processing. The technique provides some of the benefits of distributed systems but without the added control overhead. Client/server participants operate by requesting and receiving services as needed. Servers hold resources and can provide service to clients. Clients require held resources and can request service from the server. The server grants service to the clients based on the present use and the sharing policy in place at the server. The methodology does not offer the tight synchronization one would find with distributed systems, but it does offer a simple means to access and share remote resources in a uniform fashion. Its simplicity has added to its popularity and growth.

### Remote procedure call policies and mechanisms

A similar remote access mechanism is the remote procedure call mechanism. As with local procedures, a requester must know the procedure's name and the proper parameters. The requester calls the remote procedure and the blocks awaiting the remote procedure's response. The called procedure performs the requested service, and, on return of control to the caller, the caller unblocks and continues processing. The procedure is exactly the same as the conventional procedure call except that the call is over a remote channel to another site. Further details of network software and specifics related to databases will be described in later chapters.

## 2.9.3　Fault detection and recovery

An operating system has a requirement to monitor the system for errors, faults, and failures and to provide mechanisms to correct these conditions or to reconfigure around them. To detect errors or faults in the first place an operating system uses a few basic functions. The first relies on hardware detection of errors—for example, parity check bits, cyclic redundancy checks, and computational checks such as overflows and divide by zero. These provide for detection of intermittent or hard errors within the communications and computational infrastructure of the machine. To check for more subtle or buried errors requires the periodic initiation of fault-monitoring software. This software collects information from these basic hardware elements and from running software using predefined test points. These collected data are then periodically analyzed for patterns that may indicate software or hardware errors present in the system. This software is referred to as program-monitoring software.

Once an error condition has been detected using the operating system's error-monitoring mechanisms, the next job is to determine where the error is coming from and then to isolate the error down to some predetermined hardware or software granularity—for example, for hardware down to a replaceable board or a component such as an integrated circuit; for software down to a module, process, function, or possibly a block or line of code; for data within the file, down to the record or data item level. The level of isolation provided will depend on the overhead and price the system is willing to pay for the detection and isolation. This mechanism is typically called fault localization. Fault localization operates by using known test drivers and known responses to walk through system hardware and software elements testing for erroneous outputs. It is not, however, sufficient to simply detect an erroneous output condition and assume this is the component at fault. Errors can propagate through numerous layers of hardware and software, only showing up in later stages. The goal of fault localization is to detect an error, and then test back through all interacting elements to isolate the fault or error to the appropriate culprit.

On isolation of a faulty hardware or software element, the operating system must determine an appropriate action to relieve the system of the error. The process of performing this function is called recovery and reconfiguration. The most common method is to perform some recovery action first.

The recovery may be as simple as reload and restart or just resetting the already loaded software. More elaborate techniques include maintaining partial execution history (register status, computation state) and to reset and restart from some intermediary point in the software. If an error is more elaborate, it may require the removal and replacement of the software or hardware element to effect recovery.

If redundant hardware and software are available, the recovery can take on a more global perspective. Recovery can look to other assets available within the system to work around the errors or failures. This form of recovery requires the reallocation of resources (both hardware and software) to fill the gap left by the failed elements. This form of recovery is referred to as reconfiguration. Reconfiguration will be discussed in further detail in later chapters.

### 2.9.4    Database management systems

A database management system is composed of five elements: computer hardware, software, data, people (users), and operations procedures. The computer hardware consists of processing elements, volatile memory, secondary storage components, archival storage devices, input and output devices, and possibly specialized computational devices and input sensors. The software for a database can be broken up into three categories: infrastructure support software, database software, and applications software. The infrastructure support software includes the operating system and network communications software. The database management system software includes components for storage management, concurrency control, transaction processing, database manipulation interface, database definition interface, and database control interface. Applications software is dependent on user needs. Data are the commodity the database system is managing. People and applications programs, as users, manipulate the stored data and, as database administrators, examine and maintain the database for the users. Operations procedures are developed and put into practice to provide additional support to the database system. Operations procedures include backing up the database onto nonvolatile mass storage, such as tapes, on a scheduled basis, and collection of operational statistics for use in tuning the database's structure and performance.

A database management system performs as an applications process under the control of the operating system. The database manager uses the operating system's file management and memory management services to store and retrieve the data in the database. Interface to the database management system is through three distinct paths: the database definition language, database manipulation language, and database control language.

### Database definition language

A database is constructed to manage data that must be maintained for future use. The data in the database are organized into structured collections based on applications' informational needs. Data are placed in the database in these predefined data structures. These data structures are defined using data definition primitives within the database's language. Data definition primitives allow the database designer to specify individual data item composition as well as more complex data structures composed of these low-level data items.

A data item represents the smallest identifiable piece of information managed within the database. These data items, or attributes, are given a unique name, and their physical structure and type are specified using data types available within the given language. In the Structured Query Language (SQL) used to define relational databases, a data item is defined at the same time that a relation is defined. As an example, to define a person relation in SQL we could use the following code:

```
CREATE TABLE person
      (name            VARCHAR(30) NOT NULL
       ssnum           INT(9) NOT NULL,
       bdate           DATE NOT NULL,
       saddr           VARCHAR(20) NOT NULL,
       city            VARCHAR(20) NOT NULL,
       state           VARCHAR(20) NOT NULL,
       zcode           INT(9) NOT NULL,
                       PRIMARY KEY (ssnum))
```

This example defines a person data entity to be composed of seven distinct data items. Each data item is given an explicit data type and a maximum size for the data item—for example, the name can be from 1 to 30 characters long; the birthday is of type date. Date is defined in SQL as having the form year-month-day and is comprised of four integers for year and two integers for both the month and day entities.

Database definition typically uses a compilation process to build and generate the database schema or data description model. The database definition process results in descriptions of the database in both logical and physical terms and the generation of a mapping between the two, as shown in the following code segment:

```
CREATE TABLE customer
     (cname            VARCHAR(10) NOT NULL,
      cnum             INT(3) NOT NULL,
      credlim          DECIMAL(6, 2),
                       PRIMARY KEY (cnum))

CREATE TABLE order
     (onum             DECIMAL(5) NOT NULL,
      cnum             DECIMAL(3) NOT NULL,
      spnum            SMALL INT NOT NULL,
      date             DECIMAL(6),
      amount           DECIMAL(6, 2),
                       PRIMARY KEY (onum))
```

These data definition constructs are from the Structured Query Language (SQL) and specify two relations. One is a customer relation and the other is an order relation. The customer relation is specified as having three attributes: a customer name, a customer number, and a credit limit. The key attribute for the relation is defined as the customer number attribute. The second relation is a customer order relation. The customer order relation is composed of five attributes: order number, customer number, supplier part number, date of the order, and dollar amount for the order. The primary key for this relation is defined as the order number. Also notice that since the customer number in the order relation is the same as the customer number in the customer relation, this attribute constitutes a foreign key into the customer relation. By using techniques such as this the relations are linked together in an informational sense.

For all database models, there exists a language for the specification of the database's structure and content. The specification is called the schema design and represents the logical view of information that is to be managed by a particular database management system. The specification gives the designer the ability to map disjoint logical user views of information into a comprehensive global view of information and finally into a mapping to physical storage structures. This separation of the logical and physical database structures results in transparency from the physical and logical dependencies of the data from the users. By doing this the database designer has the ability to alter the physical storage structure and organization in order to optimize low-level storage and retrieval efficiency without the need to alter the logical user view and its application's code.

The database design language, beyond the basic ability to define data, must also have the ability to alter specified data structures and their physical representations after the database has been specified. Features to drop a structure from the database, to insert a new structure, or to alter an existing structure need to be built into the language for completeness and for the maintenance of a database. Keep in mind that most databases will not be constructed, put in service, and removed over a short period of time. When enterprises construct and populate a database, they do so continually over the lifetime of their system. The lifetime of a database system in such an enterprise may span decades, implying that growth and change are inevitable and must be designed for up front. A database within such an environment is initially specified and put into service. After using the database, some initial adjustments will be required. In addition, as the enterprise grows and possibly changes the focus of its activities, so must its information base change in order to stay competitive. One can see that a rigid, unchangeable specification and operational structure will lead to obsolescence and degradation of performance to the very applications the database was initially specified to support. A database specification language and implementation must be flexible in order to be useful and enduring.

### Database manipulation language

The component of the database most visible and recognizable by database professionals, as well as applications developers and possibly applications users, is the data manipulation language. This component of the database can take on many forms, the most common being a programming language–like interface, which provides the ability to retrieve and store information within the database previously specified by the database design language.

The data manipulation language need not, however, take on a textual and procedural view only. The data manipulation language can be visual, as in the spatial data management system, where information is described using icons and is retrieved using pictures that can be zoomed in on for greater detail about an item—for example, given that we have a map of the United States used as the top-level view for the querying of business information, we may wish to find out what universities are within the southern region of Massachusetts closest to Cape Cod. We would first select the type of icons we wish depicted—for example, only show regions with universities by selecting the university icons. The visual display would then highlight cities where major universities are located. To isolate a particular university or to find out more about the area where a university is located, we begin by selecting the area, say southeastern New England around Cape Cod, by encircling the region. The display would then expand this area, again only depicting the universities. To select a particular university select a university icon (Figure 2.28). If we selected the University of Massachusetts

**Figure 2.28**
*Spatial data management system.*

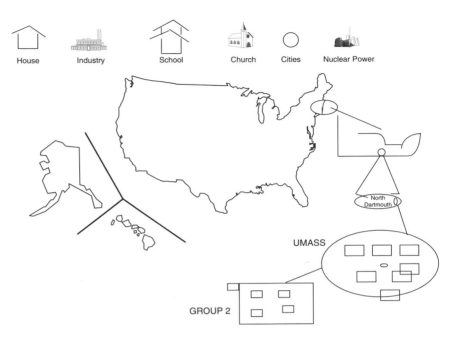

at Dartmouth, we may next get an aerial view of the university. To discover more information we could select a building, then a department, or possibly even a particular professor or course offering. In such a way the majority of information needed could be extracted and displayed in visual form. There are, however, limitations with this method. Not all information lends itself to visual-only representation. We may be forced to place only a subset of the totally available information in such a system and use a separate database interface for more textual information.

A second type of interface is related more toward business uses of databases. This type of interface uses a company's typical paper forms for information about inventory, sales, employee records, and so forth as the interface presented to the users of the database. An application or user simply selects the proper form, say an employee record form, and selects which employee or group of employee records to look at by typing in information on the form.

Figure 2.29 shows a form that may be used by a business to represent customers or suppliers. The form shows the company's major information, such as the company's name, address, phone number, fax machine number, and e-mail address, and possibly some information about the type of product or service it produces or supplies. In addition, the form may include

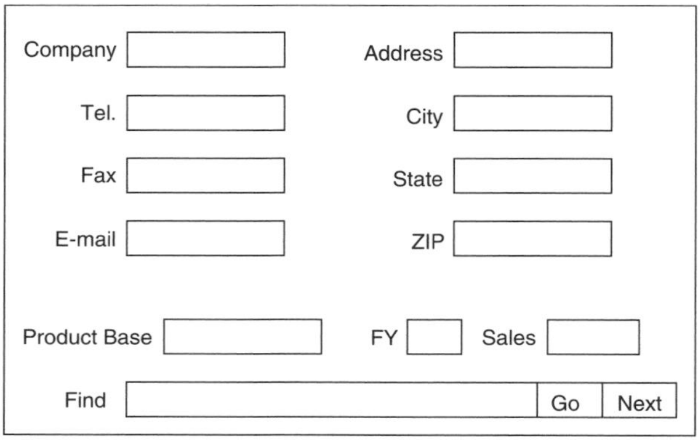

**Figure 2.29**
*Sample form.*

some extra fields, which can be used to aid in finding information. In the example screen of Figure 2.29, there is a separate field called Find on the bottom of the screen. In this field a user could input parameters to be looked for or qualifiers to aid in a search—for example, if we wished to select all companies in Boston, Massachusetts, that are stored in our database, there are two potential ways to do this. The first is to enter the names Boston and Massachusetts in the appropriate city and state fields and select Go on the bottom right of the screen. This would indicate to the database to match any records that have these qualities in these particular fields. To find additional entries with the same fields one would select the Next field on the lower-right corner. An additional means to recover the same records is to type All, Boston, and Massachusetts in the Find field of the form.

A third form of nontraditional data manipulation language is the query by example, or QBE, type of facility. In a query by example environment the user requests basic information about a record of interest—for example, a company name. The system then returns a template, which may or may not fit what is being requested. This template can then be used by the user to further refine the query and to receive additional examples to use in formulating a more precise query. The QBE interface developed for the relational model is closely tied to the forms-based interface. The examples come back in the form of tables, and the user fills in known quantities. The database then attempts to fill in a response table using this information as the restriction information.

Other data manipulation languages are based on functional evaluation. In these types of languages the users request information from the database through the use of function calls. The function calls may return text, graphics, video, sound, or a variety of data formats. The form returned is dependent on the data formats of the function called and the parameters' data types.

This form of query interface is most prevalent in object-oriented databases and in multimedia and hypermedia databases. The information that is passed between the database and the applications is in the native form of the application, not in the base form of the database. This type of interface is desirable in applications where data come in nontextual forms that nevertheless are stored and managed by a database management system.

The most prevalent form of data manipulation language today is still by far the textual and procedural languages, such as Structured Query Language (SQL) and Object Query Language (OQL). In these languages the queries are formed much like a program in any programming language. The query writer has some reserved words that provide some given functionality. The typical query includes reserved words to select multiple records, a single record, or a subset of a record; to specify where the record is to come from; and any qualifiers on the access and retrieval of the requested information. In languages of this form the queries take on the structure and execution flow of the program—for example, if we are looking at a relation Order, of the form order number, order date, customer number, product ordered, quantity ordered, unit cost, total cost, and want to find all orders (the entire tuple) from the XYZ Company for bookbindings since May 1995, the following query could be used, given that the XYZ Company has the customer number I101:

```
Range of O is order;
SELECT O.onum, O.odate, O.cnum, O.pname, O.qty, O.uic,
O.ttl
FROM Orders
WHERE O.cnum := 'C101' and O.odate > '4-30-95' and
O.pname := 'bindings';
```

In this query we first set an internal variable to range over all values of the search relation. Second, we request the search look to retrieve all the attributes of the relation Order in the same order in which they are stored. Third, we specify where to look for these attributes, namely in relation Order. And, finally, we restrict the selection to find and copy into our result relation only those tuples that have the company number attribute stored with the value of 'C101', the value for attribute order date greater than the end of April (odate > '4-30-95'), and only the parts named 'bindings'.

The procedural languages such as SQL also have operators to insert new tuples in the database, to create new relations, to modify existing relations, to delete relations, and to update the contents of a relation. An insert of a tuple into the previous relation could be readily performed by issuing the following instruction:

```
Range of O is order;
INSERT INTO Orders
VALUES ('O100', '5-21-95', 'C101', 'binding', '100',
'1.25', '125.00') ;
```

To delete the same tuple from the database requires that we first find the proper tuple, and then remove it from the relation. The code may appear as follows:

```
Range of O is order;
DELETE FROM Orders
Where O.cnum := 'O100' AND O.odate := '5-21-95', AND
O.cnum, := 'C101' AND O.pname := 'binding' AND O.qty :=
'100' AND O.uic := '1.25' AND
O.ttl := '125.00';
```

A simpler means would be to refer to the intended tuple by its primary key only. Since in a relational database the primary key by definition must uniquely define a tuple in a relation, then this alone can be used to find and delete the proper tuple. The reformed deletion operation would be as follows:

```
Range of O is order;
DELETE FROM Orders
Where O.onum := 'O100';
```

What the reader should realize from this discussion is that there is no one correct means of retrieving information from a database. There are, however, standard means [1]. The important concept is that database retrieval is different from conventional programming language processes. There is a language of informational access, which has evolved and continues to evolve along with database technology. These languages, however, will continue to be different from their programming language counterparts primarily due to the differences in the requirements for persistent data beyond the point of a program's existence and the requirements for consistency and correctness of information beyond the scope of any single process or program.

### Database control language

The last component of the language interface to a database management system is the data control language. This is also sometimes included as part of the data definition language in some descriptions. We decompose it here to help focus on some of the differences. In particular this component of a database interface is typically used by the database administrator. Typical functions provided at this layer are tools to monitor database operations; restructure underlying physical storage; reset constraint values on data items; rename relations; create additional indexes; archive data; and to grant, alter, or revoke privileges. The typical interface at this level is textual oriented with specialized analysis tools used to analyze collected information.

The database administrator could, for example, examine a set of range constraints on an attribute value and determine, based on the user's requirements, to alter them to increase the possible domain of values considered correct by this attribute—for example, if the database administrator feels that there is not a sufficient range of values to represent the job categories in a company, he or she could elect to increase the number of jobs and their titles as needed. If originally there were only three titles in the company:

```
jobtitle IN {welding, management, sales}
```

but it is determined that the data structure must be expanded to more fully meet the need of additional job categories, the data administrator simply extends the list of valid items. This instruction simply adds three new categories to the list of allowable job titles. These new titles can now be used by applications querying or modifying the database.

```
jobtitle IN (welding, management, metal cutter,
machinist, glass cutter, sales)
```

Constraints for the range of values of a data item can be altered by increasing the values assigned to boundary values—for example, if an initial constraint indicates that the customer number ranges from 1 to 500, but we now find ourselves with 501 customers, the constraint must be altered to allow storage of the new customer record. To change the constraint, simply set RANGE OF Customer.cnum 1 . . . 750. Constraints on when to perform testing functions can be altered also—for example, test constraints on reads, writes, or commit.

Beyond the alteration of constraints, database data control languages provide instructions and constructs to grant additional privileges to users or to revoke privileges. The GRANT statement is used to allow a user to perform certain manipulations—for example, to allow user Tom to read values from the Customer relation can be done by:

```
GRANT SELECT ON Customer TO Tom;
```

One could also grant the rights to multiple operations within one statement, as follows:

```
GRANT SELECT, UPDATE, INSERTION ON Customer TO Tom;
```

This statement grants selection, update, and insertion rights to the user Tom on the relation Customer. In this manner the database administrator can alter, add, or remove access rights to any items within the database. Not all database systems and models support a wide variety of data control language features. In several languages, many of these features would necessitate bringing the database off line for alteration.

# 2.10   Components of a database system's architecture

A database system is composed of much more than just the data definition language, data manipulation language, and data control language. These simply represent the interface into the actual database system. The core of a database management system is the collection of services that provide the persistence of data in the database and the functionality to guarantee the consistency and correctness of data and the adherence to ACID properties by transactions (Figure 2.30). The ACID properties include the atomic, consistent, independent, and durable execution of a transaction on the database. We will discuss these in more detail later in this chapter.

The architecture of a database system is comprised of a set of services built on top of basic operating system services, system file storage services,

**Figure 2.30**
*Architecture to support a database system.*

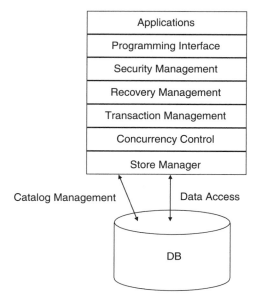

and primary memory buffer management services. The file manager is the database's interface to the persistent stored information. The information managed for the database by the file system includes the internal, conceptual, and external schema for the stored information (metadatabase); the actual database; and the database log file. The log files include before images (buffer values), after images, redo records (actions of committed transactions), undo records (actions of uncommitted transactions), commit records, abort records, and transaction begin records.

Through the basic features of process management, interprocess communications, synchronization, buffer management, and file management the database systems services can be constructed. These services include catalog management, integrity management, transaction management, concurrency control, lock management, deadlock management, recovery management, security management, query processing, communications management, and log management. On top of the database services the user's applications operate through the input/output view manager and the data manipulation manager. In the following paragraphs we will briefly review each of these. Following these brief overviews, we will review some of these in greater detail.

## 2.10.1   Catalog manager

The catalog manager maintains information about the database's information. These metadata form the schema for the database. The database administrator, using data control language and data definition language interfaces, can alter the schema. As an example, in SQL this portion of the database would keep the definition for all relations, constraints, security assertions, and mappings to physical storage.

## 2.10.2   Integrity manager

The integrity manager aids in the maintenance of the database's data items' accuracy, correctness, and validity—for example, the integrity manager may check that a data item is of the proper type through a mechanism that determines when to do the check; how to do the check; and how to recover, reject, or fix the condition when encountered. The integrity manager may check to see that a data item is within a predefined domain of correct values, such as DOMAIN FIXED (5) or Weight GREATER THAN 0 AND Weight LESS THAN 2000. These would test the ranges of values a data item may span. Integrity checks can span multiple entities or relations—for example, a referential integrity check in SQL can be used to see that the relationship of many objects has a property that must hold for them to be considered valid. Such a check could be that the SUM of all account balances at a bank must equal the bank's balance. An important aspect of this management is when to perform the specified checks—for example, there is a different cost if the checks are done at database definition time, on access to the data item, on update of a data item, on an event such as a timer, or on the commit of a transaction. The tradeoff is accuracy and validity of the data versus performance. Checks done during run time will slow down the database's processing throughput.

## 2.10.3   Transaction manager

The transaction manager controls and coordinates the execution of transactions within the database. For now just assume that a transaction is a collection of operations on the database that are bound together into a single run-time unit. The transaction manager must perform tasks to initiate transactions (scheduling); synchronize transaction execution with the database, other transactions, and the operating system; coordinate intertransaction communications; commit (completion) processing; and abort (failure) processing, transaction constraint checking, and condition handling, as well as transaction recovery (error) management. A transaction typically is of the following form:

```
TRANSACTION T (Optional Input Parameters)
Specification Part
BEGIN
BODY of T
COMMIT or ABORT of T
RECOVERY PART of T
END
END TRANSACTION T
```

The initial statement names the transaction, allowing it to be possibly precompiled and stored for later execution. The initial statement also leaves space for transferring input parameters to the transaction, such as the location of data to be executed. The specification part of the transaction is the area where local variables for the transaction's workspace are specified, as are preconditions and postconditions on transaction execution, recovery conditions, isolation level, access modes, and the diagnostic size to allocate. The body contains the executable code for the transaction. The commit and abort statements indicate the success or failure of the transaction. Finally, the recovery part specifies user- or system-supplied recovery or condition handlers for error processing and transaction completion processing.

### 2.10.4   **Concurrency control manager**

The concurrency control manager coordinates the actions of interactive access to the database by concurrently running transactions. The goal of concurrency control is to coordinate execution so that the VIEW or effect from the database's perspective is the same as if the concurrently executing transactions were executed in a serial fashion. This scheme is referred to as the serializable execution of transactions. Concurrency control's serializability theory has two basic modes: The simplest concerns the serializable execution of the read and write sets from conflicting transactions and is based on either locking, timestamp ordering, or optimistic read and write conflict resolution. The second concurrency control concept is more complex and uses semantic knowledge of a transaction's execution to aid in coordination. The major difference is that the granularity of the serialization operator is not the read and write but rather complex functions and procedures as well as complex data objects. The criterion of correct execution, however, is, nevertheless, serialization across concurrent transactions.

### 2.10.5   **Lock manager**

The lock manager is designed to control the access to the database lock table. The lock table of the database maintains the status of locks (read lock, write lock, share lock, semantic lock, etc.) for each item of the database that has been accessed. The lock manager isolates users from accessing the lock table directly. To acquire access to lock status, the lock manager provides lock and unlock primitives to database and user code. The lock can be a read lock, which is granted (if no one holds a conflicting write lock) when a transaction attempts to read a data item. A write lock can only be granted if no other transaction holds a read or write lock on the data item. Locks in a database can be viewed like semaphores in an operating system; they are used as a means to guarantee exclusive use to an item within the database's control.

### 2.10.6   **Deadlock manager**

When a locking protocol is being used, a lock held by one transaction can block a lock request from another transaction. If there are no circular waits for a lock, then the lock will ultimately be granted. If there are circular waits, then deadlock occurs. Deadlock is the condition where two or more transactions wait for resources held by another transaction that is waiting for a resource you hold. Since no one can move forward, the system cannot get any useful work done. The deadlock manager must detect when a deadlock condition holds and decide how to handle the condition. Typically, one of the involved transactions is aborted and its locks released, thus allowing other transactions to go on.

### 2.10.7   Recovery manager

The recovery manager must ensure that the database is always in a state that is recoverable consistently and correctly. This is done by ensuring that the database contains all or none of the effects of committed transactions and none from aborted or running transactions. The recovery manager uses the concept of a checkpoint (snapshot of the present state of the database) and a log file (file of operations on the database) to aid in the recovery. For conventional databases recovery attempts to bring the database back to an old state of the database and initiate processing from there. To bring the database back to a past state the recovery manager uses both undo, where uncommitted or active transaction past views are restored, and redo, where committed transactions not written to the database have their new states restored to the persistent store. These undo and redo records are applied to a checkpoint state to bring the database to some intermediate acceptable consistent state. A second form of recovery attempts to move the database forward by applying compensating transactions (to change committed effects to acceptable forms based on semantic needs), by applying extrapolations (to compute new acceptably correct and consistent future states), and by applying condition handlers to user or system semantic actions at a variety of levels within the database.

### 2.10.8   Security manager

The security manager has the task of limiting access, modification, and malicious intrusion to the database. To perform these control actions the security manager requires that users be identified, authenticated, and authorized for access and control over a data item being requested. Identification is similar to typical login capabilities, where the security manager asks the users to identify themselves. To make sure that not just anybody attempts access the database may also ask a user to authenticate his or her identity. This can be done with a password or by a variety of fairly elaborate mechanisms. Once the user is allowed access, he or she is further restricted to what can be viewed and altered. Authorization performs the function of limiting access to only a desirable predefined level—for example, read only, write only, alter capability, view restriction, and numerous other restrictions.

## 2.10.9    Query processing support manager

The query processor of a database system has the function of determining how to answer the requests for information from a user in the most optimal manner. The idea is that a query can be answered by a database system in a variety of ways. The most straightforward is the brute-force approach. This, however, is typically the most expensive in terms of time and resources consumed—for example, the cost to join two tables will be the cost of scanning each item of the first with each item of the second, or on the order of $N$ times $N$ or $N$ squared if we assume they are the same size. On the other hand, if we could reduce the size of each by a factor of 2, then the cost drops by one-half. This is easily accomplished if we perform a select first on each before a join. If the size of $N$ is large, this reduction can become significant and have a meaningful result on the database's performance. To reduce the cost of queries we look at heuristics on the order of access of relations and their combinations, relation reductions via selections and projections, pre-processing (sorting), iteration order, relation operator precedence ordering, and numerous other factors.

## 2.10.10    Communications manager

The communications manager has the role of traffic cop in the database. This service must coordinate the transfer of database data as well as status information to aid in the processing of data. Communications may be between database services, different databases, different processors, different transactions, or within a transaction. Mechanisms such as simple message-passing schemes, client/server protocols, and others have been implemented.

## 2.10.11    Log manager

The log manager has the job of coordinating the transfer of information from the active database into secondary persistent storage to aid in the recoverability of the database and to effectively mitigate the problem of the operating system paging out information prematurely. The log maintains a history of data flow in and out of the database, as well as actions that can affect the database's state. This includes transactions before images, after images, undo records, and redo records.

### Transaction management

The transaction manager has the job of providing a bounded framework around which to guarantee that the database stays consistent while concurrent operations execute on the database. The database manager, without concurrency, canguarantee this with no problem—but this is neither interesting to study nor practical in the real world. The real world of database processing typically deals with a large database with a high degree of multi-processing (concurrently executing transactions).

The execution of a transaction is similar to making a contract; both sides are involved in the contract, they negotiate for a while, and then they either come to a consensus and sign the contract, or they both walk away. A transaction is thus either all or nothing. A transaction must complete totally or must not complete at all. Now that's a concept.

The transaction is meant to be used as a consistent and reliable unit of work for the database system. A transaction interacts with the application's environment and the database's concurrency control protocols to perform its intended function (Figure 2.31a). A transaction is required to guarantee four properties when executing on a consistent database. These four properties are called the transaction's ACID properties; they include atomic, consistent, independent, and durable executions of transactions on the database.

An ACID transaction guarantees that the database the transaction begins with and the database it finishes with are consistent, that the data are durable, that the transaction acted alone on the database, and that the transaction completely finished its actions on the database (Figure 2.31b).

The transaction ACID properties are as follows:

Atomic—The atomic property implies that a transaction is an indivisible unit of execution that either completely performs its designed function or else its effect on the database is as if the transaction never began; that is, the database state an atomic transaction leaves if the transaction does not totally commit is the same database state that the transaction began with. On the other hand, if an atomic transaction completes, then the database state it leaves has all of the changes the transaction computed with no others installed.

Consistent—Consistent execution of a transaction requires that a transaction transform an initial consistent database state to another new consistent database state. The basic concept behind this transaction property is that the database is comprised of a set of data items, which have constraints defined on them. The database, to be considered consistent at any point in time, requires that these constraints on data items within the database all evaluate to true; that is, none of these constraints can be violated if we are to have a con-

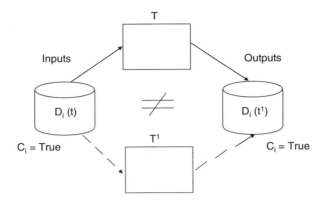

**Figure 2.31a**
*Database transaction.*

sistent database state. A valid transaction, which initially sees a database that is consistent, must, upon commit, leave a database that is still consistent.

Independent—Independence, sometimes referred to as the isolation property of transactions, requires that each transaction accessing shared data acts alone, without being affected by other concurrently running transactions. This property basically indicates that a transaction's effect on the database is as if it, and it alone, were executing on the database. The function of this property is to require the removal of any dependence of a transaction's execution on any other transaction's execution.

Durable—The durability of a transaction's execution requires that once a transaction is committed, its effects remain permanent in the database. What this property implies is that the changes a transaction makes

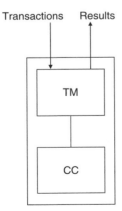

**Figure 2.31b**
*ACID transaction.*

to the database do not disappear when the transaction terminates. Data produced by a transaction and written to the database become permanent. Data once written to the database can only be altered by another transaction that reads and/or writes over this data item.

These transaction properties must hold for all transactions that execute within a database management system if consistency, correctness, and validity of the database are to be maintained. The properties must hold even when other transactions execute along with each other concurrently. In addition, if adhered to, the properties will guarantee a correct and consistent database even in the face of failures or errors. It is when we begin to envision what policies and mechanisms for transaction execution and operations can be developed to guarantee these properties that problems occur.

### *Transaction basics*

A transaction is a collection of applications code and database manipulation code bound into an indivisible unit of execution; an example is shown in the following code segment:

```
BEGIN-TRANSACTION Name
Applications Code
DB-Code
Applications Code
DB-Code
DB-Code
         .
         .
         .
Applications Code
END TRANSACTION Name
```

A transaction is framed by the BEGIN TRANSACTION and END TRANSACTION markers delineating the boundaries of the transaction—for example, if we have the following three relations that describe an airline reservation system:

```
FLIGHT(Fno, Date, Source, Destination, Seats-Sold, Capacity)
CUSTOMER(Cname, Address, Balance)
FlghtCust(FNO, Date, Cname, Special)
```

The first relation depicts the flight information—flight number, the date of the flight, the city of origin, the destination city, the number of seats sold for this flight, and the capacity of this plane. The second relation describes the customers who will be flying on a flight; it gives their names, addresses, and the balances owed on the tickets. The third relation describes the relationship between the flights and the customers. This relation in particular indicates which flight, which passengers are flying on what date, and any special requirements for these passengers—for example, maybe someone wants a McDonald's Happy Meal or a vegetarian meal.

To generate a simple transaction on these database relations, which make a reservation for a customer, we could write the following pseudocoded relational Structured Query Language request or query:

```
BEGIN TRANSACTION Reservation
BEGIN
Input (FlightNo, date, customer, specl)
EXEX SQL UPDATE FLIGHT
SET Seats-Sold = Seats-Sold + 1
WHERE Fno = 'FlightNo' AND Date = 'date';
EXEX SQL INSERT INTO FlightCust (FNO, Date, Cname, Special)
VALUES (FlightNo, date, customer, specl)
OUTPUT("Transaction Completed")
END TRANSACTION Reservation;
```

This transaction looks for input from the keyboard for the flight number, date of the flight, the customer's name, and any special requirements the customer may have. These are input to transaction variables: FlightNo, date, customer, and specl, respectively. The contents of these variables are then inserted into the proper places within the relation through the VALUES function. We update the count of seats sold for this flight by incrementing the value by one and then updating the value in the relation. The transaction then updates the FlghtCust relation with the new information. To be complete we should also update the customer relation; this will be left as an exercise for the reader. This represents a simple transaction; however, as it stands it will not guarantee the transaction ACID properties alone.

To guarantee the transaction ACID properties we need some additional features within this simple transaction model. To meet the needs of atomic execution we require a means to determine the conditions for termination of a transaction, correct or otherwise. The first concept required for correct execution and termination is the commit. Commit is used to indicate the correct and atomic termination of a transaction. It includes the processing necessary to ensure proper updating and marking of the database. The second concept, called abort, is necessary for transactions that fail or stop execution for some reason. Abort conditions will include erroneous operations, conflicts in accessing stored information, or the inability to meet the ACID requirements on transaction processing. An abort requires that all of the effects of a transaction are removed from the database before any other transaction has a chance to see them. These two added features are necessary to facilitate atomic execution, although not in isolation.

The commit action is necessary in order to synchronize the actions of other elements of the database management system to make changes to the database permanent—for example, this command may be used to cause the database buffers and activity log to be flushed (force written) to the permanent storage subsystem, thereby making the changes durable, as shown in the following code segment:

```
BEGIN TRANSACTION Reservation
BEGIN
Input(FlightNo, date, customer,specl)
SELECT Seats-Sold, Capacity FROM FLIGHT ;
IF Seats-Sold > Capacity THEN
BEGIN
EXEX SQL UPDATE FLIGHT SET Seats-Sold = Seats-Sold + 1
WHERE Fno = 'FlightNo'
AND Date = 'date';
EXEX SQL INSERT INTO FlightCust(FNO, Date, Cname, Special)
VALUES(FlightNo, date, customer, specl)
OUTPUT("Transaction Completed")
COMMIT Reservation;
ELSEABORT Reservation;
END
END TRANSACTION Reservation;
```

This altered transaction now allows us either to go on with the transaction if it has a chance to succeed, or abort the transaction if we cannot complete it. In this example we would abort the transaction if we did not have a seat remaining in the plane to give to this customer. If there is a seat, we sell this customer a seat and commit the transaction.

### Transaction formalization

A transaction, $Ti$, is composed of a set of operations, $Oj \in$ {Read, Write}, where $Oj$ is some operation from a transaction $i$ on data items from the database $D$.

Let $Osi = \cup\ Oij$ represent the union of the set of all operations $j$ from a transaction $i$.

Finally, let $Ni \in$ {Abort, Commit} represent the set of termination conditions on a transaction, either commit or abort.

A transaction is modeled as a partial ordering over its operations and end conditions. The partial ordering is represented by $P <<$, which indicates that the partial order $P$ is composed of a set of operations, denoted $S$, and an ordering relation that holds between the elements in $S$ denoted $<<$.

With these definitions we can formally describe a transaction, *Ti*, as a partial ordering of its composite operations, as follows:

$$Ti = \{Si, << i\} \tag{2.15}$$

where

1. $Si = OSi \cup Ni$ $\hspace{6cm}$ (2.16)

2. For any two operations from $Ti = Oij, Oik \in Osi$
   If $Oij = R(X)$ and $Oik = W(X)$, then for any $X$ $\hspace{1cm}$ (2.17)
   Either $Oij << i\ Oik$ or $Oik << i\ Oij$

3. And for all $Oij \in OSi, Oij << i\ Ni$ $\hspace{3.5cm}$ (2.18)

What all this says is that a transaction is made up of reads, writes, and a commit or an abort operation, and that there is an explicit ordering in a transaction so that if a conflicting read precedes a conflicting write in the history, a strict sequential ordering must always hold in this transaction for these conflicting operations. In addition, all operations from the transactions must precede the commit or the abort statements. This is an important concept for developing correctness criteria for transaction executions, especially when concurrency comes into play. The transaction ordering must not be violated, to ensure that the transaction can perform the intended operation.

Transaction processing in a database system strives for guaranteeing the ACID properties, while delivering a high degree of data availability, no loss of updates, avoidance of cascading aborts, and recoverability of the database and transactions. A high degree of data availability is realized through reduced blocking of read and write requests. No loss of updates is guaranteed by correct commit processing. The avoidance of cascading aborts is provided for by robust recovery protocols. Finally, recovery is provided by redundancy and the rules governing commit.

## 2.10.12    **Database and system mismatch**

The operating system migrates storage from primary memory to secondary storage, based on the operating system's perspective on when this should be done. Demand paging and limited storage dictate that this be performed on a page fault basis. The database, however, may not wish the page to be written back to secondary memory due to concurrency control and atomicity issues. The database may wish to hold pages in memory until transaction commit time and then flush to secondary storage. This would allow the database not to require undo of transactions on failure, simply abort, and restart.

Related to this is I/O management and device management. The database may wish to order access based on the queries being presented to it in order to maintain ACID execution, whereas the operating system simply will order the accesses to deliver the greatest throughput of data back to the CPU. The order in which it returns information may be counterproductive to the database, to the point where the database has waited so long for needed data that when the data do come the operating system pages out the database software to make room for the data, or it removes the data that the new information is to be processed against. In either case this is not conducive to optimal database processing.

The problem with the operating system for this type of problem is the I/O buffer management policies and mechanisms. The database wants to use and optimize buffers to maximize transaction throughput, while the operating system wants to maximize average process response.

The control of the processor itself by the operating system may block essential functions that the database must perform—for example, the database requires that the log of database actions be flushed to secondary storage at specific points and in an uninterruptable manner in order to guarantee recovery and correct execution. Likewise, to keep the database as consistent as possible requires the database to flush committed data to the persistent store when necessary and in an atomic operation. The operating system in its wish to be fair may time-out a database function doing specifically this operation. On another related issue, if a database is sorting and processing two large data files against each other, it may wish to maintain direct control over how and when data traverse the boundaries from the storage to the processor and back. Without direct control over the allocation and deallocation mechanisms, the database could be removed from one resource while still holding another, causing a loss of the intended operation's continuity.

The operating system's locking mechanism works well for simple file management, and for the majority of applications this is sufficient. But a database needs better control over locking to allow locking at possibly a data item level only. The reason for this is to allow more concurrency and less blocking of data. The intent is to increase data availability by only locking what is being used, not an entire file. To rectify this databases are forced to use direct addressing and direct file management features to allow for their own control over the file level of locking. However, in some operating systems the database still suffers under the control of the operating system's lock manager, regardless of what mode is used.

An operating system's interprocess communication mechanisms may be too expensive to use within a database system. Many operating systems use a form of message passing involving interrupt processing. Such mechanisms may have a high cost in terms of overhead. A database may wish to provide more simple IPC mechanisms using shared memory or semaphores, especially since a database is only another process within the operating system.

Scheduling in an operating system looks to maximize overall average response time and to share resources fairly. Scheduling only deals with the selection of a process to place onto the executing hardware. A database, on the other hand, has a multilevel scheduling problem—not only must it select which transaction to place into service at any point in time, but it must also schedule which operation to perform on the underlying database to meet concurrency control requirements. An operating system's scheduler will not and does not provide such a service.

A database requires the use of copying, backup, and recovery services of the underlying infrastructure to aid in constructing database recovery protocols. The problem is that many of the other features of an operating system may get in the way and hinder the easy operation of database recovery. The database wishes to dictate how and when it will force information out to persistent storage. This is done in order to minimize the work (UNDO and REDO) that must be done to recover the database to a known consistent state. The operating system, on the other hand, will do this based on its needs to reallocate storage for processes in execution. The operating system will not take into account that this least recently used page will actually be the next page to be used by the database. It will simply choose this page and force it out immediately, based on its needs.

To make the operating system and database interface more compatible it is desirable that the operating system use semantic information, which can be provided by the database to make sound, informed decisions. This is not to say that the database should overtake or dictate the moves of the operating system. Instead it should act in a cooperative fashion to maximize the system-oriented needs of a database, which are more diverse than those of a typical application. See [1] for further information on database systems.

## 2.11   Summary

A computer system is comprised of many elements. Primarily these are the central processing unit, the memory unit, the secondary storage unit, the input and output unit, and interconnection hardware. Each of these elements can be architected in a variety of ways, each with their own set of pros and cons. Computer systems are typically represented as either single processor units, multiple processing units, distributed processing units, or networked units. The policies for connecting these devices to meet the needs of an application will dictate the final form of the system's architecture.

The operating system and related support infrastructure services are used by an application to organize, maintain, and manipulate information on a specific computer architecture. The applications and operating system's needs and priorities do not always match. Due to this impedance mismatch, applications and have, in the past, tried to work around the operating system instead of working with it. The most notorious was in the early days of the IBM PC and the DOS operating system. Application programs typically bypassed the operating system and worked directly on the underlying hardware. The result was that programs typically ran "IBM PC or 100% compatible" machines. Another example is the operating system's management of the memory hierarchy may be fair and reasonably optimal for the average application running on the system but may not match the needs of the database management system. The operating system strives to maintain a reasonable set of data pages in memory for the application's use, but it does not attempt to go beyond its own measures of effectiveness. The concept today is to engineer systems so that they operate optimally, based on the semantic needs and intent of the applications, which may go against the operating system's average response time and fairness goals.

# 3

# Fundamental Concepts and Performance Measures

## 3.1    Introduction

Computer systems architects and designers look for configurations of computer systems elements so that system performance meets desired measures. What this means is that the computer system delivers a quality of service that meets the demands of the user applications. But the measure of this quality of service and the expectation of performance vary depending on who you are. In the broadest context we may mean user response time, ease of use, reliability, fault tolerance, and other such performance quantities. The problem with some of these is that they are qualitative versus quantitative measures. To be scientific and precise in our computer systems performance studies, we must focus on measurable quantitative qualities of a system under study.

There are many possible choices for measuring performance, but most fall into one of two categories: system-oriented or user-oriented measures. The system-oriented measures typically revolve around the concepts of throughput and utilization. Throughput is defined as the average number of items (e.g., transactions, processes, customers, jobs, etc.) processed per unit of measured time. Throughput is meaningful when we also know information about the capacity of the measured entity and the presented workload of items at the entity over the measured time period. We can use throughput measures to determine systems capacity by observing when the number of waiting items is never zero and determining at what level, based on the system's presented workload, the items never wait. Utilization is a measure of the fraction of time that a particular resource is busy. One example is CPU utilization. This could measure when the CPU is idle and when it is functioning to perform a presented program.

The user-oriented performance measures typically include response time or turnaround time. Response time and turnaround time refer to a view of the system's elapsed time from the point a user or application initiates a job on the system and when the job's answer or response is returned to the user. From this simple definition it can readily be seen that these are not clear, unambiguous measures, since there are many variables involved. For example, I/O channel traffic may cause variations in the measure for the same job, as would operating systems load, or CPU loads. Therefore, it is imperative that if this measure is to be used, the performance modeler must be unambiguous in his or her definition of this measure's meaning. These user measures are all considered random, and, therefore, their measures are typically discussed in terms of expected or average values as well as variances from these values.

In all cases, however, to make such measurements we need some basic understanding of the environment and its parameters with which we are working. One fundamental concept is that of time. To measure a physical phenomenon we need a metric to measure it against. In computer systems this metric is typically time. Time alone, however, is not sufficient; we need to have a place from which to mark time. This place is sometimes driven by an event in the system to be measured or simply a specified time. For example, in a computer system we may wish to measure the time a transaction takes to execute within a database system. We need to define the events of interest for this transaction system—for example, beginning the transaction, running the transaction, and ending or commitment of the transaction. Given that we have time and events, we next need to define when and how we measure these events and the intervals of interest for these events.

Other basic concepts needed for our discussions of computer systems performance include the means by which one measures or samples a system. Measurements can take on many forms within an evaluation project, as will be seen. Another aspect of time, which is important in computer systems performance studies, is that of intervals. An interval represents a measured distance of time representing a measured distance in a time period. For example a day, week, or month represents intervals of time. Most important to computer systems evaluation is the concept of response. Response represents a completion event for a measured entity—for example, the time between when a key is hit on a computer terminal and the user receives the result.

To utilize the basic quantities of time, events, intervals, and response, we need some additional concept concerning the relationships between all of these items. The typical concerns we have deal with the concepts of independence and randomness as they relate to the items within a computer system. Last, but not least, the concept of a workload and the relationship this plays with a modeling project must be defined.

## 3.2    Time

Time is the most fundamental of concepts needed for computer systems performance analysis. Without a clear concept of time our performance studies cannot take on quantitative qualities. Time as a quantity shows up in several ways when one investigates a computer system's performance. For example, we hear of concepts such as arrival time of an entity, the service time for an entity, time between failures, time to repair, entity lifetime, and numerous other quantities of time associated with computer systems performance. Each of these quantities requires us to have a reference point from which to determine their meanings.

In computer systems performance, we will be interested in the measurement of time related to various operational events in the computer system under study. These events will be marked by timestamp, and by using this timestamp we will have the capability to determine the relative ordering of these events in relation to each other. The timestamp of an event, $E$, would be represented as $E(t)$. The measurement or marking of the time, $t$, will only be as good as the clock we use in representing the time of an event and our ability to match the time representation with the event.

Time in a real-world system is represented in two major ways: either as a continuum or as discrete intervals or steps. The best way to think of these two measures of time is that discrete time represents a single instance of a time clock's measures, whereas continuous time represents discrete time intervals, where the intervals approach zero or are infinitely small.

Computer systems work using the concept of fixed time intervals. These intervals represent the time frame or limit into which a computer system's clock breaks down a second. Typical computer systems clocks or cycle times are measured in nanoseconds ($10^{-9}$ seconds) or in slices of about one-billionth of a second. Such fine gradations of a second help us to understand the speed of computer systems and related components.

I am sure you all can relate to hearing about a processor's speed. When we go to purchase a new personal computer, we are quoted a number of measures of computer relative time. For example, a 1.5-GHz processor implies that the processor will have a clock cycle of about 0.67 nanoseconds, or $6.67^{-10}$ seconds. This is not the only measure one needs to know when measuring or sizing up a personal computer for purchase. The CPU speed is important but is only one measure. We need to know how fast data and instructions can be transferred from the external devices into the internal primary memory, and then how fast the primary memory can transfer this information and instructions to the processor for actual execution. Even though one is quoted the CPU speed, this does not represent the actual measure of the machine's performance. We will see that the way devices are interconnected and how they interact will dictate overall speed. In this simple example, the slowest device in the system will ultimately dictate the real speed.

## 3.3    Events

Time is an important measure, but it can only become useful for us if we have a means to use it in measuring something within our computer system under evaluation. An event describes an entity of interest in our system. Events usually represent some action—for example, the beginning of a clock cycle (Figure 3.1) or the end of a clock cycle. The beginning of a computer's instruction execution cycle is another event, as is the end of the cycle, the reading of a memory location, the initiation of a block data transfer from a secondary storage device, and the initiation of a process or task. All of these represent events of interest to the computer engineer or computer architect.

Events, representing actions within our computer system, must all be controlled, so that the sequencing or ordering (partial or total ordering) of

**Figure 3.1**
*Example of a computer clock.*

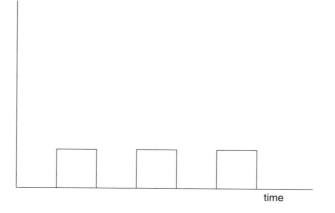

time

these actions contributes to the accomplishment of some larger event. For example, the simple computer clock cycle is used to mark the beginning of an instruction's execution in a computer. The rising edge of the clock is used by the processor to begin execution of the current instruction in the instruction register and to prepare the next instruction for execution. The multitude of parallel events being performed during each and every clock cycle of the computer system's clock must be synchronized so that the designed intentions are realized. For example, the instruction to perform was loaded into the instruction register during the last sequence, while at the same time the next instruction address was computed and possibly some parameters for the instruction moved into place. Each action must be designed and its sequencing in relation to other actions defined so that the computer will work as intended.

Each simple action, from the clock ticks to more complex actions such as an instruction's execution all become part of larger systems actions—for example, the initiation of a direct memory transfer of data from a secondary storage disk drive; the DMA transfer being used as part of the systems memory management system's paging algorithms; and the paging algorithm's relationship to the movement of one process actively running on the CPU being replaced by another due to a process switch handled by the operating system. All of these represent actions of interest to the computer analyst. Each, however, has a different temporal relationship to the measure of time. The clock cycle is measured in fractions of nanoseconds, the single assembly-level instructions in tens of nanoseconds, main memory transfers in the range of 100 nanoseconds, disk transfers in the milliseconds range, operating systems file transfers in the tens of milliseconds range, and so on.

In terms of performance assessment the system analyst must have an understanding of the events within the system under study and the relationship of these events among each other. For example, we need to know

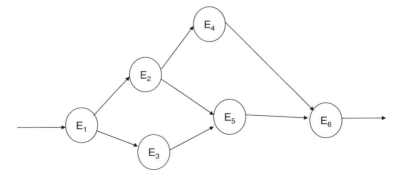

**Figure 3.2**
*Event partial
orderings.*

that a file access event is composed of the disk access event, memory page replacement algorithm event, and the main memory load and store events. In addition to knowing the events involved with a higher-order event, event orderings must also be understood. For example, it is important to know that the page replacement algorithm must be accessed first, to determine which page to move, before the new page can be loaded into the primary memory. These event orderings can be represented by simple event lists or by more complex partial orderings (Figure 3.2). These orderings dictate what events need to be considered and how the events may need to be measured, so that an accurate picture of the system's performance can be determined.

## 3.4    Measurements (sampling)

How does one measure a system or component performance? This is the main problem facing the computer systems performance analyst. To determine how to measure, when to measure, or what to measure, the analyst must first know all of the events of interest in the system and the relationship these events have with each other. The events, as we saw earlier, represent all of the real actions that occur in the computer system under study. These events form a hierarchy of relationships, where the finer, granular events are used to construct the coarse-grained events in the system. Even with these definitions, however, we do not know enough to begin measurements that will have meanings. We must know all the possible conditions that hold for events in our system and when they can be valid. Given a set of possible events and their values, we can describe a valid "state" for the computer system under study.

State is an important concept when considering any computer system. The state, $S$, is defined as the set of all events in our system along with valid values for their condition within the defined state. This can be described as follows:

$$S = \{E_1(\text{value}), E_2(\text{value}), E_3(\text{value}), \dots, E_n(\text{value})\} \qquad (3.1)$$

where each of the events must have all component events valid, and their own values must define valid states. For example, a state for a central processing unit may be defined as being composed of the following events and values:

- The program counter address held in the program counter

- The instruction held in the instruction register

- The status and value of the index register

- The status and values in the condition control register

- The value in the arithmetic logic unit temporary registers

- The value on the data bus

- The value on the address bus

- The value in the memory data register

Once we have definitions for the events and the state of the system, we can then begin to discuss the concept of measuring quantities within the system. There are three primary types of measures: A, B, and C. They can be described as follows:

> Type A looks to count a number of items over a given time period. For example, we may be interested in how often the CPU receives a new instruction during each second. This would represent the instruction speed of the processor, given the mix of instructions presented to the CPU.

> Type B measures all state variables (valid events and their values). A representation of this type of measurement may be to extract all of the values for all internal registers and devices at the beginning of an instruction execution cycle.

> Type C measures the fraction of time the system is within a state. An example of this measure may be to see what the fraction of time is that the system is executing load instructions versus all other kinds of instructions during the measured period of time.

It is not sufficient to simply determine the kind of event one wishes to measure and the values representing this event. One must also be able to recognize that a specified state has been reached and that all events and status variables for the state are valid. In addition to recognizing that a valid state has been reached, one must also be able to determine if we are at an end or transitional point within a state. These are not easy to know when one is attempting to measure a system.

In order to find out where we are within a state, we must have means to measure the systems events we are interested in. There are a number of ways to measure these events, each with its own issues. We can use hardware monitoring, software monitoring, or hybrid monitoring. The decision about which of these techniques to use is dependent on many factors, such as accessibility, event frequency, monitor artifact, overhead of monitoring, and the flexibility of the technique used.

Hardware monitoring requires that the system analyst have the ability to add instrumentation to the measured system. For example, we may attach a logic analyzer to measure the signals within the system or insert a specially designed hardware card to extract some signals from a system. This mode of measurement will allow us to measure some subset of the total system's hardware elements. We can only measure what is exposed and available to be attached to for monitoring. If the item or action we wish to monitor is not easily accessible, we may not be able to get to it using a hardware monitor. We may need to use some other means to extract the information from the system.

Another form of hardware monitoring uses integral test hardware, which is designed into the system being monitored during systems design. A common form of this monitoring scheme is found in very large scale integration (VLSI) devices. Many VLSI devices are designed so that all data items of interest can be tested in the device itself, or, at a minimum, the test data points are brought outside of the chip so additional devices can be used to gather this information and compute the health of the device.

In all of these cases it is imperative that the hardware monitoring be designed as an integral component of the system, so that it will not interfere with the operational system. It is not desirable for the monitoring equipment to interfere with the system being monitored. If this is the case, the results from the monitoring are suspect and may lead to erroneous conclusions. The monitoring hardware must be selected and designed with the device being measured in mind. The determination of sampling sites and the frequency of measurements must be designed ahead of time, not after the monitor has been put in place. The monitoring method has to be set up ahead of time also. That is, we must determine if the monitor is to act synchronously or asynchronously with the measured system. We must determine and define all aspects of the monitor's existence in the measured system. Nothing can be left out if we are to get trustworthy data.

Software monitoring requires support from the system under study if it is to be successful. Software monitoring requires that there be a means for the monitor designers to get at systems hardware elements as well as low-level software elements—for example, systems clocks, programmable timers, interrupt registers, and systems status registers. The typical software monitor is designed for trace monitoring and sampling, not for synchronous monitoring. In trace monitoring, the analyst adds additional code to a code sequence so that the code's run time can be monitored. Typically we would be interested in how often a code segment is entered, how long the code segment runs, or how much of the total systems time the code segment utilizes.

Software monitoring, as with hardware monitoring, still requires that we know ahead of time where the sampling measures are to occur within the system and the frequency of this sampling if our measurements are to have meaning.

In software monitoring, where we are using sampled monitoring techniques, we need to have access to low-level operating systems calls. This type of access is required so that we may cause a system's interrupt and take control of the system. The interrupt control would allow for entrance into the system and collection of systems state information such as the contents of registers and status flags. One positive aspect of this form of software monitoring is that it may not lead to the alteration of any code, given that all required information can be collected using available information.

A more common form of measurement uses hybrid monitoring. This form of systems monitoring uses concepts and mechanisms from both hardware and software monitoring. To utilize hardware monitoring we must go through the same set of issues as was the case for hardware monitoring as well as for software monitoring. The setup may require the synchronization of multiple hardware and software setups. We must set up the control programs to determine when and how to monitor the system under test. We must determine what to capture with hardware devices and what to capture with software means. Upon execution of the monitoring subsystem, we must determine how and how often to retrieve collected information. In addition we must also determine how and when to synchronize the measuring and measured systems.

Hybrid monitoring comes with its own set of problems. As in hardware monitoring, we must have a means to extract signals of interest from our system. We must determine which elements we wish to test are best tested with hardware and which with software. We must understand and bound the impact the monitoring software has on the monitored systems, so that correct measurements are extracted. Finally, we must always keep in mind that the measurements are only as good as the available measurement points.

# 3.5    Intervals

Measurement requires that we have a domain or environment in which we are measuring. In computer systems the environment is the systems clocks

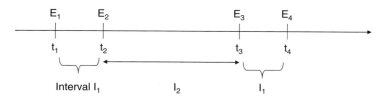

**Figure 3.3**
*Example of*
*intervals*

and the instruction execution cycle. Another major environment is the high-order systems functions. In order to measure these items we need to focus on their interval of execution. An interval represents a period of time bounding the initiation of an event sequence of interest and the end of this event sequence (Figure 3.3).

In Figure 3.3, the interval $I_1$ is composed of Event 1's time tag and Event 2's time tag. Intervals are used as a means to measure an event's sequences period of execution or the period of time between such executions (in Figure 3.3, interval 2). Two intervals are the same if they represent the same sequence of events (they are related) and the time interval between the events is equivalent. Two intervals representing two separate sequences of different events can also have equivalent intervals, but they are unrelated.

## 3.6    Response

Response is an important concept in computer systems performance studies. Response time represents a measure of the period of time a user or application must wait from the point of issuing some action or command until the completion and return of control for the requested command. The typical measure used may pit the response time (an interval) against the systems load (stream of jobs). The curve may appear similar to that shown in Figure 3.4.

The interpretation of this curve becomes an important means to evaluate our system. In Figure 3.4 we see that the response time of our measured action sequence stays within tolerable ranges (between 1.0 and 3.0) for loads below approximately 60 percent of the capacity of the measured system. As the load increases above this point, the response climbs exponentially—reaching a saturation level when the system is fully loaded, yielding an asymptotic response time approaching infinity. One can see from this simple example the importance of response time as a measurement in modeling and evaluating systems.

The problem is in trying to determine the response of what. It may not be sufficient to look at our systems performance from only one measure or

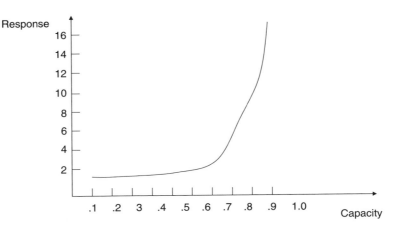

**Figure 3.4**
*Response time versus system load.*

action sequence. We may be interested in a family of such action sequences, requiring a series of separate tests to study the effect of each of these measurable sequences against system load. In addition to this form of measure, we may also be interested in how these various action sequences impact each other as load increases. This would result in a family of response curves, which need to be interpreted against each other and the loads.

## 3.7    Independence

Another very important concept in performance modeling and analysis is that of independence. An action or event is considered independent of another event or action if the occurrence of one does not influence the outcome of the other. For example, the tossing of a coin followed by the rolling of a die are independent, since the coin's toss has no impact on the outcome. If we look at these events as two separate sample spaces, the interaction of these events becomes clearer. The sample space for the coin's toss is simply the set {H,T}, and the sample space for the die is simply the set {1,2,3,4,5,6}. The sample space in Figure 3.5 is the Cartesian product of these two independent spaces.

The independence of events in a system is an important concept to consider when evaluating systems. If two events are independent, we need not

**Figure 3.5**
*Cartesian product of two independent sample spaces.*

|   | 1 | 2 | 3 | 4 | 5 | 6 |
|---|---|---|---|---|---|---|
| H | H1 | H2 | H3 | H4 | H5 | H6 |
| T | T1 | T2 | T3 | T4 | T5 | T6 |

consider these as related items requiring us to examine their response in relation to each other and their environment.

In a computer system, two programs that cannot run concurrently with each other can be viewed as independent items and analyzed as such. Even though they run on the same hardware and possibly use the same operating systems software, since they cannot interfere with each other and are not dependent in terms of sequencing, they can be evaluated as separate, unrelated items. It becomes an important part of our modeling and analysis of a system to define all elements and their relationship to each other. These definitions can then be used to aid in the determination of independence. We will discuss this property of events further when we look at probability and then map this to computer systems elements.

## 3.8    Randomness

Just as important to modeling as the concept of independence is the concept of randomness of events. Randomness is a property of an event and its reoccurrence. If an event is random, it implies that there is not a pattern that can be mapped onto the events to determine when they will occur again. Randomness is difficult, if not impossible, to prove. The converse, however, can be shown—that is, that an event is not random. We can use the assertion that a pattern does not exist as a way of indicating that the past will not aid in defining the future of an event. A random sequence of trials is the realization of the property of independence defined in the previous section.

Randomness is a mathematical concept. In mathematics we think of random numbers coming from a random infinite source. In practice, there are finite sequences of available numbers, and once they are generated they now have a pattern. For example, if we roll the die, before we roll it we have no idea which number will occur; but after it is rolled there is only one outcome.

In a computer system, the events caused by external sources (e.g., user key strokes, remote calls to a server) can be viewed as random events. Thus, their occurrence cannot be predicted ahead of time nor can the future after the last occurrence. This concept becomes very important when we wish to analyze our computer systems using mathematical concepts.

More on the concept of randomness will be discussed when we look at random variables and their use in modeling computing systems as Markov chains and Markov processes in later chapters.

## 3.9   Workloads

A concept we have been discussing throughout the book up to this point is that of workload, or, more simply, load. These terms represent an extremely important element in our computer systems modeling problem. The workload or load represents the events or event sequences presented to the system to model or drive the system under study. The load represents how many of some event sequence are being offered for execution during some given period of time. An example may be the number of instructions per second and the mix of instruction types presented for execution per second. The combination of the volume and the mix is important, as well as the duration of the load.

The duration may be all at once, requiring the system to queue up the requests and perform them as resources become available. This type of mix and load would saturate the system up front and then decay to no load as the items get processed. The duration could be endless, with the load continually refreshed to provide a constant saturation or equilibrium load to the system. Loads can be periodic, where the instructions are presented all at once for service and then allowed to be processed. The load is then reentered after the prescribed period of time has passed, providing another spike in processing requirement.

There is a science to workload development and selection for the computer systems modeler. For example, the database community has developed a set of transactional workloads aimed at testing a variety of database systems configurations. This set of transactions and the underlying database system have been developed over a number of years through the measurement of real database systems and the need to evaluate databases against each other with a known well-formed set of loads. Likewise, the personal computer industry has also developed a set of systems workloads aimed at allowing customers to assess the performance of one computer architecture against another.

## 3.10   Problems encountered in model development and use

Developing a performance assessment project for a specified system is not without its pitfalls. We must start with developing a concept for what we are evaluating and why. That is, does our performance study have as its goal to measure the existing performance of a system or future possibilities? Are we measuring the cost of the system now or in the future? Are we measuring the correctness of the system or the adequacy? How do we define these terms? What dictates correctness or adequacy? Why do we need to perform this study?

The typical analyst first begins with the primary concern, that the system performs its intended design function correctly. For example, if a computer system is to be able to perform concurrent operations, then a primary measure is that it can do just that. A secondary concern of the modeler is that the system has adequate performance and delivers this at a reasonable cost. This implies that we need some way to measure and predict what is adequate performance and what is reasonable cost.

To understand these terms we first need to put them in the context of an environment where the system is to be operational. Even before this, though, we must start by determining what is meant by the system. For example, if it is a PC, we need to know what this term entails. Do we wish to include the motherboard, processor type, memory volume and type, I/O boards, graphics cards, disk drives, and maybe network interconnects? Or do we simply mean the black box, without concern for what is inside? Once the system of interest has been defined, the modeler must define what components make up this system and what their importance is in the context of the entire system.

Given the systems definition and the components definition, we next must define the environment in which the system will operate. The environment should only include the important factors defining it, not everything. For example, if we are studying a PC architecture, we may wish to know if it will be exposed to the elements, extreme temperatures, humidity, and so on.

Once the environment is defined, we must determine what parameters are of interest to us as analyst. These may include parameters upon which the system is used or measured by. Some parameters may include things such as the PC processor speed, the size of primary memory, and so forth.

The common answer with PC users and computer systems users in general is that they cannot easily define the above terms. They typically look at computer systems performance evaluation as only answering one question: If my computer is not working up to snuff, can't I just add more of "whatever" to make it work better? The problem lies in how to know what "whatever" is needed. How much of this "whatever" is needed? The problem is that one does not readily know when adding "whatever" that a certain quantity will provide the intended result. More importantly, without performance evaluation how do we know we are done?

The problem the performance evaluator is faced with is how to determine what to measure and how to do this. There are two main classes of techniques for computer systems performance assessment. The first is to take an existing system and design some experiments involving possibly hardware, software, or both. Then measure the result to determine what is needed. The second class of modeling tool utilizes more abstract means. These involve either analytical modeling or simulations. Analytical modeling typically uses queuing theory or Petri nets theory and can provide coarse analysis of the systems under study. Simulations can provide more fidelity but at an added cost in terms of design time and analysis. Simulations can be designed as discrete event-based models, continuous-based models, or combined models.

Performance measures used by the analyst in making a determination of performance include responsiveness, use levels, missionability, dependability, productivity, and predictability. Responsiveness indicates the system's ability to be provided commands and to deliver answers within a reasonable time period. Use level indicates the system's degree to which it is loaded— for example, is the system 50 percent loaded or 100 percent saturated? Missionability refers to the system's ability to perform as it was intended for the duration demanded. For example, a spaceship must be highly missionable. Dependability is related to the last measure but indicates the system's ability to resist failure or to stay operational. Productivity indicates a measure of the throughput of the given system. And predictability indicates a measure of a system's ability to operate as required under all or most conditions.

All of these measures have a place, given specific classes of systems. For example, a general-purpose computing facility must possess the qualities of being responsive, have good use levels, and be productive. High-availability systems, such as transaction processing or database systems, must not only be responsive but must possess a higher degree of dependability than the general-purpose computing environment. Real-time control systems require high responsiveness, dependability, and predictability. Mission-oriented systems, such as avionic control systems, require extremely high reliability over short durations and must be responsive. Long-life applications, such as spacecraft and autonomous underwater vehicles, must be highly dependable, missionable, and responsive.

There are common errors or mistakes computer systems performance analysts make or must avoid when performing their tasks. The first and most common is having no goals or ill-defined goals for the performance study. The goals should include a specification for a model of the system or component under study and definition of the techniques, metrics, and workload to be used in the evaluations. The second major problem is setting biased goals. This is a very common mistake by the modeler. The goal becomes to prove that "my system is superior to someone else's system." This makes the analyst the jury, which will lead to bad judgments.

If the analyst uses an unsystematic approach to developing the model or jumps into analysis before fully understanding the problem under study, the results will be flawed. The choice of incorrect performance metrics or misleading metrics will result in erroneous results and conclusions. Choosing an unrepresentative or nonstressful workload will lead to misinterpretations of system performance boundaries. Choosing the wrong evaluation technique—for example, analytical modeling, when a testbed is the right choice—will lead to overly simplistic or complex analysis. Overlooking important system parameters or not examining the interaction among systems parameters may lead to erroneous conclusions about sensitivities and dependencies among system elements. Inappropriate experimental design or bad choice of the level of detail can cause misleading conclusions. Erroneous analysis, no sensitivity analysis, or even no analysis lead to failure. Ignoring input, internal or output errors, or the variability of these can cause misleading interpretations of results. Not performing sensitivity analysis, outlier analysis, or ignoring change can also cause problems in interpreting or trusting results. Performing too complex an analysis or improper presentation or interpretation of results, as well as the omission of assumptions and limitations, will yield a failed analysis.

To try to alleviate these problems the analyst should ask the following questions before, during, and after an analysis has been done:

1.    Is the system correctly defined and the goals of the analysis clearly stated?

2.    Are the goals stated in an unbiased manner?

3.    Have all the steps of the analysis been followed systematically?

4.    Is the problem clearly understood before analysis is begun?

5.    Are the performance metrics relevant for this problem?

6.    Is the workload correct for this problem?

7.    Is the evaluation technique appropriate?

8.    Is the list of parameters that affect performance complete?

9.    Have all parameters that affect performance been chosen as factors to be used in experimental design?

10.     Is the experimental design efficient in terms of time and results expected?

11.     Is the model's level of detail sufficient?

12.     Are the measured data presented with analysis and interpretation?

13.     Is the analysis statistically correct?

14.     Has the sensitivity analysis been done?

15.     Would errors in the input cause an insignificant change in the results?

16.     Have the outliers in the input or outputs been treated properly?

17.     Have the future changes in the system and workload been modeled?

18.     Has the variance of input been taken into account?

19.     Has the variance in results been analyzed?

20.     Is the analysis easy and unambiguous to explain?

21.     Is the presentation style suitable for its intended audience?

22.     Have the results been presented graphically as much as possible?

23.     Are the assumptions and limitations of the analysis clearly documented and accounted for?

When developing a performance study the sage performance analyst would follow a systematic approach, which has the following point as its components:

1.     State goals and define the system to be studied.

2.     List services and outcomes clearly and completely.

3.     Select the performance metrics.

4.     List all systems parameters of interest.

5.     Select the factors for the study.

6.     Select the evaluation technique to apply.

7.     Select the workload.

8.     Design the experiments.

9.     Analyze and interpret results.

10.    Present results clearly and unambiguously.

11.    Repeat if needed.

# 3.11   A case study

If we wished to study the issue of remote pipes versus remote procedure calls, we could go through the following modeling effort. The first step is to define the system we wish to study. This entails developing a model that contains all of the major components of interest. In Figure 3.6 we postulate such a definition.

The services we wish to focus on are small and large data transfers. We will not be concerned with other details of the services.

The metrics we wish to focus on as well as some assumptions include that there are no errors and no failures in the system. We wish to focus on defining rates of access, time for performance, and resource requirement per service. The resources we will focus on are the client, server, and network elements.

These metrics and assumptions may lead us to focus on measurements to be collected, such as elapsed time per call, maximum call rate per unit of time, time required to complete a block of $N$ successive calls, local CPU time per call, remote CPU time per call, number of bytes sent over the link per call, and so on.

These in turn will require us to focus on definition of the system's parameters—for example, the speed of the local and remote CPUs, the speed of the network, operating system overhead for interfacing with the channels, operating system overhead for interfacing with the network, reliability of the network, and so forth.

The workload parameters used to define the presented workload may include the time between successive calls, the number and sizes of the call parameters, number and size of the results, the type of channel used, and other background loads on the local and remote site as well as on the network.

Factors we may wish to study could include type of channel (RPC or remote pipes), size of the network (long distance, local area network), size of the calls (small, large), and the number of successive calls (can vary from one, five, ten up to some saturation load).

The assumptions made may include fixing the type of CPU and operating system, ignoring retransmissions due to network errors, and doing measurements with no other loads on hosts and networks.

The evaluation technique may be chosen as a prototype along with analytical models to validate or bound the expected results. The workload is

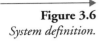

**Figure 3.6**
*System definition.*

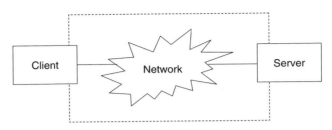

constructed using synthetic constructs. The experimental design will vary all factors, resulting in a full factorial experimental design with 88 experiments used. This represents the varying of all factors described over their entire range of postulated values. The data analysis will involve determining the variance of results and comparing these against each factor. This would be followed by the plotting of all results in graphical form to better show performance variations.

## 3.12   Summary

In this chapter we briefly described some of the fundamental concepts required to initiate the analysis of computer systems. The first dealt with the basic concept of time and how this unit can be used as a fundamental means to measure performance. This description was then followed by a description of the definition of events or actions within a domain. The concepts of time and event were then melded to yield a means to identify points from which to initiate measurement. The methods of measuring a system were then described, focusing on hardware and software monitoring and issues associated with each.

The next step in our investigation was to develop the concept of related actions making up larger actions and the duration of these activities. The duration was defined as the interval of a complex action or the time between successive repetitions of a specified sequence.

With the concept of intervals we could then focus on measuring a sequence of related actions. The focus of this section was to define response time in relationship to a computer system's modeling and performance analysis.

The concept of these complex interactions was addressed next. The concepts of dependent and independent actions were developed. These were then followed by the development of a definition for randomness of such events within a computer system. It was pointed out that this concept of randomness is an important one in simplifying some of our analysis techniques.

This discussion was then followed up with an introduction to the concept of a workload and what it represents in computer systems performance. The final section in this chapter discussed some of the hurdles facing the computer systems analyst in the design, development, operation, and completion of a performance study.

# 4

# *General Measurement Principles*

In modeling computer systems, we typically are interested in the service times of entities that utilize system resources. Entities in our discussion can represent a variety of operations on a computer system. For example, we may be interested in the time it takes to service an operating interrupt or, in a database system, the time to lock a data item in the database. The resources we are interested in are computer hardware elements and software resources. The entities represent the operations that are performed using the resources of the computer system. For example, if the resource is a central processing unit, a program operating on the CPU would have a service time composed of instruction execution (possibly driven by the instruction mix), memory management, I/O management, and secondary device access and transfer delays.

These components of the system under analysis are observable and possibly measurable. This does not mean that we need to measure all components precisely and completely as deterministic points in time. It may actually be more desirable to use average times and random service and arrivals to model these resources and programs. If the focus of review is the overall program operation, and not the components of this operation, then the service times will appear to be unpredictable and, therefore, can be assumed to be random. Without such assumptions, modeling a computer system would get bogged down in the extraction and determination of minute details, which may cloud our overall analysis.

Even though the service times for events may be unpredictable, we can still describe them in a way amenable to modeling and analysis with fairly good accuracy. For example, we can observe many event occurrences over a long period of time and deduce the composite average service time from this information with some degree of accuracy. Such approximations are sufficient for many models and for their analysis, as will be seen in later chapters.

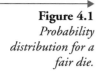

**Figure 4.1**
*Probability*
*distribution for a*
*fair die.*

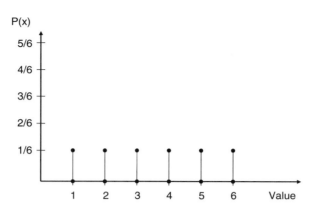

One of the most important approximations concerning events and service distributions in a modeled system is that of probability distribution. It is important in modeled systems to have a measure of the possibility of some event occurring in relation to other events. The probability distribution looks to assign discrete probability values or continuous intervals of probable values to events. The assumption is that individual service times or events are independent and identically distributed (see Chapter 3). This is a reasonable approximation to reality under most conditions.

The simplest form of a probability distribution is found when we have a finite set of possible values. For example, the rolling of a fair die can only take on the values of {1,2,3,4,5,6} and no others. In addition, the probability of these individual values being rolled, given a fair die and an exhaustive number of trials, is 1/6 each. The possible values and a graphical representation are shown in Figure 4.1.

In equation 4.1, $P(x)$ represents the probability (or relative frequency) of value $x$ occurring. In Chapter 5, we will see that $P(x)$ must possess the properties that $0 \leq P(x) \leq 1$ for all possible values of $x$ from our set of possible values, and $\sum P(x) = 1$.

When using such measures, the most important parameter when modeling is the mean or expected value. This value corresponds to the average value and is represented as:

$$E[X] = \sum_x x P(x)$$

(4.1)

Given the distribution of equation 4.1, $E[X]$ would be calculated as:

$$E[X] = 1(1/6) + 2(1/6) + 3(1/6) + 4(1/6) + 5(1/6) + 6(1/6)$$
$$= 3.5 \tag{4.2}$$

An additional generalized measurement typically used is the $n$th moment and is computed as the sum of the $x$ value raised to the $n$th power times the probability of this value of $x$ occurrence, or:

$$E[X^n] = \sum_x x^n P(x) \tag{4.3}$$

For our fair die example, the second moment would be found as:

$$E[X^2] = 1^2 (1/6) + 2^2 (1/6) + 3^2 (1/6) +$$
$$4^2 (1/6) + 5^2 (1/6) + 6^2 (1/6) = 15.167 \tag{4.4}$$

A variation and more useful measure is the $n$th central moment, which is found by examining the difference between measured values and the expected value. The central moment is found by the formula:

$$E\left[ (X - E[X])^n \right] = \sum_x (x - E[X])^n P(x) \tag{4.5}$$

For our fair die example, the second central moment would be found as:

$$E\left[ (X - E[X])^2 \right] =$$
$$1/6\left[ (-2.5)^2 + (-1.5)^2 + (-0.5)^2 + (0.5)^2 + (1.5)^2 + (2.5)^2 \right] = 2.92 \tag{4.6}$$

This measure of the second central moment has another name: the variance. The variance can be refined to give us an important measure, called the standard deviation, by taking the square root of the variance. Typically the variance is written $\sigma^2$. In our example, for the fair die, the standard deviation is found to be 1.7. The standard deviation tells us the average distance our measured values vary from the mean and can help in telling us how variable our data are. An additional measure concerning the relationship of actual values versus expected values is the coefficient of variation $C_x$. The coefficient of variation is defined as:

$$C_x = \sigma_x / E[X] \tag{4.7}$$

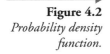

**Figure 4.2**
*Probability density function.*

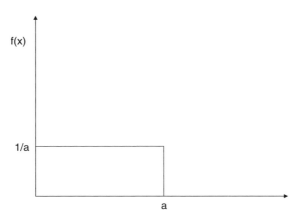

In computer systems modeling it is possible to see coefficient of variation measures from below 1 to 10 and above. Most measures, however, will tend to fall somewhere between these values.

In modeling computer systems we often must characterize arrival rates and service rates using a variety of distribution functions. Typical distributions utilized include the exponential distribution, the normal distribution, the uniform distribution, and geometric distributions. We will mention them in overview in this chapter, discussing additional details in Chapter 5.

When looking at the values for an entity of interest, we have been examining how often the value occurs in comparison to all possible values. We have used the discrete probability distribution up to this point, since our examples assumed discrete values. Often in computer systems values for an entity of interest will not be discrete; they will be continuous. For example, the amount of time the CPU takes for every job it processes will typically consist of real values, not discrete values. Such measures require that the probability of a particular value we are interested in will vary over the full range of possible values. Such probability functions are continuous and are described by functions. The function describing the possible probability values for our entity of interest is called the probability density function (Figure 4.2), while the measure showing the systems probability is described by the probability distribution function (Figure 4.3). The probability density function gives us the actual value for the probability of some entity at a specific point in the state space for the item. The distribution function provides us with a probability measure indicating what the probability is that a value is less than or equal to a specific value.

For the measures we introduced for expected values, variance, and the central moment, the following changes in formula hold.

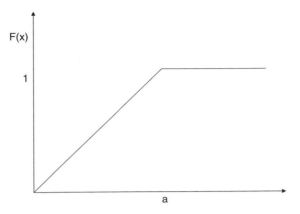

**Figure 4.3**
*Probability distribution function.*

For the mean:

$$E[X] = \int_{-\infty}^{\infty} x \, f(x_0) dx_0 \qquad (4.8)$$

for the variance:

$$E[X^2] = \int_{-\infty}^{\infty} x^2 \, f(x_0) dx_0 \qquad (4.9)$$

and for the central moment:

$$\sigma^2 = \int_{-\infty}^{\infty} (x - E[X])^2 f(x_0) dx_0 \qquad (4.10)$$

For the distribution shown in Figure 4.2 the probability density function would be described as:

$$f(x) = \begin{cases} 1/a & 0 \le x_0 \le a \\ 0 & \text{otherwise} \end{cases} \qquad (4.11)$$

and for the probability distribution function as:

$$F(x) = \begin{cases} 0 & x_0 < 0 \\ x_0/a & 0 \le x_0 \le a \\ 1 & x_0 > a \end{cases} \qquad (4.12)$$

The expected value for our example would be found as:

$$E[x] = a/2 \tag{4.13}$$

The second moment for our example would be found as:

$$E[X^2] = a^2/3 \tag{4.14}$$

and the variance called the central moment would be found as:

$$\sigma^2 = a^2/12 \tag{4.15}$$

One of the most important distributions for modeling computer systems is the exponential distribution (in particular the negative exponential). For the exponential distribution the probability density function is described as:

$$f(x_0) = \begin{cases} 0 & x_0 < 0 \\ \lambda e^{-\lambda x_0} & x_0 \geq 0 \end{cases} \tag{4.16}$$

and for the probability distribution function as:

$$F(x_0) = \begin{cases} 0 & x_0 < 0 \\ 1 - e^{-\lambda x_0} & x_0 \geq 0 \end{cases} \tag{4.17}$$

The expected value for the exponential distribution is described as:

$$E[X] = 1/\lambda \tag{4.18}$$

The second moment is found as:

$$E[X^2] = 1/\lambda^2 \tag{4.19}$$

The central moment is found as:

$$\sigma^2 = 1/\lambda^2 \tag{4.20}$$

and the coefficient of variation is found as:

$$C_x = 1 \tag{4.21}$$

In later chapters we will see the importance of this distribution when examining computer systems. This distribution can be used in ways such that we can get very close approximations of general systems operations.

# 4.1   **Scheduling algorithms**

When analyzing computer systems one ultimately must look at the scheduling algorithms applied to resource allocation. The means by which resources are allocated and then consumed are of utmost importance in assessing the performance of a computer system. For example, scheduling algorithms are applied when selecting which program runs on a CPU, what I/O device is serviced, and when or how a specific device handles multiple requests. When examining scheduling algorithms, two concepts must be addressed. The first is the major job of the scheduling algorithm, which is what job to select to run next. The second is to determine if the job presently running is the most appropriate to run and if not, should it be preempted (removed from service).

The most basic form of scheduling algorithm is first-come first-served (FCFS). In this scheduling algorithm jobs enter the system and get operated on based on their arrival time. The job with the earliest arrival time gets served next. This algorithm does not apply preemption to a running job, since the running job would still hold the criterion of having the earliest arrival time. A scheduling algorithm that operates opposite from the FCFS is the last-come first-served (LCFS) algorithm. In this algorithm the job with the most recent time tag is selected for operation. Given this algorithm's selection criteria, it is possible that this algorithm could be preemptive. The job being serviced is no longer the last to come in for service. The preemption decision must be made based on the resource's ability to be halted in midstream and then restarted at some future time. Processors typically can be preempted, since there are facilities to save registers and other information needed to restart a job at some later time. Other devices, such as a disk drive or I/O channel, may not have the ability to halt a job and pick it up at some later point.

A number and variety of scheduling algorithms are associated with processor scheduling. One of the most common processor scheduling algorithms is round robin. Round-robin scheduling is a combination algorithm. It uses FCFS scheduling, along with preemption. The processor's service is broken into chunks of time called quantum. These quanta or time slices are then used as the measure for service. Jobs get scheduled in an FCFS fashion as long as their required service time does not exceed the time of a quantum. If their required service time exceeds this, the job is preempted and placed in the back of the set of pending jobs. This motion of placing a job back into the FCFS scheduling pipe continues until the job ultimately completes. Thus, the job's service time is broken up into some number of equal, fixed-size time slices. The major issue with round-robin scheduling is the selection of quantum size. The reason quantum size selection is so important is due to the nature of preemption. Preempting a job requires overhead from the operating system to stop the job, save its state, and install a new job. If the time for these tasks is large in comparison to the quantum size, then performance will suffer. Many different rules of thumb have been developed in designing such systems. Most look to make the overhead a very small fraction of the size of the quantum—typically, orders of magnitude smaller. A method used for approximating round-robin scheduling when the quantum is very large compared with the overhead is processor sharing (PS). This model of round-robin scheduling is used in theoretical analysis, as we will see in later chapters.

Another algorithm is shortest remaining time first (SRTF). In this algorithm the job that requires the least amount of resource time is selected as the next job to service. The CPU scheduling algorithm SRTF does support preemption. When an arriving job is found to have a smaller estimated execution time than the presently running job, the running job is preempted and replaced by the new job. The problem with this scheduling algorithm is that one must know the processing requirements of each job ahead of time, which is typically not the case. Due to this limitation it is not often used. The algorithm is, however, optimal and used as a comparison with other more practical algorithms.

A useful algorithm related to SRTF is the value-driven algorithm, where both the time of execution and the value of getting the job completed within some time frame are known ahead of time. This class of algorithm is found in real-time, deadline-driven systems. The algorithm selects the next job to do based on nearness to its deadline and the computation of the value it returns if done now. The algorithm also is preemptive in that it will remove an executing job from the processor if the contending job is nearer its deadline and has a higher relative value. The interest in these classes of scheduling algorithms is that they deliver support for the most critical operations at a cost to overall throughput.

## 4.1.1   Relationship between scheduling and distributions

In determining the performance of a computer system, the usual measure is throughput. In the discussions that follow we consider this to be the mean number of jobs passing through some point of interest in our architecture during an interval of time—for example, the number of jobs leaving the

CPU per minute. In most cases we will realize the maximum value for throughput when our resources are fully utilized (busy).

In the previous section we introduced measures that we can use now. The coefficient of variation defined previously is a good way to examine the variability of our data. If the service times are highly variable, $C > 1$, then most measures will be smaller than the mean and some will be larger. For example, in the exponential distribution, $C = 1$, one would find from the probability density function that about 63 percent of the values are below the mean. Such variability would cause problems with certain scheduling algorithms—for example, the FCFS scheduling algorithm, since jobs with large resource requirements will cause added delays to the majority of jobs that will be smaller than the mean. The effect can be further compounded by other resources dependent on the FCFS scheduled resource. For example, if jobs pile up waiting for CPU service, other resources such as disk drives and I/O devices would go idle.

One scheduling algorithm that is not as susceptible to this phenomenon is the round-robin scheduling protocol. Since no job, whether large or small, can acquire and hold the resource longer than a single quantum at a time, larger jobs will not starve out smaller jobs. This fact makes the round-robin scheduling protocol a nice algorithm for measuring resource utilization with variable loads. If we were to compare the FCFS and round-robin scheduling protocols with each other for highly variable and highly correlated loads, we would see that as the loads became more correlated the algorithms performed in a more similar manner. On the other hand, as the data become more variable the round-robin scheduling protocol performs better than the FCFS.

## 4.1.2   Relationship to computer systems performance

For modeling computer systems and their components we typically will be interested in determining the throughput, utilization, and mean service times for each of the elements of interest over a wide range of loads. The analysis from a theoretical perspective will always assume equilibrium has been reached, implying that the number of arrivals at some resource is equal to the number of departures from the resource (Figure 4.4).

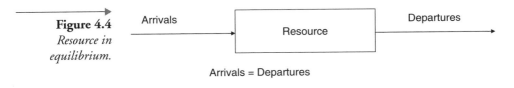

**Figure 4.4**
*Resource in equilibrium.*

Arrivals

Resource

Departures

Arrivals = Departures

The flow out of the resource is called its throughput. The mean service time is $E[X]$, as defined previously, and the mean service rate is $1/E[X]$. The utilization for this resource is defined as the fraction of time the resource is busy ($U$). The throughput of the resource must be equivalent to the service rate of the resource, when it is busy, times the fraction of the time it is busy.

This can be represented as:

$$\text{Throughput} = U/E[X] \tag{4.22}$$

If we have $n$ identical devices in our system—for example, multiple CPUs with the same properties—then the throughput for these would be described as:

$$\text{Throughput} = nU/E[X] \tag{4.23}$$

These simple relationships between utilization and expected time of service will be important measures in analyzing the performance of systems, as will be seen in later chapters.

Also of interest to the modeler is the size of the collection of jobs awaiting service at a resource and the time these jobs spend waiting for their service. First, we need to define the resource queue length. This is defined as the average number of jobs found waiting for service over the lifetime of this resource. Theoretically this can be found using the probability of having $n$ waiting jobs times the number of jobs for all values of $n$:

$$L_q = E\left[L_q\right] = \sum_{n=1}^{\infty} n\, p(n) \tag{4.24}$$

where $P(n)$ represents the probability that the resource's queue length is $n$. The mean queuing time (resource waiting time) can be found from:

$$T_q = E[q] = \int_0^{\infty} q_0 f_q\left(q_0\right) dq_0 \tag{4.25}$$

where $f_q\left(q_0\right)$ represents the probability density function for the resource's queuing times. From these observations it can be shown that:

$$L_q = \lambda T_q \tag{4.26}$$

This formula indicates that we can find the average queue length given that we know the average queuing time and the rate of arrivals $\lambda$ (or serviced items) for the resource of interest. This simple observation was discovered by J. D. Little and is referred to as Little's Law. More will be said on this formula and its application to computer systems performance analysis in later chapters.

## 4.2   Workloads

In order that we can model and analyze systems, we need to develop means to test and/or stress systems of interest. These means to test or stress systems are called workloads. A workload should be developed so it faithfully models the nature of the true load on the system of interest. Workloads are constructed based on the focus of the analysis. For example, if we are interested in examining the hardware of a computer system in comparison to another, our focus may be on the low-level instructions. We would need to measure the instruction mix seen on a running system and then develop a synthetic mix of instructions based on these measures. Another example is to measure transaction throughput through some database system. This workload would have transactional units of work that read and write data items from the database system and do some additional computational work mimicking the real system. The database community has developed such workloads for conventional databases, object relational databases, data warehouses, and data mining. These workloads are called TP benchmarks.

When designing a workload, it is important that we understand how the workload will load down the system of interest. It is not sufficient to simply provide a token load; the load must provide the means to stress the system being analyzed. We want workloads that will cause the measured system to go into saturation. We want to see where the system gets to 100 percent utilization of resources and to sustain such loads for some duration of time.

Once a workload is developed, we will want to use some form of distribution function to select items from our workload and to present them to the system for service. For example, if we have developed $n$ transaction types for our database system analysis, we may wish to use a uniform distribution to select database data items for the transactions to operate on and use the exponential distribution to present transactions to the system for processing. Using these means our workload will be presented to our system in a way that mimics the real-world situation, but which we have total control over.

Workloads also need to be developed so they test the components we want them to test. For example, if we are testing the database system, a simple instruction mix workload will not provide the kind of information we are interested in. The instructions alone are not representative of the desired load: transactions. Transactions are composed of transactional boundaries, database access and alteration commands, and data manipulation commands. More on workloads will follow in later chapters.

## 4.3    Summary

In this chapter we introduced some basic concepts needed for computer systems performance evaluation. The concept of service time–related resources is introduced, as are some basic concepts for use of these measures. The fundamental concepts involved in probability density and probability distribution functions are developed. These are then used to develop basic definitions for expected or mean values, the $n$th moment of a distribution. The special second moment, called the central moment, is developed, as is the definition and formulation for variance and coefficient of variation. The discussion then changed to scheduling algorithms used in computer systems. We introduce priority scheduling, round-robin, first-come first-served, last-come first-served, and the deadline-driven value function scheduling algorithms.

This is followed by a discussion of how these items relate to computer systems modeling. The relationship scheduling algorithms have with distribution functions is presented, as is their relationship to performance studies. The last topic presented is that of workloads. The concept of what a workload is and how it is used in computer systems modeling is presented from an introductory perspective.

# 5

# *Probability*

Queuing theory and queuing analysis are based on the use of probability theory and the concept of random variables. We utilize the concepts embodied in probability in a number of different ways. For example, we may ask what the probability is of the Boston Bruins winning the Stanley Cup this year. How likely is George W. Bush to be reelected after the events of this year? How likely is it to snow on the top of Mt. Washington in New Hampshire in January of this year? Most of the time a general answer would suffice. For example, it is highly probable that snow will fall sometime in January on Mt. Washington. Conversely, based on the last 30 years of frustration, it is also highly unlikely that the Boston Bruins will win the Stanley Cup this year. Probability theory allows us to make more precise definitions for the probability of an event occurring based on past history or on specific available measurements, as we will see. In this chapter, we will introduce the concepts of probability, joint probability, conditioned probability, and independence. We will then move on to probability distributions, stochastic processes, and, finally, the basics of queuing theory.

Before discussing queuing analysis, it is necessary to introduce some concepts from probability theory and statistics. In basic probability theory, we start with the ideas of random events and sample spaces. Take, for instance, the experiment that involves tossing a fair die (an experiment typically defines a procedure that yields a simple outcome, which may be assigned a probability of occurrence). The sample space of an experiment is simply the set of all possible outcomes—in this case the set {1,2,3,4,5,6} for the die. An event is defined as a subset of a sample space and may consist of none, one, or more of the sample space elements. In the die experiment, an event may be the occurrence of a 2 or that the number that appears is odd. The sample space, then, contains all of the individual outcomes of an experiment. For the previous statement to hold, it is necessary that all possible outcomes of an experiment are known.

The fundamental tenet of probability states that the chance of a particular outcome occurring is determined by the ratio of the number of favorable outcomes (successes) to the total number of outcomes (the sample space). Expressed as a formula for some event, $A$:

$$P(A) = \frac{\text{Number of successful outcomes}}{\text{Total number of possible outcomes}} \qquad (5.1)$$

From the previous example, the probability of rolling a 2, stated as $P(2)$, using a fair die, is equal to the ratio 1/6 or 0.167. In this experiment, 1 represents the favorable outcome or success of our experiment, and 6 represents the total number of possible outcomes from rolling the die. Likewise, we could determine the probability of rolling an odd number (1, 3, or 5) stated as $P(\text{odd})$, as 3/6 or 0.5. In this experiment, 3 represents the number of possible outcomes that represent favorable outcomes for this experiment, and 6 represents the total number of possible outcomes from rolling the die. Another example using playing cards may further refine this definition. If we have a well-shuffled deck of cards with 52 possible cards that could be drawn, and we wish to know the probability of drawing a king, this could be stated as:

$$P(\text{drawing a king})$$
$$= \frac{\text{Total number of successful outcomes (e.g., a king} = 4)}{\text{Total number of outcomes (e.g., 52 cards in the deck)}}$$
$$= 4/52 \text{ or } 0.077 \qquad (5.2)$$

One could ask the probability of drawing the king of hearts as:

$$P(\text{drawing a king})$$
$$= \frac{\text{Total number of successful outcomes (e.g., \# of king of hearts} = 1)}{\text{Total number of outcomes (e.g., 52 cards in the deck)}}$$
$$= 1/52 \text{ or } 0.019 \qquad (5.3)$$

In all cases, the value for the probability of an event occurring within a range of all possible events must span from 0, where the event does not occur (e.g., rolling a zero with a die; since there are no zeros on the die, this is not possible) to a maximum of 1 (e.g., the probability of rolling an odd or even number with the die) indicating the event always occurs.

In the examples cited, each number on the die must have an equal chance of being rolled. Likewise, in the cards example, each card must have an equal chance of being drawn. No number on the die face or card in the deck can be differentiated so that it would be more likely to be chosen or rolled (e.g., a weighted die is not a fair die).

The theory of probability was constructed based on the concept of mutual exclusion (disjointedness) of events. That is, events cannot occur at the same time in an experiment if they are mutually exclusive. For example, the rolling of the fair die can result in one of six possible outcomes, but not two or more of them at the same time. A second example is a fair coin—flipping the coin will result in a head or tail being displayed but not both a head and tail. Therefore, the outcome of the event rolling a die and getting a 1 versus all other numbers is said to be mutually exclusive, as is the flipping of the coin resulting in either the head or tail but not both.

Another important property within the field of probability is that of independence. For example, if we have a coin and a die, we intuitively understand that the event of flipping the coin and rolling the die have independent outcomes. That is, the result of one will not affect the outcome of the other. The sample space for the two events is composed of the Cartesian product of the two independent spaces; since all events of both are independently possible, the resulting sample space must include all possible combinations of the two independent spaces.

If we believe that this property of equal likelihood exists, then the probability of any of these outcomes must be equal and composed of the multiplicative probability of each independently. In the previous example, the fair coin flip has a sample space consisting of the elements of the set {H,T}, each with a probability of 1/2, and the fair die has a sample space consisting of the elements of the set {1,2,3,4,5,6}, each with a probability of 1/6. The probability of the combination of either of these events occurring would be derived from the Cartesian product set {H1,H2,H3,H4,H5,H6,T1,T2,T3,T4,T5,T6}, with any of these combined events, yielding an equal probability equal to $1/2 \times 1/6$, or 1/12.

In general, when events are independent, sample spaces where each event occurs are equally likely. If there are $n_1$ items in the first event space, $n_2$ in the second, and $n_m$ in the last sample space, then the sample space of the combined events space is equal to the sum of the size of each of these spaces:

$$\text{Combined sample space} = \left( n_1 + n_2 + \ldots + n_m \right) \qquad (5.4)$$

The probability of any individual event occurring is then equal to $1/(n_1 + n_2 + \ldots + n_m)$, which, in the previous example, was found to be 1/12.

We will not always be interested in the likelihood of just one event from a total sample space occurring but rather some subset of events from the total space. For example, we may be interested in the likelihood of only one head occurring during the flipping of four coins. The complete sample space for this experiment has exactly 16 possible outcomes:

{HHHH,HHHT,HHTH,HTHH,THHH,TTHH,THHT,HHTT,THTH,HTHT,HTTH, HTTT,THTT,TTHT,TTTH,TTTT}

From this space, we can see that the events meeting the desired outcome of only one head results in the subset:

{HTTT,THTT,TTHT,TTTH}

where each item in this subset is equally likely to occur from the original set, so each has the equal probability of 1/16. Their combined probability would represent the desired probability of only one head occurring and would be equal to the sum of their probability: 4/16 or 1/4. In this example, we are using the additive probabilities of these events to see the likelihood of one of these occurring from the original set. To compute the subset probability we need only know the size of the original set and the size of the subset.

More often, we are faced with the problem of determining the possibility of some event occurring given that some prior event has already occurred. For example, we may be asked the probability of our computer system failing given that one memory chip has failed. This concept of related or dependent events is called conditional probability. The effect of applying this property to two independent event spaces is to remove some of the possible combinations from the final combined space of possible values. For example, we may be asked what the probability is of getting exactly one head after the first element was found to be a tail in the four-coin toss. The initial sample space was 16, but given that we removed the events where the initial toss resulted in a tail, the resultant space now has only eight possible outcomes and from these there are only three within the subspace meeting our final desired outcome.

To compute what the probability is in this case, we can do a few things. First, we can compute the probability of realizing the tail on the first toss as 8/16 and the probability that there is one head from the last three tosses as 3/8. Many times it is easier to compute the opposite occurrence. That is, let's compute the probability that the final event does not happen. First, we may reason that the sample space now excludes all events where the first item was a head, or eight events. There are now only 16 − 8 or 8 equally likely events remaining in our space. Of these remaining 8, there are five ways in which, given a tail first, we do not get exactly one head. The probability of at least one head is then the ratio of the number of successes (3) to the total number of possible events (16 − 8) or 8, resulting in a probability of 3/8.

Several operations on the events in the sample space yield important properties of events. By definition, the intersection of two events is the set that contains all elements common to both events. The intersection of sets *A* and *B* is written *AB*. By extension, the intersection of several events contains those elements common to each event. Two events are said to be mutually exclusive if their intersection yields the null set. The union of two events yields the set of all of the elements that are in either event or in both events. The union of sets *A* and *B* is written $A \cup B$.

The complement of an event, denoted $\overline{A}$, represents all elements except those defined in the event *A*. The following definition, known as DeMorgan's Law, is useful for relating the complements of two events:

$$\overline{AB} = \overline{A} \cup \overline{B} \tag{5.5}$$

Permutations and combinations of elements in a sample space may take many different forms. Often, we can form probability measures about combinations of sample points, and the basic combinations and permutations discussed in the following text are of use in this task. By definition, a combination is an unordered selection of items, whereas a permutation is an ordered selection of items. The most basic combination involves the occurrence of one of $n_1$ events, followed by one of $n_2$ events, and so on to one of $n_k$ events. Thus, for each path taken to get to the last event, *k*, there are $n_k$ possible choices. Backing up one level, there were $n_{k-1}$ choices at that level, thereby yielding $n_{k-1} n_k$ choices for the last two events. Following similar logic backing up to the first level yields:

$$n_1 n_2 \dots n_{k-1} n_k = \prod_{i=1}^{k} n_i \tag{5.6}$$

possible paths. For example, in a string of five digits, each of which may take on the values 0 through 9, there are $10 \times 10 \times 10 \times 10 \times 10 = 100,000$ possible combinations, or $n^k$ possible outcomes, where *n* = 10 and *k* = 5 in the sample space. The assumption is that once an item has been sampled, it is returned to the space for possible resampling. This is sometimes referred to as sampling with replacement. The probability distribution for a random selection of items is uniform; therefore, each item in the sample space will have the probability of $1/n^k$.

When dealing with unique elements that may be arranged in different ways, we speak of permutations. When we have *n* things and sample *n* times, but do not replace the sample items before the next selection, we now have a selection without replacement, also referred to as a permutation. For $n$ distinct objects, if we choose one and place it aside, we then have $n - 1$ left to choose from. Repeating the exercise leaves $n - 2$ to choose from, and so on down to 1. The number of different permutations of these $n$ elements is the number of choices you can make at each step in the select and put aside process and is equal to:

$$p(n,n) = (n)(n-1)(n-2)\ldots(2)(1) = n! \qquad (5.7)$$

The common notation $P(n,k)$ denotes the number of permutations of $n$ items taken $k$ at a time. To find the numerical value for a random selection we can use similar logic. The first item may be selected in $n$ ways, the second in $n - 1$ ways, the third in $n - 2$ ways, and the $k$th or last item we choose in $n - k - 1$ ways. Choosing from $n$ distinct items taken in groups of $k$ at a time yields the following number of permutations or product space for this experiment:

$$P(n,k) = (n)(n-1)(n-2)\ldots(n-k+1) = \{n!\}/(n-k)! \qquad (5.8)$$

The permutation yields the number of possible distinct groups of $k$ items when picked from a pool of $n$. We can see that this is the more general case of the previous expression and reduces to equation (5.7) when $k = n$ (also, by definition, $0! = 1$). For example, if we wished to see how many ways we could arrange three computer servers on a workbench of five distinct servers, we would assume that the order of the servers has some meaning; therefore, we have:

$$P(5,3) = (5)(5-1)(5-2) = 60 \text{ ways} \qquad (5.9)$$

A combination is a permutation when the order is ignored. One special case occurs when there are only two kinds of items to be selected. These are called binomial coefficients or $C(n,k)$. The number of combinations of $n$ items taken $k$ at a time (denoted $C[n,k]$) is equivalent to $P(n,k)$ reduced by the total number of $k$ element groups that have the same elements but in different orders (e.g., $P[k,k]$). This is intuitively correct, because order is unimportant for a combination, and, hence, there will be fewer unique combinations than permutations for any given set of $k$ items. $P(k,k)$ is given in equation (5.7), hence:

$$C(n,k) = \{n!\}/k!(n-k!)! \qquad (5.10)$$

Alternatively, one can state that each set of $k$ elements can form $P(k,k) = k!$ permutations, which, when multiplied by $C(n,k)$, yields $P(n,k)$. Dividing by $P(k,k)$ yields:

$$P(k,k)C(n,k) = P(n,k) \tag{5.11}$$

$$C(n,k) = P(n,k)/P(k,k) = n!/(n-k)!k! \tag{5.12}$$

Now that we have characterized some of the ways that we can construct sample spaces, we can determine how to apply probabilities to the events in the sample space. The first step to achieving this is to assign a set of weights to the events in the sample space. The choice of which weighting factor to apply to which event in the sample space is not an easy task. One method is to employ observations over a sufficiently long period so that a large sample of all possible outcomes is obtained. This is the so-called "observation, deduction, and prediction cycle," and it is useful for developing weights for processes where an underlying model of the process either does not exist or is too complex to yield event weights. This method, sometimes called the "classical probability definition," defines the probability of any event as the following:

$$P(A) = N_A/N \tag{5.13}$$

where $P(A)$ denotes the probability of event $A$, $N_A$ is the total number of observations where the event $A$ occurred, and $N$ is the total number of observations made. An extension to the classical definition, called the "relative frequency definition," is given as:

$$P(A) = \lim_{n \to \infty} (N_A/N) \approx N_A/N \tag{5.14}$$

The preceding two approaches, combinations/permutations and relative frequency, are often used in practice as a means of establishing a hypothesis about how a process behaves. These methods do indeed define hypotheses because they are both based on the observation of a finite number of observations. This fact drives the desire to develop axiomatic definitions for the basic laws of probability.

Probability theory, therefore, is based upon a set of three axioms. By definition, the probability of an event is given by a positive number. That is:

$$P(A) \geq 0 \tag{5.15}$$

The following relationship is also defined:

$$P(S) = 1 \tag{5.16}$$

That is, the sum of all of the probabilities of all of the events in the total sample space $S$ is equal to 1. This is sometimes called the "certain event." The previous two definitions represent the first two axioms and necessarily restrict the probability of any event to between 0 and 1 inclusively. The third is based on the property of mutual exclusion, which states that two events are mutually exclusive if, and only if, the occurrence of one of the events positively excludes the occurrence of the other. In set terminology, this states that the intersection of the two events contains no elements; that is, it is the null set. For example, the two events in the coin-toss experiment (heads and tails) are mutually exclusive. The third axiom, then, states that the combined probability of events $A$ or $B$ occurring is equal to the sum of their individual probabilities. That is:

$$P(A \text{ or } B) = P(A) + P(B) \tag{5.17}$$

So, for example, the probability of a head being tossed or a 6 being rolled is equal to the probability of a head being tossed or 1/2, plus the probability of rolling a 6, or 1/6, which is 4/6.

The reader is cautioned that the expression to the left of the equal sign reads the probability of event $A$ or event $B$, whereas the right-hand expression reads the probability of event $A$ plus the probability of event $B$. This is an important relationship between set theory and the numerical representation of probabilities.

The three axioms of probability are as follows:

I.      $P(E) \geq 0$                                                   $(5.18)$

II.      $P(S) = 1$                                                    $(5.19)$

III.      If $AB = 0$, then $P(A + B) = P(A) + P(B)$         $(5.20)$

In equation (5.20), the terminology $AB$ is taken as the set $A$ intersected with the set $B$. The sample space is defined on the total set $\{A_1 \ldots A_k\}$ as:

$$S = A_1 + A_2 + \ldots + A_k \tag{5.21}$$

A very important topic in probability theory is that of conditional probability. Consider the following experiment in which we have the events $A$, $B$, and $AB$. For example, a disk crash and a memory failure could be event $A$ and $B$, respectively, and a disk and memory failure at the same time is event $AB$. The event $AB$ contains the events that are in $A$ and $B$. Let us say that this event ($AB$) occurs $N_{AB}$ times. Let $N_B$ denote the number of times event

*B* occurs on its own. If we want to know the relative frequency of event *A* given that event *B* occurred, we could do the following experiment and computation:

$$\text{Relative frequency } (A) = N_{AB}/N_B \tag{5.22}$$

That is, if both events *A* and *B* occur (event *AB*), the number of times event *A* occurs when event *B* also occurs is found as a fraction of the space of event *B* where event *A* intersects (see Figure 5.1). The notation for this relative frequency is denoted $P(A|B)$ and reads as the conditional probability of event *A* given event *B* also occurred. If we form the following expression from equation (4.16):

$$P(A|B) = (N_{AB}/N)/(N_B/N) = N_{AB}/N_B \tag{5.23}$$

and apply equation (5.14), we obtain the traditional conditional probability definition:

$$P(A|B) = P(AB)/P(B) \tag{5.24}$$

One interesting simplification of equation (5.23) occurs when event *A* is contained in, or is a subset of, event *B*, so that $AB = A$. In this case, equation (5.23) becomes:

$$\text{If } AB = A, \text{ then } P(A|B) = P(A)/P(B) \tag{5.25}$$

Two events, *A* and *B*, are independent if their Venn diagrams do not intersect. The independence of two events is defined by the following formula:

$$P(AB) = P(A) \times P(B) \tag{5.26}$$

or

$$P(A) = P(AB)/P(B) = P(A|B) \tag{5.27}$$

**Figure 5.1**
*Conditional probability space Venn diagram.*

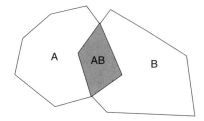

This definition states that the relative number of occurrences of event $A$ is equal to the relative number of occurrences of event $A$ given event $B$ occurred. In simpler terms, the independence of two or more events indicates that the occurrence of one event does not allow one to infer anything about the occurrence of the other.

Bayes's theorem is stated as follows: If we have a number of mutually exclusive events, $B_1$, $B_2$ ... $B_N$, whose union defines the event space (or, more formally, a subset of the sample space), for some experiment, and an arbitrary event $A$ from the sample space, the conditional probability of any event $B_k$ in the set $B_1$, $B_2$ ... $B_N$, given that event $A$ occurs, is given by:

$$P(B_k|A) = \left( P(B_k) \times P(A|B_k) \right) \Big/ \sum_{i=1}^{N} P(B_i) \times P(A|B_i) \qquad (5.28)$$

This result is an important statement, because it relates the conditional probability of any event of a subspace of events relative to an arbitrary event of the sample space to the conditional probability of the arbitrary event relative to all of the other events in the subspace. The theorem is a result of the total probability theorem, which states that:

$$P(A) = P(A|B_1)P(B_1) + ... + P(A|B_k)P(B_k) \qquad (5.29)$$

The theorem holds because the events $B_1$ ... $B_k$ are mutually exclusive, and, therefore, event $A = AS = A(B_1, B_2, ... B_k) = AB_1 + AB_2 + ... AB_k ...$ so that:

$$P(A) = P(AB_1) + P(AB_2) + ... + P(AB_k) \qquad (5.30)$$

Since events $B_1$, $B_2$ ... $B_k$ are mutually exclusive, so are events $AB_1$, $AB_2$, ... $AB_k$. Applying the conditional probability definition of equation (5.24) to equation (5.30) yields equation (5.28).

One other relationship that is often useful when examining conditional probability of two events is the following:

$$P(A + B) = P(A) + P(B) - P(AB) \qquad (5.31)$$

This formula states that for any two events, $A$ and $B$, if we wish to determine if event $A$ or $B$ occurred or that both occurred, we need to examine them in isolation and in unison. This follows from the discussions of sets of events earlier in this chapter. Since the union of the events $A$ and $B$ yields all sample points in $A$ and $B$ considered together, the sum of the events separately will yield the same quantity plus an extra element for each element in the intersection of the two events. Thus, we must subtract the intersection to form the equality, hence equation (5.30). Note that equation (5.31) is essentially an extended version of equation (5.20), where $AB$ does not equal the null set.

# 5.1    Random variables

Thus far, we have been discussing experiments, along with their associated event space, in the context of the probabilities of occurrence of the events. We will now move on to a topic of great importance, which relates the basic probability measures to real-world quantities. The concept of a random variable relates the probabilities of the outcomes of an experiment to a range or set of numbers. A random variable, then, is defined as a function whose input values are the events of the sample space and whose outcome is a real number. For example, we could have an experiment in which the outcome is the length of each message that arrives over a communication line. A random variable defined on this experiment could be the number of messages that equaled a certain character count. Often, we want to consider a range of values of the random variables—for instance, the range of messages greater than $x_1$. This is denoted here as $\{X \leq x_1\}$, where $X$ denotes the random variable and $x_1$ is a value for the random variable at a specific point. We may call this set the event where the random variable $X$ yields a value greater than $x_1$.

Continuing with the previous example, suppose we had the following outcomes from the message-length experiment: The random variable defined by the number of times a particular message length seen. Referring to Figure 5.2; the event $\{X > 2000\}$ contains the outcomes of messages 1, 4, 5, and 6.

Random variables may be either discrete or continuous. A discrete random variable is one that is defined on an experiment in which the number of events in the set of outcomes is finite or infinite (i.e., it is possible to

**Figure 5.2**
*Outcomes of the message length experiment.*

| Outcome | Message Length |
|---------|----------------|
| 1       | 2,097          |
| 2       | 500            |
| 3       | 1,259          |
| 4       | 5,794          |
| 5       | 4,258          |
| 6       | 5,205          |

assign a positive integer to each event, even if there are an infinite number of outcomes). A continuous random variable is one that is defined on an experiment in which the number of possible outcomes is infinite (i.e., defined on the real line). The concept of random variables forms the foundation for the discussion of probability distributions and density functions.

## 5.2   Jointly distributed random variables

Suppose we have an experiment that has two or more random variables defined on its event space and we wish to form a random variable that takes into account each of the individual random variables. These are called jointly distributed random variables, and they represent the intersections of the individual random variable event spaces. Jointly distributed random variables are represented with the following notation:

$$\{X \leq x_1, Y \leq y_1\} \tag{5.32}$$

Stated simply, joint random variables derive their output from a function whose domain is the set of outcomes for all of the individual random variable domains.

It should be noted here that more complicated combinations and conditions for the random variable function may be constructed. For example, consider the following random variables:

$$\{x_1 \leq X \leq x_2\} \text{ where } x_1 < x_2 \tag{5.33}$$

$$\{x_1 > X, x_2 < X\} \text{ where } x_1 > x_2 \tag{5.34}$$

$$\{x_1 \leq X \leq x_2, y_1 \leq Y \leq y_2\} \text{ where } x_1 < x_2 \text{ and } y_1 < y_2 \tag{5.35}$$

## 5.3   Probability distributions

The concept of a random variable in and of itself does not lend itself to extensive practical use. To remedy this we define a distribution function for each random variable $X$. The distribution function is typically represented as:

$$F(x) = P(X \leq x) \tag{5.36}$$

By its definition, the distribution function assumes values from 0 to 1. Also, the distribution function is nondecreasing as $x$ increases in value. These properties are summarized as follows:

Property I:    $\lim\limits_{x \to -\infty} F(x) = 0$                    (5.37)

Property II:   $\lim\limits_{x \to \infty} F(x) = 1$                    (5.38)

Property III:  $F(x_1) \le F(x_2)$ if $x_1 \le x_2$              (5.39)

Distribution functions are also called cumulative distribution functions, because at any $x$ along the distribution, the area under the curve to the left of $x$ represents the cumulative total of the probabilities of the random variables $\{x \le X\}$. Figure 5.3 shows some example distribution functions.

From Figure 5.3, it is obvious on these functions are called distribution functions because they show exactly how the probability of the random variable is distributed over the range of the random variable values.

The distribution function shown in Figure 5.3a is a continuous function, because it is based upon a continuous random variable. Figure 5.3b shows a discrete distribution function that is based upon a discrete random variable.

**Figure 5.3**
*Example distribution functions.*

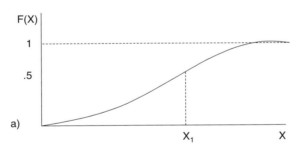

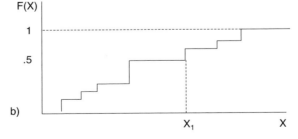

A joint distribution is one that defines how the probability is associated with each of several random variables. Thus, we can state a function that defines a joint distribution as:

$$F(x, y) = P(X \le x, Y \le y) \tag{5.40}$$

This function can be interpreted as:

$$F(x, y) = P(X \le x \text{ intersected with } Y \le y) \tag{5.41}$$

We are also interested in the individual distribution functions of $X$ and $Y$ given the joint distribution of equation (5.40). For instance, the distribution of $X$ given $F(x,y)$, also called the marginal distribution function of $X$ corresponding to $F(x,y)$, is given as:

$$F_X(x) = \lim_{y \to \infty} F_{X,Y}(x, y) \tag{5.42}$$

or

$$F_X(x) = F_{X,Y}(x, \infty) \tag{5.43}$$

The same is true for the marginal distribution of $Y$:

$$F_Y(y) = F_{X,Y}(\infty, y) \tag{5.44}$$

The marginal distributions of the random variables given previously result from the definitions of random variables and of distribution functions. Remember that a random variable is defined with a range of values along the real axis and that the distribution function is defined as the cumulative probability that the random variable will attain at least a certain value. The probability that the random variable will obtain a value less than infinity is equal to one. Thus, the marginal distribution for a random variable given a joint distribution is clear given that:

$$(X \le x) = (X \le x, Y \le \infty) \tag{5.45}$$

## 5.4  Densities

A density function defines the derivative of the distribution function, indicating the rate of change of the probability distribution:

$$f(x) = dF(x)/dx \tag{5.46}$$

This definition holds for continuous random variables. For discrete random variables, the density function is defined as the discrete probabilities that the random variable equals a specific value for its range of possible values. That is:

$$f_X(x) = P[X = x] = \sum P(X)\delta(x - X)$$ (5.47)

where $\delta(x - X)$ is a delta function that is 1 when $x = X$ and 0 elsewhere.

From the previous relationships, we can see how the distribution function is formed. For each value of the random variable, we can integrate (for a continuous function) up to that point to find the cumulative probability to that point. The probabilities are summed for discrete functions:

$$F(x) = \int_{-\infty}^{x} f(t)\,dt$$ (5.48)

$$F(x) \sum_{n-\infty}^{x} f(n)$$ (5.49)

We know from the previous discussions that $F(\infty) = 1$, so that:

$$\int_{-\infty}^{\infty} f(t)\,dt = 1$$ (5.50)

and

$$\sum_{t=-\infty}^{\infty} f(t) = 1$$ (5.51)

In a manner similar to that shown previously for finding the distribution function from the density function for a single random variable, we can find the joint distribution from the joint density. The relationship is given by:

$$F(x, y) = \int_{-\infty}^{x} \int_{-\infty}^{y} f(t, u)\, dt\, du$$ (5.52)

Similarly, a discrete distribution can be found from the discrete density:

$$F(x, y) = \sum_{i=-\infty}^{x} \sum_{j=-\infty}^{y} f(i, j)$$ (5.53)

As with singularly distributed densities, the total area under the probability density function is given by:

$$\int_{-\infty}^{\infty}\int_{-\infty}^{\infty} f(x,y)\,dx\,dy = 1 \tag{5.54}$$

Obtaining the density function from the distribution function for a continuous case is given by:

$$f(x,y) = \partial^2 F(x,y)/\partial x \partial y \tag{5.55}$$

We define the marginal density of a jointly distributed random variable as:

$$f_Y(y) = \int_{-\infty}^{\infty} f(x,y)\,dx \tag{5.56}$$

The independence property is defined on joint distributions as:

$$F(x,y) = F_X(x)F_Y(y) \tag{5.57}$$

and for joint densities as:

$$f(x,y) = f_X(x)f_Y(y) \tag{5.58}$$

In some cases, it is necessary to define combined joint distributions in which one of the variables is discrete and the other continuous. The joint density, where $y$ represents the continuous variable and $i$ represents the discrete one, is written as:

$$f(i,y) = f_{X|Y}(y|i)P_X(i) \tag{5.59}$$

This expression introduces another important point: conditional distributions. For discrete random variables, the conditional function can be defined as the following:

$$f_{X|Y}(x|y) = f(x,y)/f_Y(y) \tag{5.60}$$

Similarly, we can define the conditional density of $y$ given $x$ from equation (5.60). The following results:

$$f(x,y) = f_{X|Y}(x|y)f_Y(y) = f_{X|Y}(x|y)f_X(x) \tag{5.61}$$

This is a convenient way to relate the conditional densities for the two random variables. If the random variables $X$ and $Y$ are independent, equation (5.60) becomes:

$$f(x,y) = f_X(x) f_Y(y) \tag{5.62}$$

and the following results:

$$f_{Y|X}(y|x) = f_Y(y) \tag{5.63}$$

From equations (5.56) and (5.60), we can substitute to get:

$$f_Y(y) = \int_{-\infty}^{\infty} f_X(x) f_{Y|X}(y|x) dx \tag{5.64}$$

and also (for the marginal density of $X$):

$$f_X(x) = \int_{-\infty}^{\infty} f_Y(y) f_{X|Y}(x,y) dy \tag{5.65}$$

Combining equations (5.60), (5.61), and (5.64), we obtain Bayes's rule for continuous random variables:

$$f_{X|Y}(x|y) = \frac{f_X(x) f_{Y|X}(y|x)}{\int_{-\infty}^{\infty} f_X(x) f_{Y|X}(y|x) dx} \tag{5.66}$$

This concludes our discussion about the properties of probability distributions and densities. In the next section, we will explore some methods for obtaining often used statistics about random variables by using their distributions and densities.

## 5.5    Expectation

Although both the distribution and density functions of a random variable provide all of the information necessary to describe its behavior, we often wish to have a single quantity (or a small number of them) that provides summary information of the random variable. One such measure is the expected value, or expectation, of a random variable. The expected value is also called the mean. Expectation for a discrete random variable $X$ is defined as:

$$E[X] = \sum_x x P(x) \tag{5.67}$$

and for a continuous random variable $X$ with density function $f(x)$ as:

$$E[X] = \int_{-\infty}^{\infty} x\, f(x)\, dx \tag{5.68}$$

Suppose now that we have a function of a random variable $X$, say $g(X)$. The expectation is given as:

$$E[g(X)] = \int_{-\infty}^{\infty} g(x) f(x)\, dx \tag{5.69}$$

for continuous random variables, and as:

$$E[g(X)] = \sum_x g(x) P(x) \tag{5.70}$$

for discrete random variables.

If we have jointly distributed random variables, the expectation is defined for discrete random variables as:

$$E[g(X,Y)] = \sum_x \sum_y g(x,y) f(x,y) \tag{5.71}$$

and for continuous random variables as:

$$E[g(X,Y)] = \int_{-\infty}^{\infty} \int_{-\infty}^{\infty} g(x,y) f(x,y)\, dx\, dy \tag{5.72}$$

for the function $g(X,Y)$. These formulations for expected values are valid if the right-hand sides of the respective equations are less than infinity.

There are a few useful laws relating to expectation that we will now discuss. Suppose that we wish to find the following:

$$E[aX + b] = \int_{-\infty}^{\infty} (ax + b) f(x)\, dx \tag{5.73}$$

The expression on the right becomes:

$$a \int\limits_{-\infty}^{\infty} x f(x) dx + b \int\limits_{-\infty}^{\infty} f(x) dx \qquad (5.74)$$

From equations (5.51) and (5.69), equation (5.74) becomes:

$$E[aX + b] = a E[X] + b \qquad (5.75)$$

Setting either $a$ or $b$ to zero results in the following:

$$E[aX] = a E[X] \qquad (5.76)$$

$$E[b] = b \qquad (5.77)$$

Now suppose that we have the following:

$$E\big[g(X) + h(X)\big] = \int\limits_{-\infty}^{\infty} \big(g(x) + h(x)\big) f(x) dx \qquad (5.78)$$

The integral becomes:

$$\int\limits_{-\infty}^{\infty} g(x) f(x) dx + \int\limits_{-\infty}^{\infty} h(x) f(x) dx \qquad (5.79)$$

From equation (5.68), we obtain:

$$E\big[g(X) + h(X)\big] = E\big[g(X)\big] + E\big[h(X)\big] \qquad (5.80)$$

Similarly, for functions of two random variables, we get:

$$E\big[g(X,Y) + h(X,Y)\big] = \int\limits_{-\infty}^{\infty} \int\limits_{-\infty}^{\infty} \big(g(x,y) + h(x,y)\big) f(x,y) dy dx \qquad (5.81)$$

which becomes:

$$\int\limits_{-\infty}^{\infty} \int\limits_{-\infty}^{\infty} g(x,y) f(x,y) dy dx + \int\limits_{-\infty}^{\infty} \int\limits_{-\infty}^{\infty} h(x,y) f(x,y) dy dx \qquad (5.82)$$

From equation (5.72), we obtain:

$$E\big[g(X,Y) + h(X,Y)\big] = E\big[g(X,Y)\big] + E\big[h(X,Y)\big] \qquad (5.83)$$

Similarly,

$$E[X+Y] = E[X] + E[Y] \tag{5.84}$$

Consider the case of two independent random variables, $X$ and $Y$, by equation (5.72):

$$E[XY] = \int_{-\infty}^{\infty} \int_{-\infty}^{\infty} xy f(x,y) \, dy \, dx \tag{5.85}$$

which, because of equation (5.58), becomes:

$$\int_{-\infty}^{\infty} \int_{-\infty}^{\infty} xy f_X(x) f_Y(y) \, dy \, dx \tag{5.86}$$

Separating the integrals by integrands yields:

$$\int_{-\infty}^{\infty} x f_X(x) \, dx \int_{-\infty}^{\infty} y f_Y(y) \, dy \tag{5.87}$$

From equations (5.69) and (5.85), we get:

$$E[XY] = E[X]E[Y] \tag{5.88}$$

for the independent random variables $X$ and $Y$.

For one special function of a random variable, $g(X) = x^n$, the expectation of $g(X)$ is known as the "$n$th moment" of the random variable $X$. The first moment of $g(X)$ is defined as the mean of the random variable $X$ for $g(X) = X$. Moments, as defined previously, are centered at the origin and are thus called "moments about the origin." A more common and useful definition of moments involves the shifting of the density function so that the mean is centered at the origin. Moments defined as such are called "central moments," because they are defined on density functions that have been centered at the origin. Thus, the function of the random variable becomes:

$$g(X) = (x - \mu)^n \tag{5.89}$$

where the mean is given by:

$$\mu = E[X] \tag{5.90}$$

The central moment, or moment about the mean, is therefore defined as:

$$\mu_n = E\left[(X-\mu)^n\right] = \sum_n (x-\mu)^n f(x) \qquad (5.91)$$

for the discrete random variable $X$, and as:

$$\mu_n = \int_{-\infty}^{\infty} (x-\mu)^n f(x)\,dx \qquad (5.92)$$

for the continuous random variable $X$.

An important measure of the variability of the distribution of a function about the mean is called the "variance." This measure tells us, loosely speaking, how concentrated the values of the functions are relative to the mean. A small variance, therefore, indicates that the probability is that the range of function values is concentrated near the mean, while a large variance suggests that the values are more spread out. The variance of a random variable is defined by its second central moment and represented as:

$$\sigma^2 = \mathrm{Var}[X] = \mu_2 = E\left[(X-\mu)^2\right] = \int_{-\infty}^{\infty} (x-\mu)^2 f(x)\,dx \qquad (5.93)$$

Note the use of several different notations; all are common. For some functions, $f(x)$, the integral of equation (5.93) may be difficult to evaluate. Fortunately, we can derive an alternative expression for the variance, as follows:

$$\sigma^2 = E\left[(X-\mu)^2\right]$$
$$= E\left[X^2 - 2X\mu + \mu^2\right]$$
$$= E\left[X^2\right] - 2\mu E[X] + \mu^2$$

by equation (5.90) $\qquad (5.94)$

$$= E\left[X^2\right] - 2\mu^2 + \mu^2$$
$$\sigma^2 = E\left[X^2\right] - \mu^2$$

The standard deviation of a random variable is defined as the square root of the variance and is denoted as:

$$\sigma = \sqrt{\sigma^2} = \sqrt{E\left[X^2\right] - \mu^2} \qquad (5.95)$$

The covariance of two random variables is a measure of the degree of linear dependence, also called "correlation," of the two variables. The covariance is defined as:

$$\text{Cov}[X,Y] = E\left[(X - \mu_x)(Y - \mu_y)\right] \tag{5.96}$$

If $X$ and $Y$ are independent, the covariance is equal to zero. This results from the following:

$$
\begin{aligned}
E\left[(X - \mu_x)(Y - \mu_y)\right] &= E\left[XY - X\mu_y - Y\mu_x + \mu_x \mu_x\right] \\
&= E[XY] - \mu_y E[X] - \mu_x E[Y] + \mu_x \mu_x
\end{aligned}
\tag{5.97}
$$

by equation (5.90):

$$
\begin{aligned}
&= E[XY] - 2\mu_y\mu_x + \mu_x \mu_x \\
&= E[XY] - \mu_x \mu_y
\end{aligned}
\tag{Cont. 5.97}
$$

by using equation (5.88) we get:

$$\text{Cov}[XY] = E[X]E[Y] - \mu_y\mu_x \tag{Cont. 5.97}$$

Equation (5.97) gives a more convenient means for calculating covariance. Two random variables are said to be uncorrelated if $\text{Cov}[X,Y] = 0$.

There are several useful properties of the variance, which we will now discuss; this will be followed by the method for developing a lower bound on the probability for any random variable, given a distance from the mean measured in standard deviations.

From equations (5.75, 5.76, 5.77, and 5.94), we can easily show that:

$$
\begin{aligned}
\text{Var}[x + b] &= E\left[(X + b - E[X + b])^2\right] \\
&= E\left[(X + b - E[X] - b)^2\right]
\end{aligned}
\tag{5.98}
$$

by using (5.93):

$$= E\left[(X - \mu_x)^2\right] = \text{Var}[X] \tag{Cont. 5.98}$$

From equations (5.76) and (5.93):

$$\mathrm{Var}[aX] = E\left[(aX - E[aX])^2\right]$$
$$= E\left[a^2(X - E[X])^2\right] \qquad (5.99)$$
$$= a^2 E\left[(X - \mu_x)^2\right] = a^2 \mathrm{Var}[X]$$

For two jointly distributed random variables, $X$ and $Y$, the variance is defined as:

$$\mathrm{Var}[X+Y] = E\left[(X + Y - E[X+Y])^2\right]$$
$$= E\left[(X - \mu_x + Y - \mu_y)^2\right]$$
$$= E\left[(X - \mu_x)^2\right] + E\left[(Y - \mu_y)^2\right] \qquad (5.100)$$
$$+ 2E\left[(X - \mu_x)(Y - \mu_y)\right]$$
$$= \mathrm{Var}[X] + \mathrm{Var}[Y] + 2\,\mathrm{Cov}[X,Y]$$

Given any random variable, it is possible to derive an expression that defines the minimum probability of a random variable lying within $k$ standard deviations of its mean. The theorem is known as Chebyshev's Theorem and is stated as follows:

$$P((\mu - k\sigma) < X < (\mu + k\sigma)) \geq 1 - (1/k^2) \qquad (5.101)$$

Equation (5.101) can be derived as follows. From equation (5.93):

$$\sigma^2 = \int_{-\infty}^{\infty} (x - \mu)^2 f(x)\,dx \qquad (5.102)$$

$$\sigma^2 = \int_{-\infty}^{\mu - k\sigma} (x - \mu)^2 f(x)\,dx$$
$$+ \int_{\mu - k\sigma}^{\mu + k\sigma} (x - \mu)^2 f(x)\,dx \qquad (5.103)$$
$$+ \int_{\mu + k\sigma}^{\infty} (x - \mu)^2 f(x)\,dx$$

Because the middle integral is positive or zero, we can remove it from the expression to get:

$$\sigma^2 \geq \int_{-\infty}^{\mu-k\sigma} (x-\mu)^2 f(x)\,dx + \int_{\mu+k\sigma}^{\infty} (x-\mu)^2 f(x)\,dx \tag{5.104}$$

Within the range:

$$x \geq \mu + k\sigma$$

and                                                                                                                     (5.105)

$$x \leq \mu - k\sigma$$

we have:

$$|x-\mu| \geq k\sigma \tag{5.106}$$

so that:

$$(x-\mu)^2 \geq (k\sigma)^2 \tag{5.107}$$

Thus, we can substitute into equation (5.104):

$$\sigma^2 \geq \int_{-\infty}^{\mu-k\sigma} (k\sigma)^2 f(x)\,dx + \int_{\mu+k\sigma}^{\infty} (k\sigma)^2 f(x)\,dx \tag{5.108}$$

and divide to get:

$$\frac{\sigma^2}{(k\sigma)^2} \geq \int_{-\infty}^{\mu-k\sigma} f(x)\,dx + \int_{\mu+k\sigma}^{\infty} f(x)\,dx \tag{5.109}$$

rewriting equation (5.107):

$$\int_{-\infty}^{\mu-k\sigma} f(x)\,dx + \int_{\mu+k\sigma}^{\infty} f(x)\,dx = \int_{-\infty}^{\infty} f(x)\,dx - \int_{\mu-k\sigma}^{\mu+k\sigma} f(x)\,dx \leq 1/k^2 \tag{5.110}$$

and from equation (5.50):

$$1 - \int_{\mu-k\sigma}^{\mu+k\sigma} f(x)\,dx \leq 1/k^2 \tag{5.111}$$

From equation (5.48) we have:

$$P(\mu - k\sigma) < X < (\mu + k\sigma) = \int_{\mu - k\sigma}^{\mu + k\sigma} f(x)\,dx \qquad (5.112)$$

Thus, equation (5.101) results:

$$P(\mu - k\sigma) < X < (\mu + k\sigma) = \int_{\mu - k\sigma}^{\mu + k\sigma} f(x)\,dx \geq 1 - 1/k^2 \qquad (5.113)$$

# 5.6    Some example probability distributions

In this section, we will examine some discrete and some continuous probability distributions that will help to solidify the basic probability theory of the previous sections. Many of these distributions are commonly used to model real-world processes and to help arrive at estimates for quantities of interest in real-world systems. We will discuss the properties of each distribution and we will also discuss the process of deriving random deviates, given a certain distribution that models a real-world process.

## 5.6.1    Uniform distribution

The simplest of all probability distributions is the discrete uniform distribution. Such a distribution states that all values of the random variable are equally probable and depend only upon the number of possible outcomes of the experiment. The density function for the uniform distribution is given as:

$$f(x) = 1/k \qquad\qquad x = x_1, x_2, \ldots, x_k \qquad (5.114)$$

where $k$ is the number of possible outcomes. The experiment where the random variable $X = P(n)$, $n = 1$ to 6, and the event is the toss of a die that results in a discrete uniform probability distribution. A plot of the density function for the uniform distribution is shown in Figure 5.4.

The mean of the uniform distribution is found by equation (5.66) and is given by:

$$E[X] = \sum_{i=1}^{k} x_i (1/k) \qquad (5.115)$$

**Figure 5.4**
*Uniform density function.*

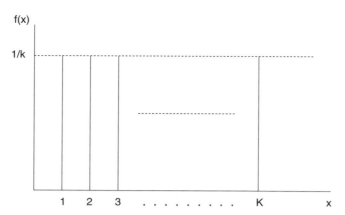

The standard deviation is found by:

$$\sigma^2 = E\left[\left(X - \mu\right)^2\right] = \sum_{i=1}^{k}\left(x_i - \mu\right)^2 f\left(x_i\right)$$

$$= \sum_{i=1}^{k}\frac{\left(x_i - \mu\right)^2}{k}$$

(5.116)

## 5.6.2   **Binominal distribution**

The concept of a Bernoulli trial is important in many discrete distributions. A Bernoulli trial is an experiment in which the outcome can be only success or failure. Random variables defined on successive Bernoulli trials make up several of the discrete density functions we will discuss.

An important discrete probability distribution is the binomial distribution. This distribution results from experiments in which there are only two possible outcomes of an experiment, such as a coin toss. For the distribution, one outcome is chosen to represent success and the other failure. A binomial experiment also requires that the probability of success remains constant for successive trials, that the trials are independent, and that each experimental outcome results in success or failure. Since the trials are independent, the total probability for an experiment with $x$ successes and $n$ trials can be found by simply multiplying the probability of each event (see equation [5.26]). If the probability of success is given as $p$ and if $q = 1 - p$, we have:

$$P\left(x \text{ successes in } n \text{ trials}\right) = p^x q^{(n-x)}$$

(5.117)

For the binomial distribution, we want to find the number of successes in $n$ independent trials, given that we know the probability of success for any individual trial. The number of successes in $n$ trials is a combination, as given in equation (5.10). The probability of $x$ successes in $n$ trials, then, is the expression for the binomial distribution:

$$f(x) = C(n,x) p^x q^{n-x} \qquad\qquad x = 1,2,3,\ldots,n \qquad\qquad (5.118)$$

Suppose we have a binomial experiment in which the outcomes of $n$ experiments can be used to represent the random variable $X$, which denotes the number of successes in $n$ trials. Thus, by equation (5.84) and by the definition of binomial random variables:

$$E[X] = E[x_1] + E[x_2] + \ldots + E[x_n]$$
$$E[X] = np \qquad\qquad\qquad\qquad\qquad\qquad (5.119)$$

Since the variance of any of the individual experiments is $pq$, by equation (5.100) the variance of a binomial density can be found to be:

$$\mathrm{Var}[X] = \mathrm{Var}[x_1] + \mathrm{Var}[x_2] + \ldots + \mathrm{Var}[x_n]$$
$$\mathrm{Var}[X] = npq \qquad\qquad\qquad\qquad\qquad\qquad (5.120)$$

Suppose that we wish to know how many Bernoulli trials occur before the first success in a sequence of trials occurs. If the first trial yields a success and the probability of success for any trial is $p$, the probability of the random variable $X$ is $p$. If the probability of failure is given as $q = 1 - p$ and we have success on the second trial, we obtain a probability of $pq$. Extending to $k - 1$ failures before an eventual success, we obtain what is known as the "geometric distribution," where:

$$f(k) = pq^{k-1} \qquad\qquad\qquad k = 1,2,\ldots \qquad\qquad (5.121)$$

Finding the expected value of the geometric density function is a bit tricky but can be accomplished as follows. By equation (5.67),

$$E[X] = \sum_{i=1}^{\infty} i\, pq^{(i-1)}$$
$$E[X] = p \sum_{i=1}^{\infty} i\, q^{(i-1)} \qquad\qquad\qquad\qquad (5.122)$$

$$E[X] = p \sum_{i=0}^{\infty} \frac{d}{dq} q^i$$

$$E[X] = \frac{pd}{dq} \sum_{i=0}^{\infty} q^i$$

$$E[X] = \frac{pd}{dq} \left[ \frac{1}{1-q} \right]$$                                          (Cont. 5.122)

$$E[X] = \frac{p}{(1-q)^2}$$

$$E[X] = 1/p$$

The fifth line of the derivation above results because the value of $q$ is less than or equal to 1; thus, the summation converges to $1 / (1 - q)$. The variance of the geometric density is not derived here but is given as:

$$\mathrm{Var}[X] = q/p^2 \tag{5.123}$$

## 5.6.3   Poisson distribution

A widely used discrete density function that is useful for deriving statistics about the number of successes during a given time period is the Poisson distribution. The Poisson density function is popular mainly because it describes many real-word processes very well. In computer systems, requests for jobs at a CPU are often represented by a Poisson process. The Poisson density function is defined as:

$$f(x) = \left( e^{-\mu} \mu^x \right)/x! \qquad\qquad x = 0, 1, 2, \ldots \tag{5.124}$$

where the parameter $\mu$ is defined as the average number of successes during the interval. Several conditions must prevail for a Poisson density function to exist. These are that the successes for one interval are independent of the successes in any other interval, that the probability of a success during an interval of extremely short length is near zero, and that the probability of only one success during a short interval depends only upon the length of the interval. Interestingly, the mean of the Poisson distribution is part of its definition. The expected value can be found as:

$$E[X] = \sum_{x=0}^{\infty} x \, \frac{e^{-\mu}\mu^x}{x!}$$

$$E[X] = \sum_{x=1}^{\infty} \frac{xe^{-\mu}\mu^x}{x!} \tag{5.125}$$

$$E[X] = \mu \sum_{x=1}^{\infty} \frac{e^{-\mu}\mu^{x-1}}{(x-1)!}$$

Now, if we let $y = x - 1$, we arrive at a summation of the density function from 1 to infinity, which, by equation (5.51), is equal to 1:

$$E[X] = \mu \sum_{y=0}^{\infty} \frac{e^{-\mu}\mu^y}{y!} \tag{5.126}$$

$$E[X] = \mu$$

The variance of the Poisson distribution can be found by first finding $E[X(X-1)]$ and then using the result in equation (5.94):

$$E[X(X-1)] = \sum_{x=0}^{\infty} \frac{x(x-1)e^{-\mu}\mu^x}{x!} \tag{5.127}$$

The first two terms of this summation are zero, so we have:

$$E[X(X-1)] = \sum_{x=2}^{\infty} \frac{x(x-1)e^{-\mu}\mu^x}{x!}$$

$$E[X(X-1)] = \sum_{x=2}^{\infty} \frac{e^{-\mu}\mu^{x-2}\mu^2}{(x-2)!} \tag{5.128}$$

By equation (5.51), and, if we let $x = y + 2$, we get:

$$E[X(X-1)] = \mu^2 \sum_{y=0}^{\infty} \frac{e^{-\mu}\mu^y}{y!} = \mu^2 \tag{5.129}$$

By equation (5.94), we get:

$$\sigma^2 = E[X^2] - \mu^2$$

$$\sigma^2 = E[X^2] - E[X] + E[X] - \mu^2 \tag{5.130}$$

By equation (5.84), we get:

$$\sigma^2 = E\left[X^2 - X\right] + E[X] - \mu^2$$
$$\sigma^2 = E\left[X(X-1)\right] + E[X] - \mu^2 \tag{5.131}$$

By equation (5.127), we get:

$$\sigma^2 = \mu^2 + \mu - \mu^2 = \mu \tag{5.132}$$

The previous density functions provide some examples of the more common discrete random variables. Distributions such as these are useful for modeling real-world processes in which the quantities of interest are countable items.

In addition to the basic discrete density functions described earlier, there are several continuous densities. Continuous density functions are characterized by the fact that the value of $f(x)$ at any point $x$ is zero. However, the probability that any value $x$ lies between $x$ and some small delta is approximately $f(x)$ times the delta value.

## 5.6.4  Gaussian distribution

One of the most important continuous probability distributions, and probably the most widely used, is the "normal," or Gaussian distribution.

The density function of a normal random variable $X$ is given as:

$$f(x) = \frac{1}{\sigma\sqrt{2\pi}} e^{-1/2\left(\frac{x-\mu}{\sigma}\right)^2} \tag{5.133}$$

Figure 5.5 shows a few normal curves (also known as bell curves because of their bell-like shapes). The flatter curve has a larger standard deviation than the thinner curves. The expected value of the normal curve is found as follows. By equation (5.67):

$$E[X] = \int_{-\infty}^{\infty} \frac{x}{\sigma\sqrt{2\pi}} e^{-1/2\left(\frac{x-\mu}{\sigma}\right)^2} dx \tag{5.134}$$

If we substitute the following:

$$y = \frac{x-\mu}{\sigma} \quad \text{or} \quad x = \sigma y + \mu$$
$$dx = \sigma \, dy \tag{5.135}$$

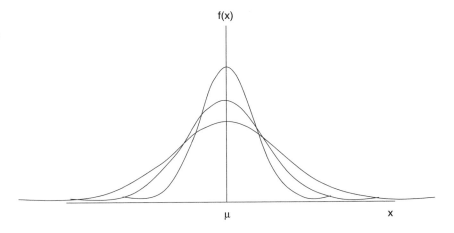

**Figure 5.5**
*A few normal
curves.*

we get:

$$E[X] = \frac{1}{\sqrt{2\pi}} \int_{-\infty}^{\infty} (y\sigma + \mu) e^{-\frac{y^2}{2}} \, dy$$

$$E[X] = \frac{\sigma}{\sqrt{2\pi}} \int_{-\infty}^{\infty} y e^{\frac{-y^2}{2}} \, dy + \frac{\mu}{\sqrt{2\pi}} \int_{-\infty}^{\infty} e^{-\frac{y^2}{2}} \, dy$$

(5.136)

If, in the second integral, we replace $y$ by the following:

$$y = (x - \mu)/\sigma$$
$$dy = 1/\sigma \, dx$$

(5.137)

we clearly see the integral of a density function, which is equal to 1:

$$E[X] = \frac{\sigma}{\sqrt{2\pi}} \int_{-\infty}^{\infty} y e^{-\frac{y^2}{2}} \, dy + \frac{\mu}{\sqrt{2\pi}} \int_{-\infty}^{\infty} e^{-\frac{1}{2}\left(\frac{x-\mu}{\sigma}\right)^2} \, dx$$

$$E[X] = \frac{\sigma}{\sqrt{2\pi}} \int_{-\infty}^{\infty} y e^{-\frac{y^2}{2}} \, dy + \mu$$

(5.138)

The expression in the remaining integral is an odd function because of the presence of $y$. Since an odd function integrated over symmetric limits is zero, the mean becomes:

$$E[X] = \mu$$

(5.139)

We can find the variance of the normal distribution as follows:

$$E\left[(X-\mu)^2\right] = \frac{1}{\sigma\sqrt{2\pi}} \int_{-\infty}^{\infty} (x-\mu)^2\, e^{-\frac{1}{2}\left(\frac{x-\mu}{\sigma}\right)^2}\, dx \tag{5.140}$$

Making the same substitution as before, we get:

$$E\left[(X-\mu)^2\right] = \frac{\sigma^2}{\sqrt{2\pi}} \int_{-\infty}^{\infty} y^2 e^{\left(-\frac{y^2}{2}\right)}\, dy \tag{5.141}$$

Now, we can integrate by parts:

Let:

$$u = y, \; v = -e^{-\frac{y^2}{2}}$$

and

$$du = dy, \; dv = ye^{-\frac{y^2}{2}} \tag{5.142}$$

then:

$$E\left[(X-\mu)^2\right] = \frac{\sigma^2}{\sqrt{2\pi}}\left[ ye^{-\frac{y^2}{2}} \Big|_{y=-\infty}^{\infty} + \int_{-\infty}^{\infty} e^{-\frac{y^2}{2}}\, dy \right]$$

As before, the first interval equals zero, and the second integral can be shown to be:

$$\int_{-\infty}^{\infty} e^{-\frac{y^2}{2}}\, dy = \sqrt{2\pi} \tag{5.143}$$

so we have:

$$E\left[(X-\mu)^2\right] = \frac{\sigma^2}{\sqrt{2\pi}}\left[0 + \sqrt{2\pi}\right]$$

$$E\left[(X-\mu)^2\right] = \sigma^2 \tag{5.144}$$

For the normal curve, the mean occurs at the mode, which is defined as the value that appears most in the distribution.

Finding the probability that a normally distributed random variable falls between two values requires the solution of the integral:

$$P(x_1 < X < x_2) = \frac{1}{\sigma\sqrt{2\pi}} \int_{x_1}^{x_2} e^{-\frac{1}{2}\left(\frac{x-\mu}{\sigma}\right)} dx \qquad (5.145)$$

This integral is not easily solvable and is best approached using numerical means. In order to be useful, however, we would need to generate a table for each value of mean and standard deviation. We would like to avoid this by having only one standard normal curve. If we make the substitution:

$$z = (x - \mu)/\sigma, \quad dx = \sigma dz \qquad (5.146)$$

in the previous equation, we obtain:

$$\frac{1}{\sqrt{2\pi}} \int_{z_1}^{z_2} e^{-\frac{z^2}{2}} dz \qquad (5.147)$$

where:

$$z = (x - \mu)/\sigma, \quad dx = \sigma dz \qquad (5.148)$$

The expression is equivalent to a normal distribution of mean equal to zero and standard deviation of one. Thus, we can transform any normal distribution into the standard normal curve with zero mean and a standard deviation of one. For example, let's compute the probability that any normally distributed random variable falls within one standard deviation of the mean. To do so, we need to generate some sort of table for the standard normal distribution. Table 5.1 gives values for the standard normal distribution integrated from minus infinity to $x$.

$$\frac{1}{\sqrt{2\pi}} \int_{-\infty}^{x} e^{-\frac{x^2}{2}} dx$$

Let:

$$x_1 = \mu - \sigma \quad \text{and} \quad x_2 = \mu + \sigma$$

then:                                                                                                              (5.149)

$$z_1 = (\mu - \sigma - \mu)/\sigma \quad \text{and} \quad z_2 = (\mu + \sigma - \mu)/\sigma$$

so:

$$z_1 = -1 \text{ and } z_2 = 1$$

The left-hand side of equation (5.143) can be rewritten as:

$$P(x_1 < X < x_2) = P(X < x_2) - P(X < x_1) \tag{5.150}$$

**Table 5.1**   *Standard Normal Curve Values*

| x+0.00 | x+0.01 | x+0.02 | x+0.03 | x+0.04 | x+0.05 | x+0.06 | x+0.07 | x+0.08 | x+0.09 |
|---|---|---|---|---|---|---|---|---|---|
| 0.50000 | 0.50401 | 0.50800 | 0.51199 | 0.51597 | 0.51996 | 0.52394 | 0.52794 | 0.53194 | 0.53594 |
| 0.53993 | 0.54391 | 0.54790 | 0.55187 | 0.55585 | 0.55981 | 0.56378 | 0.56773 | 0.57168 | 0.57562 |
| 0.57955 | 0.58348 | 0.58740 | 0.59130 | 0.59520 | 0.59909 | 0.60297 | 0.60684 | 0.61070 | 0.61455 |
| 0.61839 | 0.62221 | 0.62603 | 0.62983 | 0.63362 | 0.63739 | 0.64116 | 0.64490 | 0.64864 | 0.65236 |
| 0.65607 | 0.65976 | 0.66343 | 0.66709 | 0.67074 | 0.67436 | 0.67798 | 0.68157 | 0.68515 | 0.68871 |
| 0.69225 | 0.69578 | 0.69929 | 0.70277 | 0.70624 | 0.70970 | 0.71313 | 0.71654 | 0.71993 | 0.72331 |
| 0.72666 | 0.72999 | 0.73331 | 0.73660 | 0.73987 | 0.74312 | 0.74635 | 0.74956 | 0.75274 | 0.75591 |
| 0.75905 | 0.76217 | 0.76527 | 0.76834 | 0.77139 | 0.77442 | 0.77743 | 0.78041 | 0.78337 | 0.78631 |
| 0.78923 | 0.79212 | 0.79498 | 0.79783 | 0.80065 | 0.80344 | 0.80622 | 0.80897 | 0.81169 | 0.81439 |
| 0.81707 | 0.81972 | 0.82234 | 0.82495 | 0.82753 | 0.83008 | 0.83261 | 0.83512 | 0.83760 | 0.84006 |
| 0.84248 | 0.84487 | 0.84724 | 0.84959 | 0.85192 | 0.85421 | 0.85649 | 0.85874 | 0.86097 | 0.86317 |
| 0.86535 | 0.86751 | 0.86964 | 0.87174 | 0.87383 | 0.87589 | 0.87793 | 0.87994 | 0.88193 | 0.88389 |
| 0.88584 | 0.88775 | 0.88965 | 0.89152 | 0.89337 | 0.89520 | 0.89701 | 0.89879 | 0.90055 | 0.90228 |
| 0.90400 | 0.90569 | 0.90736 | 0.90901 | 0.91063 | 0.91224 | 0.91382 | 0.91538 | 0.91692 | 0.91844 |
| 0.91994 | 0.92142 | 0.92287 | 0.92431 | 0.92572 | 0.92712 | 0.92849 | 0.92985 | 0.93118 | 0.93250 |
| 0.93379 | 0.93507 | 0.93633 | 0.93756 | 0.93878 | 0.93998 | 0.94117 | 0.94233 | 0.94348 | 0.94460 |
| 0.94571 | 0.94681 | 0.94788 | 0.94894 | 0.94998 | 0.95100 | 0.95201 | 0.95300 | 0.95397 | 0.95493 |
| 0.95587 | 0.95679 | 0.95770 | 0.95860 | 0.95947 | 0.96034 | 0.96119 | 0.96202 | 0.96284 | 0.96364 |
| 0.96443 | 0.96521 | 0.96597 | 0.96672 | 0.96745 | 0.96817 | 0.96888 | 0.96957 | 0.97026 | 0.97093 |
| 0.97158 | 0.97223 | 0.97286 | 0.97348 | 0.97409 | 0.97468 | 0.97527 | 0.97584 | 0.97640 | 0.97695 |
| 0.97749 | 0.97803 | 0.97855 | 0.97906 | 0.97956 | 0.98005 | 0.98053 | 0.98100 | 0.98146 | 0.98191 |
| 0.98235 | 0.98279 | 0.98321 | 0.98363 | 0.98403 | 0.98443 | 0.98482 | 0.98520 | 0.98557 | 0.98593 |
| 0.98629 | 0.98664 | 0.98698 | 0.98731 | 0.98764 | 0.98795 | 0.98827 | 0.98857 | 0.98887 | 0.98916 |
| 0.98944 | 0.98972 | 0.98999 | 0.99025 | 0.99051 | 0.99077 | 0.99101 | 0.99125 | 0.99149 | 0.99172 |
| 0.99194 | 0.99216 | 0.99237 | 0.99258 | 0.99279 | 0.99298 | 0.99318 | 0.99337 | 0.99355 | 0.99373 |
| 0.99391 | 0.99408 | 0.99424 | 0.99441 | 0.99456 | 0.99472 | 0.99487 | 0.99502 | 0.99516 | 0.99530 |
| 0.99543 | 0.99556 | 0.99569 | 0.99582 | 0.99594 | 0.99606 | 0.99618 | 0.99629 | 0.99640 | 0.99650 |
| 0.99661 | 0.99671 | 0.99681 | 0.99690 | 0.99700 | 0.99709 | 0.99717 | 0.99726 | 0.99734 | 0.99742 |
| 0.99750 | 0.99758 | 0.99765 | 0.99773 | 0.99780 | 0.99787 | 0.99793 | 0.99800 | 0.99806 | 0.99812 |
| 0.99818 | 0.99824 | 0.99829 | 0.99835 | 0.99840 | 0.99845 | 0.99850 | 0.99855 | 0.99859 | 0.99864 |
| 0.99868 | 0.99873 | 0.99877 | 0.99881 | 0.99885 | 0.99888 | 0.99892 | 0.99896 | 0.99899 | 0.99902 |
| 0.99906 | 0.99909 | 0.99912 | 0.99915 | 0.99918 | 0.99920 | 0.99923 | 0.99926 | 0.99928 | 0.99930 |
| 0.99933 | 0.99935 | 0.99937 | 0.99939 | 0.99942 | 0.99944 | 0.99945 | 0.99947 | 0.99949 | 0.99951 |
| 0.99953 | 0.99954 | 0.99956 | 0.99957 | 0.99959 | 0.99960 | 0.99962 | 0.99963 | 0.99964 | 0.99966 |
| 0.99967 | 0.99968 | 0.99969 | 0.99970 | 0.99971 | 0.99972 | 0.99973 | 0.99974 | 0.99975 | 0.99976 |
| 0.99977 | 0.99978 | 0.99978 | 0.99979 | 0.99980 | 0.99981 | 0.99981 | 0.99982 | 0.99983 | 0.99983 |
| 0.99984 | 0.99984 | 0.99985 | 0.99986 | 0.99986 | 0.99987 | 0.99987 | 0.99988 | 0.99988 | 0.99988 |
| 0.99989 | 0.99989 | 0.99990 | 0.99990 | 0.99990 | 0.99991 | 0.99991 | 0.99991 | 0.99992 | 0.99992 |
| 0.99992 | 0.99992 | 0.99993 | 0.99993 | 0.99993 | 0.99993 | 0.99994 | 0.99994 | 0.99994 | 0.99994 |
| 0.99994 | 0.99995 | 0.99995 | 0.99995 | 0.99995 | 0.99995 | 0.99995 | 0.99996 | 0.99996 | 0.99996 |
| 0.99996 | 0.99996 | 0.99996 | 0.99996 | 0.99997 | 0.99997 | 0.99997 | 0.99997 | 0.99997 | 0.99997 |

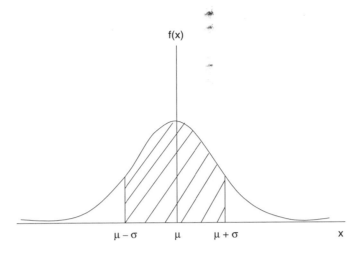

**Figure 5.6**
*Selected area under a normal distribution curve.*

The values from the table for $z = -1$ and $1$, respectively, are:

$$P(z < -1) = 0.1587$$
$$P(z < 1) = 0.8413$$

$\qquad(5.151)$

Therefore, we have:

$$P(x_1 < X < x_2) = P(X < x_2) - P(X < x_1)$$

$\qquad(5.152)$

Figure 5.6 shows the selected area under the normal curve.

### 5.6.5    **Exponential distribution**

A simpler continuous distribution, the exponential, is important in queuing theory and therefore is discussed here. Its main attraction is that it has the Markovian property, which states that the probability of occurrence of an event is completely independent of the history of the experiment. This characteristic is also called the "memoryless" property. The expression for an exponential distribution is given as:

$$f(x) = \begin{cases} \lambda e^{-\lambda x} & x > 0 \\ 0 & \text{otherwise} \end{cases}$$

$\qquad(5.153)$

The graph of an exponential curve is shown in Figure 5.7.

We will see later that the exponential distribution, because of its Markovian property, will be useful for representing service time distributions in queuing systems.

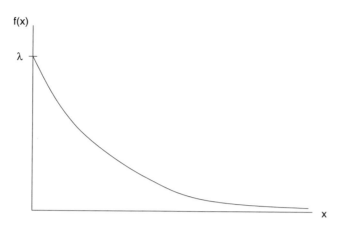

**Figure 5.7**
*Exponential
probability density
function.*

Suppose that the time a computer user spends at a system terminal is exponentially distributed over time. The probability that the user will be at a terminal for $n$ minutes is given as:

$$P(X \geq n) = \int_{n}^{\infty} f(x)\, dx$$

$$P(X \geq n) = \int_{n}^{\infty} \lambda e^{-\lambda x}\, dx \qquad (5.154)$$

$$P(X \geq n) = e^{-n\lambda}$$

The probability distribution function for the exponential function is shown in Figure 5.8 and given as:

$$F(x) = P(X < x) = \begin{cases} 1 - e^{-\lambda x} & x > 0 \\ 0 & \text{otherwise} \end{cases} \qquad (5.155)$$

As with any distribution function, we can find the same result by picking the point $n$, representing the probability that the user will be at a terminal for less than $n$ minutes, and using equation (5.19) to find the probability of the complementary event (see also Figure 5.8):

$$P(X \geq n) = 1 - F(n)$$

$$P(X \geq n) = 1 - (1 - e^{-nx}) \qquad (5.156)$$

$$P(X \geq n) = e^{-nx}$$

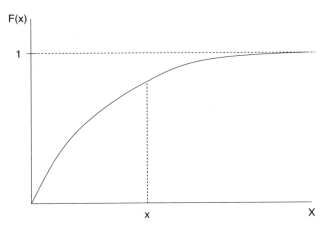

→
**Figure 5.8**
*Exponential
probability
distribution
function.*

The mean of an exponential random variable is found as:

$$E[X] = \int_0^\infty x\lambda e^{-\lambda x}\, dx \tag{5.157}$$

If we let:

$$u = x \quad \text{and} \quad v = -e^{-\lambda x}$$
$$du = dx \quad \text{and} \quad dv = \lambda e^{-\lambda x}\, dx \tag{5.158}$$

and integrate by parts where:

$$\int_a^b u\, dv = uv\Big|_a^b - \int_a^b v\, du \tag{5.159}$$

we obtain:

$$E[X] = -x e^{-\lambda x}\Big|_0^\infty - \int_0^b -e^{-\lambda x}\, dx \tag{5.160}$$

because:

$$\lim_{x \to \infty} x e^{-\lambda x} = 0$$
$$E[X] = 0 - \int_0^\infty -e^{-\lambda x}\, dx \tag{5.161}$$

$$E[X] = -1/\lambda\ e^{-\lambda x} \Big|_{0}^{\infty}$$

$$E[X] = \lim_{x \to \infty}\ 1/\lambda\ e^{-\lambda x} + 1/\lambda \qquad\qquad \text{(Cont. 5.161)}$$

$$E[X] = 1/\lambda$$

We may find the variance of the exponential random variable as follows:

$$\mathrm{var}[X] = E\left[(X-\mu)^2\right] = \int_{-\infty}^{\infty} (x-\mu)^2\, \lambda e^{-\lambda x} dx$$

$$\mathrm{var}[X] = \int_{0}^{\infty} \lambda x^2 e^{-\lambda x} dx - 2\mu \int_{0}^{\infty} \lambda x e^{-\lambda x} dx + \mu^2 \lambda \int_{0}^{\infty} e^{-\lambda x} dx \qquad (5.162)$$

We can see that by equations 5.157 through 5.161, the second interval evaluates to $1/\lambda$. The third interval evaluates to $1/\lambda$ (as shown in 5.161). To solve this first interval, we introduce the gamma function, denoted as:

$$\Gamma[t] = \int_{0}^{\infty} x^{t-1} e^{-x} dx \qquad\qquad\qquad (5.163)$$

The gamma function can be solved for a positive value of the parameter to yield:

$$\Gamma[n] = (n-1)! \qquad\qquad\qquad (5.164)$$

We can now use equation (5.164) to help find the solution to equation (5.162) and arrive at the variance for an exponential distribution:

$$\mathrm{var}[X] = 1/\lambda^2 \qquad\qquad\qquad (5.165)$$

## 5.6.6   Erlang distribution

The exponential density function is often used to represent the service time of a server at the end of a waiting line. In some cases, it is desirable to represent several identical servers with a single density function whose statistics are the same as for a single equivalent exponential server. The distribution that satisfies these conditions is called the "Erlang distribution" and is given as:

$$f(x) = \begin{cases} \dfrac{\lambda k (\lambda k x)^{k-1} e^{-\lambda k x}}{(k-1)!} & x > 0 \end{cases} \qquad\qquad (5.166)$$

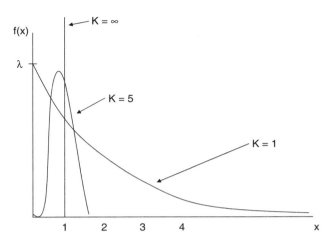

**Figure 5.9**
*Erlang density functions for selected values of k.*

with parameters $\lambda$ and $k$. Figure 5.9 shows a graph of the Erlang density function for various values of $k$ for a given value of $\lambda$. The mean and standard deviations of the Erlang density function are given as:

$$E[X] = 1/\lambda \qquad (5.167)$$

$$\text{var}[X] = 1/k\lambda^2 \qquad (5.168)$$

The probability distribution function is given as:

$$F(x) = 1 - e^{-\lambda kx}\left[1 + \sum_{i=0}^{k-1}\frac{(k\lambda x)^i}{i!}\right] \qquad (5.169)$$

It is important to note that the expected value for the Erlang density is the same as for an exponential with the same parameter, $\lambda$, and is independent of the number of Erlangian servers (e.g., parallel servers).

## 5.7 Summary

This chapter introduced some of the basic probability concepts that are useful for understanding and analyzing queuing network models. Many additional, more complex probability densities are known to be useful for representing certain types of real-world processes. These are beyond the scope of this book but may be found in many probability and statistics texts (see [2–6]). The densities presented in this book, however, are commonly used in queuing analysis due to their applicability to many arrival and service processes and because of their relative computational simplicity.

# 6

# *Stochastic Processes*

## 6.1    Introduction

Markov processes are powerful analytical tools applicable to the analysis of computer systems. They provide accurate, yet relatively simple means to construct representations of systems and to mathematically analyze a computer system. Markov processes require that we have an understanding of stochastic processes and their analysis. This chapter provides the background necessary to perform the modeling and analysis of such systems.

## 6.2    Basic definitions

A stochastic process involves the representation of a family of random variables. A random variable is represented as a function on a variable, $f(x)$, which approximates a number with the result of some experiment. The variable $X$ is one possible value from a family of variables, from a sample space represented as $\Omega$. For example, for a toss of a coin the entire sample space is $\Omega = \{$heads, tails$\}$, and the random variable $X$ may equal the mapping $x = \{1,0\}$, representing the functional mapping of the event set $\{$heads, tails$\}$ to the event random variable mapping set $\{1,0\}$. (See Table 6.1.)

A stochastic process is represented or described as a family of random variables, denoted $X(t)$, where one value of the random variable $X$ exists for each value of $t$. The random variable, $X$, has a set of possible values defined

**Table 6.1**    *Functional Mapping*

| Events | = | Heads | Tails |
|--------|---|-------|-------|
|        |   | ↓     | ↓     |
| $X$    | = | 0     | 1     |

by the state space, $X(t)$, for the random variable $X$, with values selected by the parameter set, $T$ (sometimes called the index set), whose values are drawn from a subset of the total index set $T$.

As with random variables, stochastic processes are classified as being continuous or discrete. Stochastic processes can have either discrete or continuous state spaces as well as discrete or continuous index sets. For example, the number of commands, $X(t)$, received by a timesharing computer system during some time interval $(0,t)$ can be represented as having a continuous index parameter and a discrete state space. A second example could be the number of students attending the tenth lecture of a course. This can be represented as having a discrete index set and a discrete state space. In general, if the number of states in the state space is finite, then the stochastic process has a discrete state space. Likewise, if the index set for the state space is finite and counting, then the index set is also discrete. For continuous systems, the number of possible values for the variables are not discrete (i.e., real valued). For the index set to be continuous, the set of possible values must be real and can approach infinite.

One important form of stochastic process is the counting process. A counting stochastic process is one where we wish to count the number of events that occur in some time interval, represented as $N(t)$, where $N$ is drawn from the discrete set of counting positive integers from the set $\{0,1,2,3,\ldots\}$. In addition, the index set for such a counting stochastic process is drawn from the continuous space of time, where time is from some reference point $\{t \geq 0\}$. The requirement for this stochastic process is that for the value of the index set 0, the random variable $N(0) = 0$. For values of $t < 0$, the value of $N(t)$ is undefined. This implies that the values of $N(t)$ only exist for values of the index set above 0, and the values of $N(t)$ for all ranges of $t$ above 0 are positive nonnegative values. A second property for a counting stochastic process deals with the relationship discrete values drawn from the state space have with each other. For any two values of the index set—for example, indexes $s$ and $t$, where $s < t$—the values of the random variables must have the relationship $X(s) \leq X(t)$. Finally, if we look over some interval of values for the index set—for example, values $s$ and $t$— $N(t) - N(s)$ represents the number of events from our represented events that have occurred by time $t$ after time $s$ and bounded by $t$.

When discussing stochastic processes, it is often important to be able to determine the order of a function, such that we can focus on the dominant component. One way of doing this is to use notation from computer science and analysis of algorithms. The definition of the "order" of computation for an algorithm is often referred to as the order of a function. Two common ones are little-*oh*, written *o(h)*, and big-*oh*, written *O(h)*, where *h* indicates the variable of the function. Little *oh* describes the order or size of a function as the value of the function, when divided by the value of *h*, approaches the limiting value of *o*, as it approaches 0. This is depicted as:

$$\lim_{h\to 0} \frac{f(h)}{h} = 0 \tag{6.1}$$

If a function of *h*, when divided by *h*, does not result in 0, then the function is not *o(h)*. If it does approach 0 as the limit is approached, then the function is *o(h)*. For example:

$$
\begin{aligned}
&f(x) = x^2 \qquad \text{is } o(h) \text{ because}\\
&\lim_{x\to 0}\frac{x^2}{x} = \lim_{x\to 0} x = 0\\
&f(x) = x \qquad \text{is not } o(h) \text{ because}\\
&\lim_{x\to 0}\frac{x}{x} = 1 \neq 0
\end{aligned} \tag{6.2}
$$

This concept of the order of a function can be used in understanding stochastic processes and in simplifying their analysis, as will be shown. For example, suppose *x* is an exponential random variable with parameter $\lambda$ and is described by the following probability function:

$$P[x \le h] = 1 - e^{-\lambda h} \tag{6.3}$$

We may wish to determine what the probability is that *x* is less than $t + h$ given that it is greater than *t*. (See Figure 6.1.)

$$P[x \le t + h \mid x > t] = P[x \le h] \tag{6.4}$$

Jumping ahead and applying a concept not yet described—that of the Markov property of exponential distributions—we can show that:

$$
\begin{aligned}
&= 1 - e^{-\lambda h}\\
&= 1 - [1 - \lambda h] + \sum_{n=2}^{\infty} \frac{(-\lambda h)^n}{n!}\\
&= \lambda h + o(h)
\end{aligned} \tag{6.5}
$$

This indicates that the function order is *o(h)*.

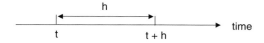

**Figure 6.1**
*Stochastic process*
*for* $P[x \leq t+h | x > t]$.

Another important property is that of independent and stationary incre-ments. A stochastic process has independent increments if events in the sample space $\{x(t), t \geq o\}$, occurring in nonoverlapping intervals, do not have the same value. For example, with regard to Figure 6.2, $x(b1) - x(a1) \neq x(b2) - x(a2)$.

A stochastic process has a stationary increment if the values of a random variable over similar ranges are equivalent. For example, if over two intervals $x(t)$, $x(s)$ and $x(t + h)$, $x(s + h)$, the value for $x(t + h) - x(s + h)$ has the same distribution as $x(t) - x(s)$ for all values of $h > 0$, then the stochastic process has stationary increments. (See Figure 6.3.)

Another way of looking at this definition is that if $x(t) - x(s) = x(t + h) - x(s + h)$, then this stochastic process has stationary increments.

As an example, we assume $N(t)$ is the number of phone calls handled by a certain central office between midnight and some time, $t$, on a workday (Figure 6.4).

This process can be looked at as possessing independent increments, not stationary increments. If we look at two values for time, 8:00 A.M. and 12:00 noon, the values from 8:00 A.M. to 10:00 A.M. and from 12:00 noon to 2:00 P.M. do not show the same value for the variable $N(t)$. Therefore, this stochastic process does not have stationary intervals but does have inde-pendent increments.

These concepts of discrete and continuous state space and index set, along with the concepts of independent and stationary increments, can be used to further understand the properties of various systems—for example, if we look at another stochastic process: tossing of a fair coin. We can describe one such stochastic process as counting the number of heads flipped during $n$ flips of a fair coin. Such a stochastic process is referred to as

**Figure 6.2**
*Independent*
*stochastic processes.*

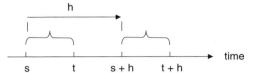

**Figure 6.3**
*Stationary stochastic processes.*

a Bernoulli process. If we let $X_1$, $X_2$, $X_3$, ... be independent identically distributed Bernoulli random variables, the property for each value of $x$ is:

$$X_i = \begin{cases} 1 & \text{with probability} \quad P \\ 0 & \text{with probability} \quad 1-P \end{cases}$$

The value of 1 represents a successful outcome (e.g., flipping a head), and 0 represents the failure of flipping a head.

$$S_n = X_1 + X_2 + X_3 + \ldots + X_n \tag{6.6}$$

Therefore, $S_n$ is a Bernoulli process (discrete parameter, discrete state).

For each $n$, $S_n$ has a binomial distribution:

$$P[S_n = k] = \binom{n}{k} P^k (1-P)^{n-k} \tag{6.7}$$
$$k = 0, 1, 2, \ldots, n$$

Starting at any point within the sample space, the number of trials, $y$, before the next success has the geometric distribution with the probability:

$$P[y = k] = (1-P)^k P \qquad k = 0, 1, \ldots \tag{6.8}$$

**Figure 6.4**
*Example phone call volume.*

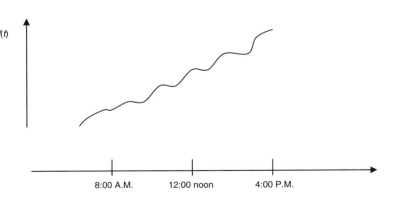

## 6.3    **Poisson process**

An important stochastic process used in computer systems performance evaluation is the Poisson process. A Poisson stochastic process has the property that events are independent, and the interarrival times of events can be described using the exponential distribution $F(t) = 1 - e^{-\lambda t}$. For example, the events described could be the arrival of a transaction for service, the completion of transaction processing, or the service time for the transaction. Given that the mean time between some event is $1/\lambda$, the rate of occurrence of the events will be $\lambda$. The Poisson process possesses the following properties:

1.    Occurrences of events during nonoverlapping intervals of time are independent.

2.    For small increments of time the probability of zero events is $1 - \lambda \Delta t$, and the probability of an event occurring during the same time is $\lambda \Delta t$.

Poisson stochastic processes have many desirable properties. If two Poisson arrival streams are merged, the resultant stream is also a Poisson stream with the rate equal to the sum of the input rates. Consider, for example, Figure 6.5 with $\{N_1(t), t \geq 0\}$ and Rate $\lambda_1$, $\{N_2(t), t \geq 0\}$ and Rate $\lambda_2$, the resultant stream, $\{N_{sum}(t), t \geq 0\}$, has Rate $\lambda_1 + \lambda_2$.

If a Poisson stream is divided into two streams, with each event going to stream $A$ with probability $P_A$ and stream $B$ with probability $P_B$, the resulting streams are Poisson with rates $P_A\lambda$ and $P_B\lambda$. (See Figure 6.6.)

Let's look at an example using some of the basic properties of the Poisson process and some of the fundamental concepts from probability. In this example, a computer center has a large number of separate system components that may fail—for example, terminals, tape drives, disks, printers, sensors, CPUs, and so on. When these items fail, they do not bring the entire computer system down. We know that for this system there are on the average 0.6 failures per day. Failures are independent. These failures can be represented by a Poisson process with rate $\lambda = 0.6$ (per day). In addi-

**Figure 6.5**
*Two Poisson arrival streams merging.*

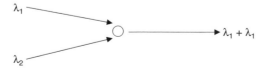

tion, the time between failures is observed to be exponentially distributed. What is the mean time between failures?

$$P[\tau_n \le s] = 1 - e^{-\lambda s} \qquad \lambda = 0.6/\text{day}$$

$$\text{E}[\tau_n] = 1/\lambda = 1.666 \text{ days} = 39.99 \text{ hours between failures} \tag{6.9}$$

Using the initial conditions, we can see that the number of failures in an interval of $t$ days has the Poisson distribution with a mean of $0.6t$. We can use this to determine the number of failures we could expect during any specific period of time. For example, we could ask what the probability is of exactly one failure in a 24-hour period.

$$P[y_t = k] = e^{-\lambda t} \frac{(\lambda t)^k}{k!}$$

$$P[y_t = 1 \text{ day}] = e^{-0.6} \frac{(0.6)}{1!} = (0.5488)(0.6) = 0.32928 \tag{6.10}$$

Or we could ask what the probability is of less than five failures in a week.

$$\begin{aligned}
P[y_7 < 5] &= \sum_{k=0}^{4} P[y = k] \\
&= \sum_{k=0}^{4} e^{-\lambda t} \frac{(\lambda t)^k}{k!} \\
&= \sum_{k=0}^{4} e^{(-0.6 \times 7)} \frac{(0.6 \times 7)^k}{k!} \\
&= e^{-4.2} \left[ \begin{array}{l} 1 + (4.2/1) + \left((4.2)^2/2!\right) \\ + \left((4.2)^3/3!\right) + \left((4.2)^4/4!\right) \end{array} \right] \\
&= 0.5898
\end{aligned} \tag{6.11}$$

This implies that we have a 0.5898 probability of getting less than five failures within this period of time.

**Figure 6.6**
*Poisson stream dividing.*

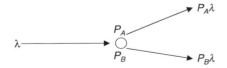

Conversely, we could start from a random point in time and determine what the probability is that no failure will occur during the next 24 hours.

$$P[\tau_n > 1 \, \text{day}] = P[y_1 = 0] = e^{-\lambda t} = e^{-0.6} = 0.5488 \tag{6.12}$$

Using the fundamental properties of the Poisson process we could postulate other questions as we discover or measure our system. For example, suppose exactly 24 hours has elapsed with no failures. What is the expected time until the next failure? The Poisson process supports the memoryless property—that is, past history does not aid in predicting future history (independent increments). The result of this question is the same as the initial question, which asked what the probability is of the next failure.

$$P[\tau_n \le s] = 1 - e^{-\lambda s} \qquad \lambda = .6 / \text{day}$$
$$E[\tau_n] = 1/\lambda = 1.666 \, \text{days} = 39.99 \, \text{hours between failures} \tag{6.13}$$

As another example, we know that four out of every five failures is a terminal problem, where each of these failures occurs with equal probability on each failure (see Figure 6.7). We may wish to determine what the process describing the terminal failure is. One must first recognize that this can be modeled as a Poisson process, where the total stream (representing failures) can be broken into a split stream, both of which also are Poisson processes. Given this assumption, we can state that this is a Poisson process with rate $P_A \lambda = (4/5) \, 0.6 = 0.48/\text{day}$ for the terminal failures.

The average time between terminal failures is 2.083 days.

We can also determine the number of terminal failures in $t$ days given by:

$$P[y = k] = e^{-\lambda t} \frac{(\lambda t)^k}{k!}$$
$$= e^{-0.48t} \frac{(0.48t)^k}{k!} \tag{6.14}$$

**Figure 6.7**
*Possibility of a terminal failure.*

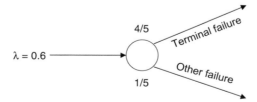

$\lambda = 0.6$

4/5   Terminal failure

1/5   Other failure

## 6.4    **Birth-death process**

The Poisson stochastic processes are related to a more general family of stochastic processes called birth-death processes. In birth-death stochastic processes we are concerned with a state space of random variables where the values range from 0, representing no members in the population, up to potentially an infinite number, representing a constantly growing population. More realistically we are interested in fixed-size populations that go through incremental additions to the population (births) and incremental deletions from the population (deaths).

For any specific level (possible range of values or specific number) in the population there is an associated birth rate and a death rate. This rate may be constant for each level but need not be. The birth-death stochastic process is described as a continuous parameter (index set) discrete state space stochastic process (Figure 6.8).

$$\{x(t), t \geq 0\} \tag{6.15}$$

$E(n)$, $n = 0, 1, 2, \ldots$ describes the state and $x(t) = n$ means $x(t)$ is in state $E(n)$ at time $t$.

For any stochastic process, $x(t)$ $t \geq 0$, to be a birth-death stochastic process, the process must be a discrete state space continuous parameter stochastic process, and it must have the following additional properties:

1.      State changes are only in increments of $\pm 1$ and the value of $E_n$ is never negative.

**Figure 6.8**
*Example birth-death process.*

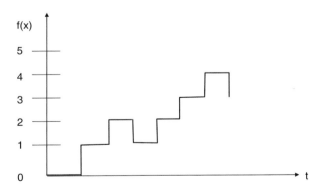

2.    If the system is in state $E_n$ at time $t$, the probability of a transition to $E_{n+1}$ during the interval $(t, t + h)$ is:

$$\lambda_n h + o(h)$$

and to $E_{n-1}$ is:

$$\mu_n h + o(h).$$

3.    The probability of more than one transition during an interval of length $h$ is $o(h)$.

If we examine a birth-death process from any particular state, $E_n$, we can see that we enter the state from only two other locations: either from state $E_{n+1}$ or $E_{n-1}$ (Figure 6.9).

Using this knowledge we can compute a variety of important perform-ance measures. All of these measures will be derived from the basis of com-puting the differential difference equations. These equations examine the birth-death stochastic process from the relationship with the initial state and the flow rates between states. We compute these focused on one node or state, as in Figure 6.9.

$$\text{Let } P_n(t) = P[X(t) = n] \tag{6.16}$$

be the probability that the system is in state $E_n$ at time $t$.

What is $P_n(t + h)$ for small $h$?

$$
\begin{aligned}
P_n(t+h) &= P_n(t)\big(1 - (\lambda_n h + o(h))\big)\big(1 - (\mu_n h + o(h))\big) \\
&\quad + P_{n-1}(t)\big(\lambda_{n-1} h + o(h)\big) \\
&\quad + P_{n+1}(t)\big(\mu_{n+1} h + o(h)\big) \\
&\quad + o(h) \\
&= \big[1 - \lambda_n h - \mu_n h\big] P_n(t) + \lambda_{n-1} h P_{n-1}(t) \\
&\quad + \mu_{n+1} h P_{n+1}(t) + o(h)
\end{aligned}
\tag{6.17}
$$

Transposing the term $P_n(t)$ and dividing by $h$:

$$
\begin{aligned}
\frac{P_n(t+h) - P_n(t)}{h} &= -(\lambda_n + \mu_n) P_n(t) \\
&\quad + \lambda_{n-1} P_{n-1}(t) + \mu_{n+1} P_{n+1}(t) + \frac{o(h)}{h}
\end{aligned}
\tag{6.18}
$$

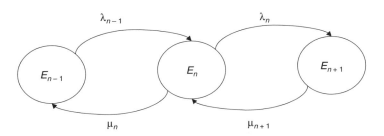

**Figure 6.9**
*Example stochastic
process state
transition diagram.*

Taking the limit as $h \rightarrow 0$:

$$\frac{dP_n(t)}{dt} = -(\lambda_n + \mu_n)P_n(t) + \lambda_{n-1}P_{n-1}(t) + \mu_{n+1}P_{n+1}(t) \text{ for } n \geq 1$$

$$\frac{dP_0(t)}{dt} = -\lambda_0 P_0(t) + \mu_1 P_1(t) \text{ for } n = 0$$

(6.19)

Equation 6.19 gives the relationship of the initial state to the first state and the initial birth and death rate. We will see the importance of this simple property of the birth-death stochastic process as we continue our development of this stochastic process and apply this to analyzing computer systems as simple queues and networks of queues.

One specialized example of the birth-death process looks at the condition when there are only births and no deaths, and, further, the birth rate is independent of the state and constant. More specifically, we make the following assumptions:

1.   There is a birth rate with mean rate $\lambda_n = \lambda > 0$.

2.   There are no deaths; therefore, the death rate is $\mu_n = 0$.

Using this information and the basic birth-death analysis previously described, we can show that:

$$\frac{dP_n(t)}{dt} = -\lambda P_n(t) + \lambda P_{n-1}(t) \text{ for } n \geq 1$$

$$\frac{dP_0(t)}{dt} = -\lambda P_0(t) \text{ for } n = 0$$

(6.20)

The probability of being in any state is:

$$P_n(t) = e^{-\lambda t}\frac{(\lambda t)^n}{n!}, \, n \geq 0 \text{ and } t \geq 0$$

(6.21)

which indicates that this is a Poisson process. The Poisson process can be modeled as a pure birth process with constant birth rate.

The general case birth-death process is a bit more complicated when finding time-dependent solutions. If, however, we look at the point where the system is nearing some limiting value, then the system can be assumed to be stationary and, therefore, equilibrium solutions exist for the system. In these equilibrium or steady-state solutions, we assume:

$$\lim_{t \to \infty} \to \frac{d\,P_n(t)}{dt} = 0 \text{ for each } n \tag{6.22}$$

and

$$\lim_{t \to \infty} \to P_n(t) = P_n \text{ for each } n \tag{6.23}$$

We can focus on the various states and compute the differential difference equations from a general node (any $n \geq 1$) and for the initial state $n = 0$, as:

1.    $$0 = \lambda_{n-1} P_{n-1} + \mu_{n+1} P_{n+1} - (\lambda_n + \mu_n) P_n, \quad n \geq 1 \tag{6.24}$$

2.    $$0 = \mu_1 P_1 - \lambda_0 P_0 \tag{6.25}$$

The solution for these differential difference equations, using a bit of algebra, is shown as:

$$P_{n+1} = \frac{\lambda_n}{\mu_{n+1}} P_n, \quad n \geq 1$$

$$\therefore \quad P_1 = \frac{\lambda_0}{\mu_1} P_0$$

$$P_2 = \frac{\lambda_1}{\mu_2} P_1 = \frac{\lambda_0 \lambda_1}{\mu_1 \mu_2} P_0 \tag{6.26}$$

$$\vdots$$

$$P_n = \frac{\lambda_0 \lambda_1 \lambda_2 \dots \lambda_{n-1}}{\mu_1 \mu_2 \mu_3 \dots \mu_n} P_0, \quad n \geq 1$$

and

$$\sum_{n=0}^{\infty} P_n = 1$$

The solutions described here focus on the use of balance equations to solve for the various state probabilities. Balance equations can be used, since

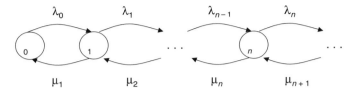

**Figure 6.10**
*Graphical representation for the birth-death process.*

we assume the system has reached equilibrium and, therefore, will migrate between stable states; no matter which state we happen to look at, this will hold. The balance equations examine each state, $E_n$, once equilibrium is reached; the rate of transition into state $E_n$ and the rate of transition out of $E_n$ are computed such that:

Rate of entering $E_n$ = rate of leaving $E_n$

From the birth-death process we find that:

1.     $$\lambda_{n-1}P_{n-1} + \mu_{n+1}P_{n+1} = (\lambda_n + \mu_n)P_n, \qquad n \geq 1 \tag{6.27}$$

2.     $$\mu_1 P_1 = \lambda_0 P_0 \tag{6.28}$$

Also:

$$\sum_{n=0}^{\infty} P_n = 1 \tag{6.29}$$

A graphical representation for the birth-death process is shown in Figure 6.10.

The rate transition diagram of an equilibrium analysis for a single server with no waiting line is shown in Figure 6.11. The example has Poisson arrivals with a rate of $\lambda$ and exponential service with a rate of $\mu$. The balance equations for this example are:

$$\mu p_1 = \lambda p_0$$

and                                                                              (6.30)

$$p_1 + p_0 = 1$$

**Figure 6.11**
*Transition rate diagram.*

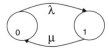

Solving the balance equations yields:

$$p_1 = (\lambda/\mu)\, p_0 \ \text{ and } \ p_0 + (\lambda/\mu)\, p_0 = 1 \tag{6.31}$$

Therefore:

$$p_0 = \frac{\mu}{\lambda + \mu} \tag{6.32}$$

The importance of this initial overview of the birth and death stochastic process, the representation of this process using transition rate diagrams, and the assumption of equilibrium and solution techniques using equilibrium will make more sense as we begin to look at general representations and mappings to computer systems.

## 6.5   Markov process

A Markov process is a stochastic process with some additional properties. If stochastic processes' future state probabilities only depend on the present state probabilities and not how they reached this state, then it is a Markov process.

More formally, a stochastic process $\{X(t),\ t \in T\}$ is a Markov process if for any set of $n + 1$ values $t_1 < t_2 < \ldots < t_n < t_{n+1}$ in the index set and any set of states $\{x_1, x_2, \ldots, x_n, x_{n+1}\}$:

$$
\begin{aligned}
P\big[X(t_{n+1}) = x_{n+1}\,\big|\,X(t_1) = x_1, X(t_2) = x_2, \ldots X(t_n) = x_n\big] \\
= P\big[X(t_{n+1}) = x_{n+1}\,\big|\,X(t_n) = x_n\big]
\end{aligned}
\tag{6.33}
$$

**Figure 6.12**
*Mapping of Markov process to other stochastic processes.*

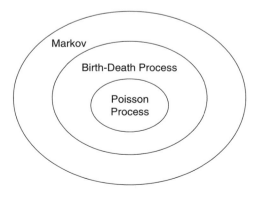

Markov

Birth-Death Process

Poisson Process

All birth-death processes are Markov processes; hence, the Poisson process is also a Markov process (Figure 6.12).

A discrete-state Markov process is called a Markov chain. Markov chains consist of discrete states $\{E_0, E_1, E_2, ...\}$. These states typically are described using nonnegative integers $\{0,1,2,3,4, ...\}$ instead of the more formal description given previously. A discrete time Markov chain makes state transitions at times $t_n$, $n = 1,2,3, ...$ (possibly into the same state). The notation for this transition and the resultant state is:

$$\{X(t_n), t_n = 0,1,2,...\} \rightarrow \{X_n\} \tag{6.34}$$

We will normally be interested only in Markov chains that have stationary state transition probabilities:

$$\begin{aligned} P\big[X_{n+1} = j \big| X_n = i\big] &= P\big[X_{m+1} = j \big| X_m = i\big] \\ &= p_{ij} \forall m,n,i,j \end{aligned} \tag{6.35}$$

The state transition probability, $p_{ij}$, represents the probability of transitioning from state $i$ to state $j$. For an entire Markov chain, we represent the collection of all such transition probabilities as a state transition matrix $\mathbf{P}$, as shown in Figure 6.13.

**Figure 6.13**
*Example probability state transition matrix.*

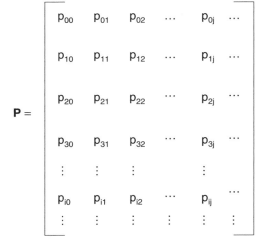

$$\mathbf{P} = \begin{bmatrix} p_{00} & p_{01} & p_{02} & \cdots & p_{0j} & \cdots \\ p_{10} & p_{11} & p_{12} & \cdots & p_{1j} & \cdots \\ p_{20} & p_{21} & p_{22} & \cdots & p_{2j} & \cdots \\ p_{30} & p_{31} & p_{32} & \cdots & p_{3j} & \cdots \\ \vdots & \vdots & \vdots & & \vdots & \\ p_{i0} & p_{i1} & p_{i2} & \cdots & p_{ij} & \cdots \\ \vdots & \vdots & \vdots & \vdots & \vdots & \vdots \end{bmatrix}$$

**Figure 6.14**
*State transition
diagram.*

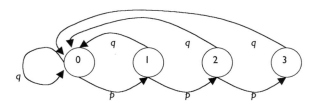

The requirements for entries in the state transition probability matrix are as follows:

$$p_{ij} \geq 0 \qquad i, j = 0,1,2,\ldots \qquad (6.36)$$

$$\sum_{j=0}^{\infty} p_{ij} = 1 \qquad i = 1,2,3,\ldots \qquad (6.37)$$

An example using such a matrix will involve a sequence of Bernoulli trials. In a Bernoulli experiment there can only be success or failure. An experiment succeeds with a probability of $p$ and fails with a probability of $q = 1 - p$. In this example, we assume that the state at trial $n$, with the value $X_n$, is the number of uninterrupted successes (i.e., length of consecutive successes). In the example suppose the following experiments occur. The values for the sample space, index $n$ and $X_n$, are shown as:

Sample:    trial:  $F$ $S$ $S$ $F$ $F$ $S$ $S$ $S$ $F$
           $n \;=\; 0\;\;1\;\;2\;\;3\;\;4\;\;5\;\;6\;\;7\;\;8$
           $X_n = \;0\;\;1\;\;2\;\;0\;\;0\;\;1\;\;\;2\;\;3\;\;0$

The state transition diagram is shown in Figure 6.14.

The resulting probability state transition matrix is composed of the following elements, as seen in Figure 6.15.

**Figure 6.15**
*Transition
probability matrix.*

$$\mathbf{P} = (p_{ij}) = \begin{bmatrix} q_{00} & p_{01} & 0 & 0 \\ q_{10} & 0 & p_{12} & 0 \\ q_{20} & 0 & 0 & p_{23} \\ q_{30} & 0 & 0 & 0 \end{bmatrix}$$

Using these probabilities we now wish to compute the state probabilities for the entire graph, assuming equilibrium as before.

If we let $\Pi_j^{(n)}$ represent the probability of being in state $j$ after the $n$th step (transition):

$$\Pi_j^{(n)} = P\left[X_n = j\right] \tag{6.38}$$

then:

$$\Pi_j^{(n+1)} = \sum_{i=0}^{\infty} \Pi_i^{(n)} p_{ij}^{(n)}, \forall j \tag{6.39}$$

Finite states: $j = 0,1,2,\dots, n-1$:

$$\Pi_j^{(n+1)} = \sum_{i=0}^{n-1} \Pi_i^{(n)} p_{ij}^{(n)}, \forall j \tag{6.40}$$

let $\boldsymbol{P}^{(n)} = \left[ p_{ij}^{(n)} \right], N \times N$ matrix:

$$\underset{\sim}{\Pi}^{(n)} = (\Pi_0^{(n)}, \Pi_1^{(n)}, \dots \Pi_{n-1}^{(n)}) \tag{6.41}$$

Then in vector notation:

$$\underset{\sim}{\Pi}^{(n+1)} = \underset{\sim}{\Pi}^{(n)} \bullet \boldsymbol{P}^{(n)} \tag{6.42}$$

Stationary (homogeneous) transition probabilities:

$$\begin{aligned} \boldsymbol{P}^{(n)} &= \boldsymbol{P}^{(m)}, \forall n,m \\ &= \boldsymbol{P} \end{aligned} \tag{6.43}$$

$$\underset{\sim}{\Pi}^{(n+1)} = \underset{\sim}{\Pi}^{(n)} \bullet \boldsymbol{P}$$

An example, assume we have a communications system that transmits the digits 0 and 1 through several stages (Figure 6.16). We assume that at each stage there is a probability of 0.75 that the output will be the same digit as the input.

**Figure 6.16**
*Communications systems stages.*

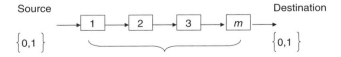

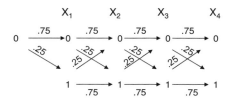

**Figure 6.17**
*Transition*
*probabilities for the*
*communications*
*systems of*
*Figure 6.16.*

One question we may ask is what the probability that a 0 entering the first stage is output as a 0 from the fourth stage. The solution requires representing the problem as a Markov chain and probability a matrix solution: Let the state at steps $n$, $X_n$, denote the value output by the $n$th stage.

Assume a 0 is input to stage 1 as shown in Figure 6.17.

What is the probability that $X_4 = 0$?

$$\prod^{(n+1)} = \prod^{(n)} P \tag{6.44}$$

Let:

$$
\begin{aligned}
\prod^{(0)} &= (1,0) \\
\prod^{(1)} &= \prod^{(0)} P \\
\prod^{(2)} &= \prod^{(1)} P = \prod^{(0)} P^2 \\
\prod^{(3)} &= \prod^{(2)} P = \prod^{(0)} P^3 \\
\prod^{(4)} &= \prod^{(3)} P = \prod^{(0)} P^4
\end{aligned}
\tag{6.45}
$$

Given the probability state transition matrix:

$$
P = \begin{vmatrix} 0.75 & 0.25 \\ 0.25 & 0.75 \end{vmatrix}
$$

$$
P^2 = \begin{vmatrix} 0.625 & 0.375 \\ 0.375 & 0.625 \end{vmatrix}
$$

$$
P^4 = \begin{vmatrix} 0.53125 & 0.46875 \\ 0.46875 & 0.53125 \end{vmatrix}
$$

$$\therefore \left( \Pi_0^{(4)}, \Pi_1^{(4)} \right) = (1,0)\, P^4$$

$$= (0.53125,\ 0.46875)$$

The general solution using stationary Markov chains yields:

$\Pi^{(n)} = \Pi^{(0)} P^n$, $n$ step transition probability matrix.

### 6.5.1 Markov chain definitions

State $j$ is said to be reachable from state $i$ if it is possible for the chain to proceed from state $i$ to state $j$ in a finite number of transitions:

$$P_{ij}^n > 0, \text{ for some } n > 0 \qquad (6.46)$$

If every state is reachable from every other state, the chain is said to be irreducible. Using the Bernoulli coin toss trials as before, we get the transition state diagram shown in Figure 6.18.

In Figure 6.18, we can see that if we are in any of the states, we can reach every other state in some number of steps. For example, if we are in state 3 we can reach state 0 by transitioning through arch 3,0. We can then get to state 1 by arch 0,1 and then to state 2 by transitioning by arch 1,2. One other point to note is that if we are in state 0, we can transition back to state 0 by the arch 0,0. After checking all paths from all pairs we can see that this Markov chain is irreducible.

In the second example (Figure 6.19), this graph is reducible, since there is at least one path (arch 0,11) that will not allow the elements of one subchain (consisting of nodes 11, 12, 13, and 14) from connecting to subchains 21, 22, 23, and 24.

We will generally be interested in the behavior of processes that can be represented by irreducible chains, since they are more easily solved and equilibrium can be achieved or assumed in such systems.

**Figure 6.18**
*Transition state diagram (Bernoulli trials, coin toss).*

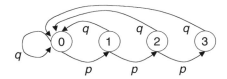

**Figure 6.19**
*Reducible
transition diagram.*

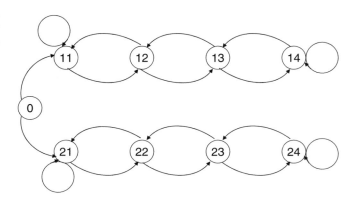

Another property of interest in Markov chains is the concept of ergotic chains. A discrete time Markov chain is said to be ergotic if (1) you can get from any state to any other state (i.e., irreducible), (2) for each of these states there are paths of various lengths back to that state (i.e., not all multiples of the same integer [aperiodic]), (3) upon leaving the state you will return with probability 1 within a finite mean time (positive recurrent). This last property implies the first, in that a path must exist and it must visit at most all of the arches.

A Markov chain is said to have a stationary distribution if:

$$\underset{\sim}{\Pi} = (\Pi_0, \Pi_1, \Pi_2, \ldots, \Pi_{n-1}) \atop n \text{ states}$$

(6.47)

and if there is a vector $\underset{\sim}{\Pi}$ such that:

$$\underset{\sim}{\Pi} = \underset{\sim}{\Pi} P$$

(6.48)

with

$$\Pi_i \geq 0 \; \forall_i$$

(6.49)

and

$$\sum \Pi_i = 1$$

(6.50)

Equivalently:

$$\lim_{n \to \infty} \Pi_j^{(n)} = \Pi_j, \text{ for } j = 0, 1, \ldots$$

(6.51)

For an ergotic Markov chain, the limit:

$$\underset{\sim}{\Pi}\; \lim_{n\to\infty} \underset{\sim}{\Pi}^{(n)} = \lim_{n\to\infty}\; \underset{\sim}{\Pi}^{(0)} \boldsymbol{P}^n \tag{6.52}$$

always exists and forms a stationary probability distribution that is independent of the initial state:

$$\underset{\sim}{\Pi}^{(0)} \tag{6.53}$$

The limiting distribution is the unique solution to the equations:

$$\underset{\sim}{\Pi} = \underset{\sim}{\Pi}\boldsymbol{P} \qquad \text{1) balance equation}$$
$$\sum_j \Pi_j = 1 \qquad \text{2) sum of probabilities} \tag{6.54}$$

Furthermore, for each state:

$$\Pi_j = 1/m_i \tag{6.55}$$

where $m_i$ is the mean recurrence time for state $i$, the mean number of steps taken to return to the state after leaving.

### Example: Communication system

What is the limiting probability that a 0 entered into the first stage is output as a 0 from the $n$th stage as $\lim n \to \infty$ (Figure 6.20)?

1.   Balance equation:

$$\underset{\sim}{\Pi} = \underset{\sim}{\Pi}\boldsymbol{P}$$
$$= \Pi \begin{bmatrix} 0.75 & 0.25 \\ 0.25 & 0.75 \end{bmatrix}$$

rate entering = rate leaving

$$\Pi_0 \times 0.75 + \Pi_0 \times 0.25 = \Pi_1 \times 0.25 + \Pi_0 \times 0.75$$
$$\Pi_0 = \Pi_1 \tag{6.56}$$

2.   Sum of probabilities:

$$\Pi_0 + \Pi_1 = 1$$

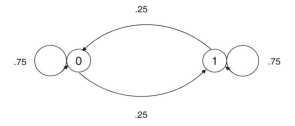

**Figure 6.20**
*State diagram.*

Hence:

$$\Pi_0 = 0.5 \text{ and } \Pi_1 = 0.5$$
$$\underset{\sim}{\Pi} = (0.5, 0.5)$$

which is a stationary distribution.

## 6.6    Summary

In this chapter, we introduced some of the basic concepts related to random variables and stochastic processes. It was shown that stochastic processes have some fundamental properties that allow them to be readily applied to the study of computer systems. One of these is the concept of the Poisson process and its application to the concept of expected arrival rates or service rates for events within stochastic processes. One special stochastic process is the birth-death process. This process was used to develop the concepts of equilibrium states and balance equations. These were used to determine state probabilities. A further refinement on the birth-death process is the Markov chain. The Markov chain has additional properties that lend it to the application of computer systems modeling. The reader is encouraged to consult [2–5] for further details.

# 7

# *Queuing Theory*

In this chapter, we will build upon the basic probability theory covered in Chapter 5 and stochastic processes covered in Chapter 6. The discussions will lead to the definition and analysis of several useful queuing models for the behavior of many types of service systems. The methods discussed herein complement those provided by simulation analysis. Frequently, the development of a general queuing model for a particular system will aid in the development of a refined Petri net model or a detailed simulation of specific parts of the system. Also, the results and behavior observed from simulation help to tune the analytical models.

This chapter is organized into three general topics: queuing models, estimation, and computational methods for theoretical systems analysis. Stochastic processes form the basis for many of the analytical techniques that apply to the queuing systems that we will discuss. The section on estimation provides some methods for defining the values that parameterize the queuing models with real-world data.

## 7.1    Queuing systems

In this section, we will cover the basic analysis techniques associated with queuing systems. The prime motivation for performing queuing analysis is to assess local system behavior under a variety of assumptions, initial conditions, and operational scenarios. The modeling aspect seeks to represent the behavior of system components as processes that have calculable statistics and that adequately reflect reality. Thus, the use of queuing analysis provides us with a set of techniques for calculating quantities, such as wait time for service, throughput of a server, the effect of different servers or queuing strategies, and the effects of coupled and closed networks of queues.

The assumption that we must make in order to take advantage of these techniques is that the system under observation can be adequately represented by a queuing system. In the remainder of this section, we will first look at analytical modeling in general, at the characteristics of the systems that we are interested in modeling, and then at the suitability of queuing models in general and their use in particular.

What are we seeking to quantify when we set out to model a system? The answer can be summed up in just one word: performance. This one word, however, may have very different meaning for different people. Take automobile performance, for instance. For the speed enthusiast, performance is how fast the car can go and how quickly it can get to that speed. For the back-road driver, it is the ability to corner without difficulty under severe conditions. For the economist, high performance means fuel efficiency and low maintenance costs. The list goes on. So it is for the performance of a computer system as well. At issue here are performance measures, such as the utilization of the system components, effective throughput, average waiting time for a potential user, average number of users in the system at any given time, and the availability of service resources.

In addition, trade-off analyses and "what if" studies can be performed to establish performance measures such as speedup and improved availability. In general, such studies provide the ability to analyze the sensitivity of the previously mentioned measures to changes in the system under study.

The general process of analytical modeling involves mapping the behavior of a complex system onto a relatively simpler system, solving the simpler system for the measures of interest, and then extrapolating the results back to the complex system. Sometimes this process has several levels, where models are broken into submodels. Here, the lowest-level models are solved (or partially solved) first, their results propagated up to the next higher layer for inclusion in that layer's solution, and so on to the top level.

In some cases, portions of a model can be replaced by a technique called decomposition, or isolation. Here, a queuing subsystem is replaced with a flow-equivalent server, where the server output is precalculated for each number of units (or customers) in the system. Thus, the job flow through the flow-equivalent server can be implemented using a simple lookup table indexed by the number of customers currently in the system. This technique is appropriate if the impact of the removed subsystem is minimal when compared with the effect of other model subsystems.

The basic premise behind the use of queuing models for computer systems analysis is that the components of a computer system can be represented by a

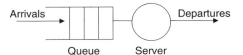

**Figure 7.1**
*Single server model.*

network of servers (or resources) and waiting lines (queues). A server is defined as an entity that can affect, or even stop, the flow of jobs through the system. In a computer system, a server may be the CPU, I/O channel, memory, or a communication port. A waiting line is just that: a place where jobs queue for service. To make a queuing model work, jobs (or customers or message packets or anything else that requires the sort of processing provided by the server) are inserted into the network. A simple example, the single server model, is shown in Figure 7.1. In that system, jobs arrive at some rate, queue for service on a first-come first-served basis, receive service, and exit the system. This kind of model, with jobs entering and leaving the system, is called an open queuing system model.

By cascading simple queuing models and allowing the existence of parallel servers, networks of queues and servers may be formed. These combinations are formally called queuing networks, although we will also call them network models and queuing systems. Figure 7.2 shows one such model of a computer system with a fixed number of jobs competing for a CPU and two I/O processors.

In Figure 7.2, jobs that have finished I/O service loop back into the CPU queue for another cycle of computation and I/O. A system like this, where the number of customers remains constant, is called a closed queuing network system model.

A combination of open and closed concepts is certainly possible if one considers each job to have an associated class. For example, a computer system may contain two job classes, interactive and system, where interactive jobs come and go as users log on and off and where system jobs execute continually. A system that contains both open and closed class customers is called mixed.

The concept of customer classes also allows different classes to receive different treatment at the same server, as well as the definition of a group of

**Figure 7.2**
*Queuing network model.*

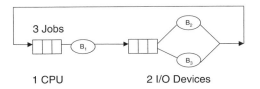

customers as open or closed. A system with more than one customer class is called multiclass, and it may be either open, closed, or mixed.

Once we have a network model established, the collection of $n_1$ customers at server 1, $n_2$ at server 2, and so on for the entire collection of queues in the network system defines the state of the network model. An analytical model for a queuing network would provide a method for calculating the probability that the network is in a particular state (i.e., that the number of customers is at certain levels for each queue and service center). In addition, network throughput, mean queue length for any server, and mean response time (wait time and service time) for any server can be found by a variety of methods.

In a network model, a server typically has associated with it a service time distribution, from which customer service times are drawn. Upon arrival at a server, a customer receives service, the duration of which is determined by the service time distribution.

We will now turn our attention to some of the more well-known queuing systems, the notation used to represent them, the performance quantities of interest, and the methods for calculating them. We have already introduced many notations for the quantities of interest for random variables and stochastic processes. Figure 7.3 reviews these and adds a host of others that will be useful for the analysis of queuing systems. The following text briefly discusses the more important parameters.

The arrival rate for a queuing system defines the stream of arrivals into a queue from some outside source. This rate is defined as an average rate, which is derived from an arrival process. The average interarrival time for a given arrival process is denoted as:

$$E[\tau] = 1/\lambda \tag{7.1}$$

The service rate parameter is defined in a way that is similar to the arrival rate. This rate is also an average rate, which defines how many customers are processed per unit time when the server is busy. The service rate can be cast in terms of the service time random variable as:

$$\mu = 1/E[s] \tag{7.2}$$

Often, we wish to know the probability that the system will contain exactly $n$ customers at steady state. Accounting for all of the probabilities for $n$ ranging from zero to infinity defines the probability distribution for the number of customers in the system.

**Figure 7.3**
*Stochastic processes
and random
variable notation.*

| | |
|---|---|
| $\lambda$ | Arrival rate at entrance to a queue |
| $\mu$ | Service rate (average) of a server |
| $P_n$ | Probability that there are $n$ customers in the system at steady state |
| C | Number of identical servers in the queuing system |
| N | Random variable for the number of customers at steady state |
| L | $E[N]$, expected number of customers in the system at steady state |
| $W_q$ | Random variable for customer waiting time in a queue |
| S | Random variable for customer service time |
| $N_q$ | Random variable for the number of customers in a queue at steady state |
| $L_q$ | $E[N_q]$, expected number of customers in a queue at steady state |
| $N_s$ | Random variable for the number of customers at a server at steady state |
| W | $W_q+S$, random variable for the total time in a system |

The number of identical servers in a system indicates that a customer leaving a queue may proceed to one of $C$ servers as soon as one becomes nonbusy (free).

Of interest for any queuing system is the average number of customers ($N$) in the system at steady state. This value can be thought of as the sum of all customers in queues ($N_q$) and at servers ($N_s$):

$$N = N_q + N_s$$
$$L = E[N] = E[N_q] + E[N_s]$$

(7.3)

The total time a customer spends in the system can also be thought of as the sum of wait time in the queues ($q_t$) and time at the servers ($s_t$). The total time, and expected total time at steady state, therefore, are given as:

$$W = W_q + S$$
$$E[W] = E[W_q] + E[S]$$

(7.4)

**Figure 7.4**
*Kendall notation.*

A/B/c/K/m/Z

where

| | |
|---|---|
| A | arrival process definition |
| B | service time distribution |
| c | number of identical servers |
| K | maximum number of customers allowed in the system (default = $\infty$) |
| m | number of customers allowed to arrive before the arrival process stops (default = $\infty$) |
| Z | discipline used to order customers in the queue (default = FIFO) |

**Figure 7.5**
*Kendall notation
symbol definitions.*

D   deterministic service time or arrival rate

G   general service time or arrival rate

M   Markovian (exponential) service time or arrival rate

In addition to the notation described previously for the quantities associated with queuing systems, it is also useful to introduce a notation for the parameters of a queuing system. The notation we will use here is known as the Kendall notation, illustrated in Figure 7.4.

The symbols used in a Kendall notation description also have some standard definitions. Figure 7.5 shows the more common designators for the $A$ and $B$ fields of the notation.

The service discipline used to order customers in the queue can be any of a variety of types, such as first-in first-out (FIFO), last in first out (LIFO), priority ordered, random ordered, and others. Next, we will examine several queuing systems and give expressions for the more important performance quantities.

### 7.1.1   The M/M/1 queuing system

The M/M/1 queuing system is characterized by a Poisson arrival process and exponential service time distributions, with one server, and a FIFO queue ordering discipline. The system, shown in Figure 7.6, may represent an input buffer holding incoming data bytes, with an I/O processor as the server. A few of the quantities that we will be interested in for this type of queuing system are the average queue length, the wait time for a customer in the queue, the total time a customer spends in the system, and the server utilization.

Let's look at the exponential service distribution first. It is given as:

$$S = \mu \, e^{-\mu t} \tag{7.5}$$

and is shown in Figure 7.7. In the figure, $E[S]$ is the average service time of a customer at the server. Next, let's derive the steady-state equations for the M/M/1 system.

**Figure 7.6**
*M/M/1 queuing
system model.*

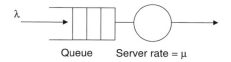

λ

Queue          Server rate = μ

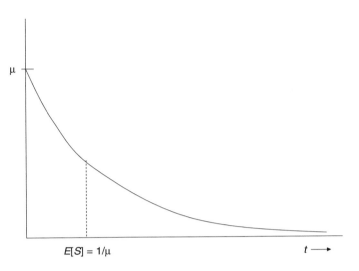

**Figure 7.7**
*Exponential service distribution.*

The M/M/1 system is a birth-death process, as discussed in Chapter 6. Let us assume that:

$$P_n(t) = \text{probablility that } n \text{ customers are in the system at time } t \quad (7.6)$$

From earlier discussions about birth-death processes, we know that:

$$\begin{aligned} P_n(t+h) &= P_n(t)\left[1 - \lambda_n h - \mu_n h\right] \\ &\quad + P_{n-1}(t)\lambda_{n-1}h + P_{n+1}(t)\mu_{n+1}h + o(h) \end{aligned} \quad (7.7)$$

and

$$P_0(t+h) = P_0(t) - P_0(t)\lambda_0 h + P_1(t)\mu_1 h + o(h) \quad (7.8)$$

Following the same reasoning for deriving the steady-state probabilities as we did for the general birth-death process, we obtain the steady-state equations for the M/M/1 system:

$$\lambda P_0 = \mu P_1 \quad (7.9)$$

$$(\lambda + \mu)P_n = \lambda P_{n-1} + \mu P_{n+1} \quad \text{for } n > 0 \quad (7.10)$$

Now, if we let $u$ denote the average server utilization, we define this quantity as the mean service time of a single customer divided by the mean interarrival time (see equations [7.1] and [7.2]), then:

$$u = (1/\mu)/(1/\lambda) = \lambda/\mu \quad (7.11)$$

Solving the steady-state equations (7.9) and (7.10), we obtain:

$$P_1 = \frac{\lambda}{\mu} P_0 \qquad \qquad \text{for } n = 0 \qquad \qquad (7.12)$$

Similarly, for n = 1

$$
\begin{aligned}
(\lambda + \mu) P_1 &= \lambda P_0 + \mu P_2 \\
\mu P_2 &= (\lambda + \mu) P_0 - \lambda P_0 \\
P_2 &= (1 + \lambda/\mu) P_1 - (\lambda/\mu) P_0 \\
P_2 &= (1 + \lambda/\mu)(\lambda/\mu) P_0 - (\lambda/\mu) P_0 \\
P_2 &= (\lambda/\mu)^2 P_0 \qquad \qquad \text{for } n = 1
\end{aligned}
\qquad (7.13)
$$

Similarly:

$$
\begin{aligned}
P_3 &= (\lambda/\mu)^3 P_0 \\
P_n &= (\lambda/\mu)^n P_0 \qquad \qquad \text{for } n > 0 \\
P_n &= \mu^n P_0 \qquad \qquad \text{for } n > 0
\end{aligned}
\qquad (7.14)
$$

We assume here that $u$ is less than 1 so that we have a finite queue length. Now, we know that:

$$\sum_{n=0}^{\infty} P_n = 1$$

and

$$\sum_{n=0}^{\infty} P_n = P_0 \sum_{n=0}^{\infty} u^n = 1 \qquad \qquad (7.15)$$

so:

$$P_0 = 1 \bigg/ \left( \sum_{n=0}^{\infty} u^n \right)$$

The right-hand side of equation (7.15) is recognized as a geometric progression that has the following solution:

$$
\begin{aligned}
P_0 &= \frac{1}{1/(1-\mu)} \\
P_0 &= 1 - u = 1 - (\lambda/\mu)
\end{aligned}
\qquad (7.16)
$$

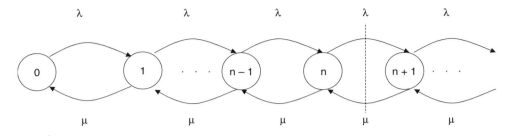

**Figure 7.8**    *M/M/1 system state transition diagram.*

Combining equations (7.14) and (7.16), we arrive at the steady-state probability that there are $n$ customers in an M/M/1 system:

$$P_n = \left(1 - (\lambda/\mu)\right)(\lambda/\mu)^n \tag{7.17}$$

Figure 7.8 shows the state transition diagram for the M/M/1 queuing system.

Now let's look at the average number of customers in the system at steady state. This is given as the expected value of $N$, which can be found by:

$$
\begin{aligned}
E[N] &= \sum_{n=0}^{\infty} n P_n \\
&= \sum_{n=0}^{\infty} n\left(1 - (\lambda/\mu)\right)(\lambda/\mu)^n \\
&= \left(1 - \lambda/\mu\right)\sum_{n=0}^{\infty} n(\lambda/\mu)^n \\
&= \left(1 - (\lambda/\mu)\right)\left((\lambda/\mu) + 2(\lambda/\mu)^2 + 3(\lambda/\mu)^3 + \ldots\right) \\
&= \left(1 - (\lambda/\mu)\right)(\lambda/\mu)\left(1 + 2(\lambda/\mu)^1 + 3(\lambda/\mu)^2 + \ldots\right) \\
&= \left(1 - (\lambda/\mu)\right)(\lambda/\mu)\sum_{n=1}^{\infty} n(\lambda/\mu)^{n-1} \\
&= \frac{\left(1 - (\lambda/\mu)\right)(\lambda/\mu)}{\left(1 - (\lambda/\mu)\right)^2} \\
E[N] &= \frac{\lambda/\mu}{1 - (\lambda/\mu)}
\end{aligned}
\tag{7.18}
$$

The average amount of time that a customer must wait in the queue, assuming that other customers are already in the queue, is given as the number of customers ahead divided by the average service time of the server:

$$E\left[W_q \mid n = i\right] = i/\mu \qquad (7.19)$$

The expected wait time in the queue, then, is a function of the average wait time and the steady-state probability of having $i$ customers in the system:

$$
\begin{aligned}
E\left[W_q\right] &= \sum_{i=1}^{\infty}(i/\mu)P_i \\
&= (1/\mu)E[N] \\
E\left[W_q\right] &= \frac{(\lambda/\mu^2)}{1-(\lambda/\mu)}
\end{aligned}
\qquad (7.20)
$$

Combining the queue waiting time (equation [7.20]) and the expected service time $E[s]$ (equation [7.2]) yields the total customer time in the system, called the expected wait time:

$$
\begin{aligned}
E[W] &= E\left[W_q\right] + E[S] \\
&= \frac{(\lambda/\mu^2)}{1-(\lambda/\mu)} + \frac{1}{\mu} \\
&= \frac{1}{\mu}\left(\frac{(\lambda/\mu)}{1-(\lambda/\mu)} + 1\right) \\
&= \frac{1}{\mu}\left(\frac{1}{1-\lambda/\mu}\right) \\
E[W] &= 1/(\mu - \lambda)
\end{aligned}
\qquad (7.21)
$$

If we rewrite equation (7.18) as:

$$E[N] = \lambda/(\mu - \lambda) \qquad (7.22)$$

using equation (7.21), we obtain Little's result:

$$E[N] = \lambda E[W] \qquad (7.23)$$

Little's result holds in general for any queuing system in steady state that conforms to the flow balance assumption discussed earlier. As such, it gives us an important relationship for the effect of arrival rate and queue length on total customer wait time. A related result, also attributed to Little, states the equivalent for queue length and queue waiting time and also holds for queuing systems in steady state:

$$E\left[N_q\right] = \lambda E\left[W_q\right] \tag{7.24}$$

This second version of Little's result says that the expected queue length can be found directly from the arrival rate times the expected queue wait time.

The total waiting time in the system, then, can be found by using Little's result or by summing the queue wait time and the expected service time.

Server utilization is a useful quantity for determining how many equivalent servers must be provided to service a given arrival process. The method is straightforward and involves solving an M/M/1 queuing system using the methods indicated previously. Suppose, for instance, that we have an M/M/1 system with an arrival rate of six customers per minute and a service time of ten seconds. Then the server utilization, as given by equation (7.11), is 1. This means that the server can be expected to be busy 100 percent of the time, but that it can, in fact, process enough customers so that infinite queue buildup is prevented. Suppose now that the arrival rate increases to 60 customers per minute so that the server utilization becomes 10, an overload situation. If we speed up the server by 10, however, or provide ten servers of the original speed, the utilization would again be 1. In general, then, if the utilization is less than 1, the server can keep up with the flow of customers and an infinite queue will not result. If, however, the utilization is greater than 1, the utilization, rounded up to the next largest integer, gives an indication of the number of identical servers that is necessary to keep up with the customer flow.

A final interesting property of the M/M/1 queuing system is the fact that the queue waiting time and total waiting time both have exponential distributions. For instance, the queue wait time can be found as follows:

$$P\left[0 < W_q \le t\right] = \sum_{n=1}^{\infty} P_n \int_0^t f_{W_q|n}\left(X|n\right) dx \tag{7.25}$$

From equation (7.14) and the distribution (Poisson), we get:

$$P\left[0 < W_q \le t\right] = \sum_{n=1}^{\infty} (\lambda/\mu)^n \left(1 - (\lambda/\mu)\right) \int_0^t \frac{\mu^n x^{n-1}}{(n-1)!} e^{-\mu x} dx$$

$$= \int_0^t \lambda e^{-\mu x} \left(1 - (\lambda/\mu)\right) \sum_{n=1}^{\infty} \frac{(\lambda x)^{n-1}}{(n-1)!} dx$$

$$= \int_0^t \lambda e^{-\mu x} \left(1 - (\lambda/\mu)\right) e^{\lambda x} dx \qquad (7.26)$$

$$= \lambda/\mu \int_0^t (\mu - \lambda) e^{-(\mu-\lambda)x} dx$$

$$= \lambda/\mu \left[1 - e^{-t(\mu-\lambda)}\right]$$

From equation (7.21), we substitute to get:

$$P\left[0 < W_q \le t\right] = \lambda/\mu \left[1 - e^{-t/E[W]}\right] \qquad (7.27)$$

Including $P[W_q = 0]$:

$$P\left[W_q \le t\right] = P_0 + \lambda/\mu \left[1 - e^{-t/E[W]}\right] \qquad (7.28)$$

By substituting $W_q[0] = 1 - \dfrac{\lambda}{\mu}$ :

$$P\left[W_q \le t\right] = 1 - \lambda/\mu \left[e^{-t/E[W]}\right] \qquad (7.29)$$

From these distributions, we can find the percentiles for the expected wait time for $r$ percent of the total number of customers. The percentile of any random variable is defined as:

$$P\left[x \le \pi(r)\right] = r/100 \qquad (7.30)$$

In the case of queue wait time, for example, if we wish to find the wait time that 90 percent of the customers in the system will not exceed, we have:

$$1 - e^{-\pi(90)/E[W]} = 0.9$$

$$0.1 = e^{-\pi(90)/E[W]}$$

$$\ln(0.1) = \frac{-\pi/(90)}{E[W]}$$

$$\pi(90) = 2.3 E[W]$$

$$(7.31)$$

## 7.1.2   The M/M/I/K system

An interesting and realistic variation on the basic M/M/1 system is a system with a finite queue size. In this system, once the queue is full, new arrivals are lost and are never provided service. This is quite realistic, for example, in an input system with finite input buffer space and no flow-control protocol. The birth-death state transition diagram for the M/M/1/K system is shown in Figure 7.9.

As for the M/M/1 system, we have:

$$P_n = (\lambda/\mu)^n P_0 \qquad \text{for } n \geq n \geq 0 \tag{7.32}$$

Using the law of total probability, we also have:

$$\sum_{i=0}^{K} P_1 = 1$$

$$\sum_{i=0}^{K} (\lambda/\mu)^i P_0 = 1 \tag{7.33}$$

$$P_0 \sum_{i=0}^{K} (\lambda/\mu)^i = 1$$

The summation is a geometric series, which yields:

$$P_0 \frac{1-(\lambda/\mu)^{K+1}}{1-(\lambda/\mu)} = 1 \quad \text{if } \lambda \neq \mu$$

so:

$$P_0 = \frac{1-(\lambda/\mu)}{1-(\lambda/\mu)^{K+1}} \tag{7.34}$$

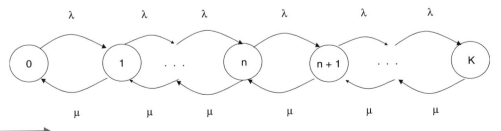

**Figure 7.9**   *State diagram for the M/M/1/K system.*

Substituting into equation (7.32) yields:

$$P_n = \frac{1-(\lambda/\mu)}{1-(\lambda/\mu)^{K+1}}\left(\frac{\lambda}{\mu}\right)^n \text{ for } K \geq n \geq 0 \tag{7.35}$$

If the arrival rate is equal to the service rate, we have:

$$P_0 \sum_{i=1}^{K}(\lambda/\mu)^i = 1 \qquad\qquad \text{for } \lambda = \mu$$
$$P_0 = 1/(K+1) \qquad\qquad \text{for } \lambda = \mu \tag{7.36}$$

and

$$P_n = 1/(K+1) \qquad\qquad \text{for } K \geq n \geq 0 \text{ and } \lambda = \mu \tag{7.37}$$

The expected number of customers in the system, for a system with nonequal arrival and service rates, is found as:

$$E[N] = \sum_{i=0}^{K} iP_i$$
$$= \sum_{i=0}^{K} i\left[\frac{1-(\lambda/\mu)}{1-(\lambda/\mu)^{K+1}}\right]\left(\frac{\lambda}{\mu}\right)^i \tag{7.38}$$
$$E[N] = \frac{1-(\lambda/\mu)}{1-(\lambda/\mu)^{K+1}}\sum_{i=0}^{K} i\left(\frac{\lambda}{\mu}\right)^i$$

After some algebra and simplification of the summation, we get:

$$E[N] = \frac{(\lambda/\mu)}{1-(\lambda/\mu)} - \frac{(K+1)(\lambda/\mu)^{K+1}}{1-(\lambda/\mu)^{K+1}} \text{ for } \lambda \neq \mu \tag{7.39}$$

We can see that, for very large values of $K$, the second term approximates zero and we get the same expression as for the M/M/1 system.

For the case where the arrival and service rates are equal:

$$E[N] = \sum_{i=0}^{K} iP_i$$

$$E[N] = \frac{1}{K+1} \sum_{i=0}^{K} i \qquad (7.40)$$

$$E[N] = K/2 \qquad (\text{for } \lambda = \mu)$$

To compute the wait time distribution for the M/M/1/K system, we must compute the probability for the number of customers in the queue when a customer arrives, given that the customer is admitted to the system. This is given as:

$$P(n \text{ customers in system} | N < K) = P_n/(1 - P_k) \qquad (7.41)$$

From this, we can arrive at the wait time distribution:

$$P(w \le t) = 1 - \sum_{N=0}^{K-1} P_n/(1 - P_K) \sum_{K=0}^{N} e^{-\mu t} \frac{(\mu t)^K}{K!} \qquad (7.42)$$

This quantity can be found in the same way as the statistic for the M/M/1 system.

### 7.1.3   The M/M/C system

The M/M/C system, shown in Figure 7.10, consists of a single waiting line that feeds $C$ identical servers. The arrival process is considered to be Poisson, and the servers have exponential service times. The state transition diagram for an M/M/C system is shown in Figure 7.11. Now let's write some of the flow balance equations for the state transition diagram.

**Figure 7.10**
*An M/M/C system,*
*for C = 3.*

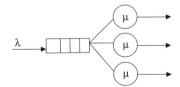

$$P_1 = \frac{\lambda}{\mu} P_0$$

$$P_2 = \frac{\lambda^2}{2\mu^2} P_0$$

$$P_3 = \frac{\lambda^3}{6\mu^3} P_0$$

$$\vdots$$

$$P_C = \frac{\lambda^C}{C!\mu^C} P_0$$

$$P_{C+1} = \frac{\lambda^{C+1}}{CC!\mu^{C+1}} P_0$$

$$\vdots$$

$$P_N = \frac{\lambda^N}{C^{N-C}C!\mu^N} P_0$$

(7.43)

so that:

$$P_N = \begin{cases} \dfrac{\lambda^N p_0}{N!\mu^N} & \text{for } N \leq C \\[2ex] \dfrac{\lambda^N p_0}{C^{N-C}C!\mu^N} & \text{for } N > C \end{cases}$$

**Figure 7.11**
*State transition diagram for an M/M/C system, for C = 3.*

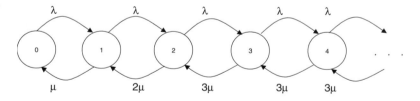

To find the probability of no customers in the system, we sum all probabilities:

$$1 = P_0 \begin{bmatrix} 1 + \lambda/\mu + (\lambda/\mu)^2/2 + \ldots + (\lambda/\mu)^C/C! + \\ (\lambda/\mu)^{C+1}/CC! + \ldots + (\lambda/\mu)^N/C^{N-C}C! + \ldots \end{bmatrix}$$

$$1 = P_0 \left( \sum_{i=1}^{C} (\lambda/\mu)^i / i! + \sum_{i=C}^{\infty} \left( \frac{\lambda}{\mu} \right)^i \Big/ \left( C^{i-C}C! \right) \right) \qquad (7.44)$$

$$1 = P_0 \left( \sum_{i=1}^{C} (\lambda/\mu)^i / i! + (\lambda/\mu)^C / C! \left( 1 - (\lambda/C\mu) \right) \right)$$

The expected queue length can be found by subtracting the number of customers in service from the expected number of customers in the system:

$$E\left[ N_q \right] = \sum_{N=C}^{\infty} (N - C) P_N$$

$$E\left[ N_q \right] = \frac{P_0 (\lambda/\mu)^C (\lambda/C\mu)}{C! \left( 1 - (\lambda/C\mu) \right)^2} \qquad (7.45)$$

Using Little's result, we can compute the queue wait time:

$$W_q = E\left[ N_q \right] / \lambda \qquad (7.46)$$

The total wait time is:

$$w = W_q + E[s]$$

$$w = \left( E\left[ N_q \right] / \lambda \right) + (1/\mu) \qquad (7.47)$$

The total number of customers in the system is:

$$E[N] = \lambda w$$

$$E[N] = E\left[ N_q \right] + (\lambda/\mu) \qquad (7.48)$$

For some multiple server systems, no queue is provided for customers to wait for service. In this case, a customer who arrives when all servers are busy is turned away, perhaps to try again later. The state transition diagram is shown in Figure 7.12. This system is often referred to as the M/M/C loss system, because customers who arrive when all servers are busy are lost.

**Figure 7.12**
*M/M/C loss system.*

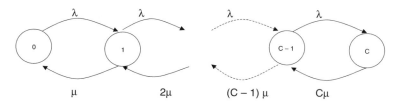

Writing the flow balance equations, we obtain the steady-state probabilities as we did for the M/M/C system:

$$P_N = (\lambda/\mu)^N / N! = 1 + (\lambda/\mu) + (\lambda/\mu)^2 / 2! + \ldots (\lambda/\mu)^C / C! \qquad (7.49)$$

The probability that a customer will be turned away, then, can be found from the previous expression with $N = C$. Since there is no queue, the queue length and queue waiting time are zero, and the total wait time is the expected service time.

## 7.1.4   The M/G/1 system

The queuing systems that we have discussed so far have all had the Markov property for arrival and service processes, making it possible to model the system as a birth-death process and to write the flow balance equations by inspection. Next, we will look at a system in which the service time does not have the Markov property. In the M/G/1 system, each customer has different and independent service times. Because service times are not guaranteed to be Markovian, the system is not representative of a Markov chain and we must resort to other methods to derive meaningful statistics. One approach commonly taken is to look at the process that describes jobs leaving the system, which is a stochastic process that also happens to be a Markov chain. It has been shown [3] that, in the limit, the distribution for the number of jobs in the system at any point in time and the number of jobs in the system observed when a customer departs from the system, are identical.

Summarizing the procedure, then, we can analyze certain aspects of the system that are described by a non-Markovian process by observing a Markovian subportion of the system (in this case the departure process) and extrapolating the results back to the original system. This type of analysis relies on what is known as an embedded Markov chain. The derivation of the statistics for the M/G/1 system is beyond the scope of this book.

The general M/G/1 system is useful in many situations, because we can characterize a known service process in terms of its moments and then evaluate its performance in the presence of a random arrival process.

### 7.1.5  The G/M/I system

In the previous section, we discussed the situation in which a system had a non-Markovian service process. Next, we will consider the case in which the service time is random and the arrival process is non-Markovian. We will assume that the interarrival times are independent and identically distributed. Again, we can find an embedded Markov chain in this system whose behavior is essentially equivalent to the system's behavior at steady state. In this case, the random variable defining the number of customers in the system, at precisely the time when another arrival occurs, forms a process that is a Markov chain. As with the other systems that we have discussed, the statistics of interest use the probability of having an empty system in calculating their values.

## 7.2  Networks of queues

Until now, we have been considering queuing systems that contain only one station. That is, the systems that we have looked at have a single queue and a single server or set of servers, and customers arrive only at that queue and depart only following service. This situation is fine for relatively simple systems that are either not connected to other systems or that can be considered isolated from other, connected systems. Now, we will consider the case in which several queuing systems are interconnected and attempt to find meaningful statistics on such a system's behavior.

Referring to section 7.1, we recall that a network of queues results from connecting the departure stream of one queuing system to the queue input of another, for an arbitrary number of queuing systems connected in an arbitrary way. Also, we discussed the concept of open and closed networks in which an open network was defined as one in which arrivals from, and departures to, the outside world are permitted, and a closed network is one in which they are not permitted. We will discuss general classes of both types here.

### 7.2.1  Closed networks

Consider the closed three-stage network of queues shown in Figure 7.13. Assume that the service time for each server is exponentially distributed and unique to that server and that the system contains two customers. We can

**Figure 7.13**
*A three-stage closed
queuing network.*

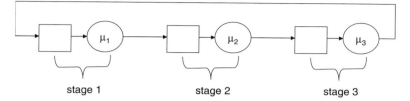

describe this system as a Markov process with each state in the process
defined as the triplet:

$$\text{State} = \{N_1, N_2, N_3\} \tag{7.50}$$

where $N_i$ is the number of customers in the $i$ queue. Also, since we have two
customers:

$$\sum_{i=1}^{3} N_i = 2 \tag{7.51}$$

The state transition diagram for the system, with the states labeled as
defined in equation (7.50), is shown in Figure 7.14. The labels on the edges
denote customer movements from stage to stage and are dependent upon
the service rate for the stage from which a customer is departing.

To find the steady-state probabilities for each state in the system, we can
write flow balance equations. As discussed earlier, the flow balance assumption states that we can represent the steady-state probabilities of a Markov
process by writing the equations that balance the flow of customers into and
out of the states in the network. For each individual state, then, we can
write a balance equation that equates flow into a state with flow out of a
state. For the states of Figure 7.14, we can write the following balance equations:

$$\pi(2,0,0)\mu_1 = \pi(1,0,1)\mu_3 \tag{7.52}$$

$$\pi(1,1,0)(\mu_1 + \mu_2) = \pi(2,0,0)\mu_1 + \pi(0,1,1)\mu_3 \tag{7.53}$$

$$\pi(0,2,0)\mu_2 = \pi(1,1,0)\mu_1 \tag{7.54}$$

$$\pi(1,0,1)(\mu_3 + \mu_1) = \pi(1,1,0)\mu_2 + \pi(0,0,2)\mu_3 \tag{7.55}$$

$$\pi(0,1,1)(\mu_2 + \mu_3) = \pi(0,2,0)\mu_2 + \pi(1,0,1)\mu_1 \tag{7.56}$$

$$\pi(0,0,2)\mu_3 = \pi(0,1,1)\mu_2 \tag{7.57}$$

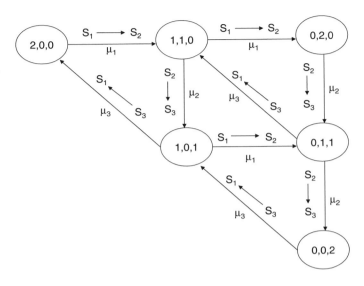

**Figure 7.14**
*State transition
rate diagram for a
simple closed
system.*

when:

$$\pi(N_1, N_2, N_3) = \text{Probability of state}\{N_1, N_2, N_3\}$$

Keeping in mind that the sum of all of the state probabilities must equal 1, this network has the solution:

$$\pi(N_1, N_2, N_3) = K\left(1/\mu_1\right)^{N_1}\left(1/\mu_2\right)^{N_2}\left(1/\mu_3\right)^{N_3} \tag{7.58}$$

where $K$ is a normalization constant to ensure that the probabilities sum to 1:

$$K = \frac{1}{\displaystyle\sum_{i=0}^{2}\sum_{j=0}^{2}\sum_{k=0}^{2}\pi(i,j,k)} \tag{7.59}$$

Now, using equations 7.52 through 7.59, and the fact that all probabilities sum to 1, we can solve the flow balance equations for the individual state probabilities. Once we have the state probabilities, we can find the expected length at any of the servers, as follows:

$$E\left[N_q\right] = \sum_{i=1}^{\#\text{ states}} iP\left[N = i \text{ at queue } k\right] \tag{7.60}$$

Because the state probabilities at the queues are not the same as for the queuing systems in isolation, we cannot find the expected wait time in a queue by simply multiplying the number of customers by the service time at that queue. Instead, we will first calculate the throughput for each queuing system and then apply Little's result using the throughput as a measure of the arrival rate at a particular queue. Therefore, the throughput at a particular queue can be found by multiplying the probability of having a customer in that queue (e.g., the server is busy) times the expected service rate:

$$\lambda_i = P(\text{server is busy})\mu \tag{7.61}$$

Now, using Little's result, we can calculate the time spent in each queue by a customer at the respective queues:

$$W_q = E[N_k]/\lambda_i \tag{7.62}$$

The total round-trip waiting time for a customer in the system can be found by summing up all of the queue waiting times. It can also be found directly by using Little's result and the average throughput for the system. Thus, for two customers, we have:

$$W_q = 2/\lambda_{\text{avg}} \tag{7.63}$$

Next, let's consider an arbitrary closed network with $M$ queues and $N$ customers. Assume that all servers have exponential service time distributions. For the sake of discussion, the network in Figure 7.15 will represent our arbitrary network. Let's define a branching probability as the probabil-

**Figure 7.15**
*Arbitrary closed system.*

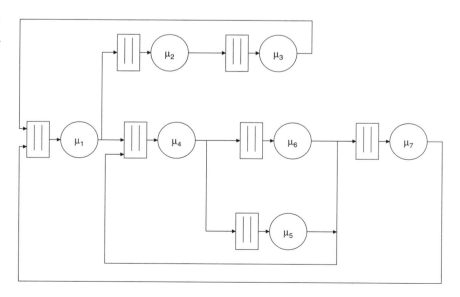

ity of having any customer follow a particular branch when arriving at a branch point. Therefore, let:

$$P_{ij} = \text{Probability that a customer leaving server } i \text{ goes to queue } j \quad (7.64)$$

For any server $i$:

$$\sum_{\text{all } j} P_{ij} = 1 \tag{7.65}$$

The conservation of flow in the system requires that:

$$\lambda_j = \sum_{i=1}^{M} \lambda_i P_{ij} \tag{7.66}$$

Define the relative throughput of a server, $i$, as:

$$B(j) = \sum_{i=1}^{M} B(i) P_{ij} \tag{7.67}$$

Since the $B$ terms are relative, we can arbitrarily set one of them equal to 1 and solve for the others. Once we have all of the terms, the steady-state probabilities are given by:

$$P(N_1, N_2, N_3, N_4, \ldots, N_M) = K \prod_{i=1}^{M} \left( \frac{B(i)}{\mu_i} \right)^{N_i} \tag{7.68}$$

Equation (7.67) can be derived by assuming the conservation of flow for a particular state and then by solving the system of equations as we did for the previous example. Let's pick a state, $S$, so that:

$$S = (k_1, k_2, k_3, \ldots, k_M) \tag{7.69}$$

and examine the effects of arrivals and departures of customers from queue $j$. Define another state, $A$, that is identical to $S$ except that it has one more customer at queue $i$ and one less customer at queue $j$ than $S$. Thus, $A$ is a neighbor state of $S$. We are postulating that the rate of entering state $S$ due to an arrival at queue $j$ is balanced by the rate of leaving state $S$ due to a departure from queue $j$. Since there may be more than one state $A$, where there is one more customer at queue $i$ and one less at $j$, we must balance all such states against state $S$. Equating the flows results in:

$$\sum_{i=1}^{M} P[A_i] \mu_i P_{ij} = P[S] \mu_j \tag{7.70}$$

From equation (7.68):

$$P[A_i] = K \prod_{j=1}^{M} \left( \frac{B(j)}{\mu_j} \right)^{N_j} \frac{B(i)}{\mu_i}$$

$$P[S] = K \prod_{j=1}^{M} \left( \frac{B(j)}{\mu_j} \right)^{N_j} \frac{B(j)}{\mu_j}$$

(7.71)

The last term in each of the previous two expressions arises from having a customer in service at the respective servers. Substituting these expressions into equation (7.70) and simplifying, we get:

$$\sum_{i=1}^{M} B(i) P_{ij} = B(j)$$

(7.72)

which is what we postulated in equation (7.67).

Now that we have equation (7.72), we can generate a set of equations that we can solve simultaneously by setting one of the $B$ terms equal to 1. In a manner similar to the previous example, we can also find the normalization constant $K$ and therefore solve equation (7.68) for the system's steady-state probabilities and also for the expected queue lengths using equation (7.60).

If we consider the closed network over a long period of time, the relative throughput terms can be thought of as indicators of the relative number of times a customer visits the associated server, also called the visit ratio. This interpretation is useful for determining which server is the most utilized, also known as bottleneck analysis. Define the relative amount of work done by a server, $i$, as:

Relative work by the server $i = B(i)/\mu_i$

(7.73)

Since this value is also the relative utilization of that server, the server with the highest such ratio is the system bottleneck.

## 7.2.2   Open networks

Next, we will discuss another class of queuing networks: those that contain sources and sinks. We will assume that customers may arrive at any queue from an outside source according to a Poisson process that is specific for that queue. We can think of these arrival processes as all originating from a single arrival process with branches, each with an associated branching probability. Figure 7.16 shows such an arrival process and a hypothetical open network with $M$ queues and associated servers.

We also assume exponential service rates for all servers in the system. In this case, the aggregate arrival rate is equivalent to the sum of all of the individual arrival rates discussed earlier. If each individual arrival rate is defined as:

$$\text{Arrival rate of queue } i = \gamma_i \qquad (7.74)$$

the aggregate rate is given as:

$$\lambda = \sum_{i=1}^{M} \gamma_i \qquad (7.75)$$

and the branching probabilities as:

$$P_{0i} = \gamma_i / \lambda \qquad (7.76)$$

Customers leaving the system also do so with the probabilities defined as:

$$P_{i0} = 1 - \sum_{j=1}^{M} P_{ij} \qquad (7.77)$$

This definition states that the probability of a job leaving the system is equal to the complement of the probability that a job will remain in the system.

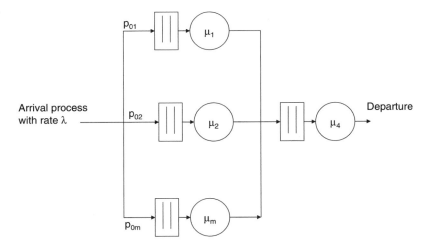

**Figure 7.16**
*Open system model.*

As with the closed network discussed earlier, we can propose a set of throughput terms, denoted $B(i)$ for each queue and server $i$. Thus:

$$B(i) = \sum_{j=0}^{M} B(j)P_{ij}$$

$$B(i) = \sum_{j=1}^{M} B(j)P_{ij} + \gamma_i \tag{7.78}$$

Since we know the throughput arriving from the outside source, we can set:

$$B(0) = \lambda \tag{7.79}$$

and solve for the remaining $B$ terms. In the case of an open network, the $B$ terms will represent actual, not relative, throughput at a server, $i$, because they are derived from the aggregate arrival rate. Because of this, we can define each server's utilization as:

$$U_i = B(i)/\mu_i \tag{7.80}$$

After solving for all of the $B(i)$ terms, the steady-state probabilities are given as:

$$P(N_1, N_2, N_3, N_4, \ldots, N_M) = K\prod_{i=1}^{M}\left(\frac{B(i)}{\mu_i}\right)^{N_i}$$

$$= K\prod_{i=1}^{M} U_i^{N_i} \tag{7.81}$$

where, again, $K$ is a normalization constant. We can sum all of the state probabilities and solve for $K$ to obtain:

$$K = \prod_{i=1}^{M}(1 - U_i) \tag{7.82}$$

Thus, the expression for the steady-state probabilities becomes:

$$P(N_1, N_2, N_3, N_4, \ldots, N_M) = \prod_{i=1}^{M}(1 - U_i)U_i^{N_i} \tag{7.83}$$

If we look at equation (7.17), we see that the expression just derived is actually the product of terms that can be obtained by treating each queue and server as an M/M/1 queue system in isolation. This result is known as Jackson's theorem, and it states that, although the arrival rate at each server in an open system may not be Poisson, we can find the probability distribution function for the number of customers in any queue, as if the arrival process were Poisson (and, thereby, use equation [7.17] for the M/M/1 system). Jackson's theorem further states that each queue system in the network behaves as an M/M/1 system, with arrival rate defined by:

$$\lambda_i = \gamma_i + \sum_{j=1}^{M} P_{ij}\lambda_i \qquad (7.84)$$

which is simply equation (7.78) recast in more familiar terms.

It is worthwhile to note that Jackson's theorem applies to open systems in which the individual queue systems are $M/M/C_i$. That is, each server may actually be comprised of a different number ($i$) of identical servers. Thus, the steady-state probabilities for each queue system in the network are also given by the equation for such a system in isolation with the arrival rate, as described in equation (7.84). The full proof of Jackson's theorem is given in [8].

# 7.3   Estimating parameters and distributions

Now that we have discussed various aspects of queuing theory, we should review some of the ways that we can parameterize the models that we choose. In this section, we will discuss various methods that can be used to determine whether a certain statistic or distribution appropriately describes an observed process. Specifically, we will cover hypothesis testing, estimators for some statistics, and goodness of fit tests. We will start with hypothesis testing in general.

A hypothesis test is a technique used to determine whether or not to believe a certain statement about a real-world phenomenon and to give some measure as to what degree to believe the statement. A hypothesis is usually stated in two parts: the first concerning the statistic or characteristic that we are hypothesizing about and the second concerning the value that is postulated for the statistic. For example, we may hypothesize that the mean value of an observed process is less than 10 or that the observed process is Gaussian. The positive statement of a hypothesis is usually called the null hypothesis and is denoted as $H0$. Associated with the null hypothesis is an alternative, denoted $H1$. The idea here is to have the two hypotheses complement each other so that only one will be selected as probable. The two hypotheses, $H0$ and $H1$, form the basis for the hypothesis test methodology outlined in the following paragraph.

A hypothesis test is usually performed in four general steps, which lead to the acceptance or rejection of the initial hypothesis. The first step is to formulate the null hypothesis $H0$ and the alternative hypothesis $H1$. Next, decide upon a statistic to test against. The statistic is typically the sample mean or variance. Third, a set of outcomes for the test statistic is chosen so that the outcome of the test statistic will fall within the set with a specific probability, given that $H0$ is true. That is, if $H0$ is true, we say that the value of the test statistic will fall within the set selected (sometimes called the critical region) with probability $P$ (also called the test's level of significance). The idea is to select a critical region so that the probability of the test statistic value falling within the region is small, typically between 0.01 and 0.05. An occurrence of this event, then, indicates that the hypothesis $H0$ is not a good choice and should be rejected. Conversely, we could select a large probability, say 0.9, in which case the occurrence of the event indicates that the null hypothesis should be accepted. The final step in the process is to collect some sample data and to calculate the test statistic.

The next immediate problem for performing a hypothesis test is to define the expressions that describe the sample statistics we are interested in. These are commonly referred to as estimators, because they estimate the statistic that could be derived from a distribution that exactly models the real process. The most commonly used estimators are the sample mean and the sample variance.

In order to calculate the sample statistics, we must first obtain a random sample from the experimental population. A random sample is defined here as a sequence of observations of the real-world process, where each value observed has an equal probability of being selected and where each observation is independent of the others in the sample. Thus, a random sample is a sequence of random variables that are independent and identically distributed.

For a random sample of size $n$, where $n$ is the number of samples obtained, the sample mean is defined as:

$$\overline{X} = \frac{1}{n}\sum_{i=1}^{n} X_i \tag{7.85}$$

The sample variance is defined as:

$$S^2 = \frac{1}{n-1}\sum_{i=1}^{n}\left(X_i - \bar{X}\right)^2 \qquad\qquad (7.86)$$

The sample standard deviation is defined as it was for the standard deviation of a distribution and is repeated here as:

$$S = \sqrt{S^2} \qquad\qquad (7.87)$$

In the above three expressions, the random variable $X_i$ represents the $i$th observation in the random sample.

Now that we can calculate the statistics for a random sample of some phenomenon, how can we relate these estimates to the actual statistics of the underlying process? For this, we use a theorem known as the sampling theorem. It states that, for a random sample, as previously described, with a finite mean, the sample mean and expected value are equivalent and the sample variance and the variance are also equivalent. That is, the sample statistics are said to be consistent, unbiased estimators. The sampling theorem also states several other important relations, including the following expression relating the variance of the sample mean and the variance of the random variable describing the process. This expression:

$$\mathrm{Var}\left[\bar{X}\right] = \mathrm{Var}\left[X\right]/n \qquad\qquad (7.88)$$

states that as the sample size gets larger, the variance of the sample mean gets smaller, indicating that it is closer to the true mean of $X$.

These estimates lead to still another question: Given that we know (or think that we know) the type of distribution that our random sample comes from, how do we estimate the parameters of such a distribution from the random sample data? There are two widely used methods for doing just this: the method of moments and the method of maximum likelihood estimation.

The method of moments is useful when we think we know the distribution of the sample but do not know what the distribution parameters are. Suppose the distribution whose parameters we wish to estimate has $n$ parameters. In this method, we first find the first $n$ distribution moments, as described in Chapter 5. Next, we calculate the first $n$ sample moments and equate the results to the moments found earlier. From this we get $n$ equations in $n$ unknowns, which can then be solved simultaneously for the desired parameters. We derive the $k$th sample moment for a sample size of $m$ samples as:

$$M_k = \frac{1}{n}\sum_{i=1}^{n} X_i^k \tag{7.89}$$

where $X_i$ is the $i$ sample point in the random sample.

In maximum likelihood estimation, we try to pick the distribution parameters that maximize the probability of yielding the observed values in the random sample. To do this, we first form what is called the likelihood function. This consists of the values of the assumed probability distribution function at the points observed in the random sample. This function, for a continuous random variable whose distribution has only one parameter, is:

$$L(\theta) = f(x_1) f(x_2) f(x_3) \ldots f(x_m) \tag{7.90}$$

For a random variable whose distribution has $n$ parameters, we will have $n$ equations, similar to equation (7.90). We then find the maximum of each equation with respect to each parameter. Finally, the set of $n$ equations in $n$ unknowns can be solved for the necessary parameters.

Now that we have outlined several methods for estimating the statistics of a distribution that describes the real-world process, we turn our attention to the reliability of our estimates. One measure of this reliability is called the confidence interval. A confidence interval is defined as a range of values, centered at the estimate of the statistic of interest, where the actual value of the statistic will fall within a fixed probability. For example, a 90-percent confidence interval for the mean of a particular random variable based upon a given sample may be defined as the range of values within a distance, $r$, of the estimated mean. In this case, $r$ is chosen so that the fraction of times that an actual mean lands within the interval is 90 percent. The general procedure for defining a confidence interval requires the construction of a known distribution, say $C$, from the estimates of the statistic being estimated. Next, we pick an interval so that:

$$P(a < C < b) = z \tag{7.91}$$

where $z$ is the desired confidence level. Finally, we evaluate $C$ using the value $X_i$ so that the relationship:

$$a < C(X_i) < b \tag{7.92}$$

is maintained. We can alternatively solve $C$ for the points $X_a$ and $X_b$, where $C(X_a) = a$ and $C(X_b) = b$. These are the end points of the 100-percent confidence interval.

This procedure assumes that we know the distribution of $C$ before we find the confidence interval. If this is not the case, and the sample size is large, we can assume that the sample distribution is normal and can obtain a reliable confidence interval for the value of the mean. In this case, we first form the statistic:

$$T = (\bar{X} - \mu)/(\sigma\sqrt{n}) \tag{7.93}$$

Since $X$ is assumed normal, $T$ in this case is also normal with a mean of 0 and a standard deviation of 1. Again, we define a percent confidence interval and determine $a$ and $b$ so that:

$$P(a < T < b) = z \tag{7.94}$$

The desired confidence interval for the mean is then given by:

$$(\bar{X} - b)\sigma/\sqrt{n} < \mu < (\bar{X} + a)\sigma/\sqrt{n} \tag{7.95}$$

Confidence intervals for the variance when the population distribution is unknown can be found using the previously described method, although the results will be poor if the actual population distribution is far from normal.

Now that we have explored several techniques for estimating the parameters of distributions, we will look at some methods for finding a distribution that fits the sampled data. Typically, we will have found the sample mean and standard deviation and now want to find a random variable that adequately represents the sample population. The tests employed here are usually called goodness of fit tests. We will discuss two tests, the chi-square test and the Kolmogorov-Smirnov test. These tests fall under the general heading of hypothesis testing, and, therefore, we use the same hypothesis-forming techniques described earlier. In both tests, we start with a null hypothesis that the population has a certain distribution, and then we obtain a statistic that indicates whether we should accept the null hypothesis.

In the chi-square test, we determine whether the distribution of the null hypothesis appropriately fits the population by comparing the categories of the collected sample value to what can be generated by the assumed distribution. The premise is that we can find $k$ bins, $B_1, \ldots, B_k$, so that each value in the random sample falls into one, and only one, bin. After finding an appropriate set of bins, we partition the samples into them and record the number of samples that land in each. Next, we take a corresponding number of samples from the hypothesized population distribution and allocate them to the same bins. If any of the second set of samples (those taken from the distribution) fail to fall in only one bin, we have not selected an appropriate set of bins and must choose another set. For whatever type of distribution that we are testing against, the appropriate distribution parameters can be found using one of the estimation techniques described earlier. Continuing with the test, we now calculate the following statistic:

$$C = \sum_{i=1}^{K} \frac{\left(NS_i - ND_i\right)^2}{ND_i} \tag{7.96}$$

where $NS_i$ denotes the number of elements in bin $i$ due to the random sample, and $ND_i$ is the number in bin $i$ due to the hypothesized distribution. The basis of this test is that the statistic of equation (7.96) has a chi-square distribution. The degree of freedom of the chi-square distribution is defined as one less than the number of sample bins minus the number of parameters in the hypothesized distribution:

$$M = k - 1 - \text{number of parameters} \tag{7.97}$$

Next, we decide on the level of significance that we wish to test for. Using the following expression, we can calculate the probability density function for a chi-square distribution with $n$ degrees of freedom:

$$f_x(x) = \begin{cases} \left(1/\left((n/2)-1\right)!\right)\left(2^{-n/2}\right)\left(x^{(n/2)-1}\right)\left(e^{-(x/2)}\right) & \text{for } x > 0 \\ 0 & \text{otherwise} \end{cases} \tag{7.98}$$

The final step is to find the value of $X$ for which the integral with respect to $x$ of equation (7.98), evaluated from $x$ to infinity, is equal to the desired level of significance. The final test states that if the value of $x$ just found is greater or equal to the chi-square statistic calculated in equation (7.96), the assumed distribution is not a good fit at the desired level of significance. That is, we reject the null hypothesis if:

$$X \geq C \tag{7.99}$$

An alternative approach for the chi-square test is to form the value $C - \varepsilon$, where $\varepsilon$ is some small value. We then use the result to find the probability that $x$ is greater than $C - \varepsilon$. The resultant probability gives us an indication as to the approximate level or significance that we may accept the null hypothesis. Several references give tables for the critical values of the chi-square distribution. These tables may be used in place of calculating the distribution values.

Another so-called goodness of fit test is the Kolmogorov-Smirnov test. The test is based upon the magnitude ordering of the sample, the calculation of the maximum difference between the sample points and the assumed distribution, and a determination of the level of fit of the assumed distribution. A formal description of this test appears in a number of statistics texts. Here we will describe a more intuitive approach, which is somewhat easier to experiment with.

As mentioned earlier, the first step of this test is to arrange the sample values in ascending order according to magnitude. For each point $x_i$ in the arranged sample, we find the fraction, $f_i$, of the number of total samples that is less in magnitude than the given value. Next, for the assumed distribution, we find the value, $K_i$, that will yield the same fraction, $f_i$, for a given number of samples. Finally, we plot $K_i$ versus $x_i$ for all $i$. The resulting plot will indicate a good fit if the data form approximately a straight line with a slope of unity. If the fit is a straight line with a slope other than unity, the assumed distribution parameters may be tuned to achieve the desired results. Otherwise, we should try another assumed distribution.

# 7.4    Computational methods for queuing network solutions

In Chapters 5 and 6 and the previous sections of this chapter, we introduced probability theory and analysis techniques for performing classical queuing system analysis. Those analyses, however, tend to be complex even for simple systems. In an effort to rectify this situation, three alternative analysis methods have emerged.

The first method, from Buzen [9], gives a technique for finding the normalization constant that is required for the solution of certain product form networks. The method does not require the solution of the normalization summation described in Chapter 5. Instead, it uses an iterative solution, which is simpler to implement.

The next method, from Buzen and Denning [10], introduced a methodology for assessing the match of a given assumption for the system under analysis. In addition, they defined the performance quantities of interest in terms of their operational relationships in the system under study. For that reason, this kind of analysis is known as operational analysis.

The third analysis method, from Reiser and Lavenberg [11], attempts to simplify the analysis of queuing networks. By using the mean waiting time and mean queue size, in conjunction with Little's result, the solution of a system of queues can asymptotically approach the exact solution, with simpler computational requirements. This type of analysis is called mean value analysis.

In this section, we will discuss these methods and models. Some of the results are specific to the type of model used, while others are more general. The specific model cases, however, can be used to approximate a given system or portion of a system and to obtain an initial feeling for the system's actual behavior.

## 7.4.1   Central server model

The central server model, shown in Figure 7.17, was originally proposed as a model for jobs in a multiprogramming computer. It is a closed network and we assume that a constant $(K)$ number of jobs are always in process. In the original model, programs are serviced by the CPU (server 1) and then are routed to one of $M - 1$ I/O devices (servers 2 through $M$). After receiving I/O service, the program again queues for CPU time. If a program completes execution, it is rerouted into the CPU queue to start another job, thereby keeping the number of jobs in the system equal to $K$. This can be

**Figure 7.17**
*Central server model.*

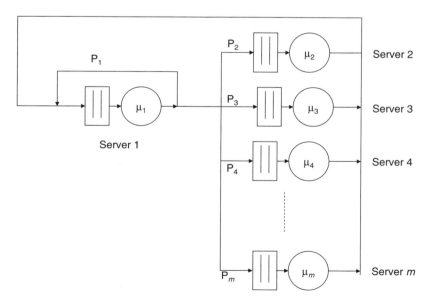

thought of as a system in which there is always a job waiting to enter the system at the CPU queue, but it will not do so until a job completes. The actual jobs in the system, therefore, may vary over time, but the number in circulation at any given time remains constant.

The central server model can be adapted to represent other systems besides a CPU and its associated I/O devices. For instance, we could choose server 1 to represent a multichannel DMA controller and servers 2 through $M$ to represent the output channels. Or, we could adjust the branching probabilities to represent a system in which the jobs remain constant and never complete (i.e., $P_1 = 0$). This could be useful for a dedicated I/O server. Alternatively, we could choose one of the servers 2 through $M$ to represent an idle period for a job or I/O channel.

Although we may be able to formulate a central server model that somewhat reflects the actual situation, the match may not be precise. The benefit of this model, however, is the computational simplicity of many of its important performance parameters. Next, we will develop the computational model for this queuing network.

In the central server model, the servers are assumed to have exponential service time distributions. As shown in Figure 7.17, the exit from the central server has several branches, each with an associated branching probability, $P_i$. There are a total of $K$ customers (jobs) in the system at any time. Let us define the state of the system:

$$S = \left( k_1, k_2, \ldots, k_M \right) \tag{7.100}$$

where $k_i$ denotes the number of customers in queue $i$. Thus:

$$\sum_{i=1}^{M} k_i = K \tag{7.101}$$

If we define $B(i)$ as the probability of going to server $i$ after service at server 1, and we let $B(1) = 1$, then:

$$B_i = P_i, \text{ for } i = 2, 3, \ldots, M \tag{7.102}$$

Using the same techniques described previously for closed queuing networks, we can obtain the state probabilities as:

$$P\left( k_1, k_2, \ldots, k_M \right) = \text{norm} \prod_{i=1}^{M} \left( \frac{P_i \mu_1}{\mu_i} \right)^{k_i} \tag{7.103}$$

This equation for the state probabilities is called product form, and it can be solved by finding the normalization constant, norm, as outlined in the earlier sections of this chapter. The described methods, however, require the solution of $M$ simultaneous equations. An alternative method with fewer computations is as follows:

Let:

$$G(k) = \sum_{\text{all states}} \frac{P(k_1, k_2 \ldots k_M)}{\text{norm}} = \frac{1}{\text{norm}} \tag{7.104}$$

$$G(k) = \sum_{\text{all states}} \prod_{i=1}^{M} \left( \frac{P_i \mu_1}{\mu_i} \right)^{k_i} \tag{7.105}$$

Let the states for the summation include all states where equation (7.101) holds. Also, we stipulate that $k_i \geq 0$. Define another function $g(k, m)$ where there are $m$ queues in the system instead of $M$. The following, then, is true:

$$g(k, m) = G(k) \tag{7.106}$$

where $k$ is the total number of customers in the system with $M$ queues. Thus, we can further define $g(k, m)$ as:

$$g(k, m) = \sum_{\text{all states}} \prod_{i=1}^{M} \left( \frac{P_i \mu_1}{\mu_i} \right)^{k_i} \tag{7.107}$$

We can break up the right-hand summation as:

$$g(k, m) = \sum_{\substack{\text{all states} \\ \text{with } k_m > 0}} \prod_{i=1}^{M} \left( \frac{P_i \mu_1}{\mu_1} \right)^{k_i} + \sum_{\substack{\text{all states} \\ \text{with } k_m = 0}} \prod_{i=1}^{M} \left( \frac{P_i \mu_1}{\mu_i} \right)^{k_i} \tag{7.108}$$

For the first summation in equation (7.108), if we always have at least one customer in queue $m$, we can think of the system as having $k - 1$ customers circulating through $m$ queues. We must also remove the product term that relates to customers in queue $m$. Similarly, in the second summation, if queue $m$ is always empty, then we can think of the system as having $m - 1$ queues and $k$ customers. Thus, equation (7.108) becomes:

$$g(k,m) = \frac{P_m \mu_1}{\mu_m} \sum_{\substack{\text{all states} \\ \text{with } k_m > 0}} \prod_{i=1}^{M} \left( \frac{P_i \mu_1}{\mu_i} \right)^{k_i} + \sum_{\substack{\text{all states with} \\ m\text{-1 queues}}} \prod_{i=1}^{M} \left( \frac{P_i \mu_1}{\mu_i} \right)^{k_i} \qquad (7.109)$$

The two summations can be rewritten, using equations (7.105) and (7.106), as:

$$g(k,m) = \frac{P_m \mu_1}{\mu_m} g(k-1,m) + g(k,m-1) \qquad (7.110)$$

For $k = 0$, and for $m = 1$, equation (7.110) becomes:

$$g(0,m) = 1 \qquad \text{for } m = 1, 2, \ldots, M \qquad (7.111)$$

$$g(k,1) = 1 \qquad \text{for } k = 0, 1, \ldots, K \qquad (7.112)$$

We now have a set of initial conditions equations ([7.111] and [7.112]) and a recursive relationship, equation (7.110), for calculating the values up to $g(K,M) = G(K)$. Then, we can use equations (7.103) and (7.104) to calculate the state probabilities. The computation is as follows:

Suppose we have a network similar to that shown in Figure 7.17, where $M = 3$, $\mu_1 = 0.9$, $\mu_2 = 0.5$, $\mu_3 = 0.9$, $p_1 = 0.7$, $p_2 = 0.2$, and $p_3 = 0.1$. Furthermore, suppose that there are $k = 2$ customers in the system. From equation (7.111), we know that:

$g(0,1) = 1$

$g(0,2) = 1$

$g(0,3) = 1$

and from equation (7.112) we know that:

$g(0,1) = 1$

$g(1,1) = 1$

$g(2,1) = 1$

We can arrange these values in a grid, as shown in Figure 7.18. The computation proceeds one row at a time and ends up with a value for $g(2,3) = G(2)$.

**Figure 7.18**
*G(k) grid
calculation.*

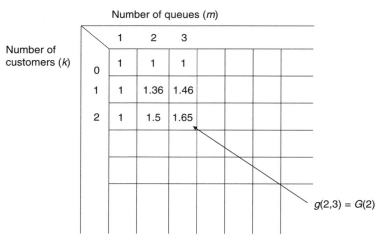

For example, to calculate $g(1,2)$, we would proceed as follows:

$$g(1,2) = \frac{P_2\mu_1}{\mu_2} g(0,2) + g(1,1)$$

$$g(1,2) = \frac{(0.2)(0.9)}{(0.5)}(1) + (1)$$

$$g(1,2) = 1.36$$

Thus, for Figure 7.18, the normalization constant is equal to 0.6. With two customers, we can now calculate the state probabilities using equation (7.103).

Buzen [9] gives several expressions for performance measures that are based upon this general computational structure. One of these measures is the device utilization, $U_i$, for server $i$. Normally, we define the utilization of a device as the sum of the state probabilities where there is at least one customer at server $i$.

$$U_i = \sum_{\substack{\text{All states} \\ \text{with } k_i > 0}} P\left(k_1, k_2, \ldots k_\mu\right) \tag{7.113}$$

$$U_i = 1/G(k) \sum_{\substack{\text{All states} \\ \text{with } k_i > 0}} \prod_{j=1}^{m} \frac{\left(P_j\mu_1\right)^{k_j}}{\mu_j} \tag{7.114}$$

Using similar reasoning, as we did for equation (7.109), we can treat equation (7.114) as a system with one less customer, multiplied by the factor that accounts for always having a customer at queue $i$. Thus, we get:

$$U_i = \frac{1}{G(k)} \frac{P_i \mu_1}{\mu_i} \sum_{\substack{\text{All states} \\ \text{with } k-1 \\ \text{customers}}} \prod_{j=1}^{m} \frac{(P_j \mu_1)^{k_j}}{\mu_j} \tag{7.115}$$

so:

$$U_i = \frac{P_i \mu_1}{\mu_i} \frac{G(K-1)}{G(K)} \tag{7.116}$$

We have already calculated the values for $G(K)$ and $G(K-1)$, as in Figure 7.18, so calculating the utilization of a device is straightforward. From this, we can find the throughput of device $i$ as:

$$\lambda_i = U_i \mu_i = P_i \mu_1 \frac{G(K-1)}{G(K)} \tag{7.117}$$

Looking back to equation (7.114), we can extend equation (7.116) to find the probability that the queue length at server $i$ will be greater or equal to some value $n$:

$$P(N_i \geq n) = 1/G(k) \sum_{\substack{\text{All states} \\ \text{with } k_i \geq n \\ \text{customers}}} \prod_{j=1}^{m} \left( \frac{P_j \mu_1}{\mu_j} \right)^{k_j} \tag{7.118}$$

so that:

$$P(N_i \geq n) = \left( \frac{P_i \mu_1}{\mu_i} \right)^n \frac{G(K-n)}{G(K)} \tag{7.119}$$

Applying equation (7.118) to the case where the queue length is $n + 1$, we can obtain the probability of $n$ customers in queue $i$.

$$P(N_i = n) = \left( \left( \frac{P_i \mu_1}{\mu_i} \right)^n \frac{G(K-n)}{G(K)} \right) - \left( \left( \frac{P_i \mu_1}{\mu_i} \right)^{n+1} \frac{G(K-n-1)}{G(K)} \right) \tag{7.120}$$

$$P(N_i = n) = \left(\frac{P_i\mu_1}{\mu_i}\right)^n \frac{1}{G(K)}\left(G(K-n) - \frac{P_i\mu_1}{\mu_i}G(K-n-1)\right) \quad (7.121)$$

Now that we have derived an expression for the probability of having $n$ customers in the queue, we can use equation (5.66) to obtain an expression for expected queue length:

$$
\begin{aligned}
E[N_i] &= \sum_{j=1}^{K} jP \qquad \text{for } N_i = j \\
&= \sum_{j=1}^{K} j\left(\left(\frac{P_i\mu_1}{\mu_i}\right)^j \frac{1}{G(K)}\left(G(K-j) - \frac{P_i\mu_1}{\mu_i}G(K-n-1)\right)\right) \\
&= \frac{1}{G(K)}\left(\frac{P_i\mu_1}{\mu_i}\left(G(K-1) - \frac{P_i\mu_1}{\mu_i}G(K-2)\right)\right) \qquad (7.122) \\
&\quad + 2\left(\left(\frac{P_i\mu_1}{\mu_i}\right)^2\left(G(K-2) - \frac{P_i\mu_1}{\mu_i}G(K-3)\right)\right) \\
&\quad + \ldots + K\left(\left(\frac{P_i\mu_1}{\mu_i}\right)^k\left(G(0) - \frac{P_i\mu_1}{\mu_i}G(-1)\right)\right)
\end{aligned}
$$

We can now expand and collect terms, keeping in mind that we have defined $G(K < 0) = 0$, to get:

$$E[N_i] = \frac{1}{G(K)}\sum_{j=1}^{K}\left(\frac{P_i\mu_1}{\mu_i}\right)^j G(K-j) \quad (7.123)$$

The expected delay through a queue, then, can be found from Little's result, using the throughput and expected queue length values just found:

$$E[W_i] = E[N_i]/\lambda_i \quad (7.124)$$

These techniques allow the efficient computation of the important statistics for the model shown in Figure 7.17. Next, we will discuss another, slightly more general computational method: mean value analysis.

## 7.4.2   **Mean value analysis**

The analyses described so far have all calculated, at one point or another, expressions for queue length distributions or state probabilities. This is perfectly acceptable for rather simple systems involving few customers and queuing systems. In the following discussion, we will explore an iterative method for finding some of the performance measures of interest without calculating the aforementioned distributions. The drawback to this is that the analysis refers only to the mean values of certain performance measures.

The techniques we are interested in here apply to closed queuing networks that have a product form solution for the state probabilities. The solutions are based on the assumption that a customer, arriving at any queue in a closed system that is at steady state, experiences a wait in the queue that is equivalent to the steady-state wait time for that queue with the arriving customer removed. Thus, the behavior of a network with one more customer is based upon the behavior before its arrival. This assumption leads to an iterative algorithm where the steady-state performance characteristics for the system with $n + 1$ customers are derived from the characteristics with $n$ customers, which are derived from a system with $n - 1$ customers, and so on down to one customer.

The general algorithm, then, allows us to compute average values for queue length, throughput, server utilization, and wait time by starting with an expression for one customer in the system and working up to any number of customers.

The main theorem behind mean value analysis states that the mean wait time for customers at any server in the network is related to the solution of the same network with one fewer customers. In conjunction with the wait time, we apply Little's result to obtain the total network throughput and then apply it again to each individual server to get the average queue length at each server.

The expression for wait time related to a network with one fewer customers is given as:

$$W(k) = 1/\mu \left[ 1 + N_q (k-1) \right] \tag{7.125}$$

where $\mu$ is the mean service time required by a customer at the server. The quantities $W(k)$ and $N_q(k-1)$ denote the mean wait time for a system with $k$ customers at the queue and the mean number of customers in the queue with $k - 1$ customers in the system, respectively. This expression holds for systems with first-come first-serve queuing disciplines with single, constant rate servers at each queue.

Next, we can apply Little's result to find the mean throughput for the network:

$$\lambda(k) = k/\text{avg. wait time} = k \Big/ \sum_{\text{all } i} \varnothing_i W_i(k) \qquad (7.126)$$

where $\varnothing$ is the visit ratio for the server considering all other servers. The visit ratio values will be discussed later in this chapter.

Finally, we can use Little's result on the servers to compare the average queue lengths:

$$\begin{aligned} N_q(k) &= \text{arrival rate} \times \text{average wait tim} \\ N_q(k) &= \varnothing_i \lambda(k) W_i(k) \end{aligned} \qquad (7.127)$$

Now we have a new expression for mean queue length that we can use in equation (7.125) to start another iteration.

The general procedure, then, is to start with an empty system ($K = 0$) and iterate equations (7.125) through (7.127) until we reach the desired value of $K$. For one iteration, we calculate the values for each queue system in the network before passing on to the next equation. Figure 7.19 shows a simple network to illustrate the technique. In the example, if we start with 0 customers, we obtain the following quantities from equations (7.125) through (7.127). In the following expressions, the subscripts denote the queue/server pair that the measure is associated with. The general iteration algorithm is as follows:

The first iteration is:

$$\begin{aligned} W_1(1) &= 1/\mu_1 \, (1 + 0) = 1/\mu_1 \\ W_2(1) &= 1/\mu_2 \, (1 + 0) = 1/\mu_2 \\ W_3(1) &= 1/\mu_3 \, (1 + 0) = 1/\mu_3 \\ \lambda(1) &= 1 \Big/ \left( \frac{\varnothing_1}{\mu_1} + \frac{\varnothing_2}{\mu_2} + \frac{\varnothing_3}{\mu_3} \right) \\ N_1(1) &= \varnothing_1 \lambda(1) W_1(1) \\ N_2(1) &= \varnothing_2 \lambda(1) W_2(1) \\ N_3(1) &= \varnothing_3 \lambda(1) W_3(1) \end{aligned} \qquad (7.128)$$

The second iteration is:

$$W_1(2) = 1/\mu_1 \left(1 + N_1(1)\right)$$
$$W_2(2) = 1/\mu_2 \left(1 + N_2(1)\right)$$
$$W_3(2) = 1/\mu_3 \left(1 + N_3(1)\right)$$
$$\lambda(2) = 1/\left(\varnothing_1 W_1(2) + \varnothing_2 W_2(2) + \varnothing_3 W_3(2)\right) \qquad (7.129)$$
$$N_1(2) = \varnothing_1 \lambda(2) W_1(2)$$
$$N_2(2) = \varnothing_2 \lambda(2) W_2(2)$$
$$N_3(2) = \varnothing_3 \lambda(2) W_3(2)$$

The visit ratios, $\varnothing_i$, are obtained as follows. Pick a server and set its visit ratio value $\varnothing_i$ to 1. Next, formulate the equations that contribute to the visit ratio for that queue by looking at all queues that feed it. Equate the feeder visit ratios, multiplied by the respective branching probabilities, to the next in line ($\varnothing_i$). Continue this process for each queue system until we have $m$ relationships in $m$ unknowns, where $m$ is the number of queuing systems. We can then solve this system of equations to obtain the desired visit ratios. Note that the visit ratios are relative quantities. For Figure 7.19, the visit ratios would be calculated as follows:

$$\varnothing_1 = 1$$
$$\varnothing_1 = P_2 \varnothing_2$$
$$\varnothing_2 = \varnothing_1 + \varnothing_3 \qquad (7.130)$$
$$\varnothing_3 = P_2 \varnothing_2$$

The algorithm is iterated until we reach the desired network population, where we can calculate the mean performance measures for the network.

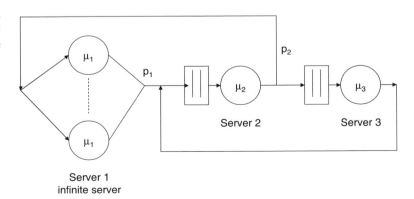

**Figure 7.19**
*Network for mean variable analysis.*

### 7.4.3  **Operational analysis**

The methods for performing queuing analysis given in the beginning of the chapter provide close approximations to the actual systems they represent. It is contended, however, that the assumption that the various distributions and relationships that we use to represent their real-world counterparts cannot be proven to be absolutely accurate. Furthermore, the stochastic models studied earlier yield relationships that cannot be absolutely proven to be valid during any observation period.

Operational analysis, on the other hand, is based upon the observation of basic, measurable quantities that can be combined into operational relationships. Furthermore, the observation period for which the system is analyzed is finite. The assumption is that the basic quantities, called operational variables, are measurable (at least in theory). The basic operational variables that are commonly found in operational analysis are as follows:

$T$ = the observation period length

$A$ = the number of arrivals during the observation period

$B$ = the server busy time during the observation period

$C$ = the number of job completions during the observation period

In addition to the measurable quantities, there are several fundamental relationships that define other useful quantities. These are as follows:

$\lambda$ = arrival rate = $A/T$

$X$ = completion rate = $C/T$

$U$ = server utilization = $B/T$

$S$ = mean service time per job = $B/C$

Several operational identities are also defined that hold under certain operational assumptions. The first, which relates server utilization to the completion rate and mean service time, is derived as follows:

$$X \cdot S = (C/T)(B/C) = B/T$$
$$X \cdot S = U$$

(7.131)

This relationship holds in all cases and is thus referred to as an operational law.

If we assume that the system is in steady-state equilibrium, we can state that the number of arrivals and the number of completions during a given observation period will be equal (i.e., the flow balance assumption). This statement may not always be true, but it can be measured and verified for any observation period of interest. Thus, it is called an operational theorem. From this, we can derive another relationship, which holds when the system is in flow balance:

$$A = C$$
$$A/T = C/T$$
$$\lambda = X \qquad\qquad\qquad (7.132)$$
$$\lambda S = XS$$
$$\lambda S = U$$

One advantageous property of operational analysis is that the technique can be used for open and closed networks. The one condition, however, that must be met is that the network under consideration must be what is called operationally connected. That is, no server may be idle during the entire observation period.

For a closed system, we know the number of jobs in circulation in the network and we find the system throughput at a particular point in the network. Other quantities can then be derived using that throughput as a starting point. In an open system, the throughput at the exit from the network is assumed to be known, and we use this to find the number of customers at the queues.

Let's look now at some basic operational quantities. Suppose that we have an arbitrary network that is observed over a period of $T$. For each queue system in the network, we observe and collect the following data:

$A_i$ = number of arrivals at queuing system $i$

$B_i$ = busy time of server $i$

$C_{ij}$ = number of times a job goes directly from server $i$ to server $j$'s queue

Jobs that arrive from an external source or that leave to an external sink are denoted by $A_{0i}$ and $C_{i0}$. The number of arrivals to and departures from the system are given by:

$$\text{Number of arrivals } A_0 = \sum_{j=1}^{m} A_{oj} \qquad\qquad (7.133)$$

$$\text{Number of departures } C_0 = \sum_{i=1}^{m} C_{io} \qquad\qquad (7.134)$$

and the total number of completions at server $i$ is given as:

$$C_i = \sum_{j=1}^{m} C_{ij} \qquad (7.135)$$

From the basic measured quantities defined previously, several other performance quantities can be derived, as follows:

Utilization of server $i$: $\qquad\qquad\qquad U_i = B_i/T$

Mean service time of server $i$: $\qquad\qquad S_i = B_i/C_i$

Output rate of server $i$: $\qquad\qquad\qquad X_i = C_i/T$

Routing frequency from server $i$ to $j$: $\quad q_{ij} = C_{ij}/C_i$

We can represent the job completion rate of such a system as:

$$X_0 = \sum_{i=1}^{m} X_i q_{i0} \qquad (7.136)$$

and the utilization of any server $i$ as:

$$U_i = X_i S_i \qquad (7.137)$$

If we think of the wait time at a particular server $i$ at each increment of time during the observation period as the sum of the service times of the customers ahead of the new arrival, the total wait time accumulated for all jobs in the system over the period is:

$$W_i = \int_{0}^{T} N_i(t)\,dt \qquad (7.138)$$

The average queue length at the server in question is given as:

$$N_i = W_i/T \qquad (7.139)$$

and the response time of the server system is given as:

$$R_i = W_i/C_i \qquad (7.140)$$

Combining equations (7.139) and (7.140), we obtain the operational equivalent of Little's result:

$$N_i = (W_i/C_i)(C_i/T) = R_i X_i \qquad (7.141)$$

If the system under study is in steady state, so that we have flow balance, we assume that the arrival rate to a queuing system is equal to the completion rate of that same system. We can also derive the server throughput rate for any server, $j$, as:

$$C_j = \sum_{i=0}^{m} C_{ij}$$

$$C_j = \sum_{i=0}^{m} \left( C_i C_{ij} \right) / C_i \qquad\qquad (7.142)$$

$$C_j = \sum_{i=0}^{m} C_i q_{ij}$$

We can obtain the same expression as stated in equation (7.136), but generalized for any server it is:

$$X_j = \sum_{i=0}^{m} X_i q_{ij} \qquad \text{for } j = 0, 1, \ldots, m \qquad\qquad (7.143)$$

The relationship derived yields a unique solution if applied to an open system, because the input throughput, $X$, is known. In a closed system, equation (7.143) will yield relative throughput rates, because we do not know the absolute value of $X_0$.

Buzen [9] defines the visit ratio $V_i$ as the number of times a particular server, $i$, will be visited, relative to a given number of inputs. We can express this quantity as the ratio of the throughput at server $i$ to the total input throughput:

$$V_i = X_i / X_0 \qquad\qquad (7.144)$$

If we assume that the flow of jobs in the network is balanced, we can set $V_0 = 1$ (since all jobs pass through the network input) and solve for all of the other visit ratios using the following expression:

$$V_j = q_{0j} \sum_{i=0}^{m} V_i q_{ij} \qquad\qquad (7.145)$$

Also, knowing the throughput of any server in the network allows us to find the throughput of any other server through a combination of equations (7.144) and (7.145).

Now let's look at the total time a job remains in the system as a function of each server's throughput and average queue length. The total wait time for any job arriving at any server depends on how many jobs are ahead of the new one in the queue and on the rate that jobs get completed by the server. At each server, we can use Little's result equation (7.141) in combination with equation (7.144) to obtain:

$$N_i / X_0 = V_i R_i \tag{7.146}$$

If we then sum equation (7.146) over all servers in the network, we obtain a general expression that can be interpreted as Little's result applied to the total system:

$$\sum_{i=1}^{m} N_i / X_0 = \sum_{i=1}^{m} V_i R_i \tag{7.147}$$

where the number of jobs in the system at any time is simply the sum of all jobs at the network's servers:

$$N = \sum_{i=0}^{m} N_i \tag{7.148}$$

So we have:

$$N / X_0 = \sum_{i=1}^{m} V_i R_i \tag{7.149}$$

The left-hand side of equation (7.149) can be thought of as an application of Little's result to the system as a whole; thus, we define the system response time as:

$$R = N / X_0 = \sum_{i=1}^{m} V_i R_i \tag{7.150}$$

The final topic that we will cover under operational analysis is bottleneck analysis in a closed system. In every network, one of the queuing systems will eventually be unable to keep up with increased service demands as the number of jobs in the network increases. This particular server will subsequently determine the maximum throughput rate of the network as a whole. A device is considered to be saturated (e.g., unable to process jobs any faster) if its utilization becomes one. In this case, the throughput will be inversely proportional to the service time, since there will always be a job in service.

$$X_0 = 1/S_0 \tag{7.151}$$

If we combine equations (7.137) and (7.144), we can express the relative utilization of any two servers in the network as follows:

$$U_i/U_j = V_iS_i/V_jS_j \tag{7.152}$$

Note that the ratios of the server utilizations do not depend upon the throughput of either server; the ratio remains constant independent of system load. Thus, the device with the largest value of $V_iS_i$ will become the network's bottleneck as load increases.

It is possible, then, to find the maximum possible system throughput when the bottleneck is in saturation. Since, for bottleneck server $b$, throughput is equal to the inverse of the service time, we can combine equations (7.144) and (7.151) to obtain the maximum system throughput:

$$
\begin{aligned}
V_b &= X_b/X_0 = 1/X_0S_b \\
X_0 &= 1/V_bS_b
\end{aligned}
\tag{7.153}
$$

The network response time, in the saturation case, is given by equation (7.150) as:

$$R = N/X_0 = N\,V_bS_b \tag{7.154}$$

and is thus limited by the bottleneck server.

Buzen and Denning [10] extend the operational results discussed previously to systems with load-dependent behavior. Also, an earlier proposal for operational analysis of queuing networks can be found in [12].

## 7.5  Summary

The areas covered in this chapter, from stochastic processes to queuing theory to basic estimation, span a wide range of topics, each with a wealth of specialities and techniques. The treatment given herein, although brief, is intended to illustrate the usefulness of statistical analysis and queuing theory and to provide a basis for understanding some of the techniques and methods used in simulation. More detailed discussions of the issues associated with basic probability and statistics are found in many basic probability texts, notably [4, 5] and, for a queuing theory slant, in reference [3]. Queuing theory topics are discussed in reference [3], and also in references [2, 6, 7, 13]. Estimation, as related to queuing systems, is treated in references [2, 3]. The application of the techniques discussed in this chapter enables one to calculate, under certain assumptions and conditions, many of the interesting performance quantities that can be found with traditional queuing theory analysis. The results obtained, however, are often more intuitive and can be more easily related to the actual system for which they are intended.

# 8

# *Simulation Analysis*

Simulation is the realization of a model for a system in computer executable form. That is, the model of the real-world system has been translated into a computer simulation language. The computer realization provides a vehicle to conduct experiments with the model in order to gain insight into the behavior and makeup of the system or to evaluate alternatives. Simulations, to be effective, require a precise formulation of the system to be studied, correct translation of this formulation into a computer program, and interpretation of the results.

Simulation is usually undertaken because the complexity of most computer systems defies use of simpler mathematical means for realistic performance studies. This complexity may occur from inherent stochastic processes in the system, complex interactions of elements that lack mathematical formulations, or the sheer intractability of mathematical relationships that result from the system's equations and constraints. Because of these constraints and other reasons, simulation is often the tool for evaluation. Simulation provides many potential benefits to the modeler. It makes it possible to experiment and study the myriad complex internal interactions of a particular system, with the complexity left up to the modeler.

Simulation allows for the sensitivity analysis of the system by providing a means to alter the model and observe the effects it has on the system's behavior. Through simulation we can often gain a better understanding of the real system. This is because of the detail of the model and the modeler's need to independently understand the computer system in order to faithfully construct a simulation of it. The process of learning about the system in order to simulate it will often lead to suggestions for change and improvements. The simulation then provides a means to test these hypotheses. Simulation often leads to a better understanding of the importance of various elements of a system and how they interact with each other. It provides a laboratory environment in which we can study and analyze many alternatives and their impact well before a real system even exists or, if one exists, without disturbing or perturbing it. Simulation enables the modeler to study dynamic systems in real, compressed, or expanded time, providing a means to examine details of situations and processes that otherwise could not be performed. Finally, it provides a means to study the effects on an existing system of adding new components, services, and so on without testing them in the system. This provides a means to discover bottlenecks and other problems before we actually expend time and capital to perform the changes.

Simulation has been used for a wide variety of purposes, as can be seen from the diversity of topics covered at annual simulation symposiums. Simulation easily lends itself to many fields, including business, economics, marketing, education, politics, social sciences, behavioral sciences, natural sciences, international relations, transportation, war gaming, law enforcement, urban studies, global systems, space systems, computer design and operations, and myriad others.

Up to this point we have used "system" to describe the intended modeled entity. In the context of simulation, it is used to designate a collection of objects with a well-defined set of interactions between them. A bank teller interacts with the line of customers, and the job the teller does may be considered a system in this context, with the customers and tellers forming the objects and the functions performed by each (deposit, withdrawal) as the set of interactions.

Systems by nature are typically described as being continuous or discrete, where these terms imply the behavior of the variables associated with the system. They provide us, the modelers, with a context in which to place the model and on which to build. In both cases, the typical relation of variables is built around time. In the case of the discrete model, time is assumed to step forward in fixed intervals determined by the events of occurrence versus some formulation, and in the continuous model, the variables change continually as time ticks forward. For example, with the bank scenario, if the variable of interest is the number of customers waiting for service, we have a dependent discrete "counting" sequence. On the other hand, if we are looking at a drive-up bank teller and are interested in the remaining fuel in each vehicle and the average, we could model the gasoline consumption as a continuous variable dependent on the time in line until exiting.

Systems can possess both discrete and continuous variables and still be modeled. In reality, this is frequently the case. Another consideration in defining a system is the nature of its processes. Processes, whether they are discrete or continuous, can have another feature, that of being deterministic or stochastic. A deterministic system is where, given an input $x$ and initial conditions $i$, you will always derive the same output: $y = f(x, i)$. That is, if we were to perform the same process an infinite number of times, with the same inputs and same initial state of the process, we would always realize the same result.

On the other hand, if the system were stochastic, this would not hold. For the same system with input held at $X$ and initial state held at $I$, we could have the output $Y$ take on one of many possible outputs. This is based on the random nature of stochastic processes. That is, they will be randomly distributed over the possible outcomes. For example, if the bank teller system is described as a discrete system, we are assuming that the service time of the server is exactly the same and the arrival rate of customers is fixed and nonvarying. However, if the same system is given some reality, we all know that service is random, based on the job the tellers must perform and how they perform it. Likewise customers do not arrive in perfect order; they arrive randomly. In both cases the model will give vastly different results.

## 8.1   Simulation process

The use of a digital computer to perform modeling and run experiments has been a popular technique for quite some time. In this environment simulation can make systematic studies of problems that cannot be studied by other techniques. The simulation model describes the system in terms of the elements of interest and their interrelationships. Once completed, it provides a laboratory in which to carry out many experiments on these elements and interactions.

Simulation programs, as with generic modeling, require discrete phases to be performed in order to realize their full potential. They are as follows:

1.   Determine that the problem requires simulation.

2.   Formulate a model to solve the problem.

3.   Formulate a simulation model of the problem.

4.   Implement the model in a suitable language.

5.   Design simulation experiments.

6.   Validate the model.

7.   Perform experiments.

The typical simulation model project will spend most of its time in phases 2, 3, and 4, because of the complexities associated with formulating the model and the conversion to simulation format and implementation in a language. Model formulation deals with the definition of critical elements of the real-world system and their interactions. Once these critical elements have been identified and defined (mathematically, behaviorally, functionally) and their interactions (cause and effect, predecessor and successor, dependencies and nondependencies, data flows, and control flow) are defined in terms of their essence, simulation model development flows into and along with systems model definition. That is, as we develop a system model we can often directly define the simulation model structure.

An important aspect of this model development is the selection of a proper level of simulation, which is directly proportional to the intended purpose of the performance evaluation, the degree of understanding of the system, its environment, and the output statistics required. On one extreme, for example, we could model our bank teller system down to the level of modeling all his or her actions. Or, on the other hand, we could model the teller service as strictly a gross estimate of time to perform service regardless of the type of service. The level to choose would be dependent on what is to be examined. In the first example, we may wish to isolate the most time-consuming aspect(s) of their functions so that we could develop ways to improve them. At the second level possibly all we wish to determine is based on the customer load, the average teller service time, and the optimal number of tellers to have on duty and when.

The intent of the performance measure drives us directly to a simulation level of detail, which typically falls somewhere in between the two extremes: too low or too high to be useful. In most cases, however, we as modelers do not or cannot always foresee how the level of detail of all components can influence the model's ultimate usefulness. A solution typically used to cope with such uncertainties is to construct the model in a modular fashion, allowing each component to migrate to the level consistent with its intent and overall impact on the simulation and system. What this typically drives us to is top-down model development, with each layer being refined as necessary.

Simulations, beyond their structure (elements and interactions), require data input and data extraction to make them useful. The most usual simulations are either self-driven or trace-driven. In self-driven simulations the model itself (i.e., the program) has drivers embedded in it to provide the needed data to stimulate the simulation. These data are typically derived by various analytical distributions and linked with a random number generator. In the example of the bank teller system, we have been using a self-driven simulation. We may use a Poisson arrival distribution to describe the random nature of customers arriving to the system. Such a use is indicative of some artificially generated stream-to-model system inputs.

In the other case, when we use trace-driven data, the simulation is being driven by outside stimuli. Typically these are extracted, reduced, and correlated data from an actual running system. For example, in our bank teller case we may wish to have a more realistic load base from which to compute the optimal number of tellers and their hours. In such a case we would measure over some period of time the dynamics of customers arriving at the bank for service. This collected information would then be used to build a stored input sequence, which would drive the simulation based on these realistic data. This type of modeling is closer to the real-world system but has the disadvantage of requiring the up-front data collection and analysis to make such data available for use.

## 8.2   Time control

In continuous and discrete simulation, the major concern in performing the simulation is time management and its use in affecting the dependent variables. Timing in simulation programs is used to synchronize events, compute state changes, and control overall interactions. Timing can take on two modes: synchronous and asynchronous.

Synchronous timing refers to a timing scheme in which time advances in fixed, appropriately chosen units of time, $t$. On each update of time the system state is updated to reflect this time change. That is, all events occurring during this time period are determined and their state adjusted accordingly. This process of advancing time (in steps) and updating the state of elements occurs until the simulation hits some boundary condition (time goes to a maximum, some event occurs, etc.). In our bank teller system timing is needed to determine arrivals and service. For the $t$-step organization on each stop we must check to see if an arrival should occur, if a service should be completed, or if a new one should be begun. An important concept or idea to keep in mind when using synchronous timing is that of step selection. If too great a step is chosen, events are seen to occur concurrently when in reality they may not be. On the other hand, too fine a granularity of time step will cause many steps to go by when nothing occurs. The latter will cause excessive computer run time but very fine differentiation between events. The former, on the other hand, will cause a distortion of everything and possibly a loss of usefulness. The important job of the modeler is to select the proper step time for the model to be useful but not be excessive in computer time.

Asynchronous, or event timing, differs from synchronous timing in that time is advanced in variable rather than fixed amounts. The concept is to keep track of events versus time steps. The time is advanced based on the next chronological event that is to occur. These chronological events are typically kept in a dynamic list, which is updated and adjusted on each event to reflect new events that are to occur in the future.

In our bank teller example the event queue, or list, will comprise two events: the next arrival and the completion of the next service. Abstractly this method appears to be easier to visualize. The events must be ordered by occurrence and adjusted as new events arrive. The issue in this, as well as in the former case, is how to insert or schedule new events or new conditions in the simulations. The next section will investigate this and other aspects of how to use time in building simulations.

# 8.3    Systems and modeling

Up to this point, we have discussed generic attributes related to simulation modeling. We have not discussed the classes of modeling techniques available or the classification of simulation implementation techniques (i.e., simulation languages). Simulation techniques include discrete event, continuous change, queuing, combined, and hybrid techniques. Each provides a specific viewpoint to be applied to the simulation problem. They will also force the modeler to fit models to the idiosyncrasies of the techniques.

## 8.3.1    Discrete models

In discrete simulation models, the real system's objects are typically referred to as entities. Entities carry with them attributes that describe them (i.e., their state description). Actions on these entities occur on boundary points or conditions. These conditions are referred to as events. Events such as arrivals, service standpoints, stop points, other event signaling, wait times, and so on are typical.

The entities carry attributes that provide information on what to do with them based on other occurring events and conditions. Only on these event boundaries or condition occurrences can the state of entities change. For example, in our bank teller simulation, only on an arrival of a customer (arrival event) can a service event be scheduled, or only on a service event can an end of service event be scheduled. This implies that without events the simulation does not do anything. This modeling technique only works on the concept of scheduling events and acting on them. Therefore, it is essential that the capability exists to place events into a schedule queue or list and to remove them based on some conditions of interest.

What this technique implies is that all actions within the simulation are driven by the event boundaries. That is, event beginnings and endings can be other events to be simulated (i.e., to be brought into action). All things in between these event boundaries, or data collection points, are now changing. A simulation model using this technique requires the modeler to define all possible events within the real system and how these events affect the state of all the other events in the system. This process includes defining the events and developing definitions of change to other states at all event boundaries, of all activities that the entities can perform, and of the interaction among all the entities within the simulated system. In this type of simulation modeling each event must trigger some other event within the system. If this condition does not hold, we cannot construct a realistic working simulation. This triggering provides the event's interaction and relationship with each other event. For example, for the model of a self-service automatic teller machine, we need to define at a minimum the following entities and events:

- Arrival events

- Service events

- Departure events

- Collection events

- Customer entities

- Server entities

The events guide how the process occurs and entities provide the medium being acted on, all of which are overseen by the collection event that provides the "snapshot" view of the system. This provides a means to extract statistics from entities. In this example, the following descriptions could be used to build a simple model:

1.    Arrival event

- Schedule next arrival (present time + $T$).

- If all tellers busy, number waiting = number waiting + 1.

- If any teller is free and no one is before the waiting customer, schedule service event.

2.    Service event

- Number of tellers busy = number of tellers busy + 1.

- Schedule service and event based on type of service.

- Take start of service statistics.

3.   End service event

- Number of tellers busy = number tellers busy − 1.

- Schedule arrival of customer.

- Take end of service statistics.

4.   Entities

- Tellers

  —Number of tellers

  —Service rates and types

  —Service types

- Customers

  —Arrival rate

  —Dynamics (service type required)

A discrete event simulation (with an appropriate language) could be built using these events and entities as their basis. A model built this way uses these conditions to schedule some number of arrivals and some end conditions. The relationships that exist between the entities will keep the model executing, with statistics taken until the end condition is met. This example is extremely simplistic and by no means complete, but it does provide a description of some of the basic concepts associated with discrete event simulations.

## 8.3.2   Continuous modeling

Continuous simulations deal with the modeling of physical events (processes, behaviors, conditions) that can be described by some set of continuously changing dependent variables. These in turn are incorporated into differential, or difference, equations that describe the physical process. For example, we may wish to determine the rate of change of speed of a falling object shot from a catapult (see Figure 8.1) and its distance, $R$, from the catapault. Neglecting wind resistance, the equations for this are as follows. The velocity, $v$, at any time is found as:

$$v_x = v_0 \cos\theta$$
$$v_y = v_0 \sin\theta_0 - gt \tag{8.1}$$

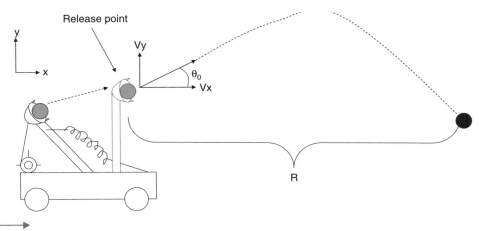

**Figure 8.1**   *Projectile motion.*

and the distance in the $x$ direction is:

$$R = V_x t = t v_0 \cos \theta \qquad\qquad (8.2)$$

These quantities can be formulated into equations that can be modeled in a continuous language to determine their state at any period of time $t$.

Using these state equations, we can build state-based changed simulations that provide us with the means to trigger on certain occurrences. For example, in these equations we may wish to trigger an event (shoot back when $v_y$ is equal to 0). That is, when the projectile is not climbing any more and it has reached its maximum height, fire back. In this event the equation may look like this:

$$v_y = 0; \text{ begin execution of shoot back} \qquad\qquad (8.3)$$

Another example of this type of triggering is shown in Figure 8.2. In this example, two continuous formulas are being computed over time; when their results are equivalent (crossover event), schedule some other event to occur. This type of operation allows us to trigger new computations or adjust values of present ones based on the relationship of continuous equations with each other.

Using combinations of self-triggers and comparative triggers (less than, greater than, equal to, etc.) we can construct ever more involved simulations of complex systems. The main job of a simulator in this type of simulation model is to develop a set of equations that define the dynamics of the system under study and determine how they are to interact.

**Figure 8.2**
*Continuous variable plot.*

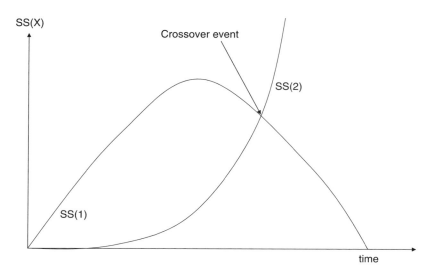

### 8.3.3   Queuing modeling

Another class of generic model is the queuing model. Queuing-based simulation languages exist (AWESIM, GPSS, Q-gert, Slam II) and have been used to solve a variety of problems. As was indicated earlier, many problems to be modeled can easily be described as an interconnection of queues, with various queuing disciplines and service rates. As such, a simulation language that supports queuing models and analysis of them would greatly simplify the modeling problem. In such languages there are facilities to support the definition of queues in terms of size of queue, number of servers, type of queue, queue discipline, server type, server discipline, creation of customers, monitoring of operations, departure collection point, statistics collection and correlation, and presentation of operations. In addition to basic services there may be others for slowing up customers or routing them to various places in the queuing network. Details of such a modeling tool will be highlighted later in this chapter.

### 8.3.4   Combined modeling

Each of the techniques described previously provides the modeler with a particular view upon which to fit the system's model. The discrete event-driven models provide us with a view in which systems are composed of entities and events that occur to change the state of these entities. Continuous models provide a means to perform simulations based on differential equations or difference formulas that describe time-varying dynamics of a system's operation. Queuing modeling provides the modeler with a view of systems comprised of queues and services. The structure comes from how they are interconnected and how these interconnections are driven by the outputs of the queue servers.

The problem with all three techniques is that in order to use them, a modeler must formulate the problem in terms of the available structure of the technique. It cannot be formulated in a natural way and then translated easily. The burden of fitting it into a framework falls on the modeler and the simulation language. The solution is to provide a combined language that has the features of all three techniques. In such a language the modeler can build simulations in a top-down fashion, leaving details to lower levels. For instance, in our bank teller system, we could initially model it as a single queue with $n$ servers (tellers). The queuing discipline is first-come, first-served, and the service discipline can be any simple distribution, such as exponential. This simple model will provide us with a sanity check of the correctness of our model and with bounds to quickly determine the system's limits. We could next decide to model the teller's service in greater detail by dropping this component's level down to the event modeling level.

At this point we could model the teller's activity as a collection of events that need to be sequenced through in order for service to be completed. If possible, we could then incorporate continuous model aspects to get further refinement of some other feature. The main aspect to gather from this form of modeling is that it provides the modeler with the ability to easily model the level of detail necessary to simulate the system under study.

### 8.3.5  Hybrid modeling

Hybrid modeling refers to simulation modeling in which we incorporate features of the previous techniques with conventional programming languages. This form of modeling could be as simple as doing the whole thing in a regular language and allowing lower levels of modeling by providing a conventional language interface. Most simulation languages provide a means to insert regular programming language code into them. Therefore, they all could be considered a variant of this technique.

## 8.4  Simulation languages

As the use of simulation has increased, so has the development of new simulation languages. Simulation languages have been developed because of the unique needs of the modeling community to have system routines to keep track of time, maintain the state of the simulation, collect statistics, provide stimulus, and control interaction. All of these previously had to be done by each individual programmer.

Early languages provided basic services by adding a callable routine from programming languages. These early languages provided for time and event management but little else. This chapter will look at four languages and discuss the aspects they possess that aid in the simulation process. We will not, however, cover languages that are built on top of basic simulation languages, such as Network II.5 and others.

## 8.4.1  GASP IV

GASP IV was developed in the early 1970s as a general-purpose simulation language and is still in use with variations today. As such we use this as a basic model for most languages in existence today. GASP IV is a FOR-TRAN-based simulation language that provides routines and structure to support the writing of discrete events, continuous and combined discrete events, and continuous simulation models. Discrete event models in GASP IV are written as a collection of system and user FORTRAN subroutines. GASP IV provides the user with the following routines: time management, file management (event files, storage and retrieval, copying of events, and finding of events), and data collection and analysis (both observation-based and time-based statistics). The user must develop a set of event routines that define and describe the mathematical-logical relationships for modeling the changes in state corresponding to each event and their interactions.

As an example of GASP IV's use and structure, our bank teller problem will be examined once again. In order to model this problem in GASP we must determine the events of interest, their structure, and the boundaries upon which they are triggered. To simplify the example, it is assumed that there is no time delay between the ending of service for one customer and the beginning of another (if there is one waiting). The important measures or states will be the number of customers in the system and the teller's status. From these two system events a customer's arrival and a teller's end of service occur. These are also chosen as the points at which significant changes to a system's status occur. The activity that occurs is the beginning of service; this can be assumed to occur either when a customer arrives at an empty line or when the teller ends service to a customer.

Entities in GASP are represented by arrays of attributes, where the attributes represent the descriptive information about the entity that the

**Figure 8.3**
*Basic model of GASP IV control.*

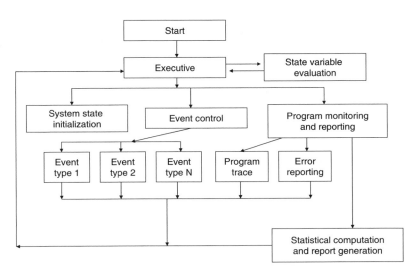

modeler wishes to keep. Entities are the elements that are acted on during the simulation. Their attributes are adjusted based on occurrences of interest. A variable "busy" is used to indicate the status of the teller, and attribute (1) of customer is used to mark the customer's arrival time to the teller line. To make the simulation operate, the system-state must be initialized to some known values; in this case the teller is initialized not busy and the first arriving customer must be scheduled to arrive. Additionally, to keep the model running, the arriving customer must schedule another customer's arrival in the future based on a selected random time distribution. Statistics will be taken when service completes on the length of wait time and the number of customers waiting, in service, and in total. When we look at the GASP code we need to examine the structure of a typical GASP program (see Figure 8.3). As indicated by this figure, GASP IV exists as a single program in FORTRAN. Therefore, making it function requires a main pro-

**Figure 8.4**
*GASP IV main FORTRAN program.*

```
Dimension nset (1000)
common/gcom/atrib (100, DP(100), DDL (100, DTNOW,
II,MFA,MSTOP,NCLNR,NCRDR,NPRINT,NNRUN,
NNSET,NTAPE,SS(100),SSL(100),TNEXT,TNOW,XX(100)
Common Q Set
Equivalence Nset(1),Qset(1))
NNSet=1000
NCRDR=5
NPRINT=6
NTAPE=7
Call GASP
Stop
End
```

**Figure 8.5**

*Subroutine Event for bank teller problem.*

```
Subroutine Event (I)
Goto (1,2), I
1 Call arrival
  return
2 Call end SRU
  return
End
```

gram and a call to the GASP program that will begin the simulation. Another function of the main program is to set up limits on the system, such as number of files, input, output, limits on events, and so on. Figure 8.4 depicts the main program for our example.

Once GASP has been called, the program runs under control of the GASP subprogram calling sequences. The GASP system's executive takes over and initializes the simulation using the user-supplied routine Intlc. Once initialized, it begins simulation by examining the event list; if any events exist, it pulls them out, executes them, and takes statistics. The loop continues until the end conditions are met or an error occurs. To control events and make sense of them in FORTRAN requires the user to supply an event-sequencing routine called Event. This event-control routine is called with the attribute number of the intended event. It will use this to call the actual event. For our bank teller example this routine is illustrated in Figure 8.5 with its two events shown. When this routine is called with an appropriate number, the intended event is called, executed, and control is returned to the event routine, which in turn returns control to the executive routine.

These events are called based on what Filem (1) has stored in it. Filem (1) is operated on in a first-come, first-served basis, removing items one at a time. The events are stored in Filem (1) as attributes: attribute (1) is the time of the event, attribute (2) is the event type, and all other attributes are added user attributes for the entity. Figure 8.6 gives an example of how the file is initialized.

**Figure 8.6**

*Subroutine Intlc for bank teller problem.*

```
Subroutine INTLC
common/gcom/atrib (100, DP(100), DDL (100, DTNOW,
II,MFA,MSTOP,NCLNR,NCRDR,NPRINT,NNRUN,
NNSET,NTAPE,SS(100),SSL(100),TNEXT,TNOW,XX(100)
Equivalence (xx(1), Busy)
Busy=0
Atrib(2)=1
Call filem
return
end
```

**Figure 8.7**

*Arrival routine
Event code.*

```
Subroutine Arrival
common/gcom/atrib (100, DP(100), DDL (100, DTNOW,
II,MFA,MSTOP,NCLNR,NCRDR,NPRINT,NNRUN,
NNSET,NTAPE,SS(100),SSL(100),TNEXT,TNOW,XX(100)
Equivalence (xx(1), Busy) TIMST(Busy,TNOW,ISTAT)
Attrib(1)=TNOW+expon(20.,1)
Attrib(2)=1
Call filem(1)
Call filem(2,attrib(1))
if (Busy=0) go to return
10 Busy =1
attrib(1)=TNOW+unfrm(10.,25,1)
attrib(2)=1
attrib(3)=TNOW
Call filem(1)
return
end
```

Figure 8.6 illustrates the initialization routine for the bank teller simulation. Filem (1), the event file, is loaded with the first arrival event (a customer) and the teller is set to not busy.

Once Filem (1) has an event stored, the simulation can begin. The first event is a customer arrival indicated by the contents of attribute (2) of Filem (1), which is the only event at this time. The arrival event (see Figure 8.7) performs the scheduling of the next arrival.

After the next arrival is scheduled, the preset arrival is placed in the queue (Filem [2]). Then a test is made to see if the teller is busy. If so, we return to the main program or else we schedule an end of service event for the preset time plus a number chosen uniformly between 10 and 25.

The second event, the end of service, is shown in Figure 8.8. This code determines statistics of time in system and busy statistics. The code also checks to see if there is any user in the queue, removes one if there is, and schedules another end of service for this user.

**Figure 8.8**

*End of service
routine.*

```
Subroutine end SRU
common/gcom/atrib (100, DP(100), DDL (100, DTNOW,
II,MFA,MSTOP,NCLNR,NCRDR,NPRINT,NNRUN,
NNSET,NTAPE,SS(100),SSL(100),TNEXT,TNOW,XX(100)
TIMST(subusy,TNOW,T,ISTAT)
TSYS=TNOW-Attrib(3)
Call col CT(TSYS,1)
if(NNQ(2), 6T,0) go to 10
busys=0
return
10 Call schd((2,unfrm(10.,25,1) attrib)
return
end
```

This simple example shows how GASP could be used to model a wide array of event-based models. Details of this language can be found in [14].

## 8.4.2   GPSS

General-Purpose Simulation System (GPSS) is a process-oriented simulation language for modeling discrete systems. It uses a block-structuring notation to build models. These provide a set of standard blocks (see Figure 8.9) that provides the control and operations for transactions (entities). A model is translated into a GPSS program by the selection of blocks to represent the model's components and the linkage of them into a block diagram defining the logical structures of the system. GPSS interprets and executes the block diagram defined by the user, thereby providing the simulation. This interpretation is slow and, therefore, the language cannot be used to solve large problems.

To illustrate GPSS we will again examine our bank teller system. It is viewed as a single-server queuing system with our teller and $n$ customer arrivals (see Figure 8.10). Customers arrive with a mean interarrival time of 10 minutes, exponentially distributed. The teller provides service to the customers in a uniform time between 5 and 15 minutes. The simulation will take statistics on queue length, utilization of teller, and time in system. The simulator builds the diagram shown in Figure 8.10 from the model of a queuing system based on the statistics to be taken. This structure is then translated to the code seen in Figure 8.11. The code is broken down into four sections. The top section is used to define the data needed to approximate an exponential distribution and set up markers for the time-dependent statistics.

The second segment is the main simulation code, and it performs the tasks of generating customers (14), taking statistics on arrival time (15), queuing up arriving customers (16), scheduling service (17; when free, take control), departing the waiting line (18), delaying the exit by the appropriate service time of the teller (19), releasing the teller for the next customer (20), taking statistics on the customer's time in the system (21), and exiting the system (27).

The third segment is a timing segment and is used to schedule the end of service routine. The model will schedule a dummy transaction at time 480, which will cause the terminate instruction to execute (counter set to 0). The fourth section, the control segment, begins the simulation by setting the termination counter and giving control over to the model segment.

| Block Symbol | Functional Description of Block |
|---|---|

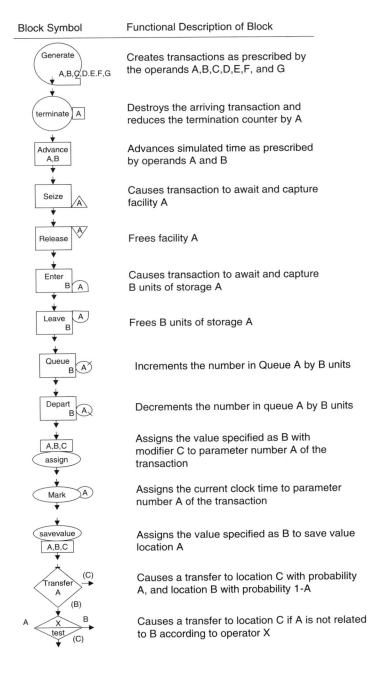

**Figure 8.9**
*Basic GPSS modeling component blocks.*

Generate
A,B,C,D,E,F,G — Creates transactions as prescribed by the operands A,B,C,D,E,F, and G

terminate A — Destroys the arriving transaction and reduces the termination counter by A

Advance A,B — Advances simulated time as prescribed by operands A and B

Seize A — Causes transaction to await and capture facility A

Release A — Frees facility A

Enter B A — Causes transaction to await and capture B units of storage A

Leave A B — Frees B units of storage A

Queue B A — Increments the number in Queue A by B units

Depart B A — Decrements the number in queue A by B units

A,B,C assign — Assigns the value specified as B with modifier C to parameter number A of the transaction

Mark A — Assigns the current clock time to parameter number A of the transaction

savevalue A,B,C — Assigns the value specified as B to save value location A

Transfer A (C) (B) — Causes a transfer to location C with probability A, and location B with probability 1-A

A X test B (C) — Causes a transfer to location C if A is not related to B according to operator X

**Figure 8.10**
*GPSS model for
the bank teller
problem.*

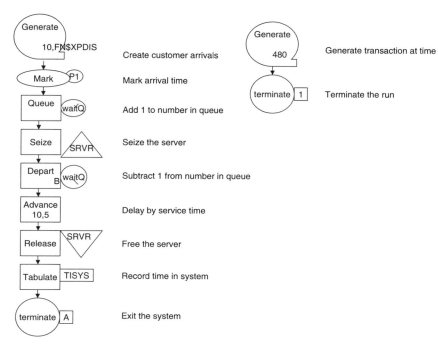

**Figure 8.11**
*GPSS code for the
bank teller
problem.*

```
1 *
2 Simulate
3 *
4 XPDIS function RN1,C24
5 0.0, 0.0/0.1, 0.104/0.2, 0.222/0.3, 0.355/0.4, 0.509/0.5, 0.69
6 0.6, 0.915/0.7, 1.2/0.75, 1.38/0.8, 1.6/0.84, 1.83/0.88, 2.12/0.9
7 2.3/0.92, 2.52/0.94, 2.81/0.95, 2.99/0.96, 3.2/0.97, 3.5/0.98
8 4.0/0.99, 4.6/0.995, 5.3/0.998, 6.2/0.999, 7.0/0.9997, 8
9 *
10 TISYS table MP1,0,5,20
11 *
12 * model segment
13 *
14 Generate 10, FN$XPDIS
15 Mark P1
16 Queue Waitq
17 Seize SRVR
18 Depart Waitq
19 Advance 10,5
20 Release SRVR
21 Tabulate TISYS
22 Terminate
23 *
24 * timing segment
25 *
26 Generate 480
27 Terminate 1
```

This example shows some features of GPSS. GPSS is a simple modeling method that became widely used. However, this language was doomed by its interpretive operation, which made it extremely slow. The reader is encouraged to consult [15] for details of the language.

### 8.4.3   Simscript

Simscript was developed in the late 1960s as a general-purpose simulation language. See [16] for details about the language. It provides a discrete simulation modeling framework with English-like free-form syntax making for very readable and self-documenting models. Simscript supports two types of entities: permanent and temporary. For example, in the bank teller problem, the teller is permanent and the clients are temporary. Permanent entities exist for the entire duration of the simulation, whereas the temporary entities come and go during it. Attributes of the entities are named, increasing their readability and meanings.

A Simscript simulation is built of three pieces: a preamble, a main program, and event subprograms. The preamble defines the components of the model (entities, variables, arrays, etc.). The main program initializes all elements to begin the simulation. The events define the user events used to model a system. To define these components we will again use the bank teller problem. We will assume arrivals are 10 minutes apart on average and exponentially distributed, and the teller service time is uniformly distributed between 5 and 15 minutes. Figure 8.12 depicts code for this problem. It indicates many of Simscript's features, as follows:

- Line 2 describes the wait time as being a system entity that has statistics associated with it, and it is a permanent entity since it is not indicated as being temporary. Therefore, we can keep statistics on it over the life of the model.

- Line 3 defines a temporary entity customer and indicates that it belongs to the wait time.

- Lines 6 and 7 define the event names and their attributes.

- Lines 9–14 define statistics to be taken on this entity.

The main program or section is shown in section B. This portion sets up the initial conditions (i.e., setting the status of the teller to idle, scheduling the first arrival, and scheduling a stop in the simulation). The next three sections define the arrival, departure, and stop events. The arrival event schedules the next arrival to keep the event flow going, creates a customer, gives it time information, places it in the wait line, and schedules a teller

A:
1 Preamble
2 the system owns a wait line and has a status temporary entities
3 every customer has an enter time and may belong to the wait line
4 event notices include arrival and stop simulation
5 every departure has a teller
6 define busy to mean 1
7 define idle to mean 0
8 define time in bank as a real variable
9 tally no customers as the number, AV time and the mean,
10 and Var time as the variance of time in bank
11 accumulate avg util as the mean, and Var util as the
12 Variance of status
13 accumulate Ave waitline length as the mean, and
14 var waitline length as the variance of N wait line
15 end

B:
1 main
2 let status=idle
3 schedule an arrival now
4 schedule a stop simulation in 8 hours
5 start simulation
6 end

C:
1. Event arrival
2 schedule an arrival in exponential F(10.,1) minutes
3 create a customer
4 let enter time (customer)=time V
5 if status=busy
6 file the customer in the wait line
7 return
8 else
9 let status=busy
10 schedule a departure given customer in Uniform F(56.,15.,1) minutes
11 return
12 end

D:
1 event departure given customer
2 define customer as an integer variable
3 let time in back=1440.*(time v-enter time(customer)
4 destroy the customer
5 if the wait line is empty
6 let status=idle
7 return
8 else
9 remove the first customer from the wait line
10 schedule a departure given customer in Uniform F(5., 15., 1) minutes
11 return
12 end

E:
1 event stop simulation
2 start new page
3 skip 5 lines
4 print 1 line thus
5 single teller wait line example
6 skip 4 lines
7 print 3 lines with no customers, av time, and var time thus
8 Number of customers = *********
9 Average time in bank = ****.****
10 Variance of time in bank = ****.****
11 skip 4 lines
12 print 2 lines with avg util and var util thus
13 Average teller utilization = ****.****
14 Variance of utilization = ****.****
15 Skip 4 lines
16 print 2 lines with avg queue length and var queue length thus
17 Average wait line length = ****.****
18 Variance of wait time = ****.****
19 stop
20 end

**Figure 8.12**   *Simscript bank teller pension code.*

service if the line is empty. The departure event computes a customer's time in the bank, removes the customer, and schedules the next customer. The stop event outputs the collected statistics.

## 8.4.4  Slam II

Slam II, a simulation language for alternative modeling, was developed by Pritsker and Associates, West Lafayette, Indiana, in the late 1970s. It is a combined modeling language providing for queuing network analysis, discrete event, and continuous modeling in integrated form. Slam II provides features to easily integrate the three forms.

At the highest end the modeler can use a network structure consisting of nodes and branches representing queues, servers, and decision points to construct a model of a system to be simulated. This, in turn, can be easily translated into Slam II code. Additionally, Slam provides the ability to mix events and continuous models with network models by use of event nodes that call event code for discrete and/or continuous models. As in the previous languages, the event-oriented Slam models are constructed of a set of events and the potential changes that can occur with each of them. These events define how the model interprets the event and state changes. Slam provides a set of standard support subprograms to aid the event-oriented modeler. As was the case in GASP, the Slam continuous models are built by specifying a set of continuous differential, or difference, equations that describe the dynamic behavior of the state variables. These equations are coded in FORTRAN (Slam's base language) using Slam's state variables.

Slam II uses a set of basic symbols to describe the system being modeled, as does GPSS. Figure 8.13 depicts the basic Slam II symbols and their associated code statements. Only the first three characters of the statement names and the first four characters of node labels are significant. They will be used in the example of the bank teller. As before, we wish to have customers arriving on an average of every 10 minutes with an exponential distribution and the first one to start at time 0. Additionally, the teller services the customers with a uniform distribution from 5 to 15 minutes. The resulting Slam network model is shown in Figure 8.14. References to nodes are made through node labels (NLBLs). When a node label is required, it is placed in a rectangle and appended to the base of the symbol.

**Figure 8.13**
*Basic symbols and statements for Slam models.*

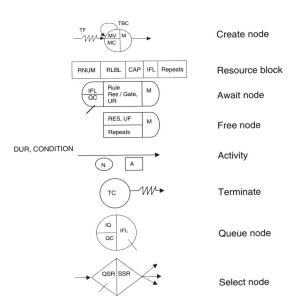

Create node

Resource block

Await node

Free node

Activity

Terminate

Queue node

Select node

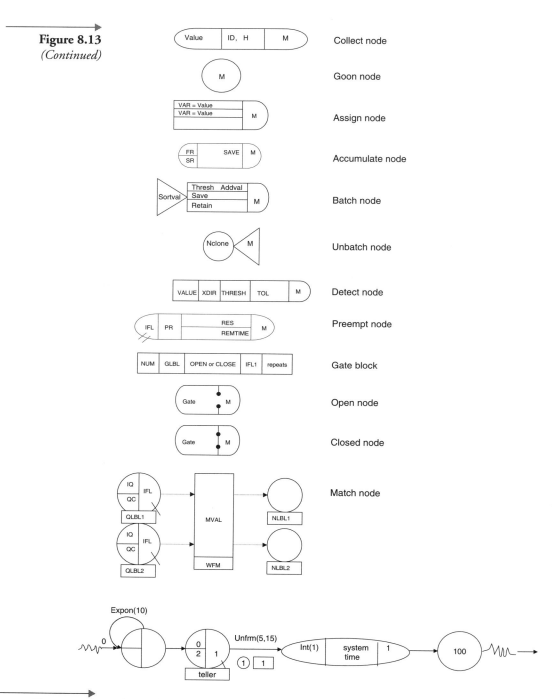

**Figure 8.13**
(*Continued*)

Collect node

Goon node

Assign node

Accumulate node

Batch node

Unbatch node

Detect node

Preempt node

Gate block

Open node

Closed node

Match node

**Figure 8.14**   *Slam II bank teller problem network model.*

**Figure 8.15**
*Slam II bank teller problem code.*

```
1    Gen, Fortier, Bankteller, 5/22/2002,1;
2    Limits, 2,1,100
3    Network
4    Create, Expon(10.), 0, 1;
5    Teller Queue(1),0,~;
6    Activity (1)/1, Unifrm(5.,15.);
7    Term 100; Colct, Ini(1), system time,,1;
8    end networks;
```

The code for this network is shown in Figure 8.15. The first line of the code defines the modeler, the name of the model, and its date and version. The second line defines the limits of the model and files one USR attribute and up to 100 concurrent entities in the system at a time. Line 3 identifies this code as network code, and line 4 creates customers with a mean of 10 minutes exponentially distributed. Line 5 defines queue 1 as a teller with no initial customers in its queue, an infinite queue with service uniformly distributed from 5 to 15 minutes. Line 7 takes statistics or time in system from entities as they leave the server. Line 8 indicates that the simulation will run for 100 entities and then end.

This code is extremely simple and provides much flexibility as to how to expand the system. To look at the tellers' operations in more detail, the queue could be replaced by an event node and the code for the teller event supplied to model (very similar to the code seen in earlier figures). (See [17].)

## 8.5  Applications of simulation

To illustrate the use of simulation a few example problems are given and models developed in the Slam II simulation language. The first example is an industrial plant with five stations building a production in assembly line fashion. The problem can be viewed in Figure 8.16.

The plant takes in subassemblies and finishes them off in five steps. There is storage room at the beginning of the line, but once in the line a maximum of one unit per station is possible. The statistics we wish to determine are workstation utilization, time to process through stations, number of units waiting, and total produced. The resulting Slam network is shown

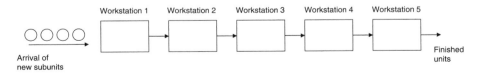

**Figure 8.16**   *Assembly line example.*

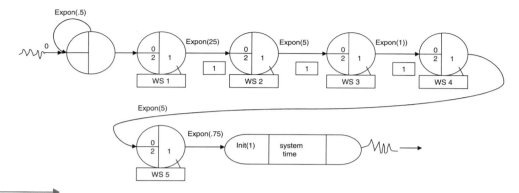

**Figure 8.17** *Slam II network model for the assembly line problem.*

in Figure 8.17. The resultant code would allow us to examine the items of interest without causing any loss of detail from the intended model.

A second, more detailed example shows how simulation can be used to model a distributed database management system. The model is shown in Figure 8.18. Depicted is the process or servers in a node that services user database transactions. Users provide requests, and the operating system services them by pipelining the database requests to the transaction manager, which, in turn, provides reduced requests to the network database

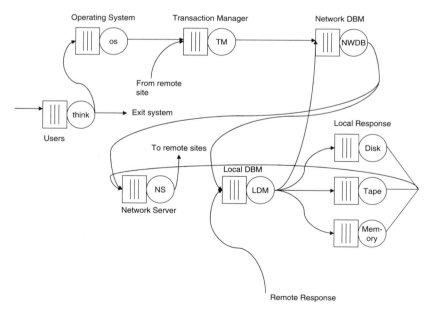

**Figure 8.18** *Queuing model of a distributed database system.*

server, which determines where the actual access is to be performed. The local site chosen then accesses the information from the appropriate device. The details at each level were commensurate with the intended model. The queues were all modeled as events and then the code necessary to simulate them was developed. This simulation is being used to analyze optimization algorithms for distributed database systems. The Slam network is shown in Figure 8.19.

**Figure 8.19**
*Slam II network simulation model for a distributed database system.*

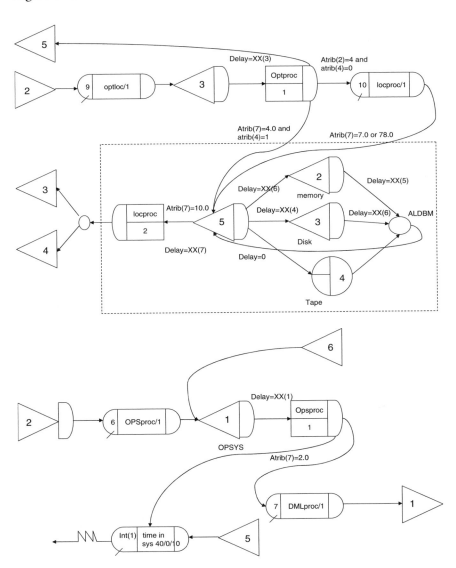

**Figure 8.19**
*(Continued)*

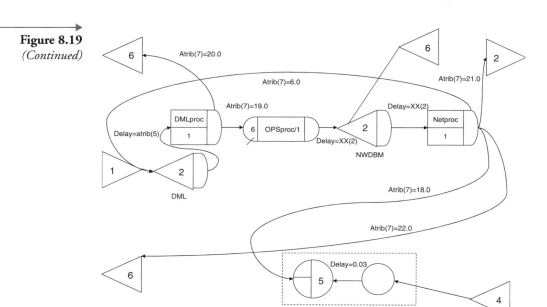

## 8.5.1   **The simulation program**

The simulation program constitutes the realization of the simulation model. It is constructed as a modular software package allowing for the interchanging of simulated database management components without causing undue stress to the other components of the model. The simulation program is composed of a set of Slam II network statements and detailed discrete event code (similar to GASP IV), which model the major computational aspects of a distributed database management system, as previously defined. To provide the capability to model a wide range of topologies and database management architectures, the model is driven by a set of information tables that hold characteristics of the network topology and communications, location of the data items, the contents of the data items, and statistics of use. The Slam II network code to realize this model is shown in Figure 8.20. This code clearly depicts the major components of the simulation program. Additionally, note that the EVENT 5 shown indicates that the particular node is not a simple queue representation; it also indicates a drop in detail into discrete event simulation code. Such events allow for greatly expanding the details of the aspect of the model.

**Figure 8.20**

*Slam II network model code.*

This is a list of the activities in the network

1 Enter to OPSYS 2 OPSYS to DML
3 OPSYS to User 4 Optimize to LDBM
5 Optimize to User 6 NWDBM to DML
7 LDBM to memory 8 LDBM to disk
9 LDBM to tape 10 LDBM to DLOC
11 Memory to RLDBM 12 disk to RLDBM
13 Tape to RLDBM 14 RLDBM to LDBM
15 DLOC to NWDBM 16 DLOC to REQN
17 REQN to NWDEL 18 NWDEL to NWDBM
19 DML to NWDBM 20 DML to OPSYS
21 NWDBM to Optimize 22 NWDBM to User
23 LDBM to REQN 24 NWDBM to User

The following statements are network input statements:

Gen, P. Fortier, DBMS Queue SIMPROG, 5,22,2002,1;
Limits, 10,20,500;
Stat,1,hits on directory,10,1.,1.;
Stat,2 hits on dictionary, 10,1.,1.;
Stat,3,processing time,20,0.,10.;
Stat,4,remote time,10,0.,.05;
Stat,5,failure rate,10,1.,1.;
Stat,6,optimizer time,10,0.,10.;
Stat,7,Optimizer algorithm delay,10,0.,10.;
Stat,8,parsing delay,10,0.,.0015;
Stat,9,illegal operations,10,1.,1.;
Stat,10, translate delay, 10,0.,.01;
Stat,11,dictionary search,10,0.,.00002;
Network
Resource/Opsproc(1),6;
Resource/DMLproc(1),7;
Resource/Netproc(1),8;
Resource/Optproc(1),9;
Resource/Locproc(1),10;

Tape queue(4);
act/13,,,RLDBM;
Mem queue(2);
act/11,XX(5),,RLDBM;
Disk queue(3);
act/12,XX(6),,RLDBM;
RLDBM GOON; Request LDBM
act/14,,,LDBM;
DLOC Free, locproc/1;
act;
goon;
act/15,,atrib(8).eq.15, NWDBM ret route, local source
act/16,0.02,atrib(8).eq.16; ret route, remote source
reqn goon;
act/17,0.02;
NWDEL queue(5); Network delay
act/18,0.03,,NWDBM
user colct,int(1), tim in sys, 40,0.,10.;
act/20;
terminate;
endnetwork;
init,0;
fin;

Enter, 1;
act/1;
Opsys await(6),opsproc/1;
event,1; operating system
act,XX(1);
free, opsproc/1;
act/3,,atrib(7).eq.3,user; service completed
act/2,,atrib(7).eq.2;
DML await(7),DMLproc/1;
event,4;
act,atrib(5);
free, DMLproc/1;
act/20,,atrib(7).eq.20,opsys service completed
act/19,,atrib(7).eq.19,NWDBM;
NWDBM await(8), Netproc/1;
event,2; Network database manager
act, XX(2);
free, Netproc/1;
act/6,,atrib(7).eq.6,DML processing completed
act/22,,atrib(7).eq.22,user; data doesn't exist
act/21,,atrib(7).eq.21;
optim await(9), optproc/1;
event,3; Query optimization
act,XX(3);
free, optproc/1;
act/4,,atrib(7).eq.4.0and atrib(4).eq.0,WLDBM;
act/26,,atrib(7).eq.4 and atrib(4).eq.1,LDBM;
act/5,,atrib(7).eq.5, user; illegal query
WLDBM await(10), locproc/1;
LDBM event,5; local database manager
act/7,XX(4),atrib(7).eq.7 or atrib(7).eq.78, mem;
act/8,XX(4),atrib(7).eq.8 or atrib(7).eq.78, disk;
act/9,999999,atrib(7).eq.10,DLOC;
act/23,atrib(7).eq.23,REQN;

# 8.6    **Summary**

This chapter introduced the use of simulation in building and analyzing a wide range of systems. Simulations were shown to be extremely versatile in their ability to model systems at varying levels of detail. They provide quick and precise models of systems to allow any studies to be performed at will. The main simulation techniques of discrete event, continuous, queuing, combined, and hybrid methods were described, as were four widely used languages: GASP, GPSS, Simscript, and Slam. This was followed by two simple examples to show how simulation can be used to study a real-world system.

# 9

# *Petri Nets*

## 9.1   Introduction

Every tool applied to the modeling and analysis of computer systems has its place. Petri nets have a place in computer systems performance assessment, ranging somewhere between analytical queuing theory and computer simulation. This is due to the nature of Petri nets and their ability to model concurrency, synchronization, mutual exclusion, conflict, and system state more completely than analytical models but not as completely as simulations. They have a fundamental theory dictating their analysis, but they act more like simulations in that they allow the modeler to examine single entities within the system, as well as their movement and effect on the state of the entire system.

Petri nets (PNs) provide a graphical tool as well as a notational method for the formal specification of systems. The systems they model tend to include more than simply an arrival rate and a service rate. They are used in situations where each entity passing through the system can bring individual state information, which can be used to more completely and accurately model complex interactions such as contention and concurrency.

Petri nets were first introduced in 1966 to describe concurrent systems. This initial introduction was followed by continual improvements—for example, the addition of timing to transitions, priority to transitions, types to tokens, and colors depicting conditions on places and tokens. These have been followed by the development of software tools to aid in the modeling and analysis of systems using Petri net concepts.

## 9.2   Basic notation

Petri nets represent computer systems by providing a means to abstract the basic elements of the system and its informational flow using only four fun-

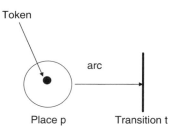

**Figure 9.1**
*Basic Petri net components.*

damental components. These four Petri net modeling components are place, transition, arc, and token. Places are represented graphically as a circle, transitions as a bar, arcs as directed line segments, and tokens as dots (Figure 9.1). Places are used to represent possible system components and their state. For example, a disk drive could be represented using a place, as could a program or other resource. Transitions are used to describe events that may result in different system states. For example, the action of reading an item from a disk drive or the action of writing an item to a disk drive could be modeled as separate transitions. Arcs represent the relationships that exist between the transitions and places. For example, disk read requests may be put in one place, and that place may be connected to the transition, "removing an item from a disk," thus indicating that this place is related to the transition. You can think of the arc as providing a path for the activation of a transition. Finally, tokens are used to define the state of the Petri net. Tokens in the basic Petri net model are nondescriptive markers, which are stored in places and are used in defining Petri net marking.

The marking of a Petri net place by the placement of a token can be viewed as the statement of the condition of the place. For example, Figure 9.2 illustrates a simple Petri net with only one place and one transition. The place is connected to the transition by an arc, and the transition is likewise connected to the place by a second arc. The former arc is an input arc, while the latter arc is an output arc. The placement of a token represents the active marking of the Petri net state. The Petri net shown in Figure 9.2 represents a net that will continue to cycle forever.

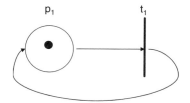

**Figure 9.2**
*Example perpetual motion Petri net.*

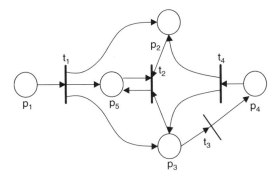

**Figure 9.3**
*Petri net example.*

Petri nets are described both graphically and using set notation. As described previously, a Petri net is composed of places ($P$), transitions ($T$), arcs (consisting of input functions, $I$, and output functions, $O$), and tokens, which form the marking of the net ($MP$). Using this notation, we can describe a Petri net as a five tuple, $M = (P, T, I, O, MP)$, where $P$ represents a set of places, $P = \{p_1, p_2, \ldots, p_n\}$, with one place for each circle in the Petri net graph; $T$ represents a set of transitions, $T = \{t_1, t_2, \ldots, t_m\}$, with one for each bar in the Petri net graph; $I$ represents a bag of sets (bags is a generalization allowing for duplicates) of input functions for all transitions, $I = \{I_{t1}, I_{t2}, \ldots, I_{tm}\}$, mapping places to transitions;, $O$ represents a bag of sets of output functions for all transitions, $O = \{O_{t1}, O_{t2}, \ldots, O_{tm}\}$, mapping transitions to places; and $MP$ represents the marking of places with tokens. The initial marking is referred to as $MP_0$. $MP_0$ is represented as an ordered tuple of magnitude $n$, where $n$ represents the number of places in our Petri net. Each place will have either no tokens or some integer number of tokens. For example, the Petri net graph depicted in Figure 9.3 can be described using the previous notation as:

$$
\begin{aligned}
M &= (P, T, I, O, MP) \\
P &= \{p_1, p_2, p_3, p_4, p_5\} \\
T &= \{t_1, t_2, t_3, t_4\} \\
I(t_1) &= \{p_1\} \\
I(t_2) &= \{p_2, p_3, p_5\} \\
I(t_3) &= \{p_3\} \\
I(t_4) &= \{p_4\} \\
O(t_1) &= \{p_2, p_3, p_5\}
\end{aligned}
$$

(9.1)

**Figure 9.4**
*Dual of Petri Net
from Figure 9.3.*

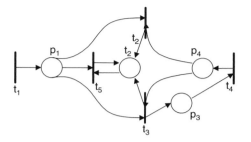

$$O(t_2) = \{p_5\}$$
$$O(t_3) = \{p_4\}$$
$$O(t_4) = \{p_2, p_3\}$$
$$MP = (0,0,0,0,0)$$

(Cont. 9.1)

The graphical notation depicts Petri nets as a directed bipartite graph. The graph, $G$, is described as a two tuple, $G = (V,A)$, where $V$ represents a set of vertices, $V = \{v_1, v_2, v_3, \ldots, v_s\}$; and A represents a bag of directed arcs, $A = \{a_1, a_2, a_3, \ldots, a_j\}$. An arc, which is an element of $A$, is composed of a tuple with two vertices, $a_i = (v_j, v_k)$, where $v_j, v_k \in V$. The set of vertices of the graph can be partitioned into two disjoint sets, $P$ and $T$, where these sets have the properties $V = P \cup T$ and $P \cap T = 0$. In addition, for an arc $a_i \in A$, if $a_i = (v_j, v_k)$, then either $v_j \in P$ and $v_k \in T$ or vice versa. That is, the two ends of the arc cannot be drawn from the same set; if $v_j \in P$, then $v_k \in T$ and cannot be an element of $P$.

A Petri net model, as with many mathematical models, has a dual. The dual of a Petri net is defined as a Petri net where transitions are changed to places and places are changed to transitions. (See Figure 9.4.) The input and output functions are changed in that the inputs defined for the transition

**Figure 9.5**
*Inverse of Petri Net
from Figure 9.3.*

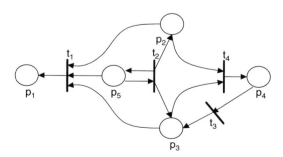

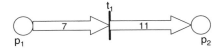

**Figure 9.6**
*Multipath arc.*

now represent inputs to places. Since this is not possible, the inputs become output functions and output functions become input functions.

A Petri net can also have an inverse defined for it. The inverse of a Petri net keeps all places and transitions the same and switches the input functions with the output functions (Figure 9.5).

Petri nets are defined also as multigraphs, since a place can represent multiple inputs and/or outputs from or to a transition. This implies that there could be several arcs between a single place and a transition. We could model these as single arcs but that could become cumbersome as the number of arcs grows. A better way to model multiple arcs is either to represent the multiple arcs as a thick arc with the number of representative arcs embedded inside (Figure 9.6), or as a bold arc with a number attached to it as a label (Figure 9.7).

Petri nets have a state. This state is defined by the cardinality of tokens and their distribution throughout the places in the Petri net. This marking can be represented as a function, $\mu$, defined over each place, $p$, and results in a value, $N$, from the set of counting integers 0, 1, ... ,$\infty$:

$$\mu : p \rightarrow N \tag{9.2}$$

The marking, $\mu$, can also be defined as an $n$ vector. The vector $\mu$ provides token information for each place, $p_i$, in a Petri net. The token information represents the number of tokens in the particular place (number of tokens in place, $p_i$, is $\mu_i$):

$$\mu = \left(\mu_1, \mu_2, \mu_3, \dots, \mu_n\right), \tag{9.3}$$

where

$$n = |P| \text{ and each } \mu_i \in N, i = 0, \dots, n$$

**Figure 9.7**
*Multipath arc as bold line.*

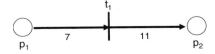

**Figure 9.8**
*Marked Petri net.*

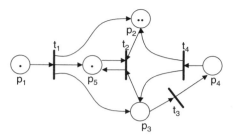

Place markings represented as a function and place markings represented as a vector are related by $\mu(p_i) = \mu_i$. The markings at a specific point in time represent the state of the Petri net at that time. A marked Petri net, $M = (C, \mu)$, is represented as a Petri net structure, $M = (P, T, I, O)$ and its marking: $MP$ or $\mu$. This is also typically represented as $M = (P, T, I, O, \mu)$. The marking $\mu$ changes as the Petri net changes state and is therefore typically represented with a subscript $t$. Therefore, the true representation is:

$$M = (P, T, I, O, \mu_t) \tag{9.4}$$

where represents the state of the Petri net at time $t$, where $t$ is drawn from the set of nonnegative integer values.

The marking of a Petri net is specified by placing tokens, which are represented as dots in the graphical notation (Figure 9.8) in the places. The marking for the Petri net shown in Figure 9.8 represented as a vector would be $\mu_t = (1, 2, 0, 0, 1)$. If we assume this is the initial marking of this Petri net, then the definition becomes $\mu_0 = (1, 2, 0, 0, 1)$, since this would be the 0th state this Petri net has visited. The number of tokens that may be assigned to a place is unbounded (though in later refined models we will see this can be limited). The set of all possible markings for a Petri net with $n$ places is simply the set of all $n$ vectors, $N^n$, where $N$ represents all possible states and $n$ the number of places.

# 9.3   Classical Petri nets

Given the basic definitions and notation from the prior section, we can now begin to examine how these fundamental elements can be used in modeling aspects of computer systems and ultimately entire systems. The first new notation required is that of Petri net state transitions. To move from one state to another state, a Petri net will fire all transitions that are enabled. The exact moment of firing can be pictured as occurring as a clock signal in

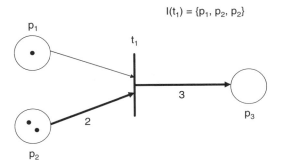

**Figure 9.9**
*Enabled transition.*

$I(t_1) = \{p_1, p_2, p_2\}$

a computer system. When the clock begins a cycle (e.g., a rising edge) all gates that have signals enabling their execution do so during the cycle. Similarly, in a Petri net all transitions that are enabled will fire once during this cycle.

Before we look at firing, we need to address the conditions required. Having tokens available in places is fundamental to the concept of enabling transitions. Therefore, it is important to know the state of the entire Petri net before preparing to fire enabled transitions. The enabling of a transition is caused by tokens being available in places that are members of a transition's input function. Only if all of the places named in a transition's input functions have tokens available is a transition enabled (Figure 9.9).

The Petri net shown in Figure 9.9 has the marking $\mu_0 = (1,2,0)$, input function $I(t_1) = \{p_1, p_2, p_3\}$, and output function $O(t_1) = \{p_3, p_3, p_3\}$. Given this initial marking and the defined input and output functions, transition $t_1$ is enabled, since it requires one token contributed by $P_1$ and two tokens contributed by $P_2$ to have all of its input functions satisfied with tokens available in the named places and in the required quantities. The tokens in these places are referred to as the transition's enabling tokens. Given that a transition is enabled at the beginning of a Petri net's firing cycle, it will fire the transition, causing the movement of the number of tokens from its input places to its output places, as modeled by the output function's arity. The result of this firing will be a new Petri net state, $\mu_1$. For example, in Figure 9.9, given the initial state $\mu_0$, transition $t_1$ will fire at the beginning of the firing cycle, removing one token from place $p_1$ and two tokens from place $p_2$ and placing these three tokens into place $p_3$. The resulting new Petri net state is represented by the marking $\mu_1 = (0,0,3)$, and is depicted in Figure 9.10. The firing action is considered an atomic action, in that it appears as if all of the tokens are removed from the input places and deposited into the output places instantaneously.

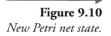
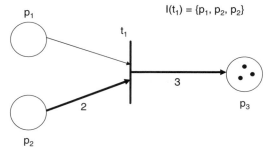

**Figure 9.10**
*New Petri net state.*

The firing of the Petri net provides the movement from one state to a new state. The new state is the only state reachable in a single total transition firing of all the enabled transitions. The collection of all possible states that can be represented by this Petri net and its initial markings is called state-space. The collection of all states in the state-space of this Petri net can only be reached in sequence from the initial state to the final state by single step, state-space changes. This implies that a Petri net can only fire enabled transitions, and, after they fire, they cannot fire any newly enabled transitions until the next cycle. This single state Petri net state-change can be described using a next-state function, $\delta$. This function, $\delta$, when applied to a Petri net state, $\mu_i$, will cause the Petri net to transition from state $\mu_i$ to a new state: $\mu_{i+1}$. The function $\delta$ is then defined as:

$$\delta\left(\mu_i\{t\}\right) = \mu_{i+1} \tag{9.5}$$

The set $\{t\}$ represents the set of all enabled transitions within this Petri net. If a transition is not enabled, then this function is undefined.

Beyond the basics defined here, Petri nets have been developed for the modeling of conditions not typically available through queuing theory. For example, synchronization, conflict, and concurrency are concepts not easily defined and modeled by queuing theory.

To clarify some of the concepts covered we will take a look at a simple example: that of resource sharing. In this example, shown in Figure 9.11, we model two user processes requesting a specific resource ($p_{res\_idle}$). If the resource is idle, there is a token present in the $p_{res\_idle}$ place. If a process wanting this resource has a token in its place (e.g., $P_{1\_req}$), and the resource is idle (a token in $p_{res\_idle}$), then the transition (e.g., $t_{1\_start}$) is enabled and can fire on the next cycle. When the transition fires, the resource now becomes unavailable (it is busy), and the second process must wait until the resource is released (Figure 9.12).

**Figure 9.11**
*Resource sharing
example.*

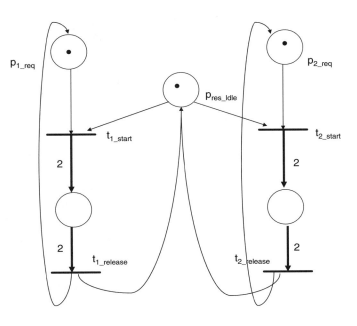

**Figure 9.12**
*Allocated resource.*

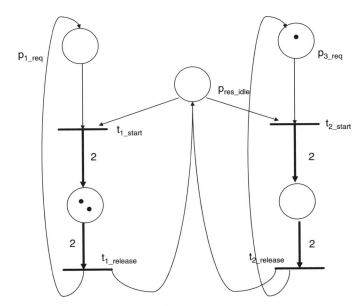

With these basic concepts we can now move on to more advanced ones. Very often in a computer system, when one process is accessing or even attempting to access some resource, others are blocked from trying to enter. This is the concept of a gate, lock, or semaphore. In the case of such items, when one job has control over the resource, others are blocked from attempting to access the resource, even if they have all the other resources they need to move forward with their execution. To model this concept of a lock or semaphore, Petri net modelers developed the concept of the inhibitor. An inhibitor is a function that relates a place (as a blocker) to a transition. If a place, $p$, has an inhibitor relationship with a transition, $t$, then, when place $p$ has a token present, transition $t$ cannot fire, even if all input functions are satisfied and the transition would be otherwise enabled. For example, Figure 9.13 depicts the reader and writer problem. The problem states that when a writer is in the mode of writing, all readers must be blocked from accessing the held resource. In the example, the inhibitor is shown as an undirected arc with a small circle at the transition being inhibited by the place at the other end of the arc. The example shows that place, $p_6$ is acting as the inhibitor to transition $t_5$. The Petri net is now described using the six-tuple, $M = (P, T, I, O, N, H)$. In the set notation the inhibitor is described as $H\{t_5\} = \{p_6\}$.

A Petri net's state, $\mu$, is said to be reachable from some other state, $\mu'$, if there exists some finite number of firings of the Petri net beginning at state $\mu$, which will result in the final marking $\mu'$. A reachability set $[RS(\mu)]$ from each valid marking of our Petri net, $M$ starting in state $N$, is defined as the set of all possible markings reachable through any set of firings. There is no reachability set possible for a Petri net with an initial null marking.

**Figure 9.13**
*Petri net with an inhibitor.*

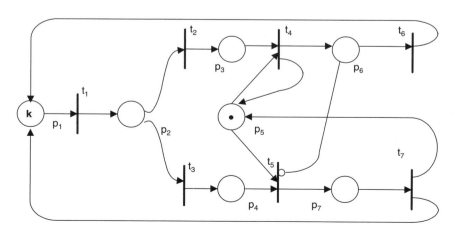

The reachability set for a Petri net with an initial marking, $\mu_0$, is denoted $RS(\mu_0)$ and is defined as the smallest set of markings, so that:

$$\mu_0 \in RS(\mu_0) \text{ and } \mu_1 \in RS(\mu_0)$$
$$\exists t \in T : \delta(N,(t)) \rightarrow \mu_2(t+1) \tag{9.6}$$
$$\Rightarrow \mu_2 \in RS(N_0)$$

To determine the reachability set, we must begin from the initial state, $\mu_0$, and incrementally define each step possible emanating from this initial state and all states derivable from this state. Once a marking has been considered, during any iteration, it cannot be considered again. The reachability set for the reader and writer graph shown in Figure 9.13 is as follows for $k = 2$.

$$\mu_0 = 2p_1 + p_5$$
$$\mu_1 = p_1 + p_2 + p_5$$
$$\mu_2 = 2p_2 + p_5$$
$$\mu_3 = p_1 + p_3 + p_5$$
$$\mu_4 = p_1 + p_4 + p_5$$
$$\mu_5 = p_2 + p_3 + p_5$$
$$\mu_6 = p_2 + p_4 + p_5$$
$$\mu_7 = p_1 + p_5 + p_6$$
$$\mu_8 = p_1 + p_7$$
$$\mu_9 = 2p_3 + p_5$$
$$\mu_{10} = p_3 + p_4 + p_5$$
$$\mu_{11} = p_2 + p_5 + p_6$$
$$\mu_{12} = 2p_4 + p_5$$
$$\mu_{13} = p_2 + p_7$$
$$\mu_{14} = p_3 + p_5 + p_6$$
$$\mu_{15} = p_4 + p_5 + p_6$$
$$\mu_{16} = p_3 + p_7$$
$$\mu_{17} = p_4 + p_7$$
$$\mu_{18} = p_5 + 2p_6$$

The reachability set contains no information about which transitions fired to reach the state markings. Such information can be found in a reachability

**Figure 9.14**
*Reachability graph
for the reader and
writer problem.*

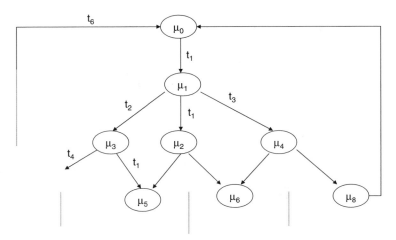

**Figure 9.14**
*Reachability graph
for the reader and
writer problem.*

graph, shown in Figure 9.14. In this graph each node represents a state of the Petri net and each arc represents a direct transition, which is possible from one end of the directed arc to the other end due to a single transition's firing. For example, you can see that if we fire transition $t_1$ from $\mu_0$ we can get to a new state, $\mu_1$, where a token has moved from place 1 to place 2.

It is often desirable to model logical conditions. For example, to only fire a transition when there are more than $n$ tokens in a place, we simply need to include an arc with arity $n + 1$. Since the basic condition on a transition firing is that its connected input places meet the conditions of the transition's input function, by including $n + 1$ redundant set items for the input place we can accomplish what we need (Figure 9.15).

If we wish instead to test for the condition of equal to some value but not greater than the value, we can use an inhibitor of arity $n + 1$ to block a

**Figure 9.15**
*Petri net
component to test
condition greater
than M.*

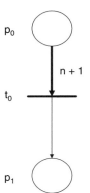

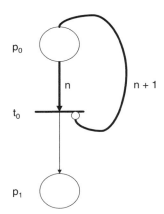

**Figure 9.16**
*Petri net component to test condition equal but not greater than M.*

transition if there are more than $n$ tokens in place 0. To meet the equal condition we use the arc weighted at $n$ to remove $n$ items if there are $n$ and only $n$ items (Figure 9.16). If we wish to test for less than $n$ items and remove the items, we could use the Petri net shown in Figure 9.17. Again, this Petri net uses an inhibitor function to block movement of the desired number of tokens.

An important property required when modeling computer systems is that of conflict (Figure 9.18). In this example, when there is a token in place $p_0$, both transitions $t_1$ and $t_2$ are enabled. However, only one of them may fire, since there is only one token available. As soon as one fires, say $t_1$, it removes the token from place $p_0$ and transfers it to place $p_1$. As soon as transition $t_1$ removes the token, transition $t_2$ is no longer enabled. If there were two tokens in place $p_0$, then both of the transitions would be enabled and could fire during this firing cycle. Very often we wish to indicate which of

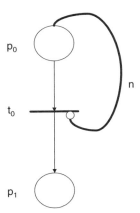

**Figure 9.17**
*Petri net modeling conflict.*

**Figure 9.18**
*Petri net
component to test
condition less than.*

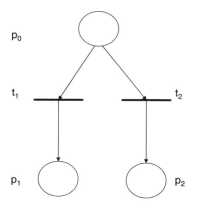

these transitions is to fire when only one can, and in which order if they both are able to fire. We will discuss some of these extended controls when we look at colored Petri nets and generalized Petri nets later in this chapter.

Another important property required when modeling computer systems and software processes is concurrency. Concurrency is characterized by the concurrent or parallel execution of activities. For a Petri net to have concurrent activities, it is required that we have concurrently enabled transitions. For example, in Figure 9.19, transitions $t_1$ and $t_2$ are considered concurrent, since they are both enabled at the same time in the Petri net marking. In our example, $\mu = (1,2,0,0)$ has transitions $t_1$ and $t_2$ enabled, and, therefore, they can fire concurrently.

Very often a computer system can have both conflict and concurrency occur at the same time. In Figure 9.20 we have an initial marking, $\mu =$

**Figure 9.19**
*Petri net modeling
concurrency.*

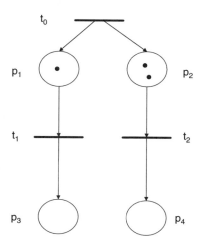

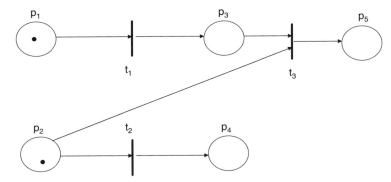

**Figure 9.20**
*Petri net modeling confusion.*

(1,1,0,0,0), which results in transitions $t_1$ and $t_2$ being enabled, the condition of concurrent transitions. If $t_1$ fires first, then we now have two transitions enabled, $t_2$ and $t_3$. This then depicts conflict, since the token from $p_2$ can only satisfy one of the necessary conditions for the two transitions it is enabling at this point in time.

A Petri net can have a variety of other qualities. For example, a Petri net state, $\mu$, is reachable from another state, $\mu'$, of the same Petri net if there is an integer number of intermediate steps from $\mu'$ that lead us to state $\mu$. For example, in Figure 9.21 we have an initial state $\mu_0 = (3,0,0,0)$, and a target state $\mu' = (1,1,0,1)$. We can see from our computations of state transitions that our net can reach this target state in three firings of our net. A related property is that of reversibility. Reversibility is the property where, given some initial Petri net state, $\mu$, we can return back to this state, $\mu$, in finite time. In Figure 9.21 the initial state, $\mu_0$, is not reversible, since we cannot get back to this state in a finite number of steps. On the other hand, if the

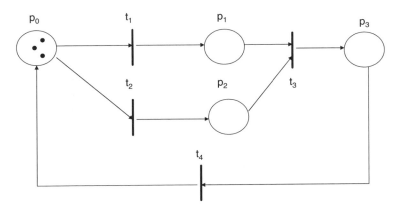

**Figure 9.21**
*Petri net indicating reachability and reversibility.*

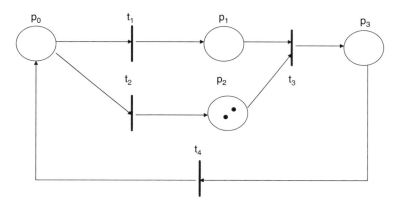

**Figure 9.22**
*Deadlocked Petri net.*

initial state is $\mu' = (0,1,0,2)$, we find that we can return to this state every four state transitions. Therefore, this state is reversible.

A Petri net is deadlocked if there are no transitions in the net that are enabled. In the example shown in Figure 9.22, the net has an initial marking, $\mu_0 = (0,0,2,0)$. This marking results in no transitions being enabled and no hope after an infinite amount of time of becoming enabled. Conversely, a Petri net is considered live if there are any transitions enabled.

A Petri net is defined to be $k$-place bounded if for all places in the network there are $k$ or less tokens in each place for all possible states of the network. For example, in the Petri net shown in Figure 9.21, we have a three-bounded net, since all places in the network have at most three or less tokens in their places for all reachable states within the Petri net.

Mutual exclusion is the final property we will define for traditional Petri nets. Mutual exclusion is defined for places and for transitions. The property holds for pairs of places or transitions within a Petri net. Two places, $p_a$ and $p_b$, are mutually exclusive in a Petri net system if for all states in the system places $p_a$ and $p_b$ are never both loaded with tokens concurrently. This implies that if one has tokens the other cannot. Similarly, for transitions, a Petri net possesses transition mutual exclusion if for all pairs of transitions in the Petri net, $t_a$ and $t_b$, only one can be enabled during any state reachable by this network. The properties presented in this section are generic and can be applied to most Petri nets.

## 9.4   **Timed Petri nets**

The Petri nets covered in the previous section had transitions that when fired took no time to move tokens from one place to another. In any real system an activity does take some finite time to perform its operation. For example, to read a file from a disk, to execute a program, or to communicate with some other machine takes some real time. Adding time to the Petri net provides the Petri net modeler with another powerful tool with which to study the performance of computer systems. Time can be associated with transitions, with selection of paths, with waiting in places, with inhibitors, and with any other component of the Petri net.

The most typical way that time is used in Petri net modeling is associated with transitions. This is because the firing of a transition can be viewed as the execution of an event being modeled—for example, a CPU execution cycle. Transitions that have time associated with them are referred to as timed transitions. These timed transitions are represented graphically as a rectangle or thick bars and are identified by designations beginning with $t$.

In Figure 9.23, transition $t_1$ is a timed transition with time $t_1$ as its interval to complete its firing once enabled. The semantics of the firing are a bit different from that of the basic Petri nets looked at previously. When a transition becomes enabled, its time period clock timer is set and begins to count down. Once the timer reaches 0, the transition fires, moving the token(s) from the input places for the transition to the output places for this transition. In the example shown in Figure 9.23, when a token arrives at place $p_1$, the timer for transition $t_1$ is set to $\tau_1$ and begins to count down. Once $\tau_1$ time units have passed, the transition fires and the token is taken from $p_1$ and moved to $p_2$. The decrement of the timer must be at a constant fixed speed for all transitions in the Petri net model. In this way the transition is made to model the operation of some element within the system being modeled.

A consideration to think about is what occurs when a transition becomes nonenabled due to the initial enabling token being used to ulti-

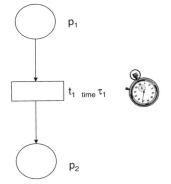

**Figure 9.23**
*Timed Petri net.*

$p_1$

$t_1$   time $\tau_1$

$p_2$

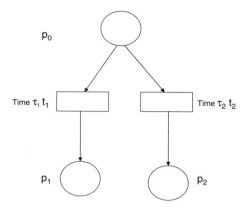

**Figure 9.24**
*Timed Petri net
with conflict.*

mately fire a competing transition. This condition is shown in Figure 9.24. If we assume that the time for transition $t_1$ is less than that for transition $t_2$, then, when place $p_1$ receives a token, the two timers would begin counting down. At some time ($\tau_1$) in the future, the timer for $t_1$ would reach its zero value, resulting in the firing of transition $t_1$. Since the token enabling $t_2$ is now gone, $t_2$ is no longer enabled and, therefore, its timer ($\tau_2$) would stop ticking down. The question now is what to do with transition $t_2$'s timer. There are two possibilities. The first is to simply reset the timer on the next cycle in which place $p_1$ has a token present, enabling $t_2$. In this case, unless place $p_1$ has a state where it has more than one token present, transition $t_2$ will never fire. The second possible way to handle this situation is to allow transition $t_2$'s timer to maintain the present clock timer value ($\tau_2 - \tau_1$). In this second case, when the next token is received at place $p_1$, the timer for transition $t_1$ resets its clock timer to $\tau_1$, and transition $t_2$ will continue counting down from time ($\tau_2 - \tau_1$). If the remaining time in transition $t_2$'s

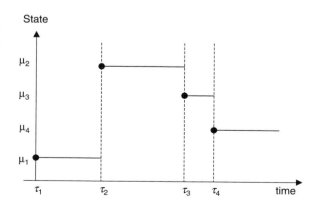

**Figure 9.25**
*State transition
timing graph.*

timer is less than transition $t$'s timer, then transition $t_2$ will fire, leaving transition $t_1$ with the remaining time $(\tau_1 - (\tau_2 - \tau_1))$. The choice of which protocol to use will depend on the system one wishes to model.

The timing need not be exclusively based on timers and counting. Some Petri net models have proposed using state transition timing graphs. In this case, each possible state, $\mu$, is enumerated, and a time period is set for each individual state to traverse from this state to the next state in the sequence (Figure 9.25). In this figure, state $\mu_1$ will require $(\tau_2$ or $\tau_1)$ time units to move from state $\mu_1$ to state $\mu_2$ and so on for all states defined in our system. This could also be represented using timed transition sequences, which depict the order of each transition in relation to all others. Such a description may appear as:

$$\left[ (\tau_1, t_1); (\tau_2, t_2); \ldots; (\tau_j, t_j); \ldots \right] \tag{9.7}$$

Transitions can also be represented as immediate transitions—that is, transitions without any time delays associated with them. To model these in timed Petri nets, we simply can use a solid bar in the graphical mode or a timer of 0 if we are using Petri net notation.

In the example shown in Figure 9.26, we use immediate transitions to capture a resource. These act like semaphores would in a real system. One

**Figure 9.26**
*Timed Petri net with immediate transitions.*

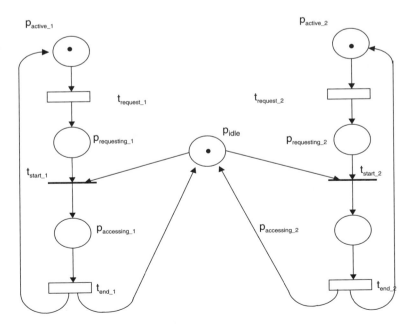

active process that is vying for the resource will win it, while the other will be forced to wait until the resource becomes free once again.

## 9.5   Priority-based Petri nets

The Petri nets defined in the previous section were improvements over the basic nets defined in the first section of this chapter. To continue this trend we next look at adding priority to a Petri net. The formal model now needs some additional elements. The Petri net is described by a nine tuple, $M = (P, T, I, O, H, \Pi, Par, Pred, \mu)$. $P$ represents the set of places of Petri net $M$. $T$ is the set of transitions of Petri net $M$. $I$ represents the set of input functions for the transitions of $M$. $O$ represents the set of output functions for the transitions of $M$. $H$ represents the inhibitor functions defined over the set of transitions in $M$. Par represents the parameter set for this Petri net, and Pred represents the predicates defining how the parameter set can be distributed. The symbol $\mu$ represents the set of markings for this Petri net, and $\Pi$ represents the priority function defined over all transitions of Petri net $M$. The function $\Pi$ maps the priority for each transition to a set of integer values representing their importance relative to each other in the net.

Now we will look at the conditions for firing under these new nets. Transitions in priority Petri nets are enabled just as in basic Petri nets. If the transitions have their input places with the right amount of tokens, then they are prepared for enabling. The term used for this is concession. If a

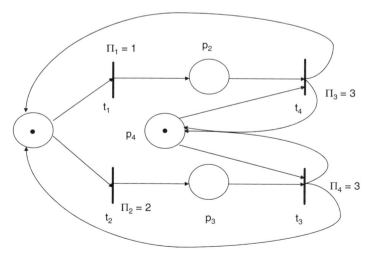

**Figure 9.27**
*Priority-based Petri net.*

transition has concession (is enabled as in basic nets) and there are no additional transitions in this network that are enabled in the present marking with priority greater than this transition's priority, then it is enabled. Formally this set of conditions is represented as:

$$t_i \text{ is enabled} \qquad \text{if} \qquad \text{and } t_j \in T \text{ only} \qquad \text{if } t_j < t_i \qquad (9.8)$$

A transition that meets these criteria can fire. The result of firing is the same as in nets without priority. In the example depicted in Figure 9.27, transition $t_1$ has the lowest priority at 1, transition $t_2$ has the next lowest at 2, and transitions $t_3$ and $t_4$ have the highest priority at 3. If we start with an initial marking, $\mu = (1,0,0,1)$, only transition $t_2$ is enabled, since it has the highest priority and has the number of tokens available from its input functions as required for enabling. If you compute the next few possible states, you would see that transition $t_1$ will never be enabled, since it does not have the priority to overcome transition $t_2$'s priority.

With the use of priority and timing we can do a more complete job of defining conditions such as contention, confusion, and concurrency. For example, the Petri net shown in Figure 9.28 has both timed and priority features. By combining these features we can now get the system to toggle between the two events. The inhibitor on transition $t_2$ causes this immediate transition to be blocked from enabling until it has completed its service. In this way it allows transition $t_1$, with the lower priority, to get service while place $p_2$ has tokens present.

**Figure 9.28**
*Timed and priority net.*

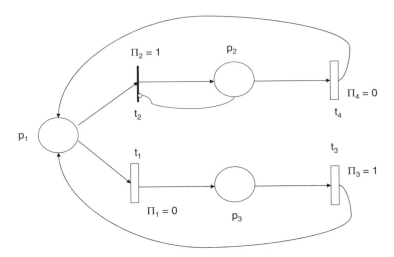

## 9.6    **Colored Petri nets**

In this section we will introduce some of the basic concepts of colored Petri nets. Colored Petri nets also add another dimension to tokens as well as to selection criteria used in determining firing by the addition of different token types. Tokens now can represent different functions. For example, we can use different tokens to represent operating system calls or different classes of jobs. These different tokens can then be used to determine which transition of multiple transitions available can operate.

To represent this graphically we use colored tokens. The set of all possible colors for the tokens represents the cardinality of the token set. Using this token set we can now redefine the definition of our Petri net, specifically, to redefine the firing rules (called link algebra) for all transitions defined in our network. For example, in Figure 9.29, there are only two token types: black and white. These could represent two different types of jobs. Transitions can have priority and time associated with them as before and can also be defined to operate on only a specific token type. As also shown in Figure 9.29, transition $t_1$ has a priority and time associated with it. Arcs also have additional details associated with them. The arc from $p_1$ to $t_1$ has a condition choose $(n, P_1)$, which selects $n$ of one of the tokens to release to the transition. Other arcs are used to select only specific types of tokens. For example, the arcs leading out of transition $t_1$ leading to places $p_2$ and $p_3$ have filters on them to only allow tokens of type black to traverse to place $p_2$ and white to traverse to place $p_3$. Conditions on arcs can be as complex as one wishes. We could use a complex condition that requires $n_1$ of one type of token, $n_2$ of some other type, and none of some third type

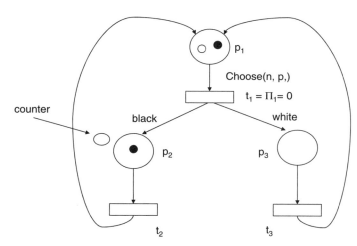

**Figure 9.29**
*Generalized Petri net.*

before we release just one token down a specified path. Using these complex methods, we can model just about any condition that may occur in a computer system we are modeling. The reader is directed to [18–20] for details about colored Petri nets.

## 9.7    Generalized Petri nets

Generalized Petri nets are used to provide yet another refinement of the models discussed up to this point. All of the other models had transitions, which, when fired, either were performed instantaneously or within some predescribed time period. The time period for a transition's firing, once set, was fixed and did not change over the course of the model's lifetime. This is adequate if we have deterministic timing in our modeled system and there is no variability. In reality we know this does not hold for most realistic systems. Generalized Petri net models alter this by providing mechanisms for associating a random, exponentially distributed firing delay with timed transitions.

The addition required to meet these new conditions for firing is a function defined over transitions in the system. This new function is called rate or weight transition function. This function, $W(t_k, \mu)$, must be defined for each transition and state in the network. If the function does not need to be defined for all markings, then we can simply refer to the function as $W(t_k)$, where $t_k \in T$. The result of this function, $W(t_k, \mu)$ or $W(t_k)$, is called the *rate* of transition $t_k$ in marking $\mu$ if $t_k$ is timed and the *weight* of transition $t_k$ in marking $\mu$ if $t_k$ is immediate. The value of this result is a random variable defined by the exponential function defined for the transition around the selected mean value.

Firing of a transition in a generalized net occurs as in a timed net except that the time to fire the transition is computed using an exponential function defined around a mean value. Each transition in the net must have a rate, $r$, defined for it. The rate is the mean value for use in computing the actual time to use in firing the transition. Once a transition is enabled, its computed timer value is decremented using a system-determined increment value until it either reaches 0 or it loses its enabling tokens. As in the timed net, we can use additional information or policies to decide how to use the state of the transition when it becomes nonenabled. We could use the remaining time in the computed time, reset the same time, or select another new time based on the same mean. All have merits based on the type of element being modeled.

Another difference in this class of system is the concept of system state. The state of the system changes from one state to another state based on the

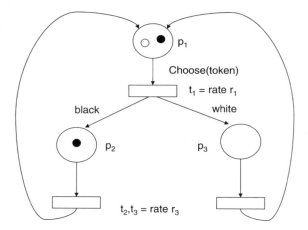

**Figure 9.30**
*Generalized Petri Net.*

firings of all active and ready transitions during this present time interval. In Figure 9.30, the initial marking is $\mu_0 = (2,0,0)$. If we use the colored net functions and simply change the transition times into rates, we now have a generalized Petri net. In the example, transition $t_1$, once enabled, will compute a transition rate using the mean rate, $r_1$, as the value fed into the negative exponential. Using the computed rate the timer would initiate decrements until it reached the firing point (timer value = 0). We would then use the selected token to determine which path to choose in leaving the transition. In the example, if the choice function chose white, then we would take the white path, resulting in a new system state, $\mu_1 = (1,0,1)$.

An important concept with these nets is that they would not compute the same state each time they executed from a given state, due to the randomness of the possible transition firing time. This is a desirable feature for such models, as it was when we used this same property for the memoryless property for arrival rates and service rates at queues.

# 9.8   Summary

Petri nets have been available as a modeling tool since the late 1960s. Since this point in time they have gone through many transitions and improvements. At first they were more of a curiosity than anything else, since there were no means available to construct and analyze models easily. Since these early days, many computerized tools have become available, allowing us to run simulations of a model's structure and to collect performance information. Some specialized Petri net analysis tools have also been developed and are widely available.

In this chapter we covered a basic introduction to Petri nets, their properties, and their modeling capabilities. This basic overview was then followed up by more refinements on the basic model. First, we added the concept of transition time to our initial model concepts. We then followed this up with the concept of priority of transitions. Next, we introduced the concept of token types and transition firing rules in colored Petri nets. Finally, we completed our overview of Petri nets with a discussion of generalized Petri nets and their capabilities.

# 10

# Hardware Testbeds, Instrumentation, Measurement, Data Extraction, and Analysis

In the previous chapters, we covered modeling from several perspectives, ranging from simulation to queuing models to Petri nets and to operational analysis. For those perspectives, only limited amounts of data are actually measured on an actual system. Often, the simplifying assumptions that are made so that model results are calculable enable us to obtain only an approximate analysis of the system's behavior. Also, the load conditions that are presented to an analytical or simulation model often are not tested in a real-world situation. These factors have two ramifications. The first is that more detailed analysis is difficult because of the lack of adequate real-world data. The second is that, even with a detailed model, validation of the model and its results must be weak at best. The latter statement is especially true for general-purpose simulation models such as those discussed throughout this book. Before a simulation can be used to predict the performance of any system, the results of its execution must be compared against a known baseline, and the simulation must be adjusted accordingly. One method of achieving this is through the instrumentation and collection of performance data on an actual system. The results of these measurements are compared with the predicted results from a simulation model of the same system. When the results agree to within some predetermined tolerance, the model is considered validated.

This chapter discusses the use of prototype hardware testbeds as a tool for ascertaining actual measures for some of the performance quantities of interest, for performing controlled experiments to determine the operational characteristics of different parts of a network, and for the validation of software simulation models. In particular, we will describe the implementation of a hardware testbed, define the measurable quantities that we are interested in, derive operational relationships for nonmeasured quantities, and give some results.

The construction of a special-purpose testbed can be costly if done solely for the purpose of estimating the final system performance. Often, however, a proof of concept prototype is constructed to test and validate design assumptions, to gain experience with the system, and to provide a vehicle for advanced development. Given that a prototype system often exists, it is advantageous to also consider instrumentation and test provisions in the prototype design. When performed within the scope of the prototyping effort, the relative cost of special performance measurement facilities becomes more acceptable. Some important facilities, which we will describe for a specific example later in this chapter, could include a system-wide time base for obtaining synchronous measurements, time-tagging hardware or software for timestamping events, counters for recording the number of occurrences of important events, and scenario drivers that can inject a known load into the system being modeled. Of course, it is desirable to make these facilities as unintrusive as possible so that their use does not interfere with the normal operation of the network under question. In some cases, portions of the final system software configuration may be substituted by special-purpose measurement facilities. The remainder of this chapter will discuss a prototype network configuration and will illustrate the techniques employed to measure its performance characteristics.

The network that we will be discussing is situated in a prototype testbed that is instrumented for data collection and can generate network traffic. Each testbed node contains a host controller that can emulate a known traffic load or generate any specified pattern of message traffic. Experiments can be repeated so that different measurements can be taken or so that a specific communication-related parameter can be varied. Thus, the prototype system's loading and recording mechanisms can be controlled in order to observe different network performance phenomena.

In constructing a prototype testbed such as the one discussed here, it is desirable to keep hardware development costs at a minimum, to provide a flexible system so that changes in network design can be accommodated, and to provide the general-purpose driver capabilities discussed previously. One method of keeping hardware development costs down is to use off-the-shelf hardware components as much as possible. All node components that are not network specific can be implemented using standard board or system-level products. For example, the host processor for a node could be implemented with a single board computer or even with a personal computer.

Flexibility in the design of the network-specific components is essential for minimizing the impact of the inevitable design changes that occur during the early network design and prototyping phase. One useful method for achieving a flexible prototype design is to reduce the speed of operation of the network. This allows some functions of the network to be implemented with more general-purpose components, such as a programmable micro-controller or state machine. After the prototype design has been analyzed and a near-final configuration decided upon, these functions can be transitioned into higher-speed implementations. The assumption here is that a uniform scaling of the speed of operation across all network-sensitive components will yield results that can be scaled back up to reflect the actual system's performance. This may not hold true in the strictest sense, such as where hardware characteristics change at higher speeds, but it will generally hold if the functionality of the network as a whole does not change.

In order to provide general-purpose network driver and data collection capabilities, it is almost always necessary to have a detached host, whose only function is to generate network traffic and collect results. Also, it may be necessary to design in additional resources, whose only functions are to assist in traffic generation of data collection. It is important to adhere as much as possible to a layered network standard such as the International Organization for Standardization's model for Open Systems Interconnection reference model (ISO's OSI model). By doing this, changes can be more or less localized to the level that is most affected, whereas the other levels can maintain their functionality. Thus, the same standards that provide a degree of interoperability among networks of different types also provide us with a useful template for building a flexible prototype system.

The hardware testbed used here, for example, consists of several network nodes connected with a token bus LAN. Each node contains two single-board computers: one that implements the simulated host functions (the host) and provides for network loading and data collection and one that provides high-level control functions for the network hardware (the input/output processor, or IOP). Additionally, each node contains a network adapter, whose function is to implement the network protocol.

In this particular case, the network testbed models a general-purpose serial communication network. With a stable host and IOP design, a number of different network types can be implemented by using different network adapters and front-end hardware. The network that we will examine uses a token access protocol. In this protocol, the node that holds the token has the option to transmit data, if there is message traffic queued for transmission by the host processor. If the node does have a message to send, it broadcasts the message over the communication bus. All other nodes listen for their identifying address in the message header and accept the message if

**Figure 10.1**
*General testbed
configuration.*

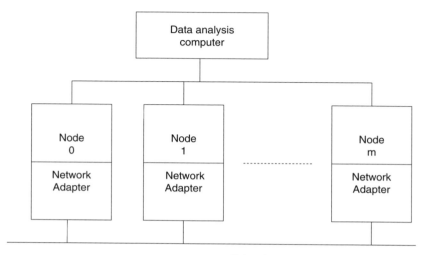

it is destined for them. After the transmission of a message has been completed, or if there is no message to send, the token is passed to the next node on the network in a round-robin manner. The next node may or may not be physically adjacent to the current node. The overall structure of the network testbed is shown in Figure 10.1.

A number of nodes, each with a network adapter, are attached to a linear token bus and also to a data analysis computer. During a test run, the network bus is used to transfer the simulated load. At the completion of the test, each node transmits its collected data to the data analysis computer for synthesis and analysis. Each node within the network testbed has an architecture, as shown in Figure 10.2.

The host computer serves two functions in this architecture. The first is to implement part of the layered protocol and to provide a simulated message load to it. The second is to collect the necessary performance data for subsequent analysis. Figure 10.3 shows the general structure of the host software that implements these functions.

The IOP controls the flow of message traffic onto and off of the network through the network adapter. It also controls the DMA channels, provides a standard interface to the host computer, and collects network-specific performance statistics. Figure 10.4 shows the IOP's functional architecture.

As mentioned earlier, it is advantageous to have the testbed components conform to a layered protocol standard. The testbed under discussion here implements levels 1 through 4, and part of level 5, of the OSI model for

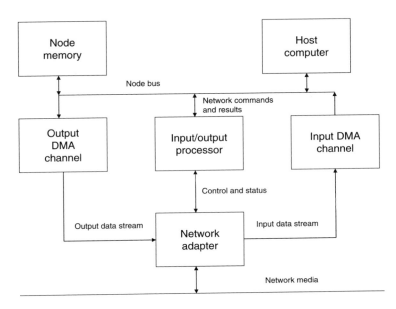

**Figure 10.2**
*Testbed node architecture.*

layered protocols. Figure 10.5 shows how the various components map to the standard. In the layered model shown in Figure 10.5, the physical level implements the electrical and physical functions that are required to link the nodes. The data link layer provides the mechanisms necessary to reliably

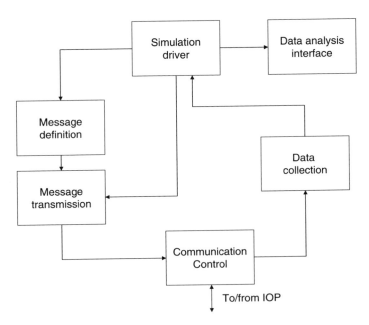

**Figure 10.3**
*Host software architecture.*

**Figure 10.4**
*IOP functional architecture.*

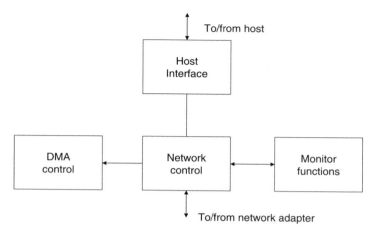

To/from host

Host
Interface

DMA
control

Network
control

Monitor
functions

To/from network adapter

transmit data over the physical link. Level 3, the network level, controls the switching of data through the network. In networks with multiple transmission paths, the level 3 function controls over which links a message will be transferred. At the transport level, an error-free communication facility between nodes is provided. Session control involves the initiation, maintenance, and termination of a communication session between processes. Level 6 provides any data translation, compaction, or encoding/decoding services that may be required by the application. At the top resides the application, which is any process that uses the communication facilities.

For the example network, levels 1 and 2 provide physical connection via coaxial cables, the serialization and packing of data, and the synchronization and detection of data onto and off of the network. Since the network

**Figure 10.5**
*Testbed/ISO correspondence.*

| ISO/OSI Level | Test-bed |
|---|---|
| Level 7: application | simulation driver |
| Level 6: transformation/presentation | not implemented |
| Level 5: session | partially implemented |
| Level 4: transport | IOP |
| Level 3: network | |
| Level 2: data link | network adapter |
| Level 1: physical | |

discussed here is a global bus, there is no need for the switching functions of level 3. In cases where this is a factor, however, the function would be implemented in the IOP. Transport control is best implemented in the IOP, because it relieves the host of performing error detection and retransmission and of managing individual message packets. Part of level 5 is implemented in the host so that messages can be assembled and queued for transmission to other nodes. Mechanisms for establishing interprocess connections are not implemented.

The network that we will study as an example requires the acknowledgment of each message packet from the receiver. A missing or bad acknowledgment results in the retransmission of the packet in error. Messages are addressed to logical process identifiers, which are mapped to each node upon initialization.

In the testbed model, a sequence of messages is treated as a series of time-ordered events. The event times are generated in the host according to a probability distribution that is representative of the desired loading characteristics. The time of message generation is recorded and collected for postrun analysis. As a message is transferred through the protocol layers and across the network, it is time-tagged, again for later analysis. In the following section, we will illustrate the use of these time tags and other collected data from a run, derive the performance evaluation parameters of interest, and show some experimental results that exemplify the techniques.

# 10.1    Derivation of performance evaluation parameters

As mentioned earlier, the message traffic for the network under examination is generated in the host. A queue of messages awaiting transmission is implemented in the node memory shown in Figure 10.2. A message is, therefore, said to enter the network from the host processor and to exit through the same.

After entering the network, the message is broken into a series of packets, each of which is transmitted serially by the network adapter under the control of the IOP. Only one network adapter may have control of the bus at any one time (i.e., only one may transmit at a time). This serial access is controlled by the circulating token. Thus, the network represents a single-server queuing system, where the service provided is the message transmission. All messages in the system are of the same priority so that the system has only one customer class.

**Figure 10.6**
*Conceptual
network server.*

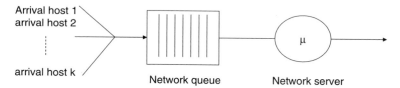

Because access to the network is serial by node and because the only server in the system is the network itself, we can consider all message packet arrivals to the server as originating from a single queue. Thus, this single conceptual queue contains the combination of all messages in the individual message queues, ordered by time. Figure 10.6 illustrates this concept.

For this example, we will assume that messages arrive at the server according to a Poisson distribution. Thus, the probability that we get $n$ arrivals at host $i$ in an interval of length $t$ is given as:

$$P(n \text{ arrivals in interval } t) = \frac{(\lambda_i t)^n e^{-\lambda_i t}}{n!} \qquad (10.1)$$

where $\lambda_i$ is the average interarrival rate at host $i$. For the Poisson distribution, the time between arrivals is exponentially distributed, and the interarrival time for messages at host $i$ is generated as:

$$A_i = 1/\lambda_i \qquad (10.2)$$

The average interarrival time for the conceptual single network server, then, can be represented as:

$$A_i = \sum_{i=1}^{k} 1/\lambda_i \qquad (10.3)$$

We can represent the state of the system during the observation period as the number of messages awaiting transmission through the network. Because of the property of the Poisson arrival process whereby the probability of no more than one arrival or completion in any time period approaches one as the interval length approaches zero, the state transitions satisfy the one-step assumption. That is, the system state only transitions to neighboring states. A state is denoted, $n(t)$, and defines the number of message packets awaiting transmission at time $t$.

We will perform an analysis that is based upon the operational analysis techniques discussed in Chapter 7. The quantities for this evaluation are as follows:

*W*—Waiting time for a message packet measured from arrival into the network queue until the completion of transmission

*B*—Busy time for the network defined as the total time that there is at least one message packet in the system

These quantities are derived from measurements of three basic quantities measured by instrumentation hardware and software in the testbed. The basic measured quantities are as follows:

$A(n)$—Number of arrivals into the system when there are $n$ message packets in the system

$C(n)$—Number of completions when there are $n$ message packets in the system

$T(n)$—Total amount of time when there are $n$ message packets in the system

Define the total over all $n$ of each of the previous quantities as follows:

$$A = \sum_{i=0}^{k} A(i) \quad \text{(arrivals)} \tag{10.4}$$

$$C = \sum_{i=0}^{k} C(i) \quad \text{(completions)} \tag{10.5}$$

$$T = \sum_{i=0}^{k} T(i) \quad \text{(observation period)} \tag{10.6}$$

In the previous summations, $k$ represents the largest number of message packets awaiting transmission during the observation interval. If we assume flow balance, the total number of arrivals will equal the total number of completions during the observation period. The waiting and busy time defined earlier can be defined in terms of these quantities as:

$$W = \sum_{i=0}^{k} iT(i) \tag{10.7}$$

$$B = \sum_{i=1}^{k} T(i) = T - T(0) \tag{10.8}$$

Along with these measures, we obtain three additional measures: message transmission time ($t_x$), message arrival time ($t_a$), and message reception

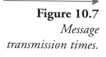

**Figure 10.7**
*Message
transmission times.*

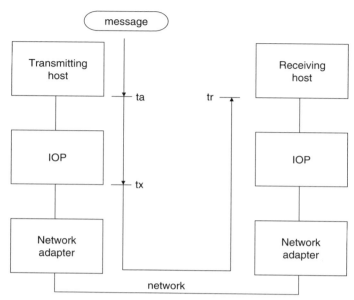

time $(t_r)$. These measures are shown in relation to a message transmission in Figure 10.7.

As in Chapter 7, we define some performance parameters in terms of the basic operational quantities. These are summarized as follows:

Mean queue length: $N = W/T$                                         (10.9)

Mean response time: $R = W/C$                                 (10.10)

Utilization: $U = B/T$                                               (10.11)

Mean job service time: $S = B/C$                               (10.12)

Network throughput: $X = C/T$                                 (10.13)

Network service time: $S = \displaystyle\sum_{\substack{\text{All} \\ \text{messages}}} t_n/C$   where $t_n = t_r - t_x$         (10.14)

The first five quantities are standard operational analysis results. The last relates to the performance of the transmission mechanisms, ignoring the queue wait time.

## 10.2  **Network performance tests**

An analysis run is performed on the testbed by initializing all network hosts with a known arrival rate generator and then by using the generated message traffic to load the network while collecting the operational measures defined previously. After the run, the measures are combined and the desired performance measures are calculated.

The example test performed on the network testbed was formulated to give an indication of when, for a certain network configuration, the network becomes saturated (i.e., the network utilization approaches 1). For the example shown here, packet lengths of 200 and 400 bytes were tested with three nodes generating network traffic. The arrival rates at all three nodes were set up to be equal, and this rate varied from approximately 600 packets per second to approximately 15,000 packets per second. A test run was made for each of several arrival rates in the interval.

The mean queue length of packets awaiting transmission over the network for various arrival rates is shown in Figure 10.8. The values for each run using the measured values for $T(i)$ and the queue lengths at each arrival time are found through a combination of equations (10.6), (10.7), and (10.9). Similarly, the mean response time was calculated using equations (10.5), (10.7), and (10.11) and is plotted in Figure 10.9.

**Figure 10.8**
*Mean queue length.*

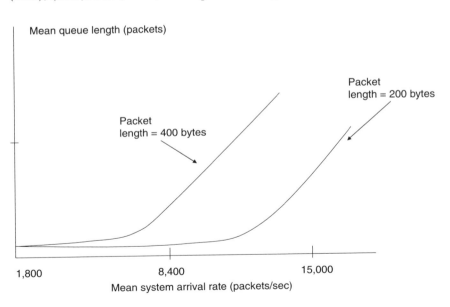

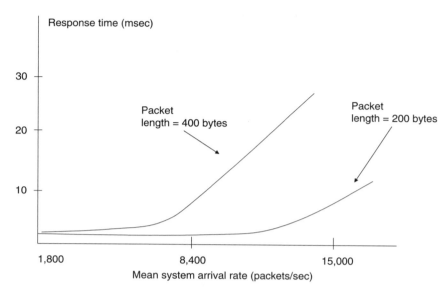

**Figure 10.9**
*Mean response
time.*

The utilization curve, shown in Figure 10.10, illustrates the percentage of the available data bandwidth that is being used to transmit message packets. From this graph, it can be seen that the particular network that we are analyzing approaches saturation (i.e., 100 percent utilization) rather quickly for the arrival rates and packet sizes shown.

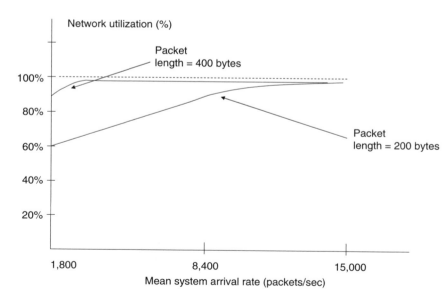

**Figure 10.10**
*Network
utilization.*

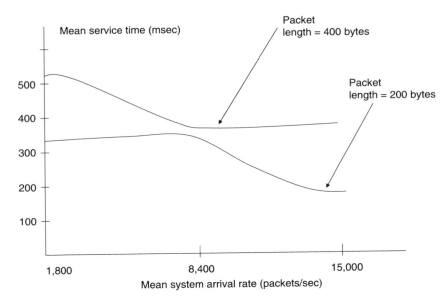

**Figure 10.11**
*Mean system service time.*

Figure 10.11 shows the effect of an increased arrival rate on service time. In this case, we have defined service time as the system busy time per completion, where the busy time considers the time a packet spends in the queue as well as the time it spends in transmission. When the system is saturated, however, there is always a packet ready to transmit, and so the queue fall-through time is hidden by this fact. Figure 10.12 illustrates this effect, which is known as pipelining.

**Figure 10.12**
*Pipeline effect on queue fall-through time.*

| Time | Queue positions | | | Transmission |
|---|---|---|---|---|
| 1 | Packet 1 | | | |
| 2 | Packet 2 | Packet 1 | | |
| 3 | Packet 3 | Packet 2 | Packet 1 | |
| 4 | Packet 4 | Packet 3 | Packet 2 | |
| 5 | | Packet 4 | Packet 3 | |
| | | | Packet 4 | |

**Figure 10.13**
*Network*
*throughput.*

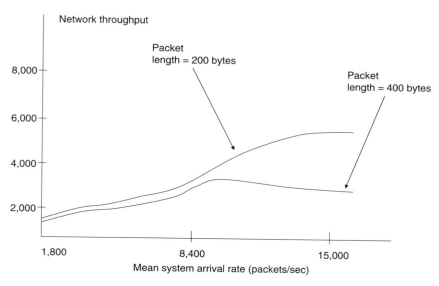

In Figure 10.13, the network throughput is plotted against the system arrival rate. The results show that after saturation, network throughput for this type of network remains constant. This is an important property for some systems, especially since some network protocols cause degraded throughput under increased system load.

**Figure 10.14**
*Network service*
*time.*

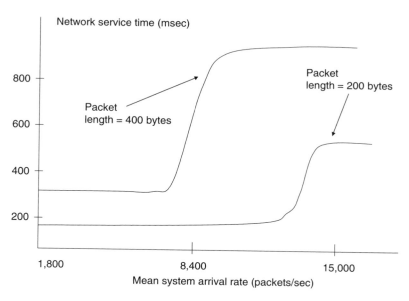

The final graph, shown in Figure 10.14, shows the time for a message to propagate through the network. This time does not include the queue wait time. When the system is lightly loaded, this time will include the time for the token to travel around the network. Under heavy load, the time includes the delay associated with transmissions of message packets at other nodes.

This example has served a dual purpose: to illustrate the usefulness of hardware modeling in certain cases and to show the application of some of the operational analysis techniques discussed in Chapter 7. For hardware modeling, assumptions about the network behavior can be validated. Operational analysis enables us to calculate quantities of interest that either are not directly measurable or that are too difficult to measure without disturbing the actual operation of the network itself.

## 10.3  General methods of data extraction

In the previous section we examined a system used to test system concepts before the final target system is constructed. Often we are faced with analyzing an existing system. This requires the computer systems analyst to develop methods for extracting information from a running system and for running experiments on an existing system.

There are three methods for extracting information from an existing system: hardware monitors, software monitors, and accounting software (e.g., the operating system). Measurements for performance analysis are typically extracted using either hardware or software monitors specifically set up for the measurements of interest. Depending on what parameters are of interest, we may be able to measure them directly, or we may need to obtain the measures from intermediate measurements.

Most computer systems, even your PC, provide means to determine resource utilization and a variety of other useful measurements. If the system is a timesharing system, one can typically determine how much CPU time was used by a process, how much memory it consumed, and possibly even how much time was spent in I/O processing. Information such as the number of users logged on to the system, number of I/O accesses performed by a user, page faults in memory, and active time for a process can be obtained.

A problem with software developed for system accounting purposes is that it may not provide information concerning the system software components, such as the operating system. In many systems, the time spent by the operating system doing its tasks may actually represent the lion's share of resource utilization. For example, most PCs will spend the majority of their time in the operating systems idle process. Due to this limitation most system accounting packages will not suffice in aiding us in analyzing a system's performance. Some of the newer operating systems provide users with many more tools for determining system resource utilization. For example, the task manager of most of the Microsoft products provides fairly good capabilities to monitor resource use and system performance. This package, however, is more closely related to software monitoring than to accounting software.

Software monitors utilize a collection of code fragments embedded in the operating system, or applications program, to gather performance data. The monitoring software must be kept to a minimum in order that its impact on the running system being measured is minimal. The main modes to construct software monitors use either a sampling or event approach. In the sampling approach, monitor code fragments are invoked periodically to determine the status of the system. Each of the monitoring code fragments has a specific function. One may be examining memory use, and another, CPU or I/O. Using the retrieved information, the monitor can over time construct a fairly accurate image of the systems behavior. The problem with sampling is that some parameters or events of interest may be missed if the sampling period does not fall into their path. The advantage of this approach, however, is its simplicity and lower systems impact. By changing the sampling frequency the load on the system can be increased or reduced as needed. The main design issue when developing a sampling scheme is to determine the appropriate sampling frequency and measurement points within the system.

The event design approach for a software monitor requires that the designers of the monitor have an understanding of the events within the system with which they can synchronize monitoring. For example, CPU task switching is an important event, as is I/O and memory allocation and deallocation. In order for the events to be monitored, the operating systems code must be altered. The code must be adjusted so that when the event occurs, required information can be extracted by the operating system and recorded to a file. For example, we may wish to record what process was allocated or deallocated memory, what process is acquiring the CPU, and the times associated with these events. The event files can then be processed at some later time to extract the performance measures for the system. If we can define all events of interest and provide handles into the operating systems code to extract information about them, then we can construct a fairly good model of the system under study. Using event traces one can determine the duration of every CPU service time and the resources consumed during each of these cycles.

If we do not have access to the operating systems code, then this approach is not feasible. One could augment applications code and be able to extract timings for this code. This would provide at least a measure of the duration of time an application holds a resource and can be used as a means to assess system performance, if the application is designed appropriately. The problem with all these approaches is that they will cause their own impact on systems performance. The sampling software will consume resources and cause additional delays to be added to the performance measurements, possibly causing them to indicate erroneous values. Studies have shown that a software monitor can consume as much as 20 percent of the systems resources, making the performance results questionable. If we choose the type of events carefully and limit added code to the minimum required to capture information, the overhead can be dropped to approximately 5 percent. The tradeoff is fidelity of information versus the overhead of the measurement software.

Besides the problem with impacting system operations, software monitors have other problems. The trace method of data collection can lead to large volumes of information to store and process, making it hard to use effectively. Software monitors also must be configured to fit into a system's architecture, making them one of a kind implementations. Due to this limitation, there are no commercially available software monitor general architectures. In addition, implementing software monitors requires significant expertise in operating systems coding, which is not an everyday capability for most programmers. Due to this limitation, this technique is not used very often. We are left to use the monitoring capabilities delivered with an operating system.

Hardware monitors provide another means to access performance information. A hardware monitor is composed of a collection of digital hardware connected to the system under measurement. For example, an oscilloscope is a general-purpose hardware monitoring device constructed to allow for the monitoring of hardware activities. Hardware monitors can be as simple as a few gates to entire computer systems including all the peripherals. Hardware monitors are readily available from commercial sources.

Hardware monitors must be connected in some way to our system in order to collect data, which are in the form of signals. The points we attach the hardware monitor to represent our test points or probe points. The test points are places in the computer system under examination accessible for measurement. For example, we may wish to probe the interrupt lines of the CPU, so we can determine when task switches are occurring. We may wish to examine specific memory locations to test when values cross some point or are altered. By attaching the monitor's test probes at these points, we can observer systems behavior over some time frame. We can also use multiple test points in conjunction with each other to synchronize when to extract signals based on the measurement or detection of some other test point. The measurements are typically done without adding any additional overhead to the measured system, a distinct advantage over the software monitoring approach.

A difficulty with hardware monitors is knowing when to use them and where to place the test points. For example, where do you measure to know if a CPU is busy? How do we know it is busy with an operating system function or an application? Most systems vendors have developed their components and systems with ready-to-use monitoring points to aid in system debug and repairs. This makes it relatively easy to determine where to place our test points. If these test points are not available, then hardware monitoring will be very difficult to implement.

The monitoring devices must have the capability to collect measured test point data and store these data for future processing and analysis. This is necessary so that we can determine the utilization of tested components within a system: the number of measured units that pass a point over some time frame—for example, how many jobs are presented to the CPU for processing over some period of time, and what percentage of this time the CPU was busy or idle.

The limitation with hardware monitoring is that we can only measure hardware signals and possibly the contents of registers or memory (if allowed). We typically will not know what the operating system is specifically doing at the point we are measuring. Due to this limitation, hardware monitors are usually used in conjunction with some form of event trace software in order to allow for later interpretation of hardware operations.

## 10.4  Testbed and model workloads

The term *workload* defines the load placed on a real system (typically measured or observed on a computer system while it runs normal operations), while the term *test* or *model workload* denotes a computer system's load constructed and applied to a system for performance studies (typically synthesized using characteristics from a real workload). For most modeling projects the use of a synthetic workload makes more sense, since we can control the load applied to the experiments. By controlling the load applied to a computer system under analysis, we can possibly predict the outcome of the experiment or force the experiment to test specific components of the system. In addition to this reason, synthetic workloads do not possibly contain real information, which may be sensitive or valuable to the system under study, and its compromise or loss would be significant. Once a valid synthetic workload has been developed, it can be reused to study additional systems. An example is the Transaction Processing Consortium (TPC) workloads developed to study database systems. These TPC workloads have been used by vendors and customers to study various database systems and to determine which is better for different applications. Some of these workloads have been specialized for data mining or for distributed databases and other specialized applications.

To study computer architectures, a variety of instruction workloads have been developed. These are focused on low-level operations and consist of mixes of loads, stores, comparisons, branches, additions, subtractions, floating-point operations, multiplications, divisions, shift operations, logical operations, and register operations. These instruction mix workloads have become standardized for specific architectures such as PCs.

Other workloads do not focus on low-level operations but wish to examine more coarse-grained architectural concepts. These would be developed using high-order languages and would be designed to test things such as file transfer, task switching, memory management policies, and other operating systems components.

Some popular benchmarks include the TPC benchmarks described previously for examining database systems, the Sieve benchmark used to examine PCs and microprocessors, Ackerman's function for testing procedure call mechanisms in computer systems, Whetstone kernel developed to test low-level assembly-level operations, the Linpack package to test floating-point operations, the Drystone benchmark for testing low-level integer operations, and the Spec benchmark suite for measuring engineering-type applications (e.g., compilation, electronic design, VLSI circuit simulation, and complex mathematics manipulations such as matrix multiplications) on a computer system.

Given that all of these and other workloads exist, modelers must still determine which to use or which method to use in constructing their own workload for a given modeling project. There are four main considerations applicable when selecting a workload for a project. They are the computer systems services exercised by the workload, the level of detail to be applied, closeness to realistic load, and timeliness.

The most important component of the workload selection is to determine the services one wishes to examine. Making this list of services can be very daunting and time consuming but is time well spent. First, one must determine the system under test. This represents the complete set of components making up a system being studied. Often we may be focusing on some single component or some small set of components for comparison, called the components under study. For example, an operating system design team may be interested in different process scheduling algorithms on the total operating systems performance. The determination of the system and its components is a very important step in workload development and should not be trivialized.

An example will illustrate the service's concept. We are interested in this example: comparing an off-line backup paging storage system using disk drive arrays (e.g., such as one would find in a large database log subsystem). The system consists of several disk data systems, each containing multiple disk drives. The disk drives have separate read and write subsystems. Each subsystem uses fixed magnetic heads for these operations. If we specify the architecture from the highest level and work down to lower levels, the services, factors, metrics, and workloads are defined as follows:

1.  Backup system

    - Services: backup pages, backup changed pages, restore pages, list backed-up pages

    - Factors: page size, batch or background process, incremental or full backup

    - Metrics: backup time, restoration time

    - Workload: a database system with log pages to be backed up—vary frequency of logging

2.  Disk data system

    - Services: read/write to a disk

    - Factors: type of disk drive

    - Metrics: speed, reliability, time between failures

    - Workload: synthetic program generating transaction-like disk I/O requests

3.  Disk drives

    - Services: read record, write record, find record

- Factors: disk drive capacity, number of tracks, number of cylinders, number of read/write heads

- Metrics: time to find record, time to read record, time to write record, data lost rate, requests per unit time

- Workload: synthetic program generating realistic operations requests to the disk drives

4. Read/write subsystem

- Services: read data, write data

- Factors: data encoding technique, implementation technology

- Metrics: I/O bandwidth, density of media

- Workload: read/write data streams with varying patterns

5. Read/write heads

- Services: read signal and write signal

- Factors: composition, head spacing, record gap size

- Metrics: magnetic field strength, hysteresis

- Workload: reads and writes of varying power strengths, disks moving at various rotational speeds

After we have completed the specification of the system and the components of interest, we need to determine the level of detail required in producing and recording requests for the defined services. A workload description can be as detailed as providing definitions for all events in the system or can simply be an aggregate or generalization of this load. Some possibilities for the detail may be average resource demand, most frequent request, frequency of request types (e.g., 25 percent reads and 75 percent writes), a timestamped sequence of specific requests, or some distribution of resource demands.

Typical modeling projects begin by using a variant of the concept of most frequently requested service. For example, in a transaction processing system we may use a simple debit-credit benchmark from the TPC benchmarks. Such a selection would be valid if a particular service is requested much more than others. A second alternative is to be more specific and construct a workload by selecting specific services, their characteristics, and frequency. The Linpack package is such a workload. It selects very specific computer operations in very prescribed patterns to test specific components of the system. The next alternative is to construct a time stamped record, where each record represents a specific request for a specific service along with details of the actual access (such a description could be constructed by taking a trace of all activities of an existing system). In most cases this type of workload may be too difficult to construct and to validate for use in all but the most complex modeling projects. The aggregate resource demand approach is similar to what we would expect to see in an analytical model. We look to characterize each request for services as averages or distributions. For example, each request may be characterized as requiring 50 units of one particular resource and 25 units of some other and making these requests every 1,000 units of time.

No matter which of these approaches we use, the modeler must determine if the selected load is representative of the real system load. Typically we will be interested in determining if the service request's load has similar arrival characteristics, resource demands, and resource utilization demands as the real load.

Finally, a developed workload should faithfully model the changes in use patterns in a timely manner. For example, the TPC benchmarks have continued to evolve to meet the needs of changing database systems design and use. The original TPC workloads were designed for the "bankers" database problem. That is, they simply were looking to provide transaction loads to well-structured, simple, flat relational database specifications. They were record oriented and had no dimensions beyond the simple relational model of the day. These have evolved now to include benchmarks for the new object relational databases and for data warehouses and data mining systems. Other important considerations in developing a workload include repeatability, external components impact, and load leveling. Repeatability looks at a workload's ability to be reproduced faithfully with little added overhead. External components impact looks to capture and characterize impacts on the system under study by nonessential components. Finally, load leveling may be of interest if our study wishes to examine a system under best-case or worst-case scenarios.

## 10.5   Experimental design

Once we have a testbed to study a computer system and a workload to load the testbed with, we need to design experiments that will help in discovering the performance limitations we as modelers are focused on. A correct experimental design will provide the maximum analysis information with the minimal number of experimental runs required. Some terminology must be introduced to make this discussion meaningful. A performance variable is a measured outcome for an experiment for a single component, process, or possibly an entire system. A factor is a variable that may have an impact on the performance variables and typically represents items that can be varied during an experiment. The steps are values a factor can take on during an experimental sequence of runs. For example, a CPU's memory may be adjusted from a minimum value to a maximum value in some distinct number of discrete steps. Each of these steps represents a value for the factor under study. Factors need not all be important. Typically, experiments on computer systems will have multiple factors, some very important (such as CPU speed) and others only peripherally important (such as terminal speed). Experiments may be repeated and are then referred to as replicants. An entire performance study for a particular system consists of a number of discrete experiments—when taken together this set of experiments constitutes the experimental design. Factors may have a correspondence to each other and must be defined as having a dependency.

Experimental design comes in a variety of ways. Three typical designs are the simple, fractional factorial, and full factorial designs. In a simple design, we start with a fixed configuration and vary one factor at a time to determine how this factor impacts performance. For example, when measuring the performance of a virtual memory management component, we may wish to study systems design by varying the size of the available primary memory. By running separate experiments, each with all conditions held stable except the memory size, we may be able to determine some useful information concerning the virtual memory management systems operations. The total number of experiments required for a simple design is simply the sum of the number of experiments for each factor. For example, if we wish to study the memory management system with three different memory sizes, using three separate CPUs and three different disk drives using three workloads, we would need:

$$N = (3 \text{ memory sizes}) + (3 \text{ CPU types})$$
$$+ (3 \text{ disk drive models}) + (3 \text{ workloads}) = 12 \qquad (10.15)$$

total experiments to be run. This form of experiment would give us some information but may not indicate to us how the various elements interact with each other. To determine how the factors interact we would need to run either fractional factorial experiments or full factorial experiments. In the fractional factorial experiments we may wish to examine only a few of our factor terms actively against each other. In this case we would require additional numbers of experiments. In our example, if we are interested in how the CPUs interact with the memory, we would be required to test all combinations of these against each other. This would require additional experiments to be run as multiples of each other. For our simple example we would now require:

$$N = (3 \text{ memory sizes})(3 \text{ CPU types})$$
$$((3 \text{ disk drive models}) + (3 \text{ workloads})) = 54 \qquad (10.16)$$

experiments to be run versus the original 12 for the simple design method. For a full factorial experimental design we simple vary all of the factors against each other. In this case we would now require that we perform:

$$N = (3 \text{ memory sizes})(3 \text{ CPU types})$$
$$(3 \text{ disk drive models})(3 \text{ workloads}) = 81 \qquad (10.17)$$

specific experiments to look at how all of these factors affect each other over their entire range of values.

When doing experiments using factorial designs it is also important to determine how necessary the various factors are in relation to each other. This is typically determined using allocation of variation. In this method the importance of a factor is measured by the portion of the total variation in the performance variable explained by this factor. For example, if two factors explain 90 percent and 5 percent of the performance variation, respectively, then the second term can be considered to have little effect on the performance variable. The sample variance for a measure is found as:

$$\text{Sample variance} = s^2 = \sum_{i=1}^{\#\text{exp}} (f_i - f)^2 / (\#\text{exp} - 1) \qquad (10.18)$$

where $f$ is the mean response time for all of the experiments combined for our measured performance variable. Many more such correlations between information must be examined and understood if we are to make sense of the performance information being returned by our models. More details on how to interpret such information can be found in the references.

## 10.6  Data presentation

If one cannot prepare and present the results of a performance study clearly and simply, then the study would be deemed a failure, no matter how much effort was put into the work. The aim of every performance study is to aid the analyst and associated client in making a decision regarding the computer system being studied. To aid in this analysis the modeler must possess the ability to determine what medium is best to use in making specific information available—for example, words, graphs, pictures, charts, animation, or some other means amenable to the domain being studied.

The old saying that a picture is worth a thousand words is one the modeler must take to heart and strive to realize. Graphics are one of the best means to convey differences between studied components or systems. It is relatively easy to see that one CPU performs better than another when they are shown clearly in graphical form and the graph clearly depicts the relative performance differences. There are many kinds of graphics available to depict such comparisons—for example, line graphs, bar charts, pie charts, histograms, and Gantt charts. In all cases it is critical that we understand what is being plotted and why, in order that we select the correct variables and styles in which to represent them.

One such value that impacts the choice of which chart to use is the type of variable displayed. Is the variable being plotted quantitative or qualitative, is it ordered or unordered, is it discrete, or is the value continuous? Qualitative variables are those where there is no specific measure present, merely a category. For example, microprocessors, servers, and mainframe computers are all classes of computers, but there is no measured value when we use these terms alone. Quantitative values are those that we can measure explicitly—for example, the number of instructions per second or the number of I/O requests per period. We would probably use a line graph to show the time-based relationship between a continuous set of variables. On the other hand, if we had discrete value variables, we may decide to use a histogram or bar chart to depict these.

When deciding what form to use it is important that the modeler keep a few important concepts in mind. First, choose a reporting mechanism that will require minimum effort from the reader. The differences you wish to depict should be clearly defined and displayed so that the client will have no problem coming to the same conclusion that the modeler did after the experiments were run. Make sure that all pertinent information is provided on the graph so the reader need not look elsewhere to fill in the blanks. Keep it simple. Even though the second item indicated to put all pertinent information on the graph, one also must make sure that no nonuseful information finds its way onto the graph. Try to use standard methods of describing and displaying information. For example, the origin of the graph is expected by most people to be labeled as the zero point in both dimensions. Finally, try to avoid ambiguity. For example, make sure all axes are labeled clearly (e.g., use names, not symbols), show the scales used clearly (e.g., log scales, decimal, etc.), and use clear differences to depict different values of variables (e.g., CPU type 1 is red, CPU type 2 is black, etc.). The scales being used should be set so they clearly depict the differences. This last important concept should not be overlooked. Choosing an inappropriate scale may make a claim look better or worse than it really is. The interested reader is pointed to texts on statistics that focus on data representation for more complete discussions and examples of some of these concepts.

## 10.7   Summary

In this chapter we introduced many new concepts. The first was the use of testbed systems to allow the modeler to construct subsets or even entire systems to be used as environments in which to iron out the performance issues with new or existing designs before they are built or before an existing system is altered. This presentation was then followed by an example of a network testbed used to analyze protocols. This example helped the reader to understand the ways in which a testbed can be effectively used as part of a larger modeling effort.

This discussion was then followed by a general discussion of measurement techniques applied within testbed and existing systems. The primary techniques described are hardware monitors and software monitors. The benefits and shortfalls of each technique were discussed along with examples of how they may be applied within a modeling project.

The discussion then changes to looking at the development of workloads to drive testbed environments. We focus on the types of workloads and how the modeler decides on which level of detail to focus the workload, how to determine the system and components the workload is to stress, and what types of services are to be mimicked. This is then followed by a presentation dealing with structuring the workload as either an average load, a real load, or something in between. We follow this up with a discussion of testbed result presentation and some concepts concerning good practice in presenting performance study outputs to the client.

# System Performance Evaluation Tool Selection and Use

Once we have decided to perform an assessment of performance for some target computer system, we still must decide which of the techniques we have discussed is the most appropriate for the proposed performance study. Many different considerations must be taken into account before we make such a decision.

## 11.1  Tool selection

The four techniques for computer systems performance evaluation include analytical modeling, Petri net modeling, simulation modeling, and empirical or testbed analysis. Depending on the criteria placed on the computer systems analysis, some rough selection metrics can be determined. The most important criterion deals with the stage of the computer systems life cycle. For example, measurements are only available as a modeling possibility if the system already exists, or something similar exists. On the other hand, if it is a new computer system, which has not been built, then analytical modeling, Petri nets, or simulation modeling makes more sense. If we are in the earliest phases of the life cycle, when we are examining tradeoffs on many components, we may wish to use analytical modeling, since it can provide relatively quick answers to tradeoff questions, allowing us to determine early on if a subset of $n$ alternatives is best for more detailed modeling. Once we have completed this rough analysis, and narrowed our choices of alternatives to some smaller subset, we would probably wish to apply Petri nets to further refine our choices. Petri nets add the ability to model and trade off concurrency, conflict, and synchronization, something impossible to accomplish with analytical modeling. Once we have completed our analysis using Petri nets and have further narrowed our choices to only a few components, we could next look toward simulation. Simulation provides the ability to produce very detailed models of a target system or just some specific contentious component. The goal at each of these early stages of a computer system's design and development is to narrow the number of choices to allow us to optimally choose the best architecture and components for a given computer system's applications requirements. Finally, once the system is constructed, we would apply empirical modeling. This would allow us to verify that our early modeling was correct and to possibly identify areas where our new system could be further refined and improved before delivery to a customer.

The next criterion for consideration when deciding on which modeling tool to use is the time we have to do the modeling task. In most situations a model is requested because some problem has occurred, and an answer to it was needed last week. There is a saying that time is money, and in computer systems modeling it is no different. If we have all the time in the world to perform our evaluations, then we probably would walk through each model, refining our analysis as was defined under the criterion of the time stage. The problem is that we typically do not have such a luxury. If time is short, then we typically can only use analytical or Petri net modeling, with analytical modeling winning out if time is very short. If time is important, but not critical, then we would look at Petri nets and simulation as being the next models of choice. Petri nets take less time to develop than simulations but would also provide us with possibly less detailed analysis information. If the system exists, then measurements may be appropriate over simulation modeling, if the number of alternatives we are looking at is small. If the number of alternatives is significant, then simulation would win out, even though it typically would take more time than measurements.

The third modeling tool selection criterion is referred to as tool availability. When we say availability we mean many different aspects. The first to come to mind is availability of a computer-based tool. For example, if we had a tool allowing us to simply define queuing models and to vary modeling factors and system component characteristics, then analytical modeling would be much easier to apply. On the other hand, if no such tool exists that can support the kind of model we are proposing, then by availability we imply that the modelers have the capability and knowledge to construct an analytical model and perform the tradeoff analysis using this model. Likewise, if we are looking to use Petri nets, we first would check if existing computer-based tools exist. Second, do we have modelers who have knowledge of the tools, and, third, if no tools exist, does our modeling staff have the knowledge to construct a Petri net model of the target computer system? If we are looking toward constructing a simulation model, we would first look to see if a simulation tool exists off the shelf that provides the class of model we require. For example, one can readily purchase a number of simulation tools aimed at network analysis, possibly some for architectures and probably none for operating systems. If a specific model exists, we must determine if it meets the needs of the modeling task, and, if not, can it be tailored to meet the demands. If existing tools do not suffice for the modeling task, we must select a general-purpose simulation language, or general-purpose programming language, and construct our simulation model from scratch. This is a time-consuming and laborious task, requiring performance modelers with the requisite simulation design and programming skills.

The selected modeling tool's ability to deliver accurate information concerning the system under analysis is also very important. Regarding accuracy, we want to know if the model delivers information that would closely map to the target system. Analytical models require the modeler to make many tradeoffs and assumptions to simplify the development of the model and to make it tractable. Such simplifications make the results also suspect. Petri nets suffer from similar problems, but they are not as severe as in the analytical model case. Simulations allow the modeler to incorporate more details from the target computer system and may require less assumptions, thereby mapping closer to the target system. Measuring the target system may provide the best results but is also subject to possible problems caused by the measurement technique applied. If we use software monitoring, the monitor load on the system may be significant enough to throw off the accuracy of the results significantly. This criterion must not be overlooked and must be fully understood when making a decision on selecting a modeling tool to use.

The fourth criterion applicable when deciding on which modeling tool to use is that of the model's ability to compare different alternatives simply and completely. If a model does not provide the capability to alter parameters and check alternatives, then it is not providing the capability required of a performance tradeoff study. The least flexible tool is the testbed and empirical models. These are very difficult to change, since we would require possibly multiple components being integrated into the environment to test alternative components or, if we are comparing entire systems, having these entire systems available. Analytical models can be quickly altered to examine different configurations or components and, therefore, make an attractive tool for analysis requiring numerous tradeoff studies. Petri nets are also similar to analytical models and lend themselves to fairly easy alteration. Simulation models can be constructed so that they also provide the ability to trade off various components against each other. For example, if we are trading off memory-management protocols, we could implement them all in one module, and keep all of the remaining components of the simulation model unchanged. Such an approach would readily allow us to focus on the differences each of these protocols would provide in the given system.

A selection criterion often overlooked by the modeling team is that of cost. Most modeling projects focus on the goal at hand and don't always treat this project like any other engineering project, where both performance and cost must be considered. The cost can include the system under study, the tool to be used in performing tradeoff studies, and the modeling staff. Intuitively, one can see that if we use empirical or testbed systems as our tools, the cost will consist of the cost of the actual system, plus the cost of setting up these systems for measurements and the cost of the performance assessment staff doing the assessment. These costs can far exceed the budget for most but the largest system development projects. In addition, the cost of altering systems between analysis runs may be prohibitive and may not even be possible. Because of this, simulations are typically used in large systems analysis projects, where many tradeoff studies are required. The simulation is much easier to alter and run than the real system or even a testbed. Finally, analytical and Petri net models may be the least expensive to produce, since they do not typically require large software developments or implementations. The major cost in these types of studies would be the analyst's salary and time.

## 11.2  Validation of results

The tool selected must produce results that are correct and consistent and, therefore, convincing to our client. If the results and assumptions used to get them are too far from the expected systems result, the analysis may be very suspect and will not be used. Analytical results readily fall into this venue, since most people are skeptical when it comes to the assumptions and simplifications required to make these models workable. Simulations also suffer from this at times, due to the nature of simulation model construction. Simulations also typically require the modeler to make tradeoffs when it comes to specific details. Some of these tradeoffs may make the model's results less realistic to the client. Also, many simulation developers suffer from one major flaw. They often do not fully validate the correctness of their models before they apply them to the problem being studied.

Once we determine which modeling tool to use and have constructed our model, we still cannot simply begin running our experiments. The selected tool and model must be validated so we believe the results they produce. The validation of one tool starts by selecting another tool or tools, and collecting information from the other tools. Using this collected information the modeler runs the new tool for the same configuration and compares the results provided by the multiple tools. The results collected from all the tools should lead the modeler to the same conclusions. There are no hard and fast rules as to how a validated tool's results should compare point to point with the tool used for validation. Many simulation studies have used a measure that looks for aggregate results not to differ by more than 5 percent, give or take a few percentage points.

The validation requires the modeler to look at a variety of components of the model. First, does the model have a correspondence to the real system under study? That is, is it a faithful representation of the real system? For example, if the model has two processors and the real system has one, it is not a faithful representation. Second, are the assumptions used by the modeler realistic in terms of the real-world system being modeled? Third, does the model's input parameters and distributions track that of the real system values, if available? If they are not available, do they track those of some other model constructed for a similar project that was validated? Finally, do the results and conclusions from the model map favorably to those of the measured system or other tools? In addition, do the conclusions from the model being validated follow those of the real system or other model consistently and correctly?

Each of these questions can be answered in a variety of ways. They can be determined using expert intuition, by measuring the system and comparing the results, or through analytical results. Expert intuition comes from an individual modeler who has performed many tests in the past. Using this wealth of knowledge, the modeler may be able to examine the results and model and determine if they appear—"in his or her opinion"—to be representative of a faithful and correct rendition of the system under study. These experts are drawn from designers, architects, implementers, analysts, maintainers, operators, and even users of the systems being studied. What we do not want is the validation expert coming from the team used to design the model being validated.

Real system measurement is the most reliable means of model validation, but it also can be the hardest to come by. This is because the real system may not exist yet, or collected information may not exist. Possibly the measurements for an existing system, if they are available, may not represent the full spectrum of information needed to corroborate the model's data. The last method for obtaining the required validation information is by using analytical results. As long as the model we are trying to validate is not an analytical model, this is an available and acceptable means of validating information. By setting the parameters for a simulation to those of an analytical model, we should in theory be able to faithfully determine the same results as those generated by the analytical model.

# 11.3   Conducting experiments

Given that we have selected a tool, constructed our model, and validated the model, we must next develop our experiments to perform the initially intended function for the performance study. To develop our experiments we must have an idea as to what the performance metrics will be (performance variables) for the study. We saw previously, in Chapter 8, that to develop a set of performance variables we must begin by developing a list of services to be offered by the system under study. Given that we have done this selection and definition of services, we next must determine all possible outcomes for the service. For example, each service can have a request for service pending, be in service, be completing service, or rejecting a service request. The results of the service request are to accept the request for future service, perform the service either correctly or incorrectly, or simply reject the request as not being possible. For example, the lock manager for a database system can accept a request for a lock and either grant it, delay it, perform the request erroneously, or refuse the lock request altogether.

If the system performs the request correctly, the performance is measured as the time taken to perform the service, the rate the service is performed at, and the resources consumed while performing the requested service. These three metrics relate to the measures of responsiveness, productivity, and utilization—all important components of any computer system's performance study. These measures have also been altered to show speed, reliability, and availability. For example, the responsiveness of a transaction processing system is measured by its response time. This consists of the time between a transaction's request for service and the response to the transaction from the server. The transaction processing systems productivity is measured by its throughput. The throughput consists of the number of transactions performed completely during some prescribed unit of time (e.g., per minute or second). The third measure, utilization, provides a measure of a resource's business. In the transaction processing example, we could see what percentage of time the server is busy serving transactions versus the time it is idle during the same interval of time as the throughput measure. Using such information we can begin to isolate problems within our system. For example, the service that is the most highly utilized may represent the system's bottleneck.

If a service is done erroneously, we also wish to capture this information. Error detection and measurement are important in determining a service's resiliency and tolerance to errors. For example, in the transaction processing system, we may want to know what caused the errors and the failure of transactions being processed. It may be important to know that an error occurred due to a hardware failure or a software failure, or was caused by contention or a poor transaction design. Each will tell us something about the product we are evaluating. If a resource cannot perform the service function at all, it may imply it is down, or 100 percent utilized. Once again, knowing what state the resource is in will aid in the determination of its overall performance.

## 11.4 Performance metrics

In studies involving computer systems we will typically be interested in many such measures, not simply one for the system. The computer systems we will model are composed of systems, components, and users. All will have their own measures reflected, and each provides a different lens into the performance of the systems as a whole. Some metrics will be systemwide or global, while others will be localized or individual. There are cases where optimizing an individual metric will impact the global metric and other times when it will have little or no effect. Also, the different levels may have different primary goals. We may be looking for high utilization at one level and low utilization at another, depending on the goals for the system and the individual components making it up. This indicates that the metrics for modeling must be chosen at differing levels so that an appropriate analysis of the true system performance can be determined. The modeler must determine the full set of metrics available for some study. Then these metrics must be examined in relation to their variability, redundancy, and completeness. If a metric has low variability, it may be assumed to be static, removing it from our list of services and measures to consider. If one variable provides the same information another provides, one of them should be dropped. For example, the queue length is equal to the number in service plus those waiting for service, so we need not keep track of them all. Completeness deals with making sure the set of variables provides as reflective a set as that from the real system.

When modeling computer systems, there are many commonly encountered performance metrics. The most common are response time (sometimes called speed, turnaround time, reaction time), throughput (sometimes called capacity or bandwidth), utilization (sometimes referred to as efficiency or business), reliability, and cost/performance ratio.

## 11.4.1  Response time

Response time is broadly defined as the time interval between a user's request for service and the services return of results, as shown in Figure 11.1. In reality this is overly simplistic and not what occurs. There are many more components on both sides of the request/response making up the true measure. If we think about the same transaction processing system we have used in our previous example, we begin with the user inputting the transaction. We assume this is a single step, but it can be much longer if the user is using an interactive interface to the transactional service. The database system must set up the appropriate data structures and provide resources for the transaction to execute. The transaction then is executed by the database engine. The transaction then completes processing and prepares the transaction results and sends them off, as shown in Figure 11.2. Each of these steps, while a bit more complete than the simplistic model, is still only a partial representation of the full transaction processing cycle in a commercial database system.

Each of these components of the transaction response time is a response time component. These components are the subparts of the total transaction response time, just as queue wait time and server time represent the job time in a queuing model.

The response time for a computer system will typically increase as the load increases. Many measures have been developed to provide rules of thumb for such scenarios. One, called the stretch factor, is computed as the expected response time over the expected service time, or:

$$\text{Stretch factor} = E[W]/E[S] \tag{11.1}$$

This measure is depicted in Figure 11.3. In most real systems we wish to see this stretch factor to have a computed value of approximately 5. If the

**Figure 11.1**
*Typical response time measurement.*

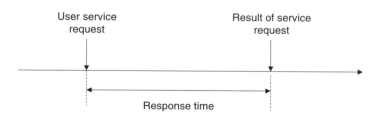

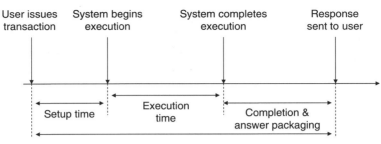

**Figure 11.2**
*Transaction processing response partitioning.*

factor rises above this approximation, this implies longer waiting times in relation to service times and, therefore, lower availability of the resource and higher utilization.

## 11.4.2   Throughput

The throughput is a measure of the number of items being measured (e.g., transactions) that receive service (e.g., complete transaction execution) over some predefined period of time. For the transaction system we have been discussing, this would be measured as transactions per second, or TPS. In computer systems' CPUs, the measure is MIPS, or million instructions per second. In communications systems it may be MPS for messages per second or BPS for bits per second. Throughput, as with response time, will grow as additional load is placed on a system. However, unlike response time, there will be a point where the throughput will maximize and possibly begin to degrade, as shown in Figure 11.4. In this figure you will note that the throughput seems to increase over a wide range of load and then slows as we reach a saturation point. In the throughput case, the throughput increases to some maximal level and then levels off. At a critical point in the load,

**Figure 11.3**
*Stretch factor compared with utilization.*

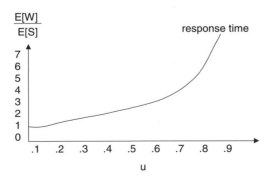

**Figure 11.4**
*Throughput curves versus response curves.*

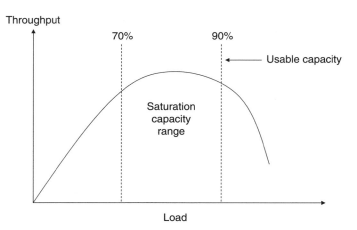

where the response time has begun to increase exponentially, the throughput begins to degrade below the maximum. Such curves are typical of computer systems where there is inadequate service capacity for the presented load. We always want to keep throughput near its peak, but not too far into the saturation region, in order that resources stay available for spikes in load.

## 11.4.3   Efficiency

Another important measure is efficiency. This measure is related to utilization and throughput. The relationships look at a ratio of the maximum achievable throughput compared with the actual throughput:

Efficiency = real throughput/theoretical throughput                     (11.2)

If we have a processor rated at 100 megaflops (floating-point operations) and, when run in a testbed we measure 90 megaflops, the processor's efficiency is 90 percent. Efficiency can also be measured for multiple resource systems. One common use is when looking at the performance speedup of having one processor versus $n$ processors. Efficiency in this class of environment is calculated as the ratio of the theoretical throughput times the number of devices divided by the speed of a single device.

In Figure 11.5 we see that the theoretical efficiency of adding more processors is a linear curve with an efficiency equal to the number of devices applied. The real measured curve shows a much different story. The efficiency is not linear and continues to degrade as more devices are added. This is due to the added overhead involved in keeping the processors effectively utilized in performing tasks.

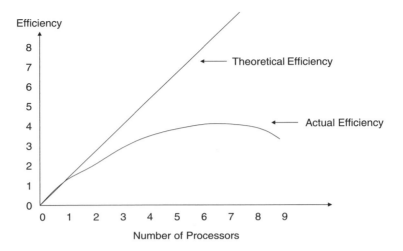

**Figure 11.5**
*Multiprocessor efficiency curve.*

### 11.4.4    Utilization, reliability, and availability

The utilization of a resource is a measure of how busy the resource is. It is computed as the fraction of time the resource is busy servicing clients divided by the entire time period:

$$\text{Utilization} = \text{time busy}/(\text{time busy} + \text{time idle}) \tag{11.3}$$

The goal in most systems is not to saturate resources (i.e., keep them 100 percent busy) but to balance the utilization so that no device is more heavily utilized than another. In principle this is the goal, but in reality this is very difficult to achieve. Utilization is an important measure when examining systems. Different devices in the system have different average utilization values. For example, processors typically will be highly utilized, while memory, disks, and other peripheral devices will all have smaller fractional use time.

Other important measures in analyzing computer systems include systems reliability and systems availability. Reliability is a measure of the probability of errors or a measure of the typical time between errors. Most computer systems are fairly reliable, with hardware being more reliable than software. The availability of a system is measured in relation to reliability. If a system is highly reliable, it will be available more likely than not. But if a system is unreliable, then it will have periods of downtime, where the system is not running or is running erroneously. In the case of failures, another important metric is the mean time to repair, or MTTR. The MTTR will indicate on average how long the system will be unavailable after an error. If errors can be quantified and predicted, we can also develop metrics such as mean time to failure, or MTTF.

A final measure used by systems analysts when comparing systems or components is the cost versus performance ratio. This measure is useful in determining which of multiple systems, having the same relative performance, is a better buy. The cost in this case includes, minimally, the hardware and software but also may include licensing, installation, maintenance, and even operations.

## 11.5  Evaluation

All these performance measurements mean nothing unless there is some relationship associated with the measure. For example, how do we know if for some given metric it is important to maximize its value or minimize its value? To make sound judgments we must understand the measures we are taking and what their relationship is to system values, as shown in Figure 11.6. For example, for a CPU do we wish to have a high number of instructions per second or a low number? Are we looking for medians or modes? It makes a difference in how the results get interpreted. To make sound decisions about how to interpret the measurements requires that we understand how they are related to each other. For example, high disk utilization may map to low system throughput. Or high CPU utilization may map to high throughput. It is important to know which is which in order to make sound decisions.

**Figure 11.6**
*Metrics versus usefulness.*

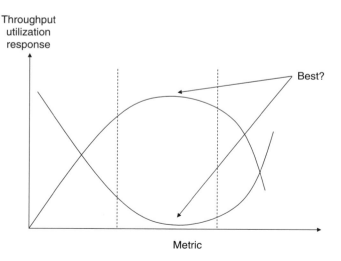

How do we know what is adequate or good performance—especially if the system for which we are considering this question does not exist as yet. The problem is that of setting performance requirements for an as yet non-existing system. Typically we specify requirements in a nonquantitative way. We may make statements such as: The system should have low overhead, the memory and processor speeds should be synchronized, there should be a low probability of failure, and so on. In all of these cases we have stated qualitative requirements, which may be very hard to measure and realize. They are nonspecific, nonmeasurable, and, therefore, unacceptable. To change this the analyst should look at what the system will be required to do, and what capacity would be needed for a typical system with the same loads. We may also wish to add in some growth factor, say 100 percent. Therefore, we would specify a system that will meet our processing requirements and still have growth capacity equal to that being used in the present system.

## 11.6 Summary

In this chapter we introduced some simple rules to consider when selecting a modeling tool for a specific modeling project. We indicated that if time and money were not a factor we would use all methods. First, we would apply analytical modeling to quickly eliminate alternative designs that would not meet the needs of the target system. Second, we would apply Petri net models to further compare and remove alternatives from consideration. Third, we would use simulation to study a few alternative components or systems. Simulation provides for very detailed modeling of components or operations if so desired. The fourth tool to apply would be testbeds. These are much more complex, and we would use this alternative when we are down to only a few alternatives, possibly only one, that need to be validated.

Since it is not a perfect world, time and money do count; therefore, our modeling tool selection would be driven by these considerations. If cost is of paramount importance, we may look to analytical modeling, since it is relatively cheap if we happen to have queuing analysts on our staff. If cost is not a problem, then building testbeds would be the way to go. If cost falls somewhere between this, we would choose simulation or Petri nets. If time is of the essence, we would also recommend queuing theory over the others, since a model can be developed and analyzed. If time is available, then simulation or testbeds would be appropriate choices.

After this discussion, the chapter moved on to examining some of the components of a modeling project that also assist us in deciding on which modeling tool to apply. The metrics we need and their fidelity or accuracy will also push us toward specific tools. If we need very accurate information, we may wish to use testbeds and empirical models, since we are measuring the real system or a prototype of it. If we are less concerned with accuracy, we may wish to use analytical models, since they can be easily constructed and provide coarse-grained analysis.

The chapter then goes on to discuss some of the implications of modeling a system—for example, how to determine if the model's data are correct, or if the results are good or bad. Interpretation of results is dependent on knowing the measurements being taken and their relationship to important systems metrics, such as throughput, utilization, and response time.

# 12

# *Analysis of Computer Architectures*

Analytical modeling and Petri net modeling were introduced in previous chapters. In these discussions, we addressed basic concepts of queuing systems and Petri net theories, their application to computer systems modeling, and an introduction to computer systems modeling. This chapter will address the use of analytical and Petri net models, specifically for their use as performance evaluation tools applied to the modeling of computer architectures.

## 12.1   Introduction

In the past several years, the use of analytical and Petri net performance models instead of the more widely used and familiar simulation methods has become increasingly popular because of their relative simplicity of implementation and robustness of application results. These analytical and Petri net models have been successful in estimating such performance measures as processor throughput, average queue length, mean response times, resource contention, and synchronization for some real systems. This chapter is an introduction to queuing and Petri net modeling techniques applied to computer architectures and is not meant as an in-depth study.

Of interest to most modelers is the classic central server model of a computer system, such as a single PC or workstation, and the multiprocessor model one would typically find in a server. For this reason, we will examine these two models as an initial example of how to apply analytical modeling techniques to the solution of a system's performance assessment.

## 12.2   Case I: Central server computer system

The central server model, shown in Figure 12.1, is typical of most desktop computers and single processor servers in service today. The main elements

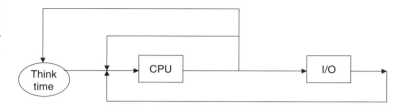

**Figure 12.1**
*Central server*
*model.*

of this model are the CPU, memory, and I/O devices (disks, network connections, etc.). In addition to these major components, the model must also depict how these components are connected to each other, forming the architecture of the central server computer system. The interconnection would consist of paths for new program initiation and for active programs to circulate through the system. The assumption here is that the number of jobs (programs) circulating in the system is steady and fixed. Each of the fixed number of jobs performs some CPU activity, followed by some I/O activity, and back to the CPU for additional service.

The modeled system would be typical of computers one would find on a person's desk in a high-capacity business office. Such a computer system would consist of a single CPU (such as a Pentium IV with onboard cache), matched speed main memory (128 MB to 1 GB), at least one disk drive, and numerous other peripheral devices. The machine would also be connected to the Internet and may service remote service calls. The operating system is one of the industry standards (Microsoft XP, LINUX).

The processing capacity of the CPU and each of the I/O devices is denoted by $\mu_i = 1/T_{S(i)}$, where $T_{S(i)}$ is the average service time for the specified device. The flow of control for a job in the system is directed by the branching probabilities, $p_1, p_2, p_3, \ldots, p_n$. On leaving the CPU a job may loop back to the CPU for more service, with probability $p_1$. The interpretation of this can be that the program is going back for more service, or it is completing and being replaced by another new program.

The remaining values are easier to interpret. The probabilities $p_2, p_3, \ldots, p_n$ determine what percentage of I/O requests go to which device. From earlier chapters you will recall that:

$$\sum_{i=1}^{n} p_i = 1 \tag{12.1}$$

The value $\mu_i$, $i = 1, 2, \ldots, n$, represents the service rates for each defined server in the model. The service rate is the number of instructions performed divided by the raw speed of the device. For example, the CPU service rate is defined as:

$$\mu_1 = \text{CPU service rate} = \frac{\text{CPU instructions per job}}{\text{CPU speed in instructions per second}} \qquad (12.2)$$

In most analyses we make the assumption that the service discipline is FCFS and that the arrival rate and service rates are exponentially distributed and the queuing discipline is FCFS. The key metrics we are interested in discovering are throughput and utilization.

The typical method to compute this is to use Buzen's algorithm. This algorithm determines the probability of having different numbers of jobs in different servers at a point in time. The number of jobs at any particular node is not independent of the remainder of the systems nodes, since the total number in the system must be kept steady. This algorithm proves that the probability of the jobs being spread around the servers in a particular distribution is:

$$\text{Prob}(k_1, k_2, \ldots, k_m) = \left(1/G(K)\right) \prod_{i=2}^{M} \left(\mu_1 \left(P_i/\mu_i\right)\right)^{k_i} \qquad (12.3)$$

Using this property and Little's Law we can compute some of the metrics of interest as:

$$
\begin{aligned}
\rho_1 \quad &= \text{CPU utilization} \\
&= G(K-1)/G(K) \\
\rho_i \quad &= \text{I/O device utilizations} \\
&= \rho_i \mu_i \left(P_i/\mu_i\right) \text{ for } i = 2, 3, \ldots, M \\
\lambda \quad &= \text{system throughput} \\
&= P_1 \rho_1 \mu_1 \text{ jobs per unit time} \\
E(k_i) \quad &= \text{average jobs at node } i \\
&= \sum_{n=1}^{K} \left(\mu_1 \left(P_i/\mu_i\right)\right)^n \frac{G(k-n)}{G(k)} \text{ for } i = 1, 2, \ldots, M
\end{aligned}
\qquad (12.4)
$$

One of the most important components of Buzen's algorithm is the function $G(k)$ for $k = 1, 2, 3, \ldots, M$. To perform this computation a partial function $g(k,m)$ is defined. The details of this function were provided in Chapter 7. Repeating some of the important aspects of computing $G(k)$:

$$g(k,1) \ =1 \ \text{for} \ k=0,1,2,\ldots,K$$
$$g(0,m) =1 \ \text{for} \ m=1,2,\ldots,M$$
$$g(k,m) = g(k,m-1)+\left(\mu_1\left(P_m/\mu_m\right)g\left(k-1,m\right)\right) \quad (12.5)$$
$$G(k) \quad = g(k,M) \ \text{for} \ k=0,1,\ldots,K$$

Details of the solution can be found in [9].

As an example of the operation of this algorithm we can set some of the values for a test system. If we assume we have a system with a CPU and three I/O devices, $M = 4$. We can set the service rate for the I/O devices as all the same $\mu_2 = \mu_3 = \mu_4 = 10$ I/Os per second. The CPU is set at $\mu_1 = 18.33$ quantum slices per job. If we set $K = 8$ tasks circulating through the system and run it through Buzen's algorithm we would find the results shown in the following chart.

| CPU Time per Request | Disk I/O Rate | CPU Utilization | Disk Utilization | Throughput Requests/sec |
|---|---|---|---|---|
| 0.6 | 10 | 0.96 | 0.53 | 1.6 |
| 0.3 | 10 | 0.67 | 0.74 | 2.23 |
| 0.6 | 15 | 1.00 | 0.37 | 1.66 |
| 0.3 | 15 | 0.88 | 0.65 | 2.92 |

A similar analysis could be developed using a Petri net instead of the queuing model. Figure 12.2 depicts a Petri net example for the single I/O device system shown in Figure 12.1.

In the depicted model, jobs get submitted through a set of terminals represented by the think place and the term transition. Once a job is requesting service, it is moved into the wait CPU place to wait for the CPU to become available. Once it is available, the waiting job acquires the CPU and models using it by moving into the use CPU place, followed by the CPU transition, which models the execution cycle of the CPU. After a job has completed its use of the CPU, it moves to the choose place. In this place a decision must be made to check if the job is complete or if more I/O is needed. If completed, the token representing a job moves back to the think place to become a new job later. If I/O is needed, the token moves to the disk wait place to busy wait for the disk resource. Once the resource is freed, the job acquires the disk and models using the disk by moving into the use disk place followed by enabling of the disk transition. Upon completion of disk use, the token (job) goes back into the wait CPU place to reacquire the CPU. If we wish to model more disk drives, we simply make more branches from the choose place and replicate the loop for the disk drive (Figure 12.3).

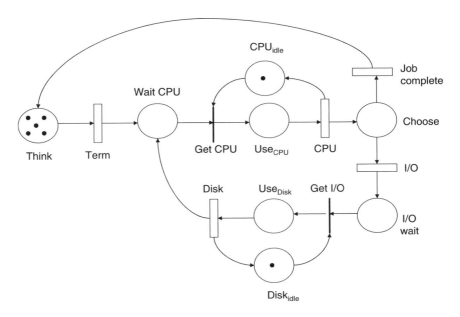

**Figure 12.2**
*Central server Petri net.*

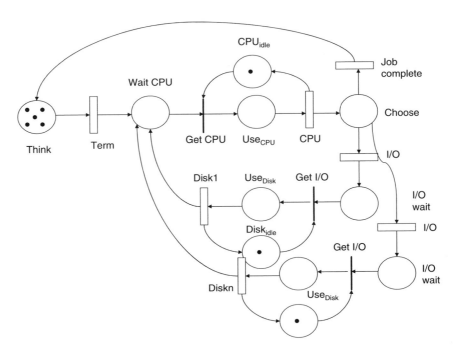

**Figure 12.3**
*Multiple disk example Petri net.*

If we set the timed transitions as follows: Term 0.1, CPU 1.0, and Disk at 0.8, and the places initially loaded with tokens as: think = 6, CPU_idle = 1, and Disk_idle = 1, we can proceed with the analysis. The first analysis must be to determine if the model is bounded and live. That is to say, there are no deadlock states and the net is configured so it can initiate firings. By examining this net we can also see that there are four major place flows through the net. Flow 1 = think, waitCPU, Use CPU, and Choose. Flow 2 = If we set = think, waitCPU, Use CPU, Choose, diskwait, and use disk. Flow 3 = CPUidle, useCPU. Flow 4 = diskidle, use disk. The first flow corresponds to jobs using the CPU and completing with no need for I/O. The second flow also represents jobs using the CPU but also requiring and using I/O devices. The third flow loop represents the CPU cycle of busy and idle, and the final flow loop represents the disk cycle of busy and idle time. Since all of the places of the Petri net are covered by these flows, the net is bounded. This also implies that this network has a finite reachability graph, and, therefore, the underlying Markov chain has a finite state space.

Using these flows we can compute the average time for jobs to flow through each loop by running this model. If we ran the model with the same data as in the queuing model, the same results would follow. More details about this model and others can be found in [10].

## 12.3   Case II: Multiple server computer system

Another classic analysis is that of the multiprocessor. In this case, we can replace the central server model with multiple examples of the same model cascaded together (Figure 12.4), or we could examine more elaborate imple-

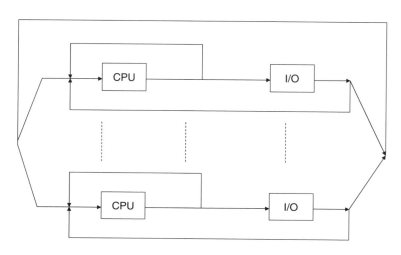

**Figure 12.4**
*Multiprocessor model using central processor.*

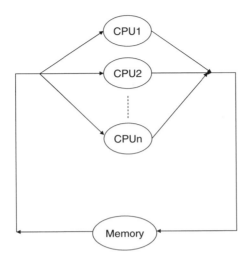

**Figure 12.5a**
*Shared memory model.*

mentations—for example, the shared memory model (Figure 12.5a) or the multiple bank shared memory model (Figure 12.5b).

The analysis of any one of these architectures would follow methodology similar to that of the single CPU case described previously. The system we choose to model here is the multiprocessor case. This is more indicative of

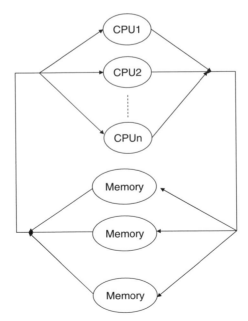

**Figure 12.5b**
*Multibank shared memory model.*

realistic systems, where multiple servers are interconnected to serve several users.

If we decide to model the system shown in Figure 12.5b, we have essentially the problem of memory allocation to processors. A processor can have all of the memory or none of the memory or anything in between. Allocations are done using the entire memory module. That is, a CPU cannot share a memory module with another CPU during a cycle.

On each CPU cycle, each processor makes a memory request. If there is a free memory meeting the CPU's request, it gets filled; otherwise, the CPU must wait until the next cycle. Each memory module for which there is a memory access request can fill only one request. When several processors make memory module requests to the same memory module, only one is served (chosen at random from those requesting). The other processors will make the same memory module request on the next cycle. New memory requests for each processor are chosen randomly from the $M$ memory modules using a uniform distribution.

Let the system state be the number of memory requests for each memory module:

$$K = \left(k_1, k_2, k_3, \ldots, k_m\right) \tag{12.6}$$

where $k_i$ represents the memory request by processors for memory bank $i$.

At the start of a cycle the sum of all requests cannot exceed the number of processors in the system, $N$:

$$k_1 + k_2 + k_3 + \ldots + k_m = N \tag{12.7}$$

The total number of possible states is related to the number of ways $N$ processor requests can be distributed to $M$ memory modules:

$$\binom{M+N-1}{N} = \binom{M+N-1}{M-1} = \frac{(M+N-1)!}{(M-1)!N!} \tag{12.8}$$

or, in other terms, how to allocate $N$ balls to $M$ cells.

For $N = 2$ and $M = 4$ (see Figure 12.6) the possible way to allocate the four memory modules to processors (indistinguishable from each other) is shown in Table 12.1.

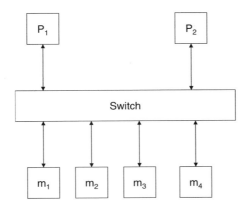

**Figure 12.6**
*Multiprocessor system with N = 2 and M = 4.*

and is found by:

$$\frac{(M+N-1)!}{(M-1)!N!} = \frac{5!}{3!2!} = \frac{5*4}{2} = 10 \tag{12.9}$$

We can see that if the number of processors requesting memory modules and the number of memory modules are increased, the number of possible states grows very quickly, making this analysis difficult for even relatively small problems, as shown in Table 12.2.

**Table 12.1**    *Possible Ways to Allocate Memory*

|  | Memory | | | |
|---|---|---|---|---|
|  | **1** | **2** | **3** | **4** |
| 1 | 0 | 0 | 0 | 2 |
| 2 | 0 | 0 | 1 | 1 |
| 3 | 0 | 0 | 2 | 0 |
| 4 | 0 | 1 | 0 | 1 |
| 5 | 0 | 1 | 1 | 0 |
| 6 | 0 | 2 | 0 | 0 |
| 7 | 1 | 0 | 0 | 1 |
| 8 | 1 | 0 | 1 | 0 |
| 9 | 1 | 1 | 0 | 0 |
| 10 | 2 | 0 | 0 | 0 |

**Table 12.2**   *Number of States for Selected Number*
*of Processors and Memory Modules*

| N | M | # States |
|---|---|----------|
| 2 | 4 | 10 |
| 3 | 5 | 35 |
| 4 | 7 | 210 |

Let $H = (h_1, h_2, ..., h_m)$ represent the intermediate state, when the memory access requested on a cycle has been filled and the new requests have not yet been made:

$$h_i = \begin{cases} k_i - 1 & \text{if } k_i > 0, \forall i \\ 0 & \text{if } k_i = 0 \end{cases} \qquad (12.10)$$

Let $G$ represent a new (feasible) system state:

$$G = (g_1, g_2, g_3, ..., g_m) \qquad (12.11)$$

First, let's define:

$$d_i = g_i - h_i \qquad \text{that is, number of new request}$$
$$x = \sum d_i \qquad (12.12)$$

**Note:** The state $G$ can be reached from state $K$ in one cycle if, and only if, $d_i \geq 0$ for each $i$.

## 12.3.1   Properties

1.   If $G$ is reachable from $K$ in one cycle, the probability it will in fact be the next state is given by:

$$P(K, G) = \frac{x!}{d_1! \, d_2! \, ... \, d_m!} \left(\frac{1}{m}\right)^x \qquad (12.13)$$

where $x$ represents the number of new requests.

2.   The system can be described by a Markov chain, since the next state probabilities at any time depend only on the current state.

3.      The system is aperiodic, since a one-step transition from a state to itself is possible at any time.

4.      The system is irreducible, since it can reach any other in a finite number of steps.

Hence, since it is a finite state process, it is also an ergotic Markov process. Also, since these conditions hold, there is an equilibrium state probability distribution, $\Pi$, so that:

$$\underset{\sim}{\Pi} = \underset{\sim}{\tilde{\Pi}} \, P \tag{12.14}$$

where $P$ is the state transition matrix (described in Chapters 6 and 7):

$$\underset{\sim}{\Pi} = \left( \Pi_1, \Pi_2, \Pi_3, \Pi_4, \ldots, \Pi_j \right) \tag{12.15}$$

A performance assessment typically made in such system configurations to determine what the effective processor power of the $N$ processors with $M$ memory system is:

$$\begin{aligned} EP(N,M) = \ & \text{the expected number of instructions} \\ & \text{excuted per second compared with an} \\ & N = 1, M = 1 \text{ system} \end{aligned} \tag{12.16}$$

Let Proc($i$) represent the number of memory requests serviced (instructions executed) when the system is in state $i$:

$$\therefore EP(N,M) = \sum_{i=1}^{j} \text{Proc}(i) \Pi_i \tag{12.17}$$

For the simple case where $N$ = 2 and $M$ = 2, we have the system illustrated in Figure 12.7.

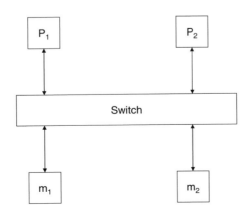

**Figure 12.7**
*Multiprocessor system with N = 2 and M = 2.*

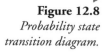

**Figure 12.8**
*Probability state transition diagram.*

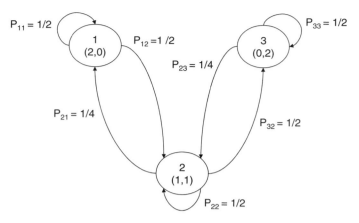

The possible states this model could be in, representing the requested memory requested by the two processors, is described as (see Figure 12.8):

States $(k_1 k_2)$:

$1(2,0)$

$2(1,1)$

$3(0,2)$

$$j = \binom{N+M-1}{N} = \binom{3}{2} = \frac{3!}{2!1!} = 3 \qquad (12.18)$$

Using the general formula:

$$P(K,G) = \frac{x!}{d_1! d_2! \dots d_m!} \left(\frac{1}{m}\right)^x \qquad (12.19)$$

$$P\big((2,0),(1,1)\big) = \left(\frac{1!}{0!1!}\right)\left(\frac{1}{2}\right)^1 = \frac{1}{2} \qquad (12.20)$$

which represents the probability of being in state (2,0) and transitioning to state (1,1). Similarly, the probability of being in state (1,1) and traversing to state (2,0) would be found as:

$$P\big((1,1),(2,0)\big) = \left(\frac{1!}{2!0!}\right)\left(\frac{1}{2}\right)^2 = \frac{1}{4} \qquad (12.21)$$

and so on.

The balance equations for this Markov chain can be found using the relationship:

$$\text{Flow In} = \text{Flow Out}$$ (12.22)

$$\text{State 1: } 1/2\,\Pi_1 + 1/4\,\Pi_2 = \Pi_1$$

$$\text{Flow In} = \text{Flow Out}$$ (12.23)

$$\text{State 2: } 1/2\,\Pi_3 + 1/4\,\Pi_2 = \Pi_3$$

Solving these simultaneous equations yields:

$$2\Pi_1 + \Pi_2 = 4\Pi_1$$
$$2\Pi_3 + \Pi_2 = 4\Pi_3$$
$$\therefore \Pi_2 = 2\Pi_1$$ (12.24)
$$\Pi_2 = 2\Pi_3$$
$$\Pi_1 = \Pi_3 = 1/2\,\Pi_2$$

and since:

$$\Pi_1 + \Pi_2 + \Pi_3 = 1$$ (12.25)

then:

$$\Pi_1 = .25$$
$$\Pi_2 = .50$$ (12.26)
$$\Pi_3 = .25$$

The discovered effective processor power is computed using the relationship:

$$EP(2,2) = \sum_i \Pi_i \, \text{Proc}(i)$$ (12.27)

where

| $i$ | $\text{Proc}(i)$ number of instructions executed in state $i$: |
|---|---|
| 1 | 1 |
| 2 | 2 |
| 3 | 1 |

$$\therefore$$
$$EP(2,2) = 1\Pi_1 + 2\Pi_2 + 1\Pi_3 = .25 + 1.0 + .25 = 1.5$$ (12.28)

**Table 12.3**   *Summary of Speed Up for* M *Memory and* N *Processors*

| M | N Processors | | | |
|---|---|---|---|---|
| Memory Modules | 2 | 3 | 4 | 5 |
| 2 | 1.5 | — | — | — |
| 3 | 1.667 | 2.048 | — | — |
| 4 | 1.750 | 2.269 | 2.62 | — |
| 5 | 1.800 | 2.409 | 2.863 | 3.199 |
| 6 | 1.833 | 2.505 | 3.036 | 3.453 |
| 7 | 1.857 | 2.575 | 3.166 | 3.648 |
| 8 | 1.875 | 2.627 | 3.265 | 3.801 |
| 9 | 1.889 | 2.668 | 3.344 | 3.925 |
| 10 | 1.900 | 2.701 | 3.407 | 4.025 |

Results for $M$ memory modules ($2 \leq M \leq 10$) and $N$ processors ($2 \leq N \leq 5$) are summarized in Table 12.3.

Limitations: The model does not take into account memory interference caused by I/O operations. It also assumes the processors and memory are synchronized, as are memory access/cycle.

# 12.4   Case III: Petri net example

We could look at the same problem from a Petri net perspective. In this case we make some of the same assumptions: There are $n_p$ processors, $n_m$ shared memory modules, and $n_b$ data buses. In the previous theoretical analysis we ignored the data buses. Each of the processors has local memory, which gets used until a page miss. At this point an access to an external memory module is required, resulting in a new page being loaded into the local processor memory. The miss rate is exponentially distributed and set at $1/\lambda$. The access time to the shared memory is also assumed to be exponentially distributed with mean $1/\mu$. If we originally set $n_p = 5$, $n_m = 3$, and $n_b = 2$, we have the initial configuration seen in Figure 12.9. The model depicted contains two places per memory module (one place for processor tokens and one place for bus tokens) and one timed transition (for memory allocation and use). There are also two immediate transitions associated with synchronizing and controlling the memory access. For the size model we postulated

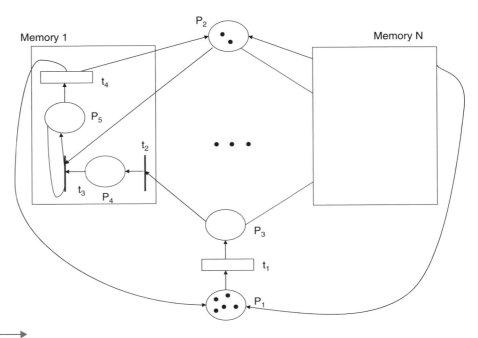

**Figure 12.9**   *Petri net model for multiprocessor system.*

we would have nine total places, four timed transitions, and six immediate transitions. Tokens in place $P_2$ represent data buses available for use. Tokens in place $P_1$ represent processors executing on their local memory. An important assumption in this model is that every processor and memory module act in an identical manner.

When a processor completes its local memory access (has a page miss resulting in firing transition $t_1$) and requires more shared memory resources, a token is moved from place $P_1$ to place $P_3$. A processor determines which memory it needs by firing the immediate transition, $t_2$, on the memory module it has chosen using a probabilistic branch. Once $t_2$ fires, a token is moved from place 3 to place 4. Once a token is in place 4, the processor is requesting access to a data bus. The bus is used to connect the processor to the memory module. The processor acquires the memory desired, and then acquires a data bus to retrieve the needed information. Once a processor has the bus, signaled by the firing of transition $t_3$, and has acquired the memory (indicated by the token in place, $p_5$), it begins to model using the memory module by initiating the timer on transition $t_4$. Upon completion of using the bus, the token representing the processor and the bus are routed back to their initial places, $P_2$ and $P_1$.

If we run this model with inputs similar to what were applied to the queuing model discussed previously, we would find results that very closely match the queuing model case. That is, we would find out that the effective processor power would be proportional to about 2.05 with the configuration as specified. We could improve on this if we made the access balanced, implying that no single processor could hold more than one memory at a time. This would increase our effective processor capacity to approximately 3.2.

## 12.5   Summary

In this chapter, we applied the analytical tools developed in Chapters 1 through 11 to the analysis of various computer architecture. We first looked at a simple central-server computer system typical of most desktop computer systems and then we looked a multiple-server computer system. We performed these analyses first analytically and then using Petri nets. This chapter is presented as a guide to the reader in analyzing computer architectures and not as a comparison of various architectures or components.

# 13

# *Analysis of Operating System Components*

This chapter is divided into the following sections. Section 13.1 covers an introduction to the specific performance evaluation conducted, its basic concepts, the types of workloads being used, the experimental design for the performance analysis, and an introduction to the simulation toolkit used for the evaluation. Section 13.2 includes the architecture of the four operating systems being used. We have tried to keep the architectures very specific to the experiments being carried out. Section 13.3 is focused on statistics, analysis of the results obtained from experiments, sensitivity analysis, cost/ performance issues, and presentation in the form of graphs and charts. Section 13.4 discusses experimental design and simulation. Section 13.5 covers conclusions about the performance analysis.[1]

## 13.1   Introduction

Computer systems users, administrators, and designers are all interested in performance evaluations, since their goal is to obtain or provide the highest performance at lowest cost. Performance evaluation is essential at every step in the life cycle of a computer system. This includes design, manufacturing, use, upgrade, and so on. We need to perform this evaluation in order to predict the adequacy of the system. In order to do this performance evaluation we must define the system correctly; define its components; state the environment in which the system resides; and define parameters, which we measure and on which the system is built. Computer systems are a backbone of an organization, which might have its clients scattered around the globe. If the system doesn't perform the way it is intended to, it results in loss of infrastructure, efficiency, and credibility of the organization. So a sound

1.    Contributed by: P. Abdelmalek, S. Bapat, K. Challapalli, I. Chen, A. Chennamraju, P. Furey, J. Joseph, R. Madiraju, S. Chowdary, A. Pisharody, V. Rajan, W. Rosa, B. Sarangarajan, S. Sharma, P. Singhal, X. Tao, K. Vangapally, T. Zhou, and Q. Yu. University of Massachusetts Dartmouth, Department of Electrical and Computer Engineering.

evaluation of the computer system is of prime importance. This encompasses not only the hardware/software performance but also a cost versus, performance measure. For any computer system performance measures such as responsiveness, missionability, dependability, and productivity are of immense importance. There are different techniques of performance evaluation. We can identify them as two major classes. One includes designing an experiment (HW/SW/Stimulus), and the second includes modeling, which might be analytical (queuing, Petri nets) or by simulation (discrete, continuous, combined). This study utilizes both of these techniques to perform a comparison among the four operating systems.

This chapter evaluates the performance of four operating systems: Microsoft's Windows XP, Windows ME, Windows NT, and LINUX 7.2. These operating system performance assessments were completed by a graduate computer systems performance evaluation class at UMass Dartmouth during the spring semester of 2002. The performance evaluation of these operating systems was performed on an x86 architecture. The operating systems' performance was examined using three specific types of workloads. The evaluation is based on the currently available major releases of these operating systems "as-is" without performance tuning. Each team was asked to design "high-level" models and convert these models into a simulation by using the AWESIM simulation toolkit. Teams came up with a common experimental design and performed specific types of performance tests to measure the response of the four operating systems pertaining to specific factors. Each team performed a comparative analysis.

## 13.2   System architectures

For the performance evaluation analysis of the operating systems, the computer systems architecture plays a prime role. This section includes the operating system architectures for LINUX 7.2, Windows ME, Windows XP, and Windows NT.

### 13.2.1   LINUX architecture

#### Red Hat LINUX 7.2

As part of the larger effort to evaluate the relative performance of LINUX versus several other operating systems, we considered key components of LINUX in order to lay the foundation for this comparison. Here we examine the LINUX policies and parameters used in the last stable version of kernel 2.4. The distribution used for our evaluation is Red Hat LINUX 7.2.

LINUX supports multitasking, which is the ability to have many programs running simultaneously. For example, it is possible to format a disk, download a file from a BBS, and edit in a word processor—all simultaneously.

### Task structure and process table

LINUX manages the processes in the system; each process is represented by a `task_struct` data structure. The task vector is an array of pointers to every `task_struct` data structure in the system. As processes are created, a new `task_struct` is allocated from system memory and added into `task_vector`. The `task_struct` structures are linked in two ways: as a hash table, hashed by pid, and as a circular, doubly linked list using `p->next_task` and `p->prev_task` pointers. The tasks are hashed by their `pid` value. The hash table is used to quickly find a task by given `pid`, which uses `find_task_pid()`. The circular doubly linked list that uses `p->next_task` and `p->prev_task` is maintained so that one could go through all tasks on the system easily.

Task flags contain information about the process states, which are not mutually exclusive. The scheduler needs the information in order to decide which process in the system deserves to run. Every process in the system has an identifier. The process identifier is not an index into `task_vector`; it is simply a number. Each process also has user and group identifiers; these are used to control this process's access to its files and devices in the system.

### Links

In a LINUX system no process is independent of any other process. Every process in the system except the initial process, called `init`, has a parent process. New processes are not created; they are copied, or rather cloned, from previous processes. Every `task_struct` representing a process keeps pointers to its parents and to its siblings (those processes with the same parent process), as well as to its own child processes. Additionally, all of the processes in the system are held in a doubly linked list, whose root is the `init` process's `task_struct` data structure. This list allows the LINUX kernel to look at every process in the system. It needs to do this to provide support for commands such as `ps` or `kill`.

### Times and timers

The kernel keeps track of each process's creation time as well as the CPU time that it consumes during its lifetime. For each clock tick, the kernel updates the amount of time in jiffies that the current process has spent in system and in user mode. LINUX also supports process-specific interval timers; processes can use system calls to set up timers and to send signals to themselves when the timers expire. These timers can be single-shot or periodic timers.

### File system

Processes can open and close files as they wish and the process's `task_struct` contains pointers to descriptors for each open file as well as pointers to two VFS i-nodes. Each VFS i-node uniquely describes a file or directory within a file system and also provides a uniform interface to the underlying file systems. The field `p->fs` contains file system information, which, under LINUX, means three pieces of information: root directory's `d_entry` and mountpoint, alternate root directory's `d_entry` and mountpoint, and current working directory's `d_entry` and mountpoint.

### Virtual memory

Most processes have some virtual memory (kernel threads and daemons do not), and the LINUX kernel must track how that virtual memory is mapped onto the system's physical memory. The fields `p->mm` and `p->active_mm` point, respectively, to the process's address space described by the `mm_struct` structure and to the active address space if the process doesn't have a real one (e.g., kernel threads).

### Paging

To approximate a least recently used (LRU) algorithm for page replacement, LINUX finds a process with the most NRU (not recently used) pages to swap pages from. Unlike a standard clock algorithm, which tends to take a few pages from all processes, this will result in taking a large number of pages from a few processes. Sometimes LINUX will deal with this situation by temporarily removing the most victimized process from the pool of concurrently running processes. Different kernels of LINUX handle these details differently.

### Kernel 2.4

Kernel 2.4 finds a compromise between kernel 2.0's aging and 2.2's lack of aging. It does so by changing the method of decreasing the age. Age is decreased exponentially as opposed to linearly. This helps prevent one process with a high page-fault rate from getting more than its share of pages and thereby hurting other processes, and it prevents a page that is only referenced once from being given the same wait as a page that is referenced 20 times.

To have memory more efficiently utilized, kernel 2.4 reintroduces the method used in kernel 2.0 for selecting processes to contribute NRU pages. Going through a process list each time, it checks only about 6 percent of the address space in each process to search for NRU pages before it goes to the next process. Similar to kernel 2.0, this method increases the possibility of thrashing.

## 13.2.2  Windows XP architecture

Windows XP Professional is built on the proven code base of Windows NT and Windows 2000, which features a 32-bit computing architecture, as well as a fully protected memory model. Windows XP Professional is designed to allow multiple applications to run simultaneously, while ensuring great system response and stability.

### Disk management

Microsoft Windows XP offers two types of disk storage: basic and dynamic.

### Basic disk storage

A disk initialized for basic storage is called a basic disk. A basic disk contains basic volumes, such as primary partitions, extended partitions, and logical drives. Additionally, basic volumes include multidisk volumes, which are created by using Windows NT 4.0 or earlier, such as volume sets, stripe sets, mirror sets, and stripe sets with parity. Windows XP does not support this multidisk basic volume.

### Dynamic disk storage

A disk initialized for dynamic storage is called a dynamic disk. A dynamic disk contains dynamic volumes, such as simple volumes, spanned volumes, striped volumes, mirrored volumes, and RAID-5 volumes. With dynamic storage, disk and volume management can be performed without the need to restart Windows. Mirrored volumes or RAID-5 volumes cannot be created on Windows XP Professional–based computers. However, a Windows XP Professional–based computer can be used to create a mirrored or RAID-5 volume on remote computers that are running Windows 2000 Server, Windows 2000 Advanced Server, or Windows 2000 Data Center Server.

Storage types are separate from the file system type. A basic or dynamic disk can contain any combination of FAT16, FAT32, or NTFS partitions or volumes.

### File systems

Windows XP supports three different file systems: File Allocation Table (FAT); FAT16, FAT32, and NTFS (NT file system); NTFS is the recommended file system. NTFS provides advanced file system features such as security, transacted operations, large volumes, and better performance on large volumes. Such capabilities are not available on either FAT16 or FAT32. Windows XP provides native support for NTFS volumes on such large sizes, while a FAT32 volume is supported only for sizes up to 32 GB. Under Windows XP, NTFS supports a maximum file size of up to the disk size. Windows XP delivers new features (such as support for acquiring and editing video files) that frequently result in creation of files that exceed 4 GB in size. NTFS is a journaling file system. NTFS writes a log of changes being made, which offers significant benefit in cases where a system loses power, experiences an unexpected reset, or crashes. NTFS can quickly return the disk to a consistent state without running CHKDSK. This yields a better user experience and results in fewer support calls.

### Memory management

Windows XP, like most modern operating systems, uses virtual memory. Windows XP regularly checks that the memory assigned to a particular application is actually in use and maintains an estimate for each application indicating the amount of memory that could reasonably be taken away without affecting performance. A reserve of memory is kept on hand to be used as needed. When this reserve sinks too low, it is replenished by trimming working sets. These estimates are used as a guideline to determine where memory should be taken from.

Virtual memory is divided among the space taken by the applications, driver code, allocated and mapped data used by the system, and the space used by the system. In Windows, physical memory has page-pooled and non-page-pooled allocations. Non-page-pooled memory is for code that is time critical, such as the Virtual Memory Manager (VMM). Page-pooled memory is mapped to disk files and allows the OS to swap the memory pages out to disk if additional physical memory is needed elsewhere. Pool memory is managed by a system of descriptors, called page table entries (PTE), that incorporates memory page frame numbers which point to physical memory pages. In addition to memory page frame numbers, the PTE contains bits on the use status of the page—in use, dirty, clean, and unused. The memory manager keeps track of page status with page table lists for fetching and reuse.

In the fight between drivers or processes for memory under low-memory conditions, the user often loses. Generally, these conditions are temporary and are relieved when a driver or process frees up its blocks. When a driver or application process needs memory, it asks the system for a memory allocation. The allocation is either provided or denied. In past versions of Windows, allocation routines that must succeed were allowed to force the system to give the driver some memory. Unfortunately, during lean memory times, it could crash the system. To help get past these low times, Windows XP no longer permits drivers to allocate must-succeed requests. If an application or driver uses a must-succeed request, it is denied. All internal Windows XP drivers have been rewritten to avoid the use of must-succeed requests. Third-party drivers will also have to comply to earn signed driver status.

Another step taken by Windows XP for more robust memory handling is I/O throttling. For performance reasons, Windows tries to do as much processing in parallel as possible. However, if memory use gets to the point where there is none left to allocate, Windows will throttle down its processing of memory to one page a time, using the resources it can. While this slows the system, it doesn't crash.

## 13.2.3 Windows NT architecture

### The Executive

NT's Executive subsystems make up the most important layer in kernel mode, and they perform most of the functions traditionally associated with operating systems. The subsystems have separate responsibilities and names. NT doesn't assign Executive subsystems to different processes; NT doesn't place the Executive subsystems in different image files.

### Object Manager

The Object Manager is one of the NT's Executive subsystems. Other Executive subsystems use the Object Manager to define and manage objects that represent resources. The Object Manager performs object-management duties that include identification and reference counting.

### Virtual Memory Manager

The Virtual Memory Manager has two main duties: to create and manage address maps for processes and to control physical memory allocation. NT 4.0 implements a 32-bit (4-GB) address space; however, applications can directly access only the first 2 GB. The 2-GB to 4-GB portion of the address space is for the kernel-mode portions of NT, and it doesn't change. The Virtual Memory Manager implements demand-paged virtual memory, which means it manages memory in individual segments, or pages. In x86 systems, a page is 4,096 bytes. The Virtual Memory Manager has advanced capabilities that implement file memory mapping, memory sharing, and copy-on-write page protection. NT uses file memory mapping to load executable images and DLLs efficiently. Copy-on-write is an optimization related to memory sharing in which several programs share common data that each program can modify individually. When one program writes to a copy-on-write page that it shares with another program, the program that makes the modification gets its own version of the copy-on-write page to scribble on. The other program then becomes the original page's sole owner. NT uses copy-on-write optimization when several applications share the writeable portions of system DLLs.

### I/O Manager

The I/O Manager is responsible for integrating add-on device drivers with NT. Device drivers, which are dynamically loaded kernel-mode components, provide hardware support. A device driver controls a specific type of hardware device by translating the commands that NT directs to the device into device-specific commands that manipulate the hardware to carry out the commands. The I/O Manager supports asynchronous, packet-based I/O. The I/O Manager supports 64-bit file offsets and layered device drivers. Using 64-bit offsets lets NT's file systems address extremely large files and lets disk device drivers address extremely large disks. Layering lets device drivers divide their labor.

### Cache Manager

The Cache Manager works closely with the Virtual Memory Manager and file system drivers. The Cache Manager maintains NT's global (shared by all file systems) file system cache. The working-set tuner assigns physical memory to the file system cache. The NT cache is file oriented rather than disk-block oriented.

### Process Manager

The Process Manager in NT wraps the kernel's process object and adds to it a process identifier (PID), the access token, an address map, and a handle table. The Process Manager performs a similar operation on the kernel's thread object, adding to it a thread identifier (TID) and statistics. These statistics include process and thread start and exit times and various virtual-memory counters.

### The kernel

NT's kernel operates more closely with hardware than the Executive does, and it contains CPU-specific code. NT's thread scheduler, called the dispatcher by NT's developers, resides in the kernel. The dispatcher implements 32 priority levels: 0–31. The dispatcher reserves priority level 0 for a system thread that zeros memory pages as a background task. Priority levels 1 through 15 are variable (with some fixed priority levels) and are where programs execute; priority levels 16 through 31 are fixed priority levels that only administrators can access. The NT dispatcher is a preemptive scheduler. The CPU's time is divided into slices called quanta. When a thread runs to the end of its quantum and doesn't yield the CPU, the dispatcher will step in and preempt it or schedule another thread of equal priority that is waiting to run. NT implements most synchronization primitives in the kernel. The kernel implements and manages its own object types, and kernel objects represent NT's synchronization primitives.

## 13.2.4   Windows ME architecture

The team documented the architecture based on Windows 98, because Millennium is based on the architecture of Windows 98 and sufficient data are unavailable on Windows Millennium.

### Memory management

In Windows 98, memory is accessed using a 32-bit linear addressing scheme. A 32-bit addressing system can access up to 4 GB of memory. Thus, in Windows 98, when an application attempts to access memory, it simply specifies a 32-bit memory address. (The minimum allocation of virtual memory is one 4-KB page.)

Windows 98's Virtual Memory Manager (VMM) controls allocating physical and logical memory. When you launch a new application, the Virtual Memory Manager initializes the virtual address space. Windows 98's VMM can address up to 4 GB, including space on your system's hard drives, so now programmers can write programs to exploit large amounts of memory without worrying about the type of memory or the amount of memory available.

Windows 98's Virtual Memory Manager provides this large, virtual memory space to applications via two memory management processes: paging and mapped file I/O.

### Paging

Every page of memory falls into one of three categories: page directories, page tables, or page frames. For time-sensitive applications and those with other special memory performance requirements, the VMM enables a user subsystem or process with special privileges to lock selected virtual pages into its working set to ensure that a critical page is not paged out of memory during the application.

In implementing the virtual memory process, Windows 98 creates a hard disk swap file to which it writes information that will not fit into physical (RAM) memory. Windows 98's swap file is dynamic and can shrink or grow based on the operations performed on the system. (The Windows 98 swap file still has to be created during system startup if it doesn't already exist, slowing startup time.)

### Mapped file I/O

If an application attempts to load a file larger than both the system RAM and the paging file (swap file) combined, Virtual Memory Manager's mapped file I/O services are used. Mapped file I/O enables the Virtual Memory Manager to map virtual memory addresses to a large file, inform the application that the file is available, and then load only the pieces of the file that the application actually intends to use. Because only portions of the large file are loaded into memory (RAM or page file), this greatly decreases file load time and system resource drainage. It's a very useful service for database applications that often require access to huge files.

### *Protection*

In Windows 98, each type of application—16 bit, 32 bit, or MS-DOS—is protected from the other. The Windows 98 memory system also helps segregate applications from other applications and from their own memory segments. Due to improved protection in Windows 98, a rebellious 16-bit-based application cannot easily bring down the system as a whole, nor can it bring down other MS-DOS applications or 32-bit applications. However, crashing 16-bit applications still can affect other running 16-bit-based applications. Each type of application—16 bit, 32 bit, or MS-DOS—has a corresponding Virtual Machine Manager. Protection improvements also include the use of separate message queues for each running 32-bit application.

### *Disk and file system overview*

### Clusters

Windows 98, as with DOS before it, allocates disk space in clusters. A cluster is a group of sectors on a disk. The number of sectors in a cluster varies according to the drive type and partition size. When Windows 98 stores a file on disk, it doesn't store the file on a sector-by-sector basis. Rather, Windows 98 allocates enough clusters to contain the file.

### The FAT

With so many clusters on a disk, Windows 98 needs some way to keep track of where each file and directory reside. Essentially, Windows 98 needs to know the starting and ending cluster for each file. The file allocation table, or FAT, provides that information. The FAT contains an entry for every cluster on the disk, and Windows 98 uses the FAT to keep track of which clusters are allocated to which files and directories. The FAT is the key that enables Windows 98 to locate, read, and write files on the disk.

### VFAT, CDFS, and VCACHE

Windows for Workgroups introduced VFAT, a virtual installable file system driver that provided a 32-bit interface between applications and the file system. VFAT operates in protected mode, enabling Windows 98 and applications, 16 bit or 32 bit, to access the file system without switching the processor from protected mode to real mode, which significantly improves performance. Working in conjunction with VFAT is a virtual cache called VCACHE, a 32-bit protected-mode disk cache. A disk cache improves file I/O performance by caching recently used data and reading these data from memory rather than disk on subsequent requests for the data. Windows 98 includes a 32-bit protected-mode CD-ROM file system driver, called CDFS. CDFS improves file I/O by enabling applications to read from the CD-ROM drive in protected mode rather than requiring the system to switch to real mode to read the CD.

### FAT32

FAT32 gets its name by using a 32-bit addressing scheme instead of a 16-bit one. FAT32 enables the root directory to live anywhere on the disk and be as long as it needs to be. FAT32 also keeps redundant backups of more critical disk information, making FAT32 partitions less susceptible to failure or data corruption. FAT32 uses space more efficiently than FAT16. Its cluster sizes are smaller, because its 32-bit addressing scheme can directly address more of them.

FAT32 has many drawbacks as well as advantages. The first downside of FAT32 as opposed to FAT16 is speed. FAT32 is slightly slower in performing many common file operations. The second downside is backward compatibility. A whole host of applications and procedures will not work with FAT32 partitions. Also, compressed drives cannot be formatted as FAT32, and removable drives should not be formatted as FAT32. Laptops will not be able to perform any suspend-to-disk functions on FAT32 drives, and if the reader's PC supports power management hibernation, it will be turned off if the drive is formatted to FAT32. Finally, a drive using FAT32 cannot have Windows 98 uninstalled.

# 13.3  Workloads

Workloads are the most crucial part of any performance evaluation project. There are some important considerations when we select workloads for the evaluation, such as services rendered by the workloads, level of details, effective representation, and timeliness.

## 13.3.1  Workloads description

Workloads can be described as follows:

1.   Processes: To test the OS's ability to handle multiple processes. This includes creating, scheduling, allocating resources, and killing the process. This can be implemented by running a C or Java program that will create a large number of processes and threads. This program will run without termination—that is, infinitely. Using this method the system is bound to crash after a certain number of processes. The program will record in a file the processes and at what time they were created. In this way we will have a good feel for what the OS can handle.

2.   Computation: To test the computational ability of each OS, assuming the hardware is the same for all the configurations. The OS handling of the ALU can be tested by forcing it to execute a large number of difficult mathematical functions.

The following sections include the detailed description of the three workloads considered for the performance evaluation of the operating systems, which are as follows:

1.  A MATLAB program, which does operations on a matrix, such as adding, multiplying, calculating the determinant, and inverse matrices.

2.  An I/O intensive C program.

3.  A C program that creates multiple processes.

### *Workload programs used by Windows ME/Windows XP/Windows NT/LINUX operating systems*

The programs that were used by the three Microsoft groups and one LINUX group are as follows. The first, `workload1`, is a C program, which opens a number of files and writes a number of bytes to them. It runs nine different experiments three times each. The second is similar to the first except that it opens up a number of processes with different sleep times between the processes to see how many the OS can handle. It runs nine experiments three times each. The third workload is a MATLAB program, which runs a number of matrix operations with different matrix sizes and number of matrices. It runs nine experiments three times each. The three programs have been written to automatically run the experiments and record the data in appropriate files.

Along with these three programs, there is a fourth program called performance monitor, which will record CPU utilization and memory utilization every 500 milliseconds. Then the CPU and memory utilization will be compared with the beginning and ending times of the experiments, and the response time of those experiments are recorded in Excel files.

The first program runs by choosing among 500, 750, and 1,000 bytes to write to a file and among 100, 500, and 1,000 files to write in. This gives a total of nine experiments. Each experiment is run three times. The response time of each of the 27 experiments is recorded in a file. This is done by opening the file, appending to it, and closing it every time a new experiment is run. The program writes the number of bytes, number of files, beginning time of experiment, ending time of experiment, and response time of the experiment in one line in the file, called `work1.txt`. This file need not be created when the program is run.

The second program is similar to the first. It chooses among 10, 100, and 1,000 processes and sleep times of 0, 100, and 1,000 milliseconds between the processes. As in `workload1`, it is written to the file with the same format as in `work1.txt`. It records the number of processes instead of number of bytes and process rate (sleep time) instead of number of files. This is written in `work2.txt`.

The third program is a MATLAB program. It is composed of two files. The first is `matrix.m`, which is a program that takes in the number of matrices and the size of the matrix and runs a number of operations on these matrices. The `matrix.m` file is run by the `workload3.m` file. This file chooses among matrices or size $10 \times 10$, $50 \times 50$, or $100 \times 100$ elements and uses either 10, 100, or 1,000 matrices. The `matrix.m` file writes to a file called `work3.txt` in the same format as `workload2` but with matrix size instead of number of processes and matrix number instead of process rate.

The fourth program is the performance monitor program. This program reads the CPU utilization and memory utilization of the system and writes them to a file specified by the experimenter. The time and the CPU and memory utilization are recorded every 500 milliseconds.

In order to derive information, we had to use the beginning and ending times of an experiment in any of the workloads and then find a timestamp immediately before the beginning time and immediately after the experiment ending time. This would give us a number of readings between the beginning and ending times. We would then take the average of the readings we are concerned with and that would complete the required information for that experiment.

### Running these programs on Windows ME

Running these programs on ME proved to be a little difficult at times. Initially, the three workloads were identical for the three OSs with the exception that ME does not have the Process `cmd.exe`, which is used in `workload2` to test the number of processes that the system can handle. Instead, we use the option of `mem.exe`. It is a similar console application. Also, in order to use the performance monitor program, we had to use our own system calls.

While running the `workload2` program, ME was not able to use the `mem.exe` program after executing a number of processes. It would run some of them and then it would run out of memory. An error message would appear indicating that `mem.exe` could not be found even though it had just run  with the number of processes or lower. This occured at about 100 processes with 100 milliseconds sleep time between processes.

### MATLAB program workload for LINUX 7.2

The purpose of this MATLAB program is to determine the memory percentage utilization and the CPU percentage utilization that occur during selected matrix operations written in MATLAB code. These operations were multiplication of matrices, addition of matrices, and inverse and determinant operations. To conduct these experiments, we varied the matrix size from $10 \times 10$ to $50 \times 50$ to $100 \times 100$ and the number of matrices from 10 to 100 to 1,000. According to the project specifications, we classified these parameters as small, medium, and large. The program was run by giving a UNIX command at the command prompt. It was of the form `matfinal` (`experiment number, matrix size, number of matrices`).

To calculate the percentage of CPU utilization, we used the MATLAB commands of `tic`, `toc`, and CPU `time`. These commands were called before and after the matrix operations previously mentioned; their results were stored and used to calculate the percentage of CPU utilization. The `tic` command starts the stopwatch timer, and the `toc` command stops the stopwatch timer. The `toc` command returns the time elapsed between its calling, and the call to `tic`; therefore `toc` measures the elapsed time for the matrix operations. The CPU `time` command gives the CPU time that has passed since MATLAB started. This value of CPU time was divided by the `toc` value to give the CPU utilization.

To calculate the percentage of memory utilization, we used a C program (`amitfinal.c`), which was called from the MATLAB program before and after the matrix operations. This C program was called from within the MATLAB program by creating a MATLAB executable (mex) format—that is, extending MATLAB with C. The C program made use of UNIX system commands to acquire system information regarding memory—the amount of RAM, available memory, cached memory, and so on. In order to capture these memory values, we wrote the output of the C program into a text file called `mem.txt`. The contents of this file were read by the MATLAB program by using `fid()` and `fopen()` commands.

Taking a look at the before and after values and by using simple mathematical formulas we calculate the memory used by the system in performing the matrix operations. Knowing the total memory used by other processes in the system, we could determine what percentage of memory our MATLAB program used. We could also verify these results by using the `top` command at the command prompt. The top-command returned the amount of memory used by the MATLAB software (including the memory used to set up the MATLAB software during initialization and the memory taken up by the operations of the MATLAB program), while the MATLAB program code we used returned the memory required for the matrix operations only. It's up to the user to decide which one to use for making appropriate conclusions. In order to run the C program from the MATLAB program, we had to include MATLAB executable commands to compile and run the C program. Finally, the required values, such as size of matrix, number of matrices, percentage of CPU utilization, and percentage of memory utilization, were printed. Since there was no way of verifying the percentage of memory use printed by the MATLAB program, we preferred to use the system monitor.

# 13.4  Experimental design and simulation

## 13.4.1  Hardware specifications for the systems used

To ensure that all the operating systems were tested on a level playing field, the four PCs that were used had identical hardware. The hardware for each of the machines was as shown in Table 13.1.

To ensure that all of the machines were indeed equal in the sense of performance capabilities, an independent group ran a PC performance benchmark to validate. The results are discussed in the next section.

## 13.4.2  PC benchmark

### Passmark: the performance test

The performance test comprises 22 individual benchmark tests, which are available in six test suites. The six different test suites are as follows:

- Integer and floating-point mathematical operations

- Tests of standard two-dimensional graphical functions

- Reading, writing, and seeking within disk files

- Memory allocation and access

- Tests of the MMX (multimedia extensions) within newer CPUs

- A test of the DirectX 3D graphics system

The test results reported are shown as relative values. The larger the number the faster the computer. For example, a computer with a result of

**Table 13.1**  *Tested Configuration*

| | |
|---|---|
| CPU | Pentium III @ 500 MHz |
| Total RAM | 256 MB |

40 can process roughly twice as much data as a computer with a result of 20. The Passmark rating is a weighted average of all the other test results and gives a single overall indication of the computer's performance. The bigger the number the faster the computer. The results we observed are shown in Table 13.2.

**Table 13.2**   *Observed Test Results for the Passmark Performance Suites**

| S. No. | Parameter Tested | Win NT | Win XP | LINUX 7.2 | Win ME |
|---|---|---|---|---|---|
| 1 | Math—Addition | 96.6 | 96.2 | 94.6 | **97.0** |
| 2 | Math—Subtraction | 96.4 | 97.1 | 96.2 | **97.6** |
| 3 | Math—Multiplication | 101.1 | 101.4 | 101.4 | **103.1** |
| 4 | Math—Division | 12.9 | 12.8 | 12.9 | **13.0** |
| 5 | Math—Floating-Point Addition | 87.7 | 87.8 | 87.6 | **88.7** |
| 6 | Math—Floating-Point Subtraction | 89.4 | 89.5 | 88.6 | **90.1** |
| 7 | Math—Floating-Point Multiplication | 91.7 | 91.7 | 90.9 | **92.3** |
| 8 | Math—Floating-Point Division | 14.8 | 14.8 | 14.8 | **14.9** |
| 9 | Math—Maximum Mega FLOPS | 171.2 | 172.2 | 170.7 | **177.6** |
| 10 | Graphics 2D—Lines | 17.5 | 17.6 | 17.5 | **17.8** |
| 11 | Graphics 2D—Bitmaps | **12.9** | **12.9** | 12.8 | **12.9** |
| 12 | Graphics 2D—Shapes | **4.7** | **4.7** | **4.7** | **4.7** |
| 13 | Graphics 3D—Many Worlds | **22.9** | **23.0** | **22.9** | **22.9** |
| 14 | Memory—Allocated Small Blocks | 86.6 | **87.6** | 87.0 | **87.6** |
| 15 | Memory—Read Cached | 67.9 | 68.4 | 68.0 | **68.5** |
| 16 | Memory—Read Uncached | 48.7 | 48.8 | **50** | 49.1 |
| 17 | Memory—Write | 40.8 | 41.1 | 40.9 | **41.4** |
| 18 | Disk—Sequential Read | 3.2 | **3.8** | 3.7 | 3.1 |
| 19 | Disk—Sequential Write | 2.9 | **3.4** | **3.4** | 2.9 |
| 20 | Disk—Random Seek | 1.2 | 2.3 | **3.6** | 2.1 |
| 21 | MMX—Addition | 97.7 | 94.5 | 97.8 | **99.4** |

*The bold text indicates the highest values for each category.

**Table 13.2**   *Observed Test Results for the Passmark Performance Suites* (continued)*

| S. No. | Parameter Tested | Win NT | Win XP | LINUX 7.2 | Win ME |
|--------|------------------|--------|--------|-----------|--------|
| 22 | MMX—Subtraction | 92.3 | 98.2 | 93.3 | **96.0** |
| 23 | MMX—Multiplication | 97.8 | 97.5 | 96.9 | **99.1** |
| 24 | Math Mark | 75.6 | 75.8 | 75.2 | **76.8** |
| 25 | 2D Mark | 46.7 | 46.9 | 46.7 | **47.1** |
| 26 | Memory Mark | 58.7 | 59.2 | 59.2 | **59.4** |
| 27 | Disk Mark | 19.3 | 25.1 | **28.4** | 21.5 |
| 28 | 3D Graphics Mark | 15.5 | **15.7** | 15.5 | 15.6 |
| 29 | MMX Mark | 48.8 | 49.2 | 48.9 | **50** |
| 30 | Passmark Rating | 45.7 | 47.2 | **47.8** | 46.7 |

*The bold text indicates the highest values for each category.

## 13.4.3   Burn-in test

What the burn-in test does is a thorough exercise of the hardware in a PC in a short period of time, in the same way as normal applications use a PC over a long period of time. It tests the following items:

1.   CPU

2.   Hard drives

3.   CD-ROMs

4.   Sound cards

5.   2D graphics

6.   3D graphics

7.   RAM

8.   Network connections and printers

The results we observed are shown in Table 13.3.

## 13.4.4   Experimental design

Operating system performance depends on several factors. In order to conduct a proper analysis, the effects of each factor must be isolated from those

**Table 13.3**    *Observed Test Results for the Burn-in Test*

| S. No. | System Information | Win XP | Win NT | Win ME | LINUX 7.2 |
|--------|-------------------|--------|--------|--------|-----------|
| 2 | Number of CPU | 1 | 1 | 1 | 1 |
| 3 | CPU manufacturer | Intel | Intel | Intel | Intel |
| 4 | CPU type | Celeron | Celeron | Celeron | Celeron |
| 5 | CPU features | MMX | MMX | MMX | MMX |
| 6 | CPU Serial # | N/A or disabled | N/A or disabled | N/A or disabled | N/A or disabled |
| 7 | CPU1 speed | 501.3 MHz | 501.3 MHz | 501.3 MHz | 501.2 MHz |
| 8 | CPU Level 2 Cache | 128 KB | 128 KB | 128 KB | 128 KB |
| 9 | RAM | 267,821,056 Bytes (256 MB) | 267,821,056 Bytes (256 MB) | 267,821,056 Bytes (256 MB) | 267,821,056 Bytes (256 MB) |
| 10 | Color depth | 24 | 24 | 24 | 24 |

of others so that meaningful estimates of their positive or negative contributions to performance can be made. For this evaluation, we created the three workloads previously mentioned to exercise the process's management, memory management, and I/O management subsystems of the operating systems under study. All three workloads exercise these subsystems, although each workload was designed to stress particular subsystems. The first workload, which performs the matrix operations, is computationally extensive and requires large memory allocations. Therefore, this workload is primarily focusing on exercising the memory management subsystem. The second workload, which creates, writes to, and deletes an array of varying sized files, focuses on exercising the file management or I/O management subsystem. The last workload, which forks UNIX and DOS shell processes, was designed to stress the process management subsystem.

The experimental design for this study is summarized in Table 13.4.

We use a full factorial design to utilize every possible combination at all levels of all factors. By limiting the number of factors and their corresponding level, we can take advantage of this design to examine all possible combinations of configuration and workload. The measures chosen for comparison are response time, CPU utilization, disk utilization, memory allocation, and stability. Table 13.4 shows the factors and their levels. To increase statistical significance while keeping the number of experiments at a reasonable level, experiments were repeated three times for every combination of factors and levels. The resulting number of experiments for this

**Table 13.4**   *A 3⁴ Experimental Design\**

| Workload | Factors and Factor Values | Replications |
|---|---|---|
| A MATLAB program performing matrix operations on an array of varying sized matrices. This program also records response times. | Size of Matrix—Small, Medium, Large (defined in program)<br><br>Number of Matrices—10, 100, 1000 | 3 |
| A C program that creates, writes to, and deletes a number of varying sized files and records response times. | Size of File—Small (1 KB), Medium (10 KB), Large (100 KB)<br><br>Number of Files—10, 100, 1000 | 3 |
| A C program that forks several UNIX/DOS shell processes. This program also records response times. | Number of Processes—10, 100, 1000<br><br>Process Arrival Rate—Slow (100 p/s), Medium (1,000 p/s), Fast (all at once) | 3 |

\*[(3 Workloads) × (3 Levels for factor1) × (3 Levels for factor2) × (3 Replications)] = 81 Experiments

design is 81, calculated as follows: (3 workloads) × (3 levels for factor1) × (3 levels for factor2) × (3 replications).

## 13.4.5   Simulation

A simulation involves many activities, including data collection, building models, executing the simulation, generating alternatives, analyzing outputs, and presenting results. Simulation systems provide software support for all the activities. AWESIM is a simulation system that supports model building, analysis of models using simulation, and the presentation of simulation results. The AWESIM user interface is built on a see-point-select philosophy employing multiple windows, a series of menus within each window, and a mouse to select menu items. Each team was assigned to prepare a high-level model before using the AWESIM simulation toolkit. The following section includes the high-level model for each group, the corresponding AWESIM model, and the reports.

### AWESIM model for LINUX 7.2

In designing the AWESIM model, the LINUX team worked closely with the NT team. The NT team focused mainly on process scheduling, whereas the LINUX team focused mainly on memory management. There was, of course, overlap in the design of both sections, and some differences emerged on the final model for each team due to differences of the operating systems and to differences of opinion over which design was best.

Before looking at the diagram it is essential to first know what resources are being modeled and what attributes the entities have. The only resources modeled were memory and CPU. CPU has an allocation unit of one, since for any point in time only one process has the CPU; memory has as many allocation units as the system being modeled has pages. The attributes are as follows: ATRIB[1] = total CPU time needed, ATRIB[2] = timestamp (used for the LRU approximation), ATRIB[3] = remaining time needed before process terminates, LTRIB[1] = priority, LTRIB[2] = total number of pages the process will ever need, LTRIB[3] = total number of reads remaining, LTRIB[4] = total number of writes remaining, LTRIB[5] = total number of pages currently held, and LTRIB[6] indicates if the entity represents the MATLAB program or the C forking program. As a note, ATRIBs are reals whereas the LTRIBs are integers. ATRIB[2] deserves more explanation. The way the LRU was approximated was by using timestamps every time a memory reference was made.

However, instead of using a timestamp for every page held (which admittedly would have been much better), a single timestamp was used for each process. The logic is that whatever process least recently referenced memory also has the least recently used page. Once this algorithm was determined acceptable, another problem came up: swapping pages. If process A has a page miss, and process B has the LRU (least recently used page), process A can take a page from process B with a preempt node using ATRIB[2] to indicate priority. The problem occurs, however, when the process itself has the LRU, since a process can clearly not preempt itself. This was solved with the combination of the node `HaveLRU` and a user-defined function.

At the `HaveLRU` node, if process A has the LRU, it will go onto the `SwapWSelf` node; otherwise, the entity will be routed to the preempt node. The user-defined function merely examines the timestamp of all entities possessing at least one page of memory. It then returns the value of the LRU's timestamp. A branch can then be used to see if the entity's timestamp equals the LRU's timestamp. Whenever an entity does preempt another entity in this manner, it becomes necessary to increment LTRIB[5] (since it now holds more than one page). Once the preceding concepts are understood, the rest of the model becomes simple to understand.

## Model

Processes are created at the create node, `create_proc`, but they are not told whether they are to simulate the MATLAB program or the C forking program until the goon-node, `Initialize`, randomly chooses to forward the entity to the assign-node `forking` or the assign-node `MATLAB`. Once the correct attributes have been set, the process must obtain a page of memory by entering the await node, `mem_wait`. After the page of memory has been obtained, the fact is recorded by incrementing the value of LTRIB[5] via the assign-node `GetFrstPg`. Once the page has been obtained, the process waits in the ready queue. From the ready queue the process goes to the pre-empt-node, `cpu_wait`, where it will either preempt the current process (provided ATRIB[3] gives it a higher priority than the current process) and send the preempted process back to the ready queue, or it will simply wait until the current running process releases the CPU. Once the entity has control of the CPU, the next sequence of steps is determined by which process the entity is to simulate.

## Forking

The entity modeling the forking program will first go to the goon-node, *fork*, from where it will release the CPU at the free-node, `cpu_free2`, and its memory at the free-node, `mem_free2`. Once both resources have been freed, the entity will split, sending one copy of itself (the parent) to the ter-minate-node `end` and the other copy of itself (the child) to the assign-node `child`, where it will record its number of pages as being zero. The `child` then attempts to get its first page of memory by going to the await-node, `mem_wait`.

## MATLAB

The entity modeling the MATLAB program will first go to the goon-node, `processmatlab`, from where it will branch, depending on whether or not it has any reads or writes to perform. If there are no reads or writes to per-form, the entity will be routed to the assign-node `Ionotreq`, where ATRIB[1] will be decremented by the duration of the time slice. Next, the CPU is released through the release-node `cpu_free`. If there is any process-ing remaining to be done, the entity will be routed back to the ready queue; otherwise, it will release its memory via the free-node *mem_free* and termi-nate by going to the terminate-node `end`.

If, however, there are any reads or writes that must be performed, the entity will first be routed to the assign-node `Ioreq`, where the value for ATRIB[1] will be decremented between zero and the value of the time slice—depending on when the I/O is requested. It will then release the CPU via the free-node `cpuio_free`, from where it will be routed to the goon-node `requestpage`.

Once a page is requested, it must first be determined whether or not the process already owns that page. The model deals with this by assuming that the probability a page is already owned is equal to the current number of pages held, divided by the total number of pages needed. The value of this probability is used for the branches. If it is determined that the process does in fact have the necessary page, the entity will be routed to the goon-node `GetPageFrame`, which simulates finding the page frame, and is then routed to the goon-node `addoffset`, which indicates that the offset is being added to the page frame. After `addoffset`, if there are any writes to perform, the entity is routed to the goon-node `write` and then to the assign-node `DecWrite`, where the timestamp is obtained and the number of writes remaining to be performed is decremented. After the write, the entity returns to the ready queue. If no writes remain, then a read needs to be performed (since we wouldn't be here in the first place if there were neither reads nor writes). The entity will first be routed to the goon-node `read`, from where it will be routed to the assign-node `DecRead`, which is similar to the `DecWrite` node. After changing the attributes, the entity is routed to the ready queue.

If the process does not have the page being requested, it needs to find the LRU and exchange it with the needed page. First, it must be determined if the process itself contains the LRU, so the entity is first routed to the goon-node `HaveLRU`, where it uses the user-defined function to determine whether or not it has the LRU and then branches accordingly. If it does have the LRU, the entity only needs to swap out its LRU and swap in the new page; this is handled through the goon-node `SwapWSelf`, after which the entity can be routed to the goon-node `GetPageFrame`. If the entity does not have the LRU, it goes to a preempt node to try to take a page away from the process with the LRU (done by using timestamp—ATRIB[2]—as the priority) and use it for itself. Once it gets a page, the number of currently held pages is incremented with the assign node, and the entity is then routed to the goon-node `GetPageFrame`. Figure 13.1 illustrates the model for INUX 7.2.

### AWESIM model for Windows XP

#### Modeling of the system

We have modeled CPU scheduling based on the Windows NT architecture. We have provided a high-level model and implemented the AWESIM model based on this high-level model. The following text describes how the CPU is scheduled in the operating system.

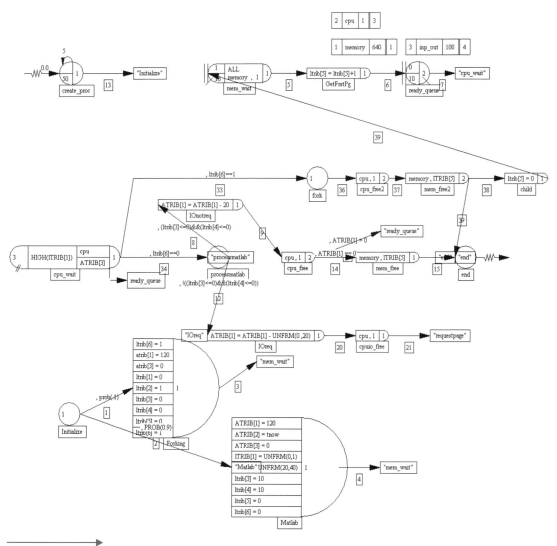

**Figure 13.1**    *Model for LINUX 7.2.*

## CPU scheduling

This operating system uses a preemptive multithreading system. That is, it lets several processes execute simultaneously and switches among them rapidly to create the illusion that each process is the only process running on the machine. This scenario assumes a uniprocessor environment.

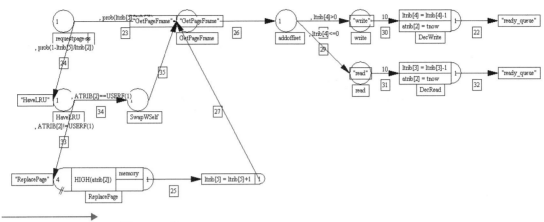

**Figure 13.1**   *(Continued)*

The basic scheduling unit is a thread. The system assigns each thread a priority number from 1 to 31, where higher numbers signal higher priorities. It reserves priorities 16 through 31 (real-time priorities) for use by time-critical operations. A process priority class is a priority level around which the process's threads get executed. New processes inherit the priority class of their parent. Process threads start at the priority level associated with their process's priority class.

The relative priorities that can change a thread's priority from its process class priority are highest, above normal, normal, below normal, and lowest. Threads must take turns running on the CPU so that one thread doesn't prevent other threads from performing work. One of the scheduler's jobs is to assign units of CPU time (quantum) to threads. A quantum is typically very short in duration, but threads receive quantum so frequently that the system appears to run smoothly—even when many threads are performing work. The scheduler must make a CPU scheduling decision every time one of the following three situations occurs:

1.   A thread's quantum on the CPU expires.

2.   A thread waits for an event to occur.

3.   A thread becomes ready to execute.

The scheduler executes the `FindReadyThread` algorithm to decide whether another thread needs to take over the CPU. If a higher-priority thread is ready to execute, it replaces (or preempts) the thread that was running. `FindReadyThread` and `ReadyThread` are the key algorithms the scheduler uses to determine how threads take turns on the CPU. Find-

ReadyThread locates the highest-priority thread that is ready to execute. The scheduler keeps track of all ready-to-execute threads in the Dispatcher Ready List. The FindReadyThread algorithm scans the Dispatcher Ready List and picks the front thread in the highest-priority nonempty queue. ReadyThread is the algorithm that places threads in the Dispatcher Ready List. When ReadyThread receives a ready-to-execute thread, it checks to see whether the thread has a higher priority than the executing thread. If the new thread has a higher priority, it preempts the current thread and the current thread goes to the Dispatcher Ready List. Otherwise, ReadyThread places the ready-to-execute thread in the appropriate Dispatcher Ready List. At the front of the queue, ReadyThread places threads that the scheduler pulls off the CPU before they complete at least one quantum; all other threads (including blocked threads) go to the end of the queue.

### High-level model

Figure 13.2 illustrates the high-level model of the CPU scheduler that we implemented in AWESIM.

### Assumptions

We have made a number of assumptions while implementing the network model. These are:

1.     Processes that have I/O are given a fixed time for those operations to occur.

2.     A fixed quantum size.

3.     Preempted processes return to the end of the queue instead of going to the head.

4.     The model will only consider I/O operations. Interrupts and forking operations will not be considered.

### AWESIM model

The AWESIM model is the implementation of the high-level model described previously. The following are the working details of the model:

1.     Each created process has the following attributes: total process time, priority I/O, and whether or not the process will perform an I/O operation.

2.     If a process has an I/O operation, then the time of occurrence and the total time for the I/O are allocated.

3.     Processes with different priorities go to the different queues.

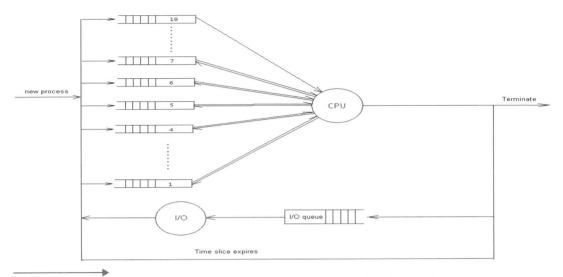

**Figure 13.2**    *High-level model of CPU scheduler implemented in AWESIM.*

4.    Since CPU is allocated to a process for a quantum, calculations are done to calculate the remaining time of the process after the quantum has expired.

5.    Preemption is done based on priority using the preempt-node, and, again, the remaining time for the process to complete is calculated.

6.    The preempted processes are sent to a queue, which goes back to the different priority queues.

7.    All the processes go to the await-node, where they wait for the CPU. When the CPU becomes available, they use it for either the full length of the quantum or until a preemption or an I/O request occurs.

8.    When an I/O request occurs, the process waits in the I/O await-node where it will be assigned one unit of the I/O resource. The processes that have finished I/O go back to the ready queue.

9.    After a resource (I/O or the CPU) is used, it is freed to be allocated to the next entity (process).

10.    After a process completes an I/O operation, its status is changed to reflect that it does not require more I/O operations.

11.    A process is terminated upon completion of the total time allocated to it.

12.    Collect-nodes were implemented to collect statistics such as the number of processes being preempted, the number of processes with different priorities, and the number of processes performing I/O.

Figure 13.3 illustrates the AWESIM model for CPU scheduling.

The design description of the AWESIM model is as follows. The high-level model concentrates on CPU scheduling; therefore the two resources in the AWESIM model are CPU and I/O. The create-node creates 100 entities (processes), which are assigned with different attributes (with each attribute defining a specific function). LTRIB[0] gives the total time of execution of the process, including the time taken for executing the I/O operation. Whether a process has I/O or not is defined by LTRIB[1]. The time at which the I/O occurs within the total execution time is indicated by LTRIB[2]. Each process is assigned a priority, which is given by LTRIB[4].

In our model, a process departing the create-node will have either a priority 1, 2, or 3. Depending on the priority value, the entities are sent to their respective queues. Here the entities branch, depending on the value of LTRIB[1]. The time required by the process for execution is compared with the time slice available on the CPU and, accordingly, the resource is made available to execute the process.

If a process with a low priority is currently being serviced by the CPU and a process with high priority comes in, then the preempt-node preempts the low-priority process and sends it to queue 4 for future service. Also, any process with I/O requirements after being serviced by the CPU will be sent to the I/O await-node, and subsequently serviced by the I/O resource. Any process with leftover execution time is sent back to the initial queues to complete its execution. The two resources are freed by using a free-node after the service.

## AWESIM model results

The summary of the output is given in a report, from which we are able to find the utilization rate of the different queues, queue lengths, utilization of service activities, and the parameters related to the other nodes. From this evaluation we have been able to find the percentages of CPU utilization and I/O utilization. The inclusion of the collect-nodes at every stage of the AWESIM model yields results, which give details about the different priorities that are attributed to the processes, the number of processes that are preempted, and whether a process has an I/O or not.

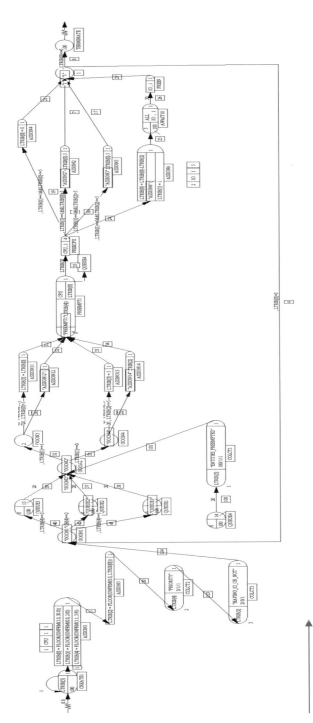

**Figure 13.3** AWESIM model for CPU scheduling.

### AWESIM model for Windows ME

#### High-level model

In the basic high-level model for Windows 98, every incoming process is directed to the operating system. The OS, depending on the type of service requested, directs the process either to the I/O or memory. If it is a memory request, then the operating system checks to see whether the requested data are present in the cache. If not, it checks for the data in the main memory and transfers the block of data into the cache. If it is not a memory request, then it is an I/O request. Eventually, after an I/O request or memory access, it finally goes to the CPU. Once the processing in the CPU is complete, it can get into the I/O or memory chain or terminate. Figure 13.4 illustrates the high-level network model.

The simulation model for Windows ME focuses on the basic functioning of two aspects: memory access and I/O. The model deals with them in the simplest way and with the level of detail necessary to simulate the conditions realistically. The simulation model for Windows focuses on basic functioning of the two main modes as closely as possible. There is one entity creation node. The entities emanating from this are fed into three assign-nodes, which assign a set of attributes to these entities to differentiate their behavior in the system. These are as follows:

1.    ATRIB[1] corresponds to the type of service needed: I/O or simple memory access.

2.    ATRIB[2] is for priority that ranges from 5 to 15.

3.    ATRIB[3] corresponds to the number of reinstalls or the number of times the entity needs to be serviced.

These entities pass through the assign-node queue in the input queue waiting to acquire their respective resources (cache, main memory, and I/O)

**Figure 13.4**
*High-level network model.*

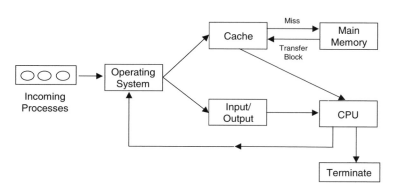

at the await-nodes. The resources are assigned based on a process's priority. After acquiring the resources, they all queue at the await-node for the CPU resource (CPU clock pulses). After getting serviced by the CPU, the entities move on and free their respective resources at the free-node and terminate. Entities that need multiple services go back to the input queue. This is done by checking ATRIB3 and changing ATRIB1 to create a realistic behavior. The model also tries to incorporate forking by creating some entities within the process. This is visible in the entity count on the activities.

Figure 13.5 illustrates the AWESIM model for Windows ME.

### AWESIM model for Windows NT

Figure 13.6 illustrates the AWESIM model for Windows NT.

In developing the AWESIM model (virtual memory part), the NT team worked closely with the LINUX team. The NT team focused mainly on CPU process scheduling, I/O scheduling, and virtual memory. We could not get into details such as file management and object manager, because the internals of the operating system were not available.

Before getting into the actual model, it is essential to look at what kind of resources are being modeled and what attributes they have.

The resources are memory, CPU, and I/O manager. Out of these, the memory and CPU are modeled as a single source of resource, whereas the I/O manager (which manages various I/O devices) is modeled as a group resource, meaning it has an $n$ number of resources instead of having only one. The CPU has an allocation unit of one, since, for any one point in time, only one process acquires the CPU; memory has as many allocation units as the system being modeled has pages.

The attributes are as follows:

ATRIB[1] = The total CPU time required by a process.

ATRIB[2] = Defines the priority of a process. This value is assigned using a probability function. If this value is 1, then it is assumed that the process belongs to a higher priority than the rest of the processes, and a zero indicates a lower priority. There was a probablity of 0.1 that a process would have a priority of one.

LTRIB[1] = The total number of pages a process needs. Again, to assign the number of pages, we used a random function, UNFRM, which generates values from 1 to 5.

LTRIB[2] = The probability that the processes might require an I/O operation such as printing, waiting on a subroutine, and so on.

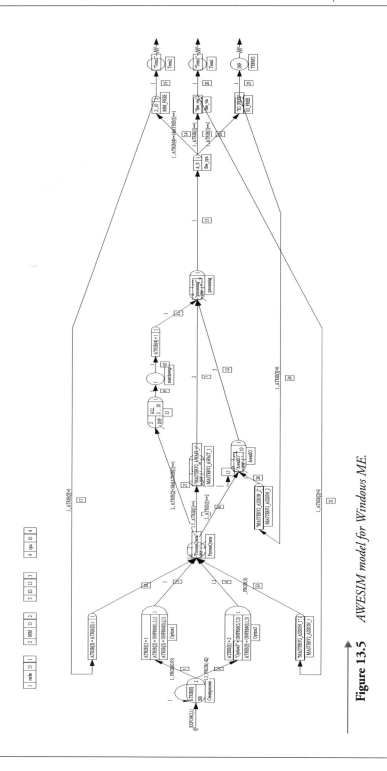

**Figure 13.5** *AWESIM model for Windows ME.*

LTRIB[3] = Number of pages requested from the memory, initially bearing a value of 0.

LTRIB[4] = The total number of pages currently held in memory.

LTRIB[5] = The timestamp, used to compute the LRU.

The way the LRU works is as follows. Every time a memory reference is made, the timestamp is updated. However, instead of using a timestamp for every page held, a single timestamp was used for each process. The logic is

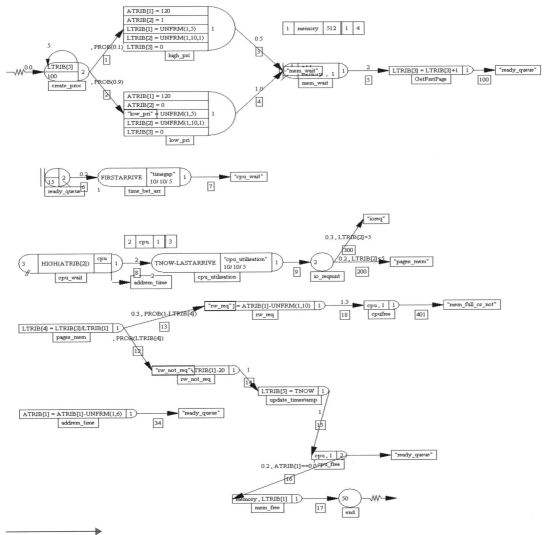

**Figure 13.6**   *AWESIM model for Windows NT.*

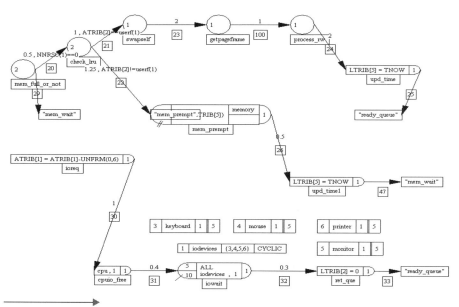

**Figure 13.6**    *(Continued)*

that whatever process least recently referenced memory also has the least recently used page.

Suppose X and Y are two processes: X has a page miss and Y has the LRU. Process X can take a page from process Y with a preempt-node using LTRIB[5] to indicate priority. But this logic has a problem whenever process X has the LRU, since it cannot preempt itself. This is solved by using a `HaveLRU`-node and a user-defined function, which simply examine the timestamp of all entries possessing at least one page of memory and returning the value of LRU's timestamp. A branch can then be used to see if the entity's timestamp equals the LRU's timestamp. At the `HaveLRU`-node, the processes then check for themselves whether they have the LRU. If so, they will go on to `SwapSelf`-node, where they simply swap themselves; otherwise, they will be routed to the preempt-node. Whenever an entity does preempt another entity in this manner, it becomes necessary to increment LTRIB[3] (since it holds more than one page).

## Network model

Processes are created at the create-node, `create_proc`. Once the correct attributes have been set, the processes must obtain a page of memory by waiting for an await-node, `mem_wait`. Initially all the processes are allocated a single page of memory. After acquiring the page, this fact is recorded by incrementing the value of LTRIB[3] via the assign-node `GetFrstPage`. Once the page has been obtained, the processes wait in the ready queue for the CPU. Thereafter, they go to a preempt-node, `cpu_wait`, where they will either preempt the current process (provided the CPU encounters a higher-priority process than the current process) and send the preempted process back to the ready queue, or they will simply wait until the current running process releases the CPU. Once the entity has control of the CPU, the next sequence of steps is determined by the node `io_reqmnt`, which determines whether it requires I/O or not depending on the value of LTRIB[2]. Here two issues arise. What if an entity requires I/O and what if it doesn't?

**What if the entities do not require I/O?**    They proceed from the node io_reqmnt toward node pages_mem, which assigns the value of LTRIB[3]/LTRIB[1] to LTRIB[4]. The logic behind doing this is to check whether or not the corresponding process has the required number of pages depending on the value of LTRIB[4]. Here two issues arise. What if a page fault occurs and what if it does not?

If there isn't a page fault, then the processes get processed and go to an assign-node, where we update ATRIB[1] and the timestamp in LTRIB[5], thereafter freeing the CPU and sending the processes back to the ready queue.

If there is a page fault, then we free the CPU from that process, since it is waiting for another page. After doing this, we need to update ATRIB[1], since we need to take into account the time that the process already spent in CPU executing up to that moment—that is, before the page fault occured. After updating ATRIB[1], the process goes to node `mem_full_or_not`, which checks whether the memory is full or not.

If the memory is not full, then the process gets the required number of pages by updating LTRIB[3] in an assign-node, `page_alloc`, and thereafter it waits for memory at the await-node, `mem_wait`.

If the memory is full, the entity is routed through a `check_lru` node, which computes the LRU using the user-defined function discussed previously and branches accordingly.

If the entity does have the LRU, the entity only needs to swap out its LRU page and swap in the new page. This is handled through the go-on node `SwapSelf`, after which the entity can be routed through the go-on node `GetPageFrame`, which simulates finding the page frame and adding the offset to it. After adding offset, the required read/write operation is performed by routing the entity through the go-on node `perform_rw`. After doing this, the entities are routed through an assign node, `upd_time`, which updates the timestamp of the entities that accessed the memory. After updating the timestamp, the entities are sent back to the ready queue, since they are done with their operation.

If the entity does not have the LRU, it goes to a preempt-node, mem_preempt, to try to take a page away from the process with the LRU (done by timestamp LTRIB[3]) and use it for itself. After preempting the LRU, the timestamp, LTRIB[5], is again updated and gets the requested page by waiting for the await-node, mem_wait, for memory resource .

**What if the entities do require I/O?**   Entities requiring I/O are freed from the CPU and routed through an assign-node, ioreq, which updates the total execution time already spent by the entity in the CPU. After this, entities wait at an await-node, iowait, on the group resource I/O block, which has various standard I/O resources, such as monitor, mouse, keyboard, and printer. After the entities are serviced by the resource, the attribute LTRIB[2] is set to zero, assuming that the entity no longer requires assitional I/O. After this the entities are routed through a free-node, free_io, where all the resources allocated to that entity are freed. Finally, the entities are routed back to the ready queue, since they are done with their execution.

### *Why isn't the AWESIM model validated by experimental results?*

The results of AWESIM were so obviously wrong (e.g., CPU utilization equals 100 percent), that without any validation it was instantly known the model was invalid. Considering that parts of the model were actually left out, this is not a surprise. Without these parts a valid model is impossible, so rather than trying to force the data to fit into a validation scheme, we will instead explain why the results were so poor, and why that cannot be changed.

The first obviously incorrect piece of data is that CPU is 100 percent utilized. This is because we do not simulate any I/O, so the only thing to make a process give up CPU is termination or end of time slice. In either case another process instantly replaces it, yielding an unrealistically high utilization rate.

All other problems run into the same general problem—we could not obtain appropriate values for attributes. An example of this is that we would like to know the number of reads or writes the MATLAB program performs, but all we are given is particular operations. These operations could represent any number of reads and writes. This forced us to use an arbitrary number for reads and writes. Also, the total number of pages a process will ever request was unknown to the simulator, forcing an arbitrary number for that as well. Other arbitrarily chosen numbers were as follows: duration of time slice, time to perform a single read, time to perform a single write, and total length of CPU time (not counting I/O times) to complete the process.

Obviously, even if the model nodes and activities are perfect, with so many arbitrary numbers the results cannot possibly be expected to be valid. The model is useful for explaining, from a high-level point of view, how the LINUX operating system works, and was also a useful educational experience to design, but as far as determining real-world behavior goes, the model is useless.

## 13.5  Experimental analysis and conclusion

This section includes the intermediate analysis of the experimental results. These results compare each workload in individual scenarios. Based on these results the final conclusion regarding the tradeoff between the operating systems concludes this chapter.

### 13.5.1  File transfer workload

For the file transfer workload, when the file size is constant and the number of files is increased, the response time and CPU utilization increase linearly, whereas memory utilization remains almost constant for XP, NT, and ME. But in the case of LINUX, the response time increases, but the CPU utilization decreases and the memory utilization remains constant.

Tables 13.5 through 13.7 show the ranges of CPU use and memory utilization, depending on the number of files for each OS.

Observations for Table 13.5: Windows ME, NT, and XP all increased their CPU use ranges, while LINUX decreased its range. LINUX perform-

**Table 13.5**  *CPU Use and Memory Utilization for File Size = 500*

| Operating System | CPU Range | Memory Utilization |
|---|---|---|
| ME | 56.5–88.8 | 10 |
| NT | 87.37–98.08 | 10 |
| LINUX | 13.0–99.9 | 0.3 |
| XP | 13.92–26.7 | 18 |

**Table 13.6**   *CPU Use and Memory Utilization For File Size = 750*

| Operating System | CPU Range | Memory Utilization |
|---|---|---|
| ME | 62.0–87.8 | 10 |
| NT | 6.35–98.49 | 10 |
| LINUX | 13.7–99.9 | 0.4 |
| XP | 16.16–32.77 | 17.99 |

ance fell within the range of 75.6–99.9 for 100 files. For file numbers of 500 and 1,000 the CPU use was between 13 and 16.8 with a varying trend.

Observations for Table 13.6: Windows ME, NT, and XP all increased their CPU utilization ranges, while LINUX decreased its utilization range; overall measurements varied greatly in the case of 100 files. CPU utilization measurements varied from 98.3 for the first experiment, 24.4 for the second experiment, and 99.9 for the third experiment. However, for 500 and 1,000 files it ranged from 13.7 to 15.9, showing less variability. Some of this variability could be smoothed out by performing more experiments at each level and averaging their results. The time allotted to our experiment did not allow us to do this, however.

Observations for Table 13.7: Windows ME, NT, and XP all increased in their CPU utilization ranges over the full spectrum of measurements, while LINUX decreased overall, staying at about 98 percent for the three experimental runs. However, for 500 and 1,000 files its CPU utilization ranged from 12.9 to 15.6.

**Table 13.7**   *CPU Use and Memory Utilization for File Size = 1,000*

| Operating System | CPU Range | Memory Utilization |
|---|---|---|
| ME | 60.0–87.8: | 10 |
| NT | 96.11–97.68 | 10–11 |
| LINUX: | 12.9–98.2 | 0.5 |
| XP | 18.156–30.91 | 17.98 |

**Table 13.8**   *CPU Use and Memory Utilization for Process Rate = 0*

| Operating System | CPU Range | Memory Utilization |
|---|---|---|
| ME | 61.67–91.2 | 10–12 |
| NT: | 3.38–85.625 | 11–26 |
| LINUX | 25–75 | 0.1 |
| XP | 47–86 | 17.23–18 |

## 13.5.2   Process creation workload

For the process creation workload, we realize that the CPU utilization is approximately linear for XP and LINUX with an increasing slope, while NT and ME vary widely in their CPU utilization. Also, for XP, the response time decreases when the number of processes rate increases. For each number of processes the performance range is higher than the previous number, but it decreases as the processes rate increases.

Tables 13.8 through 13.10 show the ranges of CPU utilization and memory utilization depending on the process rates for each OS.

Observations for Table 13.8: The Windows NT CPU utilization is approximately 22 percent for ten processes but increases to between 77 percent and 85 percent for 100 processes and drops down to about 50 percent for 1,000 processes. Also, for 1,000 processes, the memory utilization increases even though the CPU utilization decreases.

Observations for Table 3.9: For the case of a process rate of 100, NT generally increases linearly with the exception of some values where it hap-

**Table 13.9**   *CPU Use and Memory Utilization for Process Rate = 100*

| Operating System | CPU Range | Memory Utilization |
|---|---|---|
| ME | 60.05–73.25: | 10–14.56 |
| NT | 12.33–31.59 | 11–15 |
| LINUX | 37.1–73.3 | 0.1 |
| XP | 77.3–85.27 | 17.98–18.99 |

**Table 13.10**   *CPU Use and Memory Utilization for Process Rate = 1,000*

| Operating System | CPU Range | Memory Utilization |
| --- | --- | --- |
| ME | 56.13–58.85 | 1.322–11 |
| NT | 3.42–4.62 | 11–20.98 |
| LINUX | 41.6–74.1 | 0.1 |
| XP | 18.156–30.91 | 17.97–17.99 |

pens to use a little less CPU utilization. However, the memory utilization seems to increase linearly. For LINUX the process rate stays in the range of 37 to 41 for a number of processes equaling 10 and 100, but for 1,000 the utilization jumps to between 50 percent and 70 percent.

Observations for Table 3.10: NT and XP remained almost constant in their CPU, with a fluctuation of about 3 percent to 4 percent. The only OS showing a variation in the percentage of CPU utilization was LINUX, ranging from 41.6 to 74.1. On the contrary, ME showed a decrease in CPU utilization with the increase in the number of processes. As the number of processes increased, the memory utilization also increased considerably (maximum of 8 percent in NT).

## 13.5.3   MATLAB workload

For the matrix operations for the MATLAB workload, with constant matrix size and varying number of matrices, the response time and CPU utilization in the case of Windows ME, NT, and XP increase, whereas the memory utilization remains almost constant. (See Tables 13.11 through 13.14.)

Observations for Table 13.11: Windows NT and XP performed similarly, with CPU utilization exponentially increasing when the number of

**Table 13.11**   *CPU Use and Memory Utilization for Matrix Size = 10 × 10*

| Operating System | CPU Range | Memory Utilization |
| --- | --- | --- |
| ME | 51.5–76.66 | 2–2.5 |
| NT | 2–74 | 16 |
| LINUX | N/A | N/A |
| XP | 4.5–56.67 | 17.97–17.99 |

**Table 13.12**   *CPU Use and Memory Utilization for Matrix Size = 50 × 50*

| Operating System | CPU Range | Memory Utilization |
|---|---|---|
| ME | 55–99.78 | 4–11.97 |
| NT | 14–99.62 | 16–18 |
| LINUX | 46–48.37 | 4.2 |
| XP | 7.66–99.17 | 28–30.97 |

matrices was increased from 10 to 1,000. The variation was a bit less in ME, ranging from 51 percent to 77 percent. Even for ten matrices it consumed a lot of computational power. For the LINUX OS, the experiment was conducted with different parameters. The matrix size started at 50 and went up to 1,000, while for the Windows-based OS it started at 10 and went up to 100. The amount of memory consumed was considerably less in the ME system (2.5 percent) as compared with the other Windows-based operating systems. On the other hand, the percentage of variation was fairly constant in all three of them.

Observations for Table 13.12: Percentage utilization of CPU for NT and XP increased exponentially when the number of matrices was increased from 10 to 1,000. The variation was a bit less in ME, ranging from 55 percent to 100 percent. Considerably, ME consumed more CPU even for a lesser number of matrices. For the LINUX OS, the CPU consumption didn't vary much but still consumed a lot of computational power for a lesser number of matrices, similar to ME. The amount of memory consumed was considerably less in the LINUX operating system (4.2 percent) as compared with the Windows-based operating systems. On the other hand, the percentage of variation in performance was fairly constant in all four of them.

**Table 13.13**   *CPU Use and Memory Utilization for Matrix Size = 100 × 100*

| Operating System | CPU Range | Memory Utilization |
|---|---|---|
| ME | 59–99.98 | 0.30–4.25 |
| NT | 39.50–100 | 16–24.98 |
| LINUX | 81.22–81.97 | 4.2 |
| XP | 7.3–100 | 28–41 |

**Table 13.14**     *CPU Use and Memory Utilization for Matrix Size = 1,000 × 1,000*

| Operating System | CPU Range | Memory Utilization |
|---|---|---|
| LINUX | 96.76 – 96.95 | 17.95–19.5 |

Observations for Table 13.13: All three of the Windows-based machines saturated their CPU utilization when the number of matrices was about 1,000. In this scenario too, Windows ME consumed more CPU resources even for small numbers of matrices. For the LINUX operating system, the CPU consumption didn't vary much but still consumed a significant amount of computational power for small numbers of matrices, similar to ME. The amount of memory consumed was considerably less in the LINUX operating system (4.2 percent) as compared with the other Windows-based OSs.

Observations for Table 13.14: Only the LINUX team tested a matrix of this size. In this case the CPU utilization was almost pushed to the limit. The memory utilization was still less compared with the Windows-based machines.

## 13.5.4   Final conclusion

The following tables were deduced by calculating the average statistical measured values for the actual tables collected in the study for the different operating systems. The measure used is a ratio of the CPU utilization divided by the product of the memory use and overall response time for each experiment.

Table 13.15 gives the results for the process experiments.

**Table 13.15**     *Results for the Process Experiments*

| Operating System | Response Time (ms) | % CPU Utilization | % Memory Utilization | CPU/(Mem*res) |
|---|---|---|---|---|
| XP | 35,290.95 | 82.34 | 19.43 | 12E-05 |
| ME | 150,110.33 | 68.98 | 8.96 | 5.13E-05 |
| NT | 148,956.52 | 27.03 | 13.91 | 1.3E-05 |
| LINUX | 7,400.5 | 49.83 | 0.1 | 6733.3E-05 |

**Table 13.16**   *Results for the MATLAB Experiments*

| Operating System | Response Time (ms) | % CPU Utilization | % Memory Utilization | CPU/(Mem*res) |
|---|---|---|---|---|
| XP | 218.66 | 99.56 | 35.975 | 0.012657 |
| ME | 224.555 | 99.715 | 26.45 | 0.016789 |
| NT | 222.345 | 98.7 | 21.46 | 0.020685 |
| LINUX | — | 65.17 | 4.2 | 0.069941* |

\* In order to get a value for this table it was necessary to have a response time for LINUX. The response time for the other operating systems was averaged; this way the LINUX response time essentially doesn't come into play.

Table 13.16 gives the results for the MATLAB experiments.

Table 13.17 gives the results for the file experiments.

No operating system dominates in performance for all the workloads that were used in this study. Each of the operating systems outperforms other operating systems in its own way. To determine which system performs best for each workload, we used the formula in the final columns, which is equal to the CPU utilization divided by the product of the memory utilization and the response time.

LINUX performs well in forking new processes. This can be deduced from the table values for process experiments, where it utilizes the least memory, average CPU utilization, and minimum response time as compared with other operating systems, giving it the best value in the aggregate measure for performance. The second best system based on this measure is the XP operating system, which has a value worse than LINUX's by a factor of 561. Next comes NT, which has a value worse than XP's by a factor of 9.2. Finally, ME is the worst, with a value that is off by a factor of 3.9 when compared with NT.

**Table 13.17**   *Results for the File Experiments*

| Operating System | Response time (ms) | % CPU Utilization | % Memory Utilization | CPU/(Mem*res) |
|---|---|---|---|---|
| XP | 164,194 | 67.74 | 17.95 | 2.29839E-05 |
| ME | 965.36 | 74.05 | 10 | 767.0714E-05 |
| NT | 129,030 | 96.06 | 10.29 | 7.23497E-05 |
| LINUX | 42,625.88 | 89.28 | 22.6 | 9.26771E-05 |

For the experiments involving matrix operations in MATLAB, LINUX out performs the other operating systems, since it utilizes the least amount of memory and has an average CPU utilization with an aggregate performance measure of 0.069941, making it better than NT by a factor of 3.38. NT is better than ME by a factor of 1.23, and ME is better than XP by a factor of 1.33.

Windows ME manages files efficiently compared with the other operating systems, with an aggregate performance measure of 7.67E-03. This measure is then followed by LINUX, which is found to perform worse by a factor of 82.7. NT in turn performs worse than LINUX by a factor of 1.28, and XP is found to be worse than NT by a factor of 3.14.

## 13.5.5  Tabular results

Tables 13.18 through 13.20 show results for the various workloads.

**Table 13.18**   *Intermediate Data for Workload 1*

| File Size (KB) | Number of Files | Windows XP | | | Windows ME | | | Windows NT | | | LINUX | | |
|---|---|---|---|---|---|---|---|---|---|---|---|---|---|
| | | RT | CPU | MEM | RT | CPU | MEM | RT | CPU | MEM | RT | CPU | MEM |
| 500 | 100 | 39,707 | 15.26 | 18 | 125.33 | 60.33 | 10 | 16,490.34 | 89.96 | 10 | 928.67 | 91.4 | 12 |
| 500 | 500 | 116,661 | 208 | 17.94 | 786.67 | 75.08 | 10 | 80,309 | 95.64 | 10 | 30,176.67 | 15.73 | 0.3 |
| 500 | 1,000 | 175,899 | 26.4 | 17.99 | 1,985.3 | 87.6 | 10 | 161,582.3 | 97.83 | 10 | 57,875 | 14.73 | 0.3 |
| 750 | 100 | 55,589.7 | 62.83 | 17.99 | 124.66 | 62.83 | 10 | 22,121.67 | 97.75 | 10 | 2,450.67 | 74.2 | 0.4 |
| 750 | 500 | 15,743.4 | 237 | 17.99 | 790 | 75.47 | 10 | 120,286 | 96.77 | 10 | 40,080 | 15.4 | 0.4 |
| 750 | 1,000 | 227,373.7 | 30.6 | 17.9 | 1,974.67 | 84.65 | 10 | 244,661.7 | 96.65 | 10 | 85,100 | 14.5 | 0.4 |
| 1,000 | 100 | 663,324 | 18.5 | 17.97 | 126.33 | 61.16 | 10 | 30,433.67 | 96.71 | 10.98 | 1,654.3 | 97.73 | 14.7 |
| 1,000 | 500 | 180,489.3 | 26.6 | 17.9 | 793 | 76.09 | 10 | 160,618 | 96.59 | 10.98 | 56,393 | 14.83 | 82.6 |
| 1,000 | 100 | 2,958.7 | 30.9 | 17.9 | 1,982.3 | 83.29 | 10 | 324,767 | 96.67 | 10.67 | 108,974.6 | 15 | 92.3 |

**Table 13.19**  *Intermediate Data for Workload 2*

| No. of Processes | Process Rate | Windows XP | | | Windows ME | | | Windows NT | | | LINUX | | |
|---|---|---|---|---|---|---|---|---|---|---|---|---|---|
| | | RT | CPU | MEM | RT | CPU | MEM | RT | CPU | MEM | RT | CPU | MEM |
| 10 | 0 | 607.3 | 47.91 | 17.28 | 271 | 63.78 | 10 | 307.3 | 22.3 | 11 | 212.6 | 43.4 | 0.1 |
| 10 | 100 | 584 | 63.165 | 18 | 1,095 | 71.08 | 10 | 1,217 | 15.51 | 11 | 206 | 35.93 | 0.1 |
| 10 | 1,000 | 630.67 | 61.45 | 17.23 | 1,000,063 | 58.9 | 10 | 10,235 | 3.18 | 11 | 122 | 66.67 | 0.1 |
| 100 | 0 | 23,936 | 106.44 | 18.55 | 2,072.3 | 87.3 | 11.53 | 3,445 | 79.94 | 12 | 2,315.3 | 41 | 0.1 |
| 100 | 100 | 4,212.67 | 83.45 | 17.99 | 10,502.6 | 65.99 | 10.67 | 122,551.34 | 28.78 | 11 | 2,308 | 38.1 | 0.1 |
| 100 | 1,000 | 4,613.34 | 86.76 | 17.99 | 10,0513 | 56.82 | 11 | 10,361.67 | 3.82 | 11.9 | 1,335.7 | 64.67 | 0.1 |
| 1,000 | 0 | 141,076.34 | 96.72 | 24 | 24,422 | 98.7 | 1.58 | 34,522.67 | 55 | 24.22 | 23,329 | 42.3 | 0.1 |
| 1,000 | 100 | 76,894 | 97.09 | 20.98 | 105,878 | 61.64 | 13.27 | 130,361 | 30.39 | 13.80 | 23,361.3 | 42.6 | 0.1 |
| 1,000 | 1,000 | 65,064.3 | 98.1 | 22.91 | 1,006,176 | 56.69 | 2.647 | 1,027,607.67 | 4.4 | 19.3 | 13,414.7 | 73.83 | 0.1 |

**Table 13.20**   *Intermediate Data for Workload 3*

| Matrix | | Windows XP | | | Windows ME | | | Windows NT | | | LINUX | | |
|---|---|---|---|---|---|---|---|---|---|---|---|---|---|
| Matrix Size | Matrix Rate | RT | CPU | MEM | RT | CPU | MEM | RT | CPU | MEM | RT | CPU | MEM |
| 10×10 | 10 | 0.01 | 5.7 | 29 | 0.0 | 58.83 | 2 | 0.015 | 12 | 16 | 0.003 | — | — |
| 10×10 | 100 | 0.057 | 9.83 | 28 | 0.056 | 53.5 | 2 | 0.06 | 13.33 | 16 | 0.032 | — | — |
| 10×10 | 1,000 | 0.791 | 47.72 | 28 | 0.84 | 73.63 | 2.44 | 0.898 | 71 | 16 | 0.538 | — | — |
| 50×50 | 10 | 0.07 | 8.9 | 28 | 0.07 | 56.5 | 4 | 0.063 | 19.33 | 16 | 0.06 | 47.0 | 4.1 |
| 50×50 | 100 | 0.577 | 42.33 | 28 | 0.68 | 72.36 | 4.33 | 0.6403 | 77.5 | 16 | 0.68 | 47.89 | 4.1 |
| 50×50 | 1,000 | 48.55 | 99.12 | 30.97 | 50.37 | 99.46 | 11.9 | 49.93 | 99.46 | 17.99 | 50.75 | 48.376 | 4.2 |
| 100×100 | 10 | 0.324 | 34.07 | 28 | 0.33 | 62.5 | 2.33 | 0.32 | 38.9 | 16 | 0.61 | 81.34 | 4.2 |
| 100×100 | 100 | 2.92 | 79.92 | 28.87 | 3.46 | 89.30 | 4.08 | 3.14 | 19.08 | 16.8 | 5.2 | 81.76 | 4.2 |
| 100×100 | 1,000 | 388.77 | 100 | 40.98 | 398.74 | 99.97 | 41 | 394.76 | 97.95 | 24.93 | 417.7 | 81.97 | 4.2 |

## 13.6   Summary

This chapter represents the results of a graduate course in computer system performance evaluation conducted at the University of Massachusetts Dartmouth. It is presented to show the difficulties associated with evaluating the performance of real-world computer systems, particularly their operating systems.

This study attempted to perform an evaluation of four operating systems. The experiments developed appeared to provide the tests we wished to perform, but our ability to adequately collect reliable measurements led to our inability to do the study with any degree of reliability. If this study were to be done again, the teams would need to use hardware-monitoring concepts in order to get at low-level system parameters to more fully understand how the systems performed. The teams also lacked experience in performing such tests and analyzing results, leading to other problems, as one can deduce from these results. We included such a study in this book to highlight many of the problems encountered when performing such tests.

# 14

# *Database Systems Performance Analysis*

## 14.1   Introduction

The previous chapter addressed the issue of operating systems evaluation. It focused on the use of testbeds and commercial-grade software to assess the relative performance of four operating systems. This chapter follows a similar path; we will be evaluating industrial-grade software products used in many applications. We will discuss database on-line transaction processing as the overall application domain. The main focus, however, is the assessment of four commercial-grade database systems running on a fixed set of testbed hardware and systems software (the operating system).

Four database systems currently compete for the top position in the database market, each claiming to be the fastest in the world. These databases are IBM DB2, Informix UDB, Microsoft SQL Server, and Oracle 8i. This chapter demonstrates which of these four database systems is the "best" not only in terms of speed but also cost.

This chapter is divided into three main sections. First, a description of the four systems that were used to test the databases is given. In the next section the results of a PC performance benchmark are shown to prove that all the PC hardware configurations were the same. The second portion details the procedures taken by each database evaluation team to run a standard benchmark on its test database. Finally, the results of the standard benchmark and a cost analysis show which database is the "best."

## 14.2   The testbed systems

To ensure that all the databases were tested on a level playing field, the four PCs used were configured with identical hardware. The hardware for each of the machines is defined in Table 14.1.

**Table 14.1**    *Testbed Configuration*

| CPU: | Pentium III @ 500 MHz |
| --- | --- |
| **Total RAM:** | 256 MB |
| **Operating System:** | Windows NT 4.0 Service Pack 5 |

To ensure that all of the machines were equal in the sense of performance capabilities, an independent performance assessment group ran a PC performance benchmark to validate each machine's performance specifications before the actual database benchmark tests were performed. The results are discussed in the next section.

## 14.2.1   PC performance assessment benchmark

The PC computer architecture performance test utilized is comprised of 22 individual benchmark tests that are available in six test suites. The six different test suites test for the following:

- Integer and floating-point mathematical operations

- Tests of standard two-dimensional graphical functions

- Reading, writing, and seeking within disk files

- Memory allocation and access

- Tests of the MMX (multimedia extensions) in newer CPUs

- A test of the DirectX 3D graphics system

The test results reported are shown as relative values. The larger the number the faster the computer. For example, a computer with a result of 40 can process roughly twice as much data as a computer with a result of 20. The Passmark rating is a weighted average of all the other test results and gives a single overall indication of the computer's performance. The bigger the number the faster the computer. The results we observed are shown in Table 14.2.

### Assessment of results

The performance assessment test found that the computer system configured for the DB2 servers appeared to have better performance than the other systems in most of the tests. However, the Passmark rating (weighted average of all test results giving a single overall indication of performance) of the computer system configured for the SQL Server 2000 was the highest.

**Table 14.2**   *Testbed Architecture Performance Results*

| Parameter Tested | Oracle System | Informix System | SQL System | DB2 System |
|---|---|---|---|---|
| Math—Addition | 96.6 | 96.2 | 94.6 | **97.0** |
| Math—Subtraction | 96.4 | 97.1 | 96.2 | **97.6** |
| Math—Multiplication | 101.1 | 101.4 | 101.4 | **103.1** |
| Math—Division | 12.9 | 12.8 | 12.9 | **13.0** |
| Math—Floating-Point Addition | 87.7 | 87.8 | 87.6 | **88.7** |
| Math—Floating-Point Subtraction | 89.4 | 89.5 | 88.6 | **90.1** |
| Math—Floating-Point Multiplication | 91.7 | 91.7 | 90.9 | **92.3** |
| Math—Floating-Point Division | 14.8 | 14.8 | 14.8 | **14.9** |
| Math—Maximum Mega FLOPS | 171.2 | 172.2 | 170.7 | **177.6** |
| Graphics 2D—Lines | 17.5 | 17.6 | 17.5 | **17.8** |
| Graphics 2D—Bitmaps | **12.9** | **12.9** | 12.8 | **12.9** |
| Graphics 2D—Shapes | **4.7** | **4.7** | **4.7** | **4.7** |
| Graphics 3D—Many Worlds | 22.9 | **23.0** | 22.9 | 22.9 |
| Memory—Allocated Small Blocks | 86.6 | **87.6** | 87.0 | **87.6** |
| Memory—Read Cached | 67.9 | 68.4 | 68.0 | **68.5** |
| Memory—Read Uncached | 48.7 | 48.8 | **50.0** | 49.1 |
| Memory—Write | 40.8 | 41.1 | 40.9 | **41.4** |
| Disk—Sequential Read | 3.2 | **3.8** | 3.7 | 3.1 |
| Disk—Sequential Write | 2.9 | **3.4** | **3.4** | 2.9 |
| Disk—Random Seek | 1.2 | 2.3 | 3.6 | 2.1 |
| MMX—Addition | 97.7 | 94.5 | 97.8 | **99.4** |
| MMX—Subtraction | 92.3 | **98.2** | 93.3 | 96.0 |
| MMX—Multiplication | 97.8 | 97.5 | 96.9 | **99.1** |
| Math Mark | 75.6 | 75.8 | 75.2 | **76.8** |
| 2D Mark | 46.7 | **46.9** | 46.7 | 47.1 |
| Memory Mark | 58.7 | 59.2 | 59.2 | **59.4** |
| Disk Mark | 19.3 | 25.1 | **28.4** | 21.5 |
| 3D Graphics Mark | 15.5 | **15.7** | 15.5 | 15.6 |
| MMX Mark | 48.8 | 49.2 | 48.9 | **50.0** |
| Passmark Rating | 45.7 | 47.2 | **47.8** | 46.7 |

## 14.2.2 Burn-in test

The computer system hardware burn-in test is a thorough exercise of the hardware in a PC performed over a short period of time, in the same way as normal applications use a PC over a long period of time. The burn-in test assesses the following items:

- CPU
- Hard drives
- CD-ROMs
- Sound cards
- 2D graphics
- 3D graphics
- RAM
- Network connections and printers

### Burn-in test assessment

From the results shown in Table 14.3, we can see that the SQL Server 2000's CPU speed is 0.1 MHz less than the other machines. This difference

**Table 14.3**  *Burn-In Test Results*

| System Information: | Informix | Oracle | DB2 | SQL Server |
|---|---|---|---|---|
| Operating System: | Win NT4 | Win NT4 | Win NT4 | Win NT4 |
| Number of CPUs: | 1 | 1 | 1 | 1 |
| CPU Manufacturer: | Intel | Intel | Intel | Intel |
| CPU Type: | Celeron | Celeron | Celeron | Celeron |
| CPU Features: | MMX | MMX | MMX | MMX |
| CPU Serial #: | N/A or disabled | N/A or disabled | N/A or disabled | N/A or disabled |
| CPU1 Speed: | 501.3 MHz | 501.3 MHz | 501.3 MHz | 501.2 MHz |
| CPU Level 2 Cache: | 128 KB | 128 KB | 128 KB | 128 KB |
| RAM: | 267,821,056 Bytes (256 MB) | 267,821,056 Bytes (256 MB) | 267,821,056 Bytes (256 MB) | 267,821,056 Bytes (256 MB) |
| Color Depth: | 24 | 24 | 24 | 24 |

is not significant, unless the duration of performance assessment tests spans a long period of time. All other measurements indicated the four testbed machines were equivalent.

# 14.3   The database systems

## 14.3.1   Database 1—Oracle architectural structure

The components comprising the Oracle database system are executed using virtual memory structures and basic application processes. Processes are jobs or tasks that work in the memory of these computers. Oracle has always placed great emphasis on portability: providing uniform features and facilities across the greatest possible range of operating environments. Oracle implements a common architecture, which includes the following components:

- An area of memory available to all Oracle sessions, known as the system global area (SGA). This area of memory includes recently accessed data blocks (the buffer cache), SQL and PL/SQL objects (the library cache), and transaction information (the redo log buffer). The SGA may also contain session information.

- Several tasks that perform dedicated database activities, including the database writer (DBWR), redo log writer (LGWR), system monitor (SMON), process monitor (PMON), and log archiver (ARCH). Other tasks may be configured if required to support Oracle options, such as parallel query, distributed database, or multithreaded servers. We will refer to these tasks as background tasks (although they are also often referred to as background processes).

- Oracle data files, which contain the tables, indexes, and other segments that form the Oracle instance.

- Redo logs, which record critical transaction information required for roll-forward in the event of instance failure.

- A separate task created to perform database operations on behalf of each Oracle session, referred to as a dedicated server. If the multi-threaded server option is implemented, many sessions can be supported by a smaller number of shared servers.

- A SQL*Net listener task, which establishes connections from external systems.

Database and redo log files are generally implemented using the operating system's native file system or raw disk partitions, and port-specific differences at the file level are relatively minor. However, the memory and process structure of an Oracle instance will vary significantly, depending on how the operating system implements process and memory management.

The architecture of Oracle in a Windows NT environment is somewhat different from UNIX. Oracle takes advantage of NT's strong support for threads. In almost all operating systems, a process is prevented from accessing memory belonging to another process. Threads belonging to the same process, however, share a common memory address space and are able to share memory easily.

On NT, the Oracle instance is implemented as a single NT process (Figure 14.1). This process includes threads that implement each of the tasks required for the Oracle instance. Therefore, there is a thread for each of the background and server tasks plus a two-thread overhead per client connection. Because each thread shares the same memory space, there is no need to implement the SGA in shared memory; if you implement the SGA within the instance's process memory, it is available to all threads within the process.

Oracle's architecture suits the NT process/thread model. However, the single-process model restricts the total memory available to threads belong-

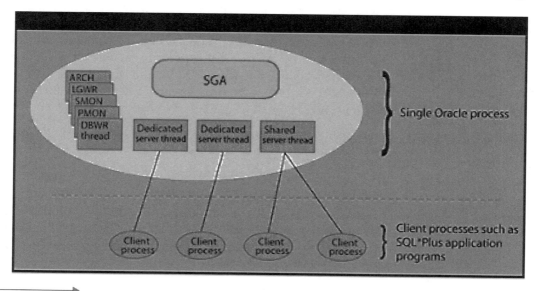

**Figure 14.1**    *Oracle process and thread structure on NT.*

ing to the Oracle instance on NT. Prior to NT version 3.51, the memory limit for a single process was only 256 MB—a severe limitation for even moderately sized Oracle instances. In NT version 4.0, a process may address up to 4 GB of virtual memory. However, 2 GB of this memory is reserved for system overhead, allowing only 2 GB for Oracle. At first glance, 2 GB might sound like a generous memory allocation for an Oracle instance. But remember that this area of memory must be sufficient to store the SGA and data segments for all Oracle sessions. Furthermore, the 2 GB is a virtual memory limit; it's possible that 2 GB of virtual memory will be expended when physical memory use is actually far lower. There are currently two options for extending the 2-GB limit: In Windows NT Server Enterprise Edition, you can reduce the system component of process memory to 1 GB, allowing up to 3 GB of memory for the Oracle instance. On Alpha NT platforms, the very large memory (VLM) option allows up to 8 GB of memory to be made available to the Oracle instance.

Oracle's multithreaded server option allows multiple client processes to share a smaller number of Oracle server processes. This approach can reduce memory requirements and process overhead. Multithreaded server is also available on NT, but only from Oracle 8 onward. Using multithreaded server under Windows NT can reduce the number of threads in the Oracle process as well as overall memory requirements. One may also be able to use the Oracle 8 connection pooling and concentrating facilities to further reduce thread and memory overhead.

### Transactions

Oracle supports many types of transactions, including read-only, read/write, and discrete transactions. Depending on the transaction type set for the transaction, the Oracle database will provide different data consistency guarantees. If no transaction type is set for a transaction, it defaults to read/write. For each transaction, Oracle must keep track of the transaction and the effect it has on the database. This is done to ensure that if the transaction does not finish, it can be rolled back and the effects of the transaction "undone" from the database. This will ensure database consistency. Oracle uses a special type of segment to record the specifics of the transaction.

**Note:** The queries run for the TPC-H experiment did not have any transaction type set, so they ran as read/write transactions.

### Query optimization

Oracle provides an internal system feature called the optimizer. The optimizer will determine one or more execution plans that it can use to execute the SQL statement. Oracle 8i has three choices: cost, rule, and choose. The cost-based optimizer will execute the SQL statement using the plan that has the lowest cost. The rule-based optimizer will execute the SQL statement according to user-defined rules set up in the database. The choose optimizer will choose the lowest-cost optimization (cost or rule) that can execute the SQL statement. In order to determine the best execution plans for SQL statements, Oracle uses statistics that are stored in the database. These statistics must be updated periodically on the database tables, indexes, and other database objects. If the database is modified after the statistics are generated (after analyzing the tables), the optimizer might not execute with the least cost; therefore, it is crucial to regularly generate statistics on the database tables.

One of the most costly execution plans is the full table scan. Full table scans require Oracle to read every row in the table. Another execution plan to find rows of a table is by searching an index of a table. Optimizers can be passed hints to allow them to choose the best execution paths for a SQL statement. One of these hints could be to use indexes. Other optimizer hints include first rows, all rows, full table scan, nested loop, merge join, use hash join, and so on. Hints can be added to SQL statements to ensure the optimizer executes the SQL statement using the specific execution plan.

---

**Note:** The TPC-H queries were run with the Oracle database optimizer set to Choose. No indexes were implemented; all of the tables were analyzed prior to running the queries. No hints were added to the TPC-H queries, since doing so would violate the comparison guidelines.

---

### Concurrency control and locking

Oracle uses locking mechanisms to protect data from being destroyed by concurrent transactions. Oracle provides both automatic and explicit locking capabilities. By default, Oracle provides locking for database resources for transactions in the database. The system will automatically set locks on tables and rows; the levels of the locks will depend on the transaction function (reads, inserts, updates, and deletes). Oracle can set locks in two lock modes: shared or exclusive. Shared locks are set on database resources so that many transactions can access the resource. Exclusive locks are set on resources that ensure one transaction has exclusive access to the database resource. Exclusive locks ensure transaction serialization. DML locks are Oracle locks that are automatically set on tables and indexes for transactions using DML operations (update, insert, delete). Oracle also automatically sets DDL locks on Oracle resources when DDL operations are used (create, alter, and drop).

### 14.3.2   Database 2—Informix Dynamic Server architectural structure

Informix Dynamic Server is a multithreaded object-relational database server that manages data stored in rows and columns in a table. It employs a single processor or symmetric multiprocessing (SMP) systems and dynamic scalable architecture to deliver database scalability, manageability, and performance. Dynamic Server can be used for on-line transaction processing (OLTP), packaging applications, data-warehousing applications, and Web solutions.

#### Dynamic scalable architecture

The foundation of Informix Dynamic Server's superior performance, scalability, and reliability is its parallel database architecture, dynamic scalable architecture (DSA), built to fully exploit the inherent processing power of any hardware (Figure 14.2). DSA enables all major database operations,

**Figure 14.2**
*Configurable pool database server.*

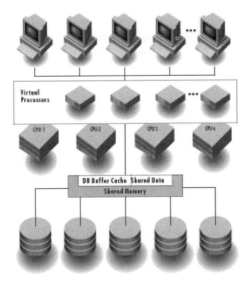

such as I/O, complex queries, index builds, log recovery, and backups and restores, to execute in parallel across all available system resources. Informix Dynamic Server's core architecture was designed from the ground up to provide built-in multithreading and parallel processing capabilities. Parallel processing is achieved through dividing large user tasks into subtasks, thus enabling processing to be distributed across all available resources.

The key advantages of Informix Dynamic Server are as follows;

- Maximum performance and scalability through a superior multithreaded parallel processing architecture

- Reduced operating system overhead through bypassing operating system limits

- Local table partitioning for superior parallel I/O operations and high-availability database administration

- Parallel SQL functionality increases performance and lets all database operations execute in parallel, thereby eliminating potential bottlenecks

- High database availability for supporting a wide range of business-critical applications on open systems platforms

- Dynamic, distributed on-line system administration for monitoring tasks and distributing workloads

- Full feature parity on Windows NT and UNIX operating systems

- Full RDBMS functionality across all hardware architectures (uniprocessor, symmetric multiprocessing, and cluster systems) and database models (relational and object relational) enables seamless migration of applications, data, and skills

### Locking, data consistency, isolation, and recovery

While high availability ensures integrity at the system level, data consistency ensures consistency at the transaction level. Informix Dynamic Server maintains data consistency via transaction logging and internal consistency checking and by establishing and enforcing locking procedures, isolation levels, and business rules.

When an operation is unable to be completed, the partially completed transaction must be removed from the database to maintain data consistency. To remove any partially completed transaction, Informix Dynamic Server maintains a historical record of all transactions in the logical logs and automatically uses these transaction records as a reference to restore the database to the state prior to the transaction.

Internal consistency checking is designed to alert the Informix Dynamic Server administrator to data and system inconsistencies. Informix Dynamic Server contains a data-level layer of checks, which can detect data inconsistencies that might be caused by hardware or operating system errors. If inconsistencies are detected, this internal mechanism automatically writes messages to the Informix Dynamic Server message log.

Other important features for maintaining data consistency are locking procedures and process isolation. These security measures prevent other users from changing data that are currently being read or modified and also helps the system detect when conflicting locks are held. Row- and page-level locking are specified when the table is created or altered. Table- and database-level locking are specified in the user's application.

The isolation level is the degree to which your read operation is isolated from concurrent actions of other database server processes: what modifications other processes can make to the records you are reading and what records you can read while other processes are reading or modifying them. Informix Dynamic Server has four isolation levels: dirty read, committed read, cursor stability, and repeatable read.

### Join methods

When Informix must join tables, it chooses any of three algorithms. All joins are minimally two-table joins; multitable joins are resolved by joining initial resultant sets to subsequent tables in turn. The optimizer chooses which join method to use based on costs, except when you override this decision by setting OPTCOMPIND. Joins are described as follows:

- Nested Loop Join: When the join columns on both tables are indexed, this method is usually the most efficient. The first table is scanned in any order. The join columns are matched via the indexes to form a resultant row. A row from the second table is then looked up via the index. Occasionally, Informix will construct a dynamic index on the second table to enable this join. These joins are often the most efficient for OLTP applications.

- Sort Merge Join: After filters are applied, the database engine scans both tables in the order of the join filter. Both tables might need to be sorted first. If an index exists on the join column, no sort is necessary. This method is usually chosen when either or both join columns do not have an index. After the tables are sorted, joining is a simple matter of merging the sorted values.

- Hash Join: Available starting in version 7, the hash merge join first scans one table and puts its hashed key values in a hash table. The second table is then scanned once, and its join values are looked up in the hash table. Hash joins are often faster than sort merge joins because no sort is required. Even though creating the hash table requires some overhead, with most DSS applications in which the tables involved are very large, this method is usually preferred.

### Cost-based query optimizer

Informix Dynamic Server's cost-based optimizer will automatically determine the fastest way to retrieve data from a database table based on detailed information about the distribution of those data within the table's columns. The optimizer collects and calculates statistics about this data distribution and will pick the return path that has the least impact on system resources—in some cases this will be a parallelized return path, but in others it might be a sequential process. All that is needed to control the degree of parallelism is the memory grant manager.

To provide users with a degree of control, Informix Dynamic Server offers optimizer directives that let users bypass the optimizer. Areas that users can control include the following:

- Access methods: This lets users specify how to access a table. For example, a user can direct the optimizer to use a specific index.

- Join methods: This lets users specify how to join a table to the other tables in the query. For example, users can specify that the optimizer use a hash join.

- Join order: This lets users direct the optimizer to join tables in a specific order.

- Optimization goal: This lets users specify whether a query is to be optimized by response time (which returns the first set of rows) or by total time (which returns all rows).

### Memory handling by Informix

All memory used by the Informix Dynamic Server is shared among the pool of virtual processors. In this way, Informix Dynamic Server can be configured to automatically add more memory to its shared memory pool in order to process client requests expeditiously. Data from the read-only data dictionary (system catalog) and stored procedures are shared among users rather than copied, resulting in optimized memory utilization and fast execution of heavily used procedures. This feature can provide substantial benefit in many applications, particularly those accessing many tables with a large number of columns and/or many stored procedures. Informix Dynamic Server also allocates an area, called the thread stack, in the virtual portion of shared memory to store nonshared data for the functions that a thread executes. The thread's stack tracks the state of a user session and enables a virtual processor to protect a thread's nonshared data from being overwritten by other threads concurrently executing the same code. Informix Dynamic Server dynamically grows the stack for certain operations such as recursive stored procedures. Informix Dynamic Server's shared memory minimizes fragmentation so that memory utilization does not degrade over time. Beyond the initial allocation, shared memory segments are automatically added in large chunks as needed but can also be added by the administrator while the database is running. The memory management system will also attempt to automatically grow the memory segment when it runs out of memory. When a user session terminates, the memory it used is freed and reused by another session. Memory can be reclaimed by the operating system by freeing the memory allocated to the database. User threads can, therefore, easily migrate among the virtual processors, contributing to Informix Dynamic Server's scalability as the number of users increases.

## 14.3.3  Database 3—IBM DB2 architectural structure

Conceptually, DB2 is a relational database management system. Physically, DB2 is an amalgamation of address spaces and intersystem communication links, which, when adequately tied together, provides the services of a relational database management system.

Beginning with DB2 version 3, each DB2 subsystem consists of three or four tasks started from the operator console 1. Each task runs in a portion of the CPU called an address space. Version 4 of DB2 provides an additional address space for stored procedures. A description of these five address spaces (Figure 14.3) follows.

- The DBAS, or Database Services Address Space, provides the facility for manipulating DB2 data structures. The default name for this address space is DSNDBM1, but each individual shop may rename any of the DB2 address spaces. The DBAS is responsible for running SQL statements and managing data buffers. It contains the core logic

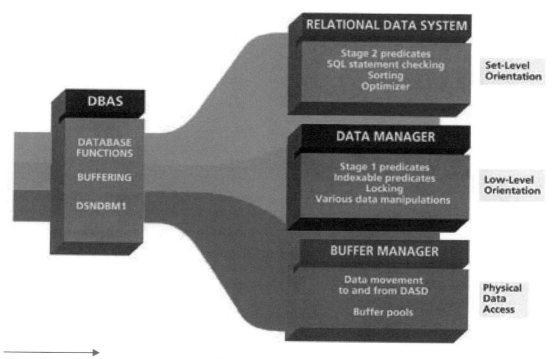

**Figure 14.3**   *Components of the database services address space.*

of the database management system. Three individual components make up the DBAS: the Relational Data System, the Data Manager, and the Buffer Manager. Each of these components performs specific tasks.

- The SSAS, or System Services Address Space, coordinates the attachment of DB2 to other subsystems (CICS, IMS/DC, or TSO). SSAS is also responsible for all logging activities (physical logging, log archival, and BSDS). DSNMSTR is the default name for this address space.

- The third address space required by DB2 is the IRLM, or Intersystem Resource Lock Manager. The IRLM is responsible for managing DB2 locks (including deadlock detection). The default name of this address space is IRLMPROC.

- The fourth DB2 version 3 address space, DDF, or Distributed Data Facility, is the only optional one. The DDF is required only if distributed database functionality is needed.

- The newest address space, SPAS, or Stored Procedure Address Space, has been added to DB2 version 4 to support stored procedures and remote procedure calls (RPCs). The SPAS runs as an allied address space providing an independent environment for stored procedures to execute. This effectively isolates the user-written stored procedure code in its own little world so that it cannot interfere with the system code of DB2 itself.

These five address spaces contain the logic to effectively handle all DB2 functionality.

### The functionality of the DBAS

Recall that the DBAS is responsible for executing SQL and is composed of three distinct components: the relational system, the data manager, and the buffer manager. Each component passes a SQL statement to the next component, and, when results are returned, each component passes the results back.

The Relational Data System (RDS) is the component that gives DB2 its set orientation. When a SQL statement requesting a set of columns and rows is passed to the RDS, it determines the best mechanism for satisfying the request. Note that the RDS can parse a SQL statement and determine its needs. These needs may include any of the features supported by a relational database (such as selection, projection, or join). When a SQL statement is received by the RDS, it checks authorization; translates the data element names being accessed into internal identifiers; checks the syntax of the SQL; and optimizes the SQL, creating an access path.

The RDS then passes the optimized SQL statement to the Data Manager (DM) component. The DM delves deeper into the data being accessed. In other words, the DM is the component of DB2 that analyzes rows (either table rows or index rows) of data. The DM analyzes the request for data and then calls the Buffer Manager to satisfy the request.

The Buffer Manager (BM) accesses data for other DB2 components. A data buffer is often referred to as a cache in other DBMSs. The BM uses pools of memory set aside for the storage of frequently accessed data in order to create an efficient data access environment. When a request is passed to the BM, it must determine whether the data are in the appropriate buffer pool. If they are, the BM accesses these data and sends them to the DM. If these data are not in the buffer pool, the BM calls the VSAM Media Manager to read the data and send them back to the BM, which in turn sends these data back to the DM. The DM receives the data passed to it by the BM and applies as many predicates as possible to reduce the answer set. Only Stage 1 predicates are applied in the DM. Finally, the RDS receives the data from the DM. All Stage 2 predicates are applied, the necessary sorting is performed, and the results are returned to the requester.

An understanding of the internal components of DB2 can be helpful when developing a DB2 application. For example, consider Stage 1 and Stage 2 predictates. It is easier to understand that Stage 1 predicates are more efficient than Stage 2 predicates, because you know they are evaluated earlier in the process (in the DM instead of the RDS). Therefore, they avoid the overhead associated with the passing of additional data from one component to another.

### DB2 memory management

The Database Manager Shared Memory is allocated when the database manager is started using the db2start command, and remains allocated until the database manager is stopped using the db2stop. This memory is used to manage activity across all database connections. From the Database Manager Shared Memory, all other memory is attached and/or allocated. The Database Global Memory (also called Database Shared Memory) is allocated for each database when the database is activated using the ACTI-

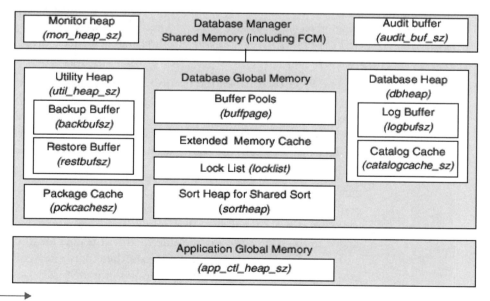

**Figure 14.4**   *Database Manager Shared Memory overview.*

VATE DATABASE command or when the first application connects to the database. The Database Global Memory remains allocated until the database is deactivated using the DEACTIVATE DATABASE command or when the last application disconnects from the database. The Database Global Memory contains memory areas such as buffer pools, lock list, database heap, and utility heap. The database manager configuration parameter, NUMDB, defines the maximum number of concurrent active databases. If the value of this parameter increases, the number of Database Global Memory segments may grow, depending on the number of active databases.

Figure 14.4 shows how memory is used to support applications. In the previous section we introduced some configuration parameters that may affect the number of memory segments. We now introduce the configuration parameters, which allow you to control the size of each memory by limiting its size.

The Database Manager Shared Memory is required for the Database Manager to run. The size of this memory is affected by the following configuration parameters:

- Database System Monitor Heap Size (MON_HEAP_SZ)

- Audit Buffer Size (AUDIT_BUF_SZ)

- FCM Buffers (FCM_NUM_BUFFERS)

- FCM Message Anchors (FCM_NUM_ANCHORS)

- FCM Connection Entries (FCM_NUM_CONNECT)

- FCM Request Blocks (FCM_NUM_RQB)

The Database Manager uses the fast communication manager (FCM) component to transfer data between DB2 agents when intrapartition parallelism is enabled. Thus, if you do not enable intrapartition parallelism, memory areas required for FCM buffers, message anchors, connection entries, and request blocks are not allocated. The maximum size of the Database Global Memory segment is determined by the following configuration parameters:

- Buffer pool size explicitly specified when the buffer pools were created or altered (the value of BUFFPAGE database configuration parameter is taken if 1 is specified)

- Maximum storage for lock list (LOCKLIST)

- Database heap (DBHEAP)

- Utility heap size (UTIL_HEAP_SZ)

- Extended storage memory segment size (ESTORE_SEG_SZ)

- Number of extended storage memory segments (NUM_ESTORE_SEGS)

- Package cache size (PCKCACHESZ)

- Application global memory is determined by the following configuration parameter: application control heap size (APP_CTL_HEAP_SZ)

### Query optimization

Query optimization is the part of the query process in which the database system compares different query strategies and chooses the one with the least expected cost. The query optimizer, which carries out this function, is a key part of the relational database and determines the most efficient way to access data. It makes it possible for the user to request the data without specifying how these data should be retrieved.

The cost of accessing a query is a weighted combination of the I/O and processing costs. The I/O cost is the cost of accessing index and data pages from disk. Processing cost is estimated by assigning an instruction count to each step in computing the result of the query. There are two approaches to optimization. They are as follows:

- Cost based: This was developed by IBM. The optimizer estimates the cost of each processing method of the query and chooses the one with the lowest estimate. Presently, most systems use this.

- Heuristic: Rules are based on the form of the query. Oracle used this at one point. Presently, no system uses this.

The query optimizer has the job of selecting the appropriate indexes for acquiring data, classifying predicates used in a query, performing simple data reductions, selecting access paths, determining the order of a join, performing predicate transformations, performing Boolean logic transformations, and performing subquery transformations—all in the name of making query processing more efficient.

### Concurrency control and locking in DB2

The granularity of locking within a database management system represents a definite tradeoff between concurrency and CPU overhead. Whenever a finer granularity of locking is desired, an increase in the use of available CPU resources may be required, because locking in general increases CPU path length. No I/O operations are done, but each lock request requires two-way communication between DB2 and the internal resource lock manager (IRLM). However, it is also possible there may or may not be an increase in the number of potential lock requests. For example, for read-only SQL with highly effective lock avoidance you may not see any increase in the number of DB2 lock requests to the IRLM.

A DB2 thread makes lock requests through IRLM services. Transaction locks are owned by the work unit or thread and managed by the IRLM. DB2 objects that are candidates for transaction locking are as follows:

- Table space
- Partition
- Table
- Page
- Row

The locking mechanisms must also perform many other operations in the name of locking—for example, manage the lock hierarchy, lock dura-tion, the modes of locks, lock escalation, lock suspension, and deadlock detection and recovery.

### Join methods

When multiple tables are requested within a single SQL statement, DB2 must perform a join. When joining tables, the access type (tablespace scan or index scan) defines how each single table will be accessed; understanding the join method defines how the result sets from multiple tables will be combined to deliver a unified result set back to the requester. While more than two tables can be joined together in a single SQL statement, DB2 will always perform the join operation in a series of steps. Each step joins only two tables together, and a composite table is passed to the next step in the series. The plan tables will describe how these tables are joined together and the order in which each table is accessed.

## 14.3.4   Database 4—Microsoft SQL Server architectural structure

Microsoft SQL Server 2000 persistently stores data in database-controlled tables organized as relations managed in physical files (Figure 14.5). When using a database, work is performed primarily with the logical components, such as tables, views, procedures, and user space. The physical implementa-tion of relations and their realization as files is largely transparent.

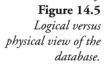

**Figure 14.5**
*Logical versus physical view of the database.*

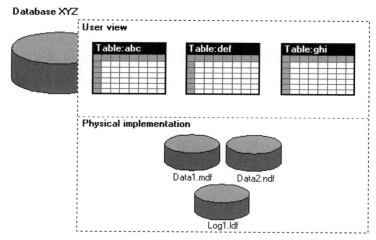

Each instance of a SQL Server has four system databases (master, model, tempdb, and msdb) and one or more user databases (Figure 14.6). Some organizations have only one user database, containing all the data for their organization. Some organizations have different databases for each group in their organization and sometimes a database used by a single application.

It is not necessary to run multiple copies of the SQL Server database engine to allow multiple users to access the databases on a server. An instance of the SQL Server Standard or Enterprise Edition is capable of handling thousands of users working in multiple databases at the same time. Each instance of SQL Server makes all databases in the instance available to all users who connect to t*he instance, subject to the defined security permissions.

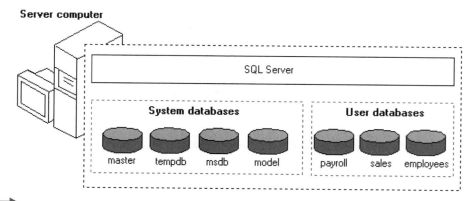

**Figure 14.6**   *Logical tablespace structures.*

When connecting to an instance of SQL Server, your connection is associated with a particular database on the server. This database is called the current database. You are usually connected to a database defined as your default database by the system administrator, although you can use connection options in the database APIs to specify another database. You can switch from one database to another using either the Transact-SQL USE database_name statement or an API function that changes your current database context.

SQL Server 2000 allows you to detach databases from an instance of SQL Server and then reattach them to another instance, or even attach the database back to the same instance. If you have a SQL Server database file, you can tell SQL Server when you connect to attach that database file with a specific database name.

The memory algorithms and use of memory by SQL Server objects are major changes in SQL Server 7.0 over SQL Server 6.5 that improve the performance of the database and also minimize the work the database administrator must do to configure memory for good performance.

Microsoft SQL Server 7.0 has dramatically improved the way memory is allocated and accessed. Unlike SQL Server 6.5, in which memory is managed by the database administrator with configuration settings, SQL Server 7.0 has a memory manager to eliminate manual memory management.

SQL Server 6.5 has a memory configuration option, which allocates a fixed amount of memory on startup—that is, memory is segmented and manually managed. If the parameter is set too high, SQL Server cannot start. The database administrator must first determine how much memory SQL Server should use versus the operating system. For example, with 256 MB of memory, SQL Server may get 200 MB and leave 56 MB for the operating system. This in itself is an art, not a science. It is very difficult to plan how much the database alone needs, much less plan what the operating system and other applications, such as Web servers running on the same computer, might need. Use of memory is not stagnant; it is possible that SQL Server may need more memory from 8:00 A.M. to 5:00 P.M., and the operating system may need more memory from 5:00 P.M. to 8:00 A.M. to run nightly batch work. Changing the memory configuration requires a shutdown and startup of SQL Server 6.5.

When SQL Server 7.0 starts, its dynamic memory allocation determines how much memory to allocate based on how much memory the Windows NT operating system and applications for Windows NT are using. For example, assume that Windows NT has a total of 512 MB of memory. When SQL Server starts up, Windows NT and the applications running on Windows NT are using 72 MB of memory. SQL Server uses available memory, leaving 5 MB free. Therefore, SQL Server uses 435 MB of memory = 512 MB total – 72 MB for active Windows NT – 5 MB of free memory. If another Windows NT–based application is started and uses the 5 MB of free space, SQL Server proactively releases memory to ensure that 5 MB of free space always remains free. Conversely, if Windows NT releases memory so that the free memory is more than 5 MB, SQL Server uses that memory for database operations.

This dynamic memory algorithm has many advantages. You no longer need to guess the correct memory percentages for Windows NT, Windows NT–based applications, and SQL Server. You can also avoid Windows NT paging during times of heavy Windows NT use, and you can use Windows NT free memory during times of light Windows NT use. The memory algorithm for SQL Server 7.0 Desktop Edition works differently. Rather than taking memory when it is free, it gives memory back to the operating system when it is not needed. This is because it is more likely that the Desktop Edition is running other applications.

### Locking architecture

Microsoft SQL Server 2000 uses locks to implement pessimistic concurrency control among multiple users performing modifications in a database at the same time. By default, SQL Server manages both transactions and locks on a per connection basis. For example, if an application opens two SQL Server connections, locks acquired by one connection cannot be shared with the other connection. Neither connection can acquire locks that would conflict with locks held by the other connection. Only bound connections are not affected by this rule.

SQL Server locks are applied at various levels of granularity in the database. Locks can be acquired on rows, pages, keys, ranges of keys, indexes, tables, or databases. SQL Server dynamically determines the appropriate level at which to place locks for each Transact-SQL statement. The level at which locks are acquired can vary for different objects referenced by the same query—for example, one table may be very small and have a table lock applied, while another, larger table may have row locks applied. The level at which locks are applied does not have to be specified by users and needs no configuration by administrators. Each instance of SQL Server ensures that locks granted at one level of granularity respect locks granted at another level. There are several lock modes: shared, update, exclusive, intent, and schema.

If several connections become blocked waiting for conflicting locks on a single resource, the locks are granted on a first come, first served basis as the preceding connections free their locks. In support of concurrent operations, SQL Server has an algorithm to detect deadlocks. If an instance of SQL Server detects a deadlock, it will terminate one transaction, allowing the other to continue.

SQL Server can dynamically escalate or de-escalate the granularity or type of locks. For example, if an update acquires a large number of row locks and has locked a significant percentage of a table, the row locks are escalated to a table lock. If a table lock is acquired, the row locks are released. SQL Server 2000 rarely needs to escalate locks; the query optimizer usually chooses the correct lock granularity at the time the execution plan is compiled.

### Structured Query Language

To work with data in a database, you have to use a set of commands and statements (language) defined by the DBMS software. Several different languages can be used with relational databases; the most common is SQL. The American National Standards Institute (ANSI) and the International Organization for Standardization (ISO) define software standards, including standards for the SQL language. SQL Server 2000 supports the entry level of SQL-92, the SQL standard published by ANSI and ISO in 1992. The dialect of SQL supported by Microsoft SQL Server is called Transact-SQL (T-SQL). T-SQL is the primary language used by Microsoft SQL Server applications.

### Summary of special features

Microsoft SQL Server 2000 gives users an excellent streamlined database platform for large-scale, on-line transactional processing (OLTP), data warehousing, and e-commerce applications. The improvements made to SQL Server version 7.0 provide a fully integrated XML environment, add a new data mining feature in analysis services, and enhance repository technology with metadata services. SQL Server 2000 enhances the performance, reliability, quality, and ease of use of SQL Server 7.0.

## 14.4  Testbed performance analysis testing

A true comparison of the four databases requires a plain benchmark that does not take advantage of any of the special features within any of the databases. In order to do this our team researched the latest benchmarks provided by the Transaction Processing Council (TPC—www.tpc.org). Three benchmarks were found that would allow us to test OLTP. These were TPC-C, TPC-H, and TPC-R. Of the three, TCP-C version 5 is designed as the latest OLTP benchmark. However, the TPC has not yet made the benchmark available for public use. As such, TPC-H and TPC-R were looked at. Both of these benchmarks are for decision-support databases in data warehousing. It was discovered that TPC-H is a revised version of TPC-R. The only difference between the two benchmarks is the implementation rules.

It was the decision of the performance evaluation team, due to the limited amount of time the group would have to learn the benchmarks, learn the databases, and do any real analysis, that it would be best to use TPC-H. This decision was made, since we would have less options to worry about during the implementation of the benchmark. This benchmark consists of a suite of business-oriented ad hoc queries and concurrent data modifications. Its main purpose is to help examine large volumes of data and execute queries with a high degree of complexity.

The next task was to determine what type of workloads the databases would run and how these loads would be run.

## 14.4.1   Workloads

The key concern in the benchmarking of a system is the specification of the workload. The workload of a computer is defined as the set of all inputs the system receives from its environment. The groups used the queries defined in the TPC-H benchmark (Table 14.4) as the basic workload.

## 14.4.2   Preparing for the testing

In order to ensure that the testing was standard, one of the performance tests in the TPC-H benchmark was chosen and modified. The planned modifications were the insertion of refreshes, as required by the TPC-H specifications, and the use of indexing. Thus, two runs would be done: one with no indexing and refreshes, and one with indexing and refreshes. Refreshes are required by the TPC-H specification, but the locations of these refreshes in the queries are left to the tester. To ensure that all databases ran the queries in the same order, performance test #1 (Appendix A of TPC-H Benchmark) was used with three predetermined refreshes.

**Table 14.4**   *TPC-H Benchmark*

| | |
|---|---|
| Query 1—Pricing Summary Report | This query will select a pricing summary report for all line items shipped as of a given date (substitution variable). The date is within 6 to 120 days of the greatest ship date contained in the database. A count of the number of line items is included in each group. |
| Query 2—Minimum Cost Supplier | This query will find, in a given region for each part of a certain type and size, the supplier that can supply it at the lowest cost. If multiple suppliers in that region offer the same lowest price for the part, the query will list the parts from the suppliers with the 100 highest account balances. |
| Query 3—Shipping Priority | This query will determine the shipping priority and potential revenue, defined as the sum of the extended price of the orders having the largest revenue among those that had not been shipped as of a given date. If more than ten unshipped orders exist, only the ten orders with the largest revenue are listed. |
| Query 4—Order Priority Checking | This query will count the number of orders that were ordered in a given quarter of a given year in which at least one line item was received later than its committed date. |
| Query 5—Local Supplier Volume | This query will list, for each country in a region, the revenue volume that resulted from line item transactions in which the customer ordering parts and the supplier filling them were both in the same country. The query only considers parts ordered in a certain year. |
| Query 6—Forecasting Revenue Change | This query will quantify the amount of revenue increase that would have resulted from eliminating certain company-wide discounts in a given percentage range in a given year. |
| Query 7—Volume Shipping | This query will determine the value of goods shipped between certain countries to help in the renegotiation of shipping contracts. |
| Query 8—National Market Share | This query will determine how the market share of a given country within a given region has changed over two years for a given part type. |
| Query 9—Product Type Profit Measure | This query determines how much profit is made on a given line of parts, broken out by supplier country and year. |
| Query 10—Returned Item Reporting | This query identifies customers who might be having problems with the parts that are shipped to them. |
| Query 11—Important Stock Identification | This query finds the most important subset of suppliers' stock in a given country. |
| Query 12—Shipping Modes and Order Priority | This query determines whether selecting less expensive modes of shipping is negatively affecting the critical-priority orders by causing more parts to be received by customers after the committed date. |
| Query 13—Customer Distribution | This query will determine the relationships between customers and the size of their orders. |

**Table 14.4**   *TPC-H Benchmark (continued)*

| | |
|---|---|
| Query 14—Promotion Effect | This query will find the percentage of revenue in a year from promotional parts (the time period is a substitution parameter selected when creating the query with the QGEN application using the Seed variable). |
| Query 15—Top Supplier | This query will find the supplier that contributed the most revenue for all parts shipped during a specific time period (the time period is a substitution parameter selected when creating the query with the QGEN application using the Seed variable). |
| Query 16—Parts/ Supplier Relationship | This query will find the count of suppliers that can supply parts that meet particular customer requirements. The brand, type, and product sizes are substitution parameters selected when creating the query with the QGEN application using the Seed variable. |
| Query 17—Small Quantity/Order Revenue | This query will find line item and part for a given brand and type and determine the average quantity of the parts ordered if the quantity is 20 percent less of the average for a seven-year period (the brand and container are substitution parameters selected when creating the query with the QGEN application using the Seed variable). |
| Query 18—Large-Volume Customer | This query will find the top 100 customers who have ever placed a large-quantity order (the quantity is the substitution parameter selected when creating the query with the QGEN application using the Seed variable). |
| Query 19—Discounted Revenue | This query will find the gross discounted revenue for all orders for three different types of parts (the part type, container, quantity, ship mode, and shipping instructions are substitution parameters selected when creating the query with the QGEN application using the Seed variable). |
| Query 20—Potential Part Promotion | This query will find the suppliers that have an excess of a given part available for a specific year (the part name and date are the substitution parameters selected when creating the query with the QGEN application using the Seed variable). |
| Query 21—Suppliers That Kept Orders Waiting | This query will find the suppliers, for a given country, whose product was part of a multiple supplier order where they failed to meet the committed delivery date (the country is a substitution parameter selected when creating the query with the QGEN application using the Seed variable). |
| Query 22—Global Sales Opportunity | This query will find the customers within a specific set of country codes who have not placed orders for seven years but still have a positive balance (the country codes are substitution parameters selected when creating the query with the QGEN application using the Seed variable). |

### No indexing

The nonindexing run was used as a baseline with which to compare an indexing run. The group knew that indexing would greatly decrease the time taken to complete the performance test but desired a quantitative result. At the time of this writing, no team had successfully completed a nonindexing run on any of the database systems. The procedures attempted are discussed later in the chapter. The primary reason for not completing a nonindexed test was lack of time. It was possible to complete an individual test of each of the queries in the performance test with no refreshes. These results are defined in greater detail in section 14.5.

### Indexing

As can be deduced from the previous section, if nonindexing was not completed neither was indexing. Representatives from each of the teams got together, however, to determine what should have been indexed. Their work is presented in Table 14.5 to provide future testers a hint as to what can be done next.

### Running all queries together

A Persistent Stored Modules (PSM) Committee was tasked to create a file that would run all queries using the TPC-H order, defined in the standard

**Table 14.5**   *Proposed Indexes for Benchmark Tests*

| |
|---|
| **Foreign Keys** |
| CREATE INDEX tpch.c_nk ON tpch.customer(c_nationkey ASC) |
| CREATE INDEX tpch.s_nk ON tpch.supplier(s_nationkey ASC) |
| CREATE INDEX tpch.ps_pk ON tpch.partsupp(ps_suppkey ASC) |
| CREATE INDEX tpch.ps_sk ON tpch.partsupp(ps_suppkey ASC) |
| CREATE INDEX tpch.1_ok ON tpch.lineitem(1_orderkey ASC) |
| **Primary Keys** |
| CREATE UNIQUE INDEX tpch.c_ck ON tpch.customer(c_custkey ASC) |
| CREATE UNIQUE INDEX tpch.p_pk ON tpch.part(p_partkey ASC) |
| CREATE UNIQUE INDEX tpch.s_sk ON tpch.supplier(s_suppkey ASC) |
| CREATE UNIQUE INDEX tpch.o_ok ON tpch.orderd(o_orderkey ASC) |
| CREATE UNIQUE INDEX tpch.ps_pk_sk ON tpch.partsupp(ps_partkey ASC, ps_suppkey ASC) |
| CERATE UNIQUE INDEX tpch.ps_sk_pk ON tpch.partsupp(ps_suppkey ASC, ps_partkey ASC) |
| **Useful Date Fields** |
| CREATE INDEX tpch.o_od ON tpch.orders(o_orderdate ASC) |
| CREATE INDEX tpch.1_sd ON tpch.lineitem(1_shipdate ASC) |

in Appendix A, for all the teams. This committee needed to determine how to keep track of the time each query ran, the total time, and how the refreshes would be handled. Unfortunately, the only team that was able to use the file was the Microsoft SQL Server team. The other teams would have had to modify the file tremendously in order for it to work on their databases. Due to a lack of time, the decision was made not to do this and instead run the queries individually.

### 14.4.3   Testbed procedures for each configuration

Four basic procedures were needed to run the benchmark on each separate configuration. First, the creation of the database and the database tables for the databases was needed. Second, the newly created tables were populated with the benchmark test data. Third, several sample runs on the individual queries were done to ensure that the systems were running properly and providing each team a way of optimizing the system prior to the test. Finally, the performance tests were run on each system.

## 14.5   The results

Table 14.6 shows the results of completed experiments by each of the teams for the four databases studied.

Note that the time for each query is measured in seconds. As can be seen from the table, a side-by-side comparison of the databases is not entirely possible. This is due to many factors, as will be discussed shortly. The major reason appears to be the memory use by each database. Only Microsoft and DB2 were able to acquire and use 100 percent of their available memory, while Oracle and Informix were able to use only one-third of the available memory. To compare all the database systems together some assumptions have been made. First, it is clearly visible by a cursory review that Microsoft SQL beats DB2 in performance from the results depicted in Table 14.6. Upon a more comprehensive review of the data presented in Table 14.6, we find that DB2 runs between 1.03 times faster than SQL Server down to 0.01 times the performance of SQL Server. Also note that DB2 only performs better than SQL Server for one test, test 18, which looks at large-volume customers. In all other cases SQL Server outperforms DB2 on average by 53 percent. Given these results, we can now focus on comparing Microsoft SQL against Informix and Oracle.

The assumption is to decrease the amount of memory that Microsoft SQL uses to the same level as Informix and Oracle. In doing this we use a

**Table 14.6**    *Results of the Testbed TPC-H Experiments*

| Query # | Informix | DB2 | SQL | Oracle |
|---|---|---|---|---|
| 1 | 510 | 510 | 431 | 335 |
| 2 | 21,600 | 3,180 | 44 | 81,840 |
| 3 | 3,180 | 842 | 465 | 532 |
| 4 | 1,530 | Error: unknown | 300 | 1,818 |
| 5 | Error: memory | Error: unknown | 314 | 20,040 |
| 6 | 250 | 388 | 245 | 269 |
| 7 | Error: unknown | Error: unknown | 311 | 466 |
| 8 | Error: syntax | 27,157 | 309 | Error: syntax |
| 9 | Error: syntax | 1,286 | 409 | Error: syntax |
| 10 | 2,760 | 30,672 | 316 | 529 |
| 11 | 95 | 144 | 41 | 199 |
| 12 | 480 | 453 | 298 | 464 |
| 13 | Not run | 126 | 89 | Error: syntax |
| 14 | 660 | 460 | 253 | 331 |
| 15 | 600 | 338 | 247 | 600 |
| 16 | 240 | 915 | 54 | 2,848 |
| 17 | Not run | 797 | 504 | 2,700 |
| 18 | 12,660 | 1,127 | 1,169 | 8,100 |
| 19 | 240 | 354 | 250 | 1,091 |
| 20 | Not run | 467 | 288 | Not run |
| 21 | Error: unknown | 1,569 | 809 | 1,560 |
| 22 | Error: unknown | 594 | 61 | Error: syntax |
| **CPU Use** | 100% | 100% | 100% | 100% |
| **Mem. Use** | 30% | 100% | 100% | 38% |

linear approach to find the new times. The theory is that if you cut the amount of memory by 50 percent, it will take twice as long. In these tests, since Informix and Oracle used one-third the memory of SQL Server, we assume that the time would be proportional to 3.33 times that of a system with one-third the memory. It should be noted that this has not been tested. Also, since not all queries could be run on Informix or Oracle, only those queries that ran on these systems have been taken into account. All other queries have been dropped. Keeping this in mind we have two new tables, Table 14.7 and Table 14.8, for Informix and Oracle.

**Table 14.7**    *Informix versus Reweighted SQL Server*

| Query # | Informix | SQL |
|---------|----------|-------|
| 1 | 510 | 1,437 |
| 2 | — | 147 |
| 3 | 3,180 | 1,550 |
| 4 | 1,530 | 1,000 |
| 5 | — | 1,047 |
| 6 | 250 | 817 |
| 7 | — | 1,037 |
| 8 | — | 1,030 |
| 9 | — | 1,363 |
| 10 | 2,760 | 1,053 |
| 11 | 95 | 137 |
| 12 | 480 | 993 |
| 13 | — | 297 |
| 14 | 660 | 843 |
| 15 | 600 | 823 |
| 16 | 240 | 180 |
| 17 | — | 1,680 |
| 18 | 12,660 | 3,897 |
| 19 | 240 | 833 |
| 20 | — | 960 |
| 21 | — | 2,697 |
| 22 | — | 203 |
| Mem. Use | 30% | 30% |

**Table 14.8**   *Oracle versus Scaled SQL Server*

| Query # | Oracle | SQL |
|---------|--------|------|
| 1 | 335 | 1,437 |
| 2 | 81,840 | 147 |
| 3 | 532 | 1,550 |
| 4 | 1,818 | 1,000 |
| 5 | 20,040 | 1,047 |
| 6 | 269 | 817 |
| 7 | 466 | 1,037 |
| 8 | — | 1,030 |
| 9 | — | 1,363 |
| 10 | 529 | 1,053 |
| 11 | 199 | 137 |
| 12 | 464 | 993 |
| 13 | — | 297 |
| 14 | 331 | 843 |
| 15 | 600 | 823 |
| 16 | 2,848 | 180 |
| 17 | 2,700 | 1,680 |
| 18 | 8,100 | 3,897 |
| 19 | 1,091 | 833 |
| 20 | — | 960 |
| 21 | 1,560 | 2,697 |
| 22 | — | 203 |
| Mem. Use | 38% | 38% |

Comparing Informix against Microsoft SQL Server using the recomputed performance values, we see that 7 of the 12 queries ran faster on Informix than on Microsoft SQL Server. As can be seen in Figure 14.7, Informix is 67 percent faster. If we look more closely at these data, we can see that the Informix database performs between 3.4 times faster down to 0.3 times the speed of the scaled SQL Server. The overall weighted differ-

**Figure 14.7**
*Informix versus
Microsoft SQL
Server.*

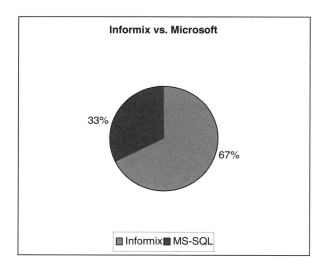

ence places Informix's performance at 1.48 times that of the SQL Server's scaled performance.

Comparing Oracle against Microsoft SQL Server using the recomputed performance values, we see that 9 of the 17 queries run faster on Oracle than on Microsoft SQL Server. As can be seen in Figure 14.8, Oracle is computed to be 57 percent faster on average. If we look more closely at these data, we can see that the Oracle database system performs between 4.2 times faster down to 0.001 times the speed of the scaled SQL Server. The

**Figure 14.8**
*Oracle versus
Microsoft SQL
Server.*

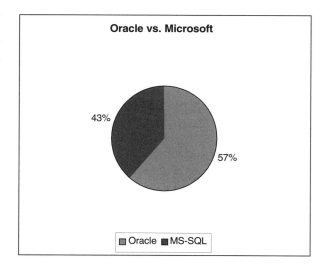

overall weighted difference places Oracle's performance at 1.76 times that of the SQL Server's scaled performance.

Thus, under our assumptions utilized to perform this weighted analysis, both Informix and Oracle perform better than SQL Server under most conditions. We still need to determine whether Informix's database is superior to Oracle's database given the same comparisons. To do this analysis we have normalized both databases' data to run at 100 percent memory use. Table 14.9 shows the new weighted results.

Comparing Informix against Oracle using the recomputed performance values, we see that 9 of the 12 queries ran faster on Oracle than on Infor-

**Table 14.9**   *Informix versus Oracle*

| Query # | Informix | Oracle |
|---------|----------|--------|
| 1       | 1,700    | 882    |
| 2       | —        | —      |
| 3       | 10,600   | 1,400  |
| 4       | 5,100    | 4,784  |
| 5       | —        | —      |
| 6       | 833      | 708    |
| 7       | —        | —      |
| 8       | —        | —      |
| 9       | —        | —      |
| 10      | 9,200    | 1,392  |
| 11      | 317      | 524    |
| 12      | 1,600    | 1,221  |
| 13      | —        | —      |
| 14      | 2,200    | 871    |
| 15      | 2,000    | 1,579  |
| 16      | 800      | 7,495  |
| 17      | —        | —      |
| 18      | 42,200   | 21,316 |

**Table 14.9**    *Informix versus Oracle (continued)*

| Query # | Informix | Oracle |
|---------|----------|--------|
| 19      | 800      | 2,871  |
| 20      | —        | —      |
| 21      | —        | —      |
| 22      | —        | —      |
| Mem. Use | 100%    | 100%   |

mix. As can be seen in Figure 14.9, Oracle is 75 percent faster on average than Informix. If we look more closely at these data, we can see that the Oracle database performs between 7.7 times faster down to 1.07 times the speed of the scaled Informix Server for all but two queries. For query 16 (parts/supplier) and for query 18 (large-volume customer) the Informix database ran significantly faster than Oracle: from 3.5 to 9.36 times faster to be exact. However, since these seem to be outlier queries, we computed the overall performance measures by removing the effect of these two and Oracle's two best performing queries. The overall weighted difference places Oracle's performance at 1.38 times that of Informix's Dynamic Server scaled performance. Thus, Oracle is the winner in terms of performance using these assumptions and tests.

**Figure 14.9**
*Informix versus Oracle.*

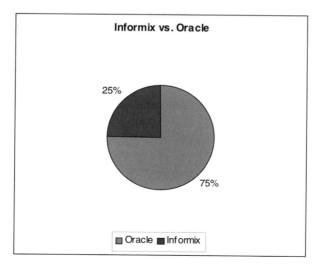

## 14.5.1   Cost versus performance

Of course, performance is not everything. Cost must be taken into account. To consider cost we obtained a rough value for the purchase cost per database system and then computed a cost per second for performance.

To provide a rough comparison on cost we have averaged the amount of time it takes each database to run all of the queries used in the models and then used that value to divide the purchase cost (Table 14.10).

**Table 14.10**   *Cost/Performance Comparison*

| Query # | Informix | DB2 | SQL | Oracle |
|---------|----------|-----|-----|--------|
| 1 | 510 | 1,700 | 1,437 | 424 |
| 2 | 21,600 | 10,600 | 147 | 103,664 |
| 3 | 3,180 | 2,807 | 1,550 | 674 |
| 4 | 1,530 | 0 | 1,000 | 2,303 |
| 5 | 0 | 0 | 1,407 | 25,384 |
| 6 | 250 | 1,293 | 817 | 341 |
| 7 | 0 | 0 | 1,037 | 590 |
| 8 | 0 | 90,523 | 1,030 | 0 |
| 9 | 0 | 4,287 | 1,363 | 0 |
| 10 | 2,760 | 102,240 | 1,053 | 670 |
| 11 | 95 | 480 | 137 | 252 |
| 12 | 480 | 1,510 | 993 | 588 |
| 13 | 0 | 420 | 297 | 0 |
| 14 | 660 | 1,553 | 843 | 419 |
| 15 | 600 | 1,127 | 823 | 760 |
| 16 | 240 | 3,050 | 180 | 3,607 |
| 17 | 0 | 2,657 | 1,680 | 3,420 |
| 18 | 12,660 | 3,757 | 3,897 | 10,260 |
| 19 | 240 | 1,180 | 833 | 1,382 |
| 20 | 0 | 1,557 | 960 | 0 |

**Table 14.10**   *Cost/Performance Comparison (continued)*

| Query # | Informix | DB2 | SQL | Oracle |
|---|---|---|---|---|
| 21 | 0 | 5,230 | 2,697 | 1,976 |
| 22 | 0 | 1,980 | 203 | 0 |
| Total Time: | 44,805 | 237,930 | 24,023 | 156,715 |
| Avg. Time: | 3,447 | 12,523 | 1,092 | 9,219 |
| Cost of DB: | 128,000 | 105,000 | 86,000 | 105,000 |
| $/Sec: | $37.14 | $8.38 | $78.76 | $11.30 |

Note that when taking the average time for each database, those queries that had 0 value were not taken into account. Table 14.10 shows that the cheapest DB in terms of cost and performance is DB2, followed by Oracle, Informix, and then Microsoft.

## 14.6   Summary

Based on the assumptions we made to compare IBM DB2 and Microsoft SQL Server 2000 with Informix UDB and Oracle 8i, it is clear that on a performance and cost level IBM's DB2 is the best choice. Of course, this is subject to interpretation. If you are not concerned with memory use on your system or do not care about configuring your system, then Microsoft SQL Server can be very appealing, since you can plug and play and be ready to go with it. Using IBM's DB2 requires more administration before the performance shown in this chapter is achieved. Ultimately, it depends on what one plans to do with the database that becomes the decision factor.

# 15

# *Analysis of Computer Networks Components*

Earlier chapters introduced the basic concepts and theories embodied in analytical modeling. Addressed were basic concepts in queuing systems theory, its application to computer systems modeling, and an introduction to network modeling. This chapter will address the use of analytical and simulation models specifically from the viewpoint of use as performance evaluation tools.

## 15.1  Introduction

In the past several years, the use of analytical performance models instead of the more widely used and familiar methods has become increasingly popular because of their relative simplicity of implementation and robustness of applications. These analytical models have been successful in estimation of such performance measures as throughputs, average queue lengths, and mean response times for a real system. This chapter is an introduction to queuing techniques for the modeling of computer communication networks, not an in-depth study.

The use of modeling to describe and imitate a real system has been with us since the beginning of the information revolution. These models are used not only to measure the performance of existing systems but also as part of the design and development of new systems. This latter goal is best attained through the use of analytical queuing models, as we will see in the following discussion of methods of performance evaluation.

The major performance evaluation tools (see Figure 15.1) other than queuing models are rules of thumb, linear projection, simulation, and benchmarking. These methods are listed in order of increasing complexity and implementation difficulty. The rules of thumb have been defined by the observation of operational systems and can be generally applied to local

**Figure 15.1**
*Spectrum of computer system modeling techniques.*

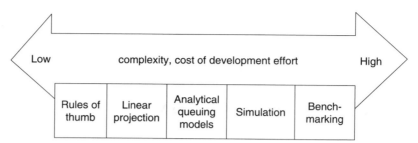

systems and extrapolated to distributed systems and networks. These rules take the following form:

1.   Generally, channel use in direct access storage devices (DASD) should not exceed 35 percent for on-line and 40 percent for batch applications.

2.   Individual DASD devices used should not exceed 35 percent.

3.   Average arm seek time on a DASD device should not exceed 50 cylinders.

4.   No block size for auxiliary storage should exceed 4 Kbytes.

These rules are useful in that they are easy to apply, economical to use, and can be applied to day-to-day operations. They are limited in the sense that they cannot be used to predict the usefulness of hardware or software upgrades.

The linear projection method has been used to pick up on the rules of thumb at the prediction limitation point. Although results can be obtained, the accuracy of the results is limited by the fact that a linear projection is used to predict the behavior of inherently nonlinear systems. This method also requires the availability of an existing system to measure the pertinent performance criteria to be used as a base for the projection and estimation of future resource requirements.

For simulation and benchmarking, there is no absolute distinction between development and implementation costs. Simulation allows the model to contain much more detail than the other methods, but this may not be an advantage when compared with queuing methods, where it has been found that too much information just serves to cloud the issue. Some simulation models are as large and cumbersome as the system they are modeling. The benchmarking method is the oldest and most used, but it is usually only helpful in the selection of the best hardware to process a known load. This is to say that the method requires existing hardware and, therefore, is not useful in the evaluation of hardware updates.

With the previous comments on other existing performance evaluation tools, we can assess the placement of queuing models and their overall usefulness. Queuing models reside between linear projection and simulation in terms of cost and complexity of implementation. Queuing models may be much simpler than the system they are modeling, because only the most pertinent performance parameters need to be accounted for. Not only do queuing models have a place in the evaluation of existing systems, but they also may be used in the design and development phase of new systems to help in the selection of hardware and hardware-software interaction to avoid system bottlenecks.

Recent advances in analytical modeling techniques are making analytical models increasingly capable of representing more and more aspects of the modeled system. Consequently, these techniques have been growing in popularity.

One method commonly used in system design is queuing analysis. Queuing models are more precise than other analytical techniques that predict performance based on average values [21]. One reason is that queuing models allow greater detail to be used in describing systems, and, hence, they capture the more important features of the system. Often, several submodels are required, as follows:

1.    Workload model. Specifies the characteristics of the resource demands on various equipment found in the system.

2.    Configuration or system structure model. Specifies the hardware characteristics of the system.

3.    Scheduling model. Specifies the scheduling algorithms whereby resources are allocated.

Queuing models can be categorized as either deterministic or stochastic in nature. If the design parameters to the model are known from prior experience or measurements, a deterministic analysis of the system may be carried out. Conversely, if the design parameters are not known, a stochastic analysis using various probability distributions is normally required.

Typical design parameters would include such items as:

1.    Interarrival rate of events

2.    Service times of these events

3.    Number of servers being modeled

4.    System capacity (i.e., number of events currently being processed and in queues)

5.    Queuing discipline employed (i.e., FIFO, LIFO, etc.)

Normally, queuing models provide some of the following performance attributes:

1.    Average queue lengths

2.    Average waiting time in queues

3.    Use statistics

4.    Average response times

Although queuing models have one overriding advantage in that they are cheap to use, there are a number of significant limitations to this method, as follows:

1.    Because these models assume the system has reached a steady state or equilibrium, peak or transient conditions are not modeled.

2.    These models are limited as to the complexity of the problems that can be solved. As problems become more complex or additional details are required, other methods must be used to model the systems.

3.    Without actually measuring various design parameters, it is difficult to determine whether the characteristics of the data used will represent the system under investigation.

# 15.2    Analytical modeling examples

To better understand how these techniques can be used to model and analyze a system, we will undertake two studies: one for the early well-known Honeywell Experimental Distributed Processing system (HXDP) and the other for the token bus. In both cases, similar quantities are sought—namely, average scan time (time for control to sequence around once) versus message size. The intent is to analyze the efficiency of the control protocol and network characteristics.

## 15.2.1    HXDP model

### Introduction

The HXDP system consists of processors connected to interface units that are joined by a bit-serial global bus. Bus allocation is governed by the vector-driven proportional access mechanism. Prior to system initialization, the 256-bit vectors are set for each processor so that for each time slice one, and only one, interface unit has a 1 in its index. The number of different schedules (possible combinations of 1s and 0s) for a system containing $N$ interface units is, therefore, theoretically equal to $N \times N^{256}$, which is exorbitant even when $N = 2$. This scheme, however, cycles through the same pattern over and over again. Nonetheless, rather than develop a model allowing for any of the possible schedules, it was decided to constrain the allowable schedules to ease the computation.

It is assumed, consequently, that the schedule mechanism is as follows: Every interface unit is assigned a 1 only once in the index, after which the initial pattern repeats itself until the 256th index for processor $N$ is set; this pattern is termed a scan block. The interface units, in turn, are sequentially logically numbered and are given a logical unit number.

One illustration of such a schedule with the corresponding scan blocks would be for four IUs (see Figure 15.2). One schedule would contain 256/4 = 64 scan blocks. Another schedule might be as shown in Figure 15.3. The sequence of events in the constrained system is then as follows: The reallocation signal arrives at logical unit 1 (the IU with the first 1 bit); if there is a message waiting service, the interface unit is granted the bus and the message is serviced. Once the message arrives at the destination, an acknowledgment is sent back to the source, after which a reallocation signal is sent out, the index is updated, and the next logical IU gets bus access. The sequence proceeds until IU $N$ is serviced, after which (because of the assumptions) logical unit 1 is serviced. This continues ad infinitum.

**Figure 15.2**
*Scan blocks.*

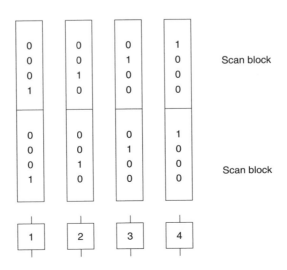

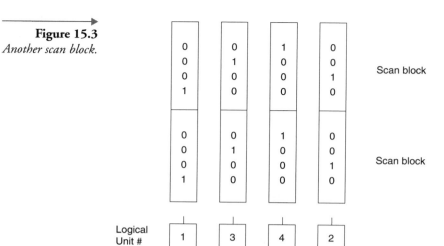

**Figure 15.3**
*Another scan block.*

The scan time is, then, the time it takes to scan through the logical sequence of IUs once—that is, through the scan block. Table 15.1 lists the terms and their definitions.

**Table 15.1**   *Symbols and Their Definitions*

| Symbol | Definition |
| --- | --- |
| $N$ | Number of interface units in the system |
| $T_{si}$ | Time requirement to service a message at interface unit $i$ |
| $T_{ri}$ | Time delay associated with the reallocation signal passing from interface unit with logical sequence $i$ to $i + 1$ |
| $\lambda_i$ | Average message arrival rate at interface unit $i$ |
| $\tau$ | Time to scan through entire sequence of IUs |
| $\bar{\tau}$ | Average or expected scan |
| $\partial_i$ | Set equal to 1 or 0 depending on whether IU has message awaiting transmittal or not |
| $T_s$ | The time it takes to send the message of predetermined constant size from $IU_i$ to $IU_{i+1}$ separated by distance $d$ |
| $T_{\text{ack}}$ | The time it takes to send the acknowledgment from $IU_i$ to $IU_{i+1}$ separated by distance $d$ |
| $T_R$ | The time it takes to send the reallocation signal from $IU_i$ to $IU_{i+1}$ separated by distance $d$ |
| $P$ | The probability of an arbitrary interface unit requiring service during one scan |

### Analytical modeling of the HXDP bus

It is assumed that the messages are arriving at an exponential rate. The probability that an arbitrary interface unit will require service during one scan is:

$$P = \int_{-\infty}^{\infty} \left(1 - e^{-\lambda t}\right) f_\tau(t) \, dt \tag{15.1}$$

where $f_\tau(t)$ is the probability density function of the scan time. For $\lambda t$ small, we use the approximation that $e^{-\lambda t} \cong 1 - \lambda t$. Thus:

$$P = \int_{-\infty}^{\infty} \left(1 - e^{-\lambda t}\right) f_\tau(t) \, dt = \lambda \overline{\tau} \tag{15.2}$$

For varying message arrival rates $= \lambda_i$, this evaluation becomes:

$$P_i = \int_{-\infty}^{\infty} \lambda_i t f_\tau(t) \, dt = \lambda_i \overline{\tau} \tag{15.3}$$

$\nabla \tau_i$, which is the segment of the scan time that can be attributed to $IU_i$, is:

$$\nabla \tau_i = \xi_i \left(T_{si} + T_{ack}\right) + T_r \tag{15.4}$$

where $T_{ack}$ is the time it takes for acknowledgment (ack) to be sent back to $i$, if there was a message received, and $T_r$ is the time it takes for the reallocation signal to go from IU logical number $i$ to IU logical $i + 1$. But $\xi_i$ can only take on values 0 or 1, and we assume that a uniform destination distribution and an IU in the HXDP system communicates with itself via the bus:

$$E\left(\xi_i \left(T_{si} + T_{ack}\right)\right) = \frac{1}{N} \sum_{k=1}^{N} \left(|i - k|\left(T_s + T_{ack}\right)\right) P_i \tag{15.5}$$

This implies that:

$$\tau = 1/N \sum_{i=1}^{N} \sum_{k=1}^{N} \left(|i - k|\left(T_s + T_{ack}\right)\right) P_I + \sum_{i=1}^{N} |i - (i+1)| T_R \tag{15.6}$$

where $|i - k|$ represents the number of interface units away from the source interface unit $i$ where interface unit $k$ is located.

Substituting $\lambda_i \bar{\tau} = P_i$ we get:

$$\bar{\tau} = \frac{\tau(T_s + T_{\text{ack}})}{N} \sum_{i=1}^{N} \left( i^2 + (1+N)(-i + (1/2)N) \right) \lambda_i$$

$$+ \sum_{i=1}^{N} |i - (i+1)| T_R \tag{15.7}$$

Thus:

$$\tau = \frac{\sum_{i=1}^{N} |i - (i+1)| T_R}{1 - \left( (T_s + T_{\text{ack}})/N \right) \left( \sum_{k=1}^{N} \left( k^2 + (1+N)(-k + (1/2)N) \right) \lambda_k \right)} \tag{15.8}$$

where index $i$ denotes the logical number of the interface unit.

The main constraint on the model is:

$$\left( (T_s + T_{\text{ack}})/N \right) \left( \sum_{k=1}^{N} \left( k^2 + (1+N)(-k + (1/2)N) \right) \right) \lambda_k \ll 1 \tag{15.9}$$

The effect on the average scan time, $\tau$, can now be determined by varying any combination of the following parameters:

1.      The number of interface units, $N$

2.      The arrival rates, $\lambda_k$

3.      The logical numbering of the interface units

4.      The distances between neighboring interface units

5.      The average size of the arriving messages

### Graphic outputs

Figures 15.4 through 15.7 show the resultant computations for the scan time versus the message size for various changes in arrival rate, processor location, and quantity. These results will be compared with those of the simulator described later in this chapter.

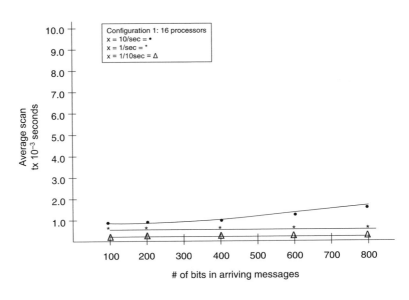

**Figure 15.4**
*Scan time versus message size, configuration 1.*

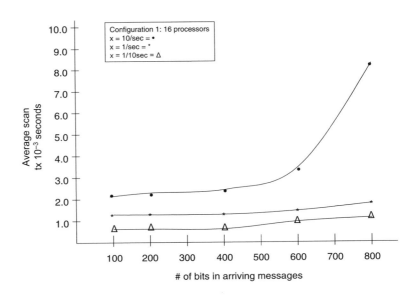

**Figure 15.5**
*Scan time versus message size, configuration 2.*

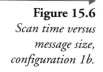

**Figure 15.6**
*Scan time versus
message size,
configuration 1b.*

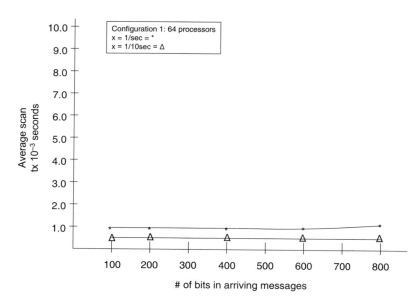

**Figure 15.7**
*Scan time versus
message size,
configuration 2b.*

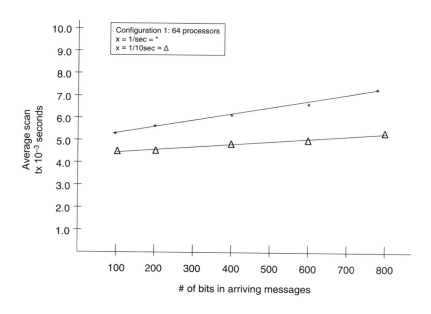

## 15.2.2   Token bus distributed system

### Introduction

The token bus distributed processing system (a local computer network) consists of processors connected to interface units, which, in turn, are connected by a common communications medium: the global bus. The allocation of the bus is controlled by the cyclic passing of tokens in a sequential manner from lowest numbered interface unit (IU) to the next highest until all numbered IUs have been interrogated and serviced. The sequential numbering is determined during power-up, and once steady state has been reached may be assumed to remain constant for modeling purposes. If an IU requires no service, control is passed to the next IU with an associated delay. The time it takes for the control to pass through the sequence completely is termed the scan time (as previously discussed).

Rather than investigating the entire token bus system, per se, emphasis will be on the bus, or the IU and bus layer, for modeling purposes. The main body of the example documents the development of the analytical models—in particular, the solution of the models for the value of the average scan time. The analytical computation of the scan time allows one to further determine such interesting and practical bus parameters as average message waiting time, average queue length, and bus use. From the derived formulas, one can readily ascertain the effect on bus parameters of increasing the number of processors, altering the sequential placement of processors, or varying the message arrival rates.

### Preliminary formulations and definitions

The message arriving at the processor is assumed to follow a Poisson distribution—in other words:

$$P(r,t) = \frac{(\lambda t)^R e^{-\lambda t}}{R!} \quad (R = 0,1,2,\ldots) \tag{15.10}$$

where $P(r,t)$ is the probability that $r$ messages arrive in time $t$, with each message being of the same size.

Service is required if there are one or more message arrivals in time $t$ or:

$$p(1 \text{ or more arrivals, } t) = 1 - P(0,t),$$

which, in turn, $= 1 - \left((\lambda t)^0 / 0!\right)e^{-\lambda t} = 1 - e^{-\lambda t}$ \tag{15.11}

Since the assumption is that steady state has been reached, we can let $f\lambda(t)$ denote the probability density function of the scan time $\tau$. The corresponding cumulative distribution is then equal to:

$$
\begin{aligned}
F\lambda(t) &= P(\tau \le t); \\
dF_\tau/dt &= f_\tau(t); \\
F\lambda(t) &= \int_{u=-\infty}^{t} f_\tau(u)\,du
\end{aligned}
\tag{15.12}
$$

Let $P$ denote the probability of an arbitrary processor requiring service during one scan:

$$
P = \int_{-\infty}^{\infty} \left(1 - e^{-\lambda t}\right) f_\tau(t)\,dt
\tag{15.13}
$$

If more than one arrival occurs at any processor in any scan, that arrival can be considered blocked. This message will then have to wait at least one scan time before it can be placed on the bus. This implies that:

$$
P(\text{blocking}) = P(\text{more than one arrival in scan time})
\tag{15.14}
$$

$$
\begin{aligned}
P\left(\begin{array}{c}\text{more than one message}\\\text{requiring service in time } t\end{array}\right) &= 1 - \left[P(0,t) + P(1,t)\right] \\
&= 1 - \left[e^{-\lambda t} + \lambda t e^{-\lambda t}\right]
\end{aligned}
\tag{15.15}
$$

To enable the evaluation of $P$, for $e^{-\lambda t} \cong 1-\lambda t$, implies that:

$$
P = \int_{-\infty}^{\infty} \left(1 - e^{-\lambda t}\right) f_\tau(t)\,dt = \int_{-\infty}^{\infty} \lambda t f_\tau(t)\,dt
\tag{15.16}
$$

which is equal to $\lambda\overline{\tau}$, by definition of expected value.

The relationship of $P \approx \lambda\overline{\tau}$ will be used for all the models for simplification purposes. For clarity and convenience, Table 15.2 contains the symbols and their corresponding definitions, which will be used in the development of the analytical models.

### Analytical modeling of the token bus

The analytical models developed for the token bus will be presented in an order reflecting an increasing degree of complexity and, consequently, a relaxation of the corresponding mathematical assumptions. In each of the

**Table 15.2**   *Symbols and Their Definitions*

| Symbol | Definition |
|---|---|
| $N$ | Number of processors and consequently number of interface units due to a one-to-one correspondence in the system |
| $T_s$ | The time required to service a message at an interface unit |
| $T_{si}$ | The time required to service a message at an interface unit $i$ |
| $T_c$ | Time delay associated with control (token) passing from an interface unit to its physically nearest neighbor interface unit |
| $T_{ci}$ | Time delay associated with control (token) passing from an interface unit with logical sequence number $i$ to its neighbor interface unit $i + 1$ |
| $\lambda$ | Average message arrival rate at interface unit |
| $\lambda_i$ | Average message arrival rate at interface unit $i$ |
| $\tau$ | Time to scan through entire sequence of IUs |
| $\overline{\tau}$ | Average or expected scan |
| $\partial_i$ | Set equal to 1 or 0 depending upon whether IU has message awaiting transmittal or not |
| $d$ | Distance between interface units $i$ and $i + 1$ |
| $t_s$ | The time it takes to send the message of predetermined constant size from $\mathrm{IU}_i$ to $\mathrm{IU}_{i+1}$ separated by distance $d$ |
| $UF$ | Bus use factor |
| $P$ | The probability of an arbitrary interface unit requiring service during one scan |

models, a steady state, constant message size, and equal spacing between processors will be assumed. In addition, once the IU has been given control of the bus, it will be assumed that the message buffer for the interface unit will be emptied instantaneously onto the bus. The underlying specific assumptions in each case will be clearly outlined.

## Case 1

In the basic analytical model, it will be assumed that the arrival rate of messages at each of the $N$ interface units is equivalent and is represented by $\lambda$. In addition, it is assumed that once steady state has been reached, the sequential (logical) numbering of the interface units is identical to the physical numbering (spatial numbering from left to right)—that is, it follows the representation shown in Figure 15.8.

**Figure 15.8**
*Physical and logical numbering of interface units.*

Interface unit physical number

Interface unit logical sequence number

If we let $T_c$ denote the time delay associated with the token (control) passing from one interface unit to another, the $T_{ci}$ for each interface unit may be considered the same, since it has been assumed that the processors are equidistant from one another, and, consequently, the control will need to traverse the same distance from a processor to its next (with next highest sequence number) neighbor.

Another essential time parameter is the time it takes to service a message for any interface unit. In a ring topology with a token-passing scheme one could consider $T_s$, which is the time required to service a processor, to average out to the same value over time for all processors. Reference [22] shows that the same conclusion cannot be reached for the bus topology. Time to service a message is a function to the destination IU. Therefore, the placement of the source IU within the bus topology will affect the average time it takes to service one of its messages. For example, if $N = 3$, we have the configuration shown in Figure 15.9.

For interface unit 1 to transmit a message to processor 2, the message will have to traverse the distance from 1 to 2; for interface unit 1 to transmit a message to 3, it will have to traverse the distance from 1 to 3. If we represent the equal distance between two neighboring interface units as $d$, and we let each of the other IUs be potential similar message destinations (e.g., a uniform distribution for message destinations is assumed):

$$E\left(T_s \middle| \text{source} = 1\right)$$
$$= \frac{1}{2}\left(\left(d/\text{velocity estimate}\right) + 1/2\left(2d/\text{velocity estimate}\right)\right) \tag{15.17}$$

where $d/\text{velocity estimate} = t_s$ = time to send the message of the chosen size from $i$ to $i + 1$:

$$= \frac{1}{2}t_s + t_s = 3/2\,t_s \tag{15.18}$$

For processor 2, as the source processor, the corresponding equation becomes:

$$E\left(T_s \middle| \text{source} = 2\right) = \frac{1}{2}t_s + \frac{1}{2}t_s = t_s \tag{15.19}$$

**Figure 15.9**
*Token bus with*
*three interface*
*units.*

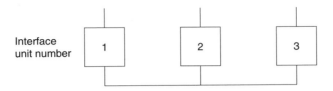

Interface
unit number

Let $T_{si}$ denote the time it takes to service a message at interface unit $i$. The time it takes for the token to pass from the $i$th IU to the $i + 1$st interface unit may then be expressed as:

$$\nabla\tau_i = \xi_i T_{si} + T_c \text{ where}$$
$$\xi_i = \begin{cases} 1, \text{ if IU has a message awaiting transmittal;} \\ 0, \text{ otherwise} \end{cases} \tag{15.20}$$

The total scan time becomes:

$$\tau = \sum_{i=1}^{N}\nabla\tau_i \text{ or } \tau = \sum_{i=1}^{N}\left(\xi_i T_{si} + T_c\right) \tag{15.21}$$

Now, taking expectations of both sides of equation (15.21) we get the average value of scan time $\overline{\tau}$ as:

$$\overline{\tau} = \sum_{i=1}^{N}E\left(\xi_i T_{si}\right) + \sum_{i=1}^{N}E\left(T_c\right) = \sum_{i=1}^{N}E\left(\xi_i T_{si}\right) + NT_c \tag{15.22}$$

Next, by definition of the expected value of product:

$$E\left(\xi_i T_{si}\right) = \sum_{\xi_i}\sum_{T_{si}}\xi_i T_{si}P\left(\xi_i T_{si}\right) \tag{15.23}$$

Since it was mentioned previously that $T_{si}$ is a function of the distance that the message has to travel, and since $\xi_i$ can only take on the value 0 to 1:

$$E\left(\xi_i T_{si}\right) = \frac{1}{N-1}\sum_{k=1}^{N}|i - k|\, t_s P \tag{15.24}$$

where $i - k$ represents the number of interface units away from the source interface unit $i$, the destination interface unit $k$ is located, and any interface unit other than $i$ has an equally likely probability of being a destination interface unit. That is, a probability $1/N - 1$.

$P$ is the probability derived in the preliminary formulation. In summary:

$$\bar{\tau} = \frac{1}{N-1}\sum_{i=1}^{N}\sum_{k=1}^{N}|i-k|t_s\,P + NT_c$$

$$= \frac{t_s p}{N-1}\sum_{i=1}^{N}\sum_{k=1}^{N}|i-k|NT_c \tag{15.25}$$

$$= \frac{t_s P}{N-1}\left(\frac{N^3-N}{3}\right) + NT_c$$

$$= t_s P\big(N(N+1)\big)/3 + NT_c$$

Substituting $P \approx \lambda\bar{\tau}$ into (15.25):

$$\bar{\tau} = t_s\lambda\bar{\tau}\big(N(N+1)\big)/3 + NT_c$$

$$\bar{\tau} = \big(1 - \big(t_s\lambda\big(N(N+1)\big)/3\big)\big) + NT_c \tag{15.26}$$

$$\bar{\tau} = (NT_c)\big/\big(1 - \lambda\big(N(N+1)t_s\big)/3\big)$$

This equation is valid, based upon the assumption and approximations if, and only if:

$$\big(\lambda\big(N(N+1)t_s\big)/3\big) \ll 1 \tag{15.27}$$

### Case II

In this model, we relax the assumptions that all the interface units have identical message arrival rates equal to $\lambda$, by allowing for message arrival rates of $\lambda_i$ for interface unit $i$. However, we retain the assumption of the hypothetical, logical, or physical configuration, which, in turn, will be eliminated in the subsequent case. The relaxation of the assumptions is being done in a gradual manner to emphasize the evolutionary nature of the development of the analytical models. The relaxation of the equivalent message arrival rates will allow for a greater realm of applicability and consequently, of testing but will, naturally, complicate the ultimate formula for $\tau$.

Since each interface unit now has a characteristic message arrival rate, $\lambda_i$ for interface unit $i$, $P$ now becomes:

$$P_i = \int_{-\infty}^{\infty} \big(1 - e^{-\lambda_i t}\big) f_\tau(t)dt \tag{15.28}$$

$$P_i \cong \lambda_i \bar{\tau}$$

Equation (15.21) is still applicable—that is:

$$\tau = \sum_{i=2}^{N} \nabla \tau_i = \sum_{i=1}^{N} \left( \xi_i T_{si} + T_c \right) \tag{15.29}$$

Furthermore, $\tau$ is still:

$$\tau = \sum_{i=1}^{N} E\left( \xi_i T_{si} \right) + N T_c \tag{15.30}$$

where:

$$E\left( \xi_i T_{si} \right) = \left( \frac{1}{N-1} \right) \sum_{k=1}^{N} |i - k| t_s P_i \tag{15.31}$$

$$\overline{\tau} = \sum_{i=1}^{N} \left( \frac{1}{N-1} \right) \sum_{k=1}^{N} \left( |i - k| t_s P_i \right) N T_c \tag{15.32}$$

$$\tau = \left( \frac{t_s}{N-1} \right) \sum_{i=1}^{N} \left( i^2 + (1+N)\left( -i + ((1/2)N) \right) P_i \right) + N T_c \tag{15.33}$$

Substituting $\lambda_i \overline{\tau} \cong P_i$

$$\overline{\tau} = \left( \frac{\tau t_s}{N-1} \right) \sum_{i=1}^{N} \left( i^2 + (1+N)\left( -i + ((1/2)N) \right) \lambda_i \right) + N T_c \tag{15.34}$$

Thus,

$$\overline{\tau} = \frac{N T_c}{1 - \left( \dfrac{t_s}{N-1} \right)\left( \displaystyle\sum_{i=1}^{N} \left( i^2 + (1+N)\left( -i + ((1/2)N)\lambda_i \right) \right) \right)} \tag{15.35}$$

## Case III

This model incorporates major modifications, which should permit the model to better reflect the actual system. In particular, it is assumed that once steady state has been reached, the logical numbering does not have to reflect the physical location, but, in fact, the steady-state configuration could be as shown in Figure 15.10.

The logical sequence numbering of the token bus system may assume any out of the $N!$ possible, different choices of the steady state with an

**Figure 15.10**
*Mapping logical to physical location.*

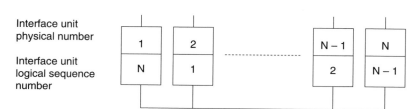

equal probability. Therefore, it is of the utmost importance to develop a model that can reflect all $N!$ of the possible combinations.

Consequently, $T_c$, now, is not a constant but must in some sense reflect the time it takes for the token to travel the distance from interface unit $i$ to interface unit $i + 1$.

Let $i$ represent the logical sequence number of the interface unit; then $\nabla \tau_i = \xi_i T_{si} + T_{ci}$; where $T_{ci}$ = the time for a token to traverse the distance from the IU with logical sequence $i$ to the IU with logical sequence $i + 1$ ($N + 1$ becomes IU 1).

In the previous models, the logical sequence number and the physical number of the interface units were identical; therefore, it was not necessary to state explicitly the correspondence of the index $i$.

The total scan time is now expressed by:

$$\tau = \sum_{i=1}^{N} \nabla \tau_i \text{ or } \tau = \sum_{i=1}^{N} \xi_i T_{si} + T_{ci} \tag{15.36}$$

The average value of scan time equals:

$$\overline{\tau} = \sum_{i=1}^{N} E\left(\xi_i T_{si}\right) + \sum_{i=1}^{N} E\left(T_{ci}\right) \tag{15.37}$$

which, for a known configuration, is equal to:

$$\overline{\tau} = \sum_{i=1}^{N} E\left(\xi_i T_{si}\right) + \sum_{i=1}^{N} \left|i - (i+1)\right| t_c \tag{15.38}$$

$N + 1$ denotes 1, due to cycling, where $t_c$ is the time it takes for the control to pass from any interface unit $k$ to physical unit $k + 1$.

We have previously evaluated:

$$\tau = \sum_{i=1}^{N} E\left(\xi_i T_{si}\right) \tag{15.39}$$

and, in order to take advantage of the results, the index $k$ will denote the physical number of the interface unit, while the index $i$ will denote the logical number of it.

Combining the results and making the substitution:

$$\lambda_k \overline{\tau} = P_k \tag{15.40}$$

we get:

$$\overline{\tau} = \frac{\displaystyle\sum_{i=1}^{N} |i - (i+1)| t_c}{1 - \left(\dfrac{t_s}{N-1}\right)\left(\displaystyle\sum_{k=1}^{N} \left(k^2 + (1+N)(-k + (1/2)N)\lambda_k\right)\right)} \tag{15.41}$$

From equation (15.41), the effect on the average scan time can be determined by varying any combination of the following variables:

1.     The number of interface units, $N$

2.     The arrival rates, $\lambda_k$, of the messages at the interface units with logical numbers, $k$

3.     Varying the logical sequential numbering of the interface units

4.     Varying the distances between neighboring interface units

5.     Varying the average size of the messages arriving at the interface units

The main constraint of the model is:

$$\left(\frac{t_s}{N-1}\right)\left(\sum_{k=1}^{N} \left(k^2 + (1+N)(-k + ((1/2)N)\lambda_k) << 1\right)\right) \tag{15.42}$$

## 15.3   Simulation modeling of local area networks

### 15.3.1   Computer networks (the model)

A computer network can be considered to be any interconnection of an assembly of computing elements (systems, terminals, etc.) together with communications facilities that provide intra- and internetwork communications.

These networks range in organization from two processors sharing a memory to large numbers of relatively independent computers connected over geographically long distances. (The computing elements themselves may be networks, in which case it is possible to have recursive systems of networks ad infinitum.) The basic attributes of a network that distinguish its architecture include its topology or overall organization, composition, size, channel type and utilization strategy, and control mechanism.

Using the nomenclature and taxonomy discussed for computer interconnection structures, a particular system can be characterized by its transfer strategy (direct or indirect), transfer control mechanism (centralized or decentralized), and its transfer path structure (dedicated or shared). Various network topologies, such as ring, bus, and star, are seen as embodiments of unique combinations of these characteristics (see Figure 15.11).

Network composition can be either heterogeneous or homogeneous, depending on either the similarity of the nodes or the attached computing elements. Network size generally refers to the number of nodes or computing elements. With respect to its communications channels, a network may be homogeneous or it may employ a variety of media. Overall network control or management is usually either highly centralized or completely distributed. If the hardware used for passing line control from one device to

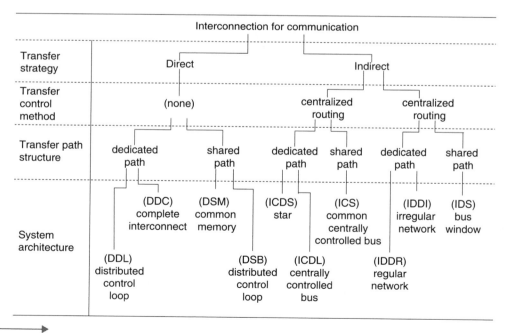

**Figure 15.11**  *Taxonomy of computer interconnection structures.*

another is largely concentrated in one location, it is referred to as centralized control. The location of the hardware could be within one of the devices that is connected to the network, or it could be a separate hardware unit. If the control logic is largely distributed throughout the different devices connected to the network, it is called decentralized control.

Implementation-independent issues that are dependent on system attributes are modularity, connection flexibility, failure effect, failure reconfiguration, bottleneck, and logical complexity. A subset of all possible computer systems is that of local computer networks (LCNs). Although no standard definition of the term exists, an LCN is generally regarded as being a network so structured as to combine the resource sharing of remote networking and the parallelism of multiprocessing. A usually valid criterion for establishing a network as an LCN is that its internodal distances are in the range of 0.1 to 10 km with a transfer rate of 1 to 100 Mbps.

### Bus-structured LCN

The range of systems to be studied will be confined to what is known in the LCN taxonomy as category 3 bus-structured systems (Figure 15.12). As opposed to such point-to-point media technologies as circuit and message

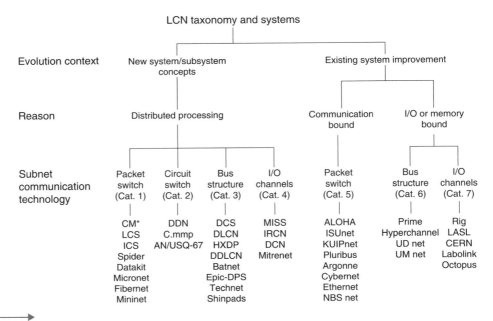

**Figure 15.12**   *Local computer networks taxonomy.*

switching, a bus-structured system consists of a set of shared lines that can be used by only one unit at a time. This implies the need for bus-control schemes to avoid inevitable bus-use conflicts.

### Network components

As a first step in developing a general LCN simulation, the network model illustrated in Figure 15.13 is established. A network consists of an arbitrary number of interconnected network nodes. Each node consists of one or more host computing elements or processors connected to an independent front-end processor termed an interface unit (IU).

The hosts are the producers and consumers of all messages, and they represent independent systems, terminals, gateways to other networks, and other such instances of computing elements. The IUs handle all nodal and network communication functions, such as message handling, flow control, and system reconfiguration. The lines represent the physical transmission media that interconnect the nodes. The IUs, together with the line interconnection structure, comprise the communication subnetwork.

The model in Figure 15.13 isolates the major hardware units involved in the transfer of information between processes in different hosts. At this level no distinction is made between instances of messages such as data blocks and acknowledgments. In order to develop and refine the model, the major elements, structures, and activities must be further defined.

**Figure 15.13**
*Generalized
distributed
computer network.*

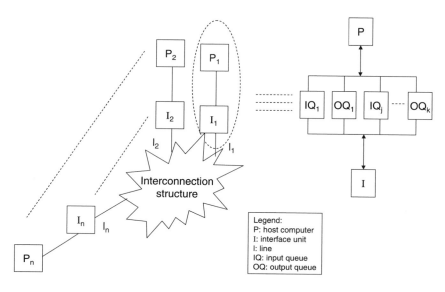

### Host processors

Host or processor components generally include computation and control elements, various levels of memory, and input and output peripherals. As far as the system is concerned, each processor's behavior can be considered to be reflected in appropriate distribution functions that describe the rate at which the processor produces and consumes interprocessor messages. These functions reflect a given processor's inherent processing power and loading based on processor parameters, exogenous communication levels, and inter-network communications.

### Queues

Queues are shared memory buffer structures through which information transfer between a processor and its IU takes place. For each node there will be an output (line) queue for messages awaiting transmission as well as one or more input (message) queues containing unprocessed receptions. The queue memory area may be located in the processor or in the IU depending on the implementation. Functionally, both are equivalent.

Associated with queues are control variables, which are maintained and monitored by both the processors and IUs to provide for the simultaneous and asynchronous access of the queues. The most common types are linear, circular, and linked queues. Linear queues (buffers) are used when the extent of a message is known and the buffer structure can be allocated in advance. The use of circular buffers is appropriate if several messages of undetermined length are to be buffered before one of them is processed. A pool of chained queues is used if the message sizes and arrival times vary over wide ranges that cannot be predicted in advance and the messages are not removed in order of their arrival.

Messages are deposited (written) into and withdrawn (read) from queues using various strategies such as FIFO (first-in, first-out), LIFO (last-in, first-out), and longest message first.

Queue access is controlled in order to prevent writing into a full queue, reading from an empty queue, and reading information as it is being written.

### Interface units

Insofar as its role in the network is concerned, the interface unit is the most complex unit with respect to both hardware and software. The basic function of the IU is to enable its processor to communicate with others in the network as well as to contribute to overall network functioning. This involves system (re)initialization, flow control, error detection, and management.

When the IU detects that its processor has a message to send, it formats the message for transmission and becomes a contender for exclusive use of the communications channels. Upon allocation of control, the controller transmits the message and, depending on the implementation, may await a response from the destination processor.

Upon completion of resource (bus) utilization, the IU must be able to pass control to the next candidate according to the allocation scheme. If there is an IU failure, the other IUs must be able to substitute for it insofar as its network control responsibilities are concerned.

### Communication lines

The lines are the physical connections between network nodes over which control and data transmissions travel. Common equivalent terms are channel and circuit. A particular circuit is either uni- or bi-directional (by nature and/or use) and supports continuous transmissions provided by analog or digital techniques.

Circuits are supported using a variety of media, such as coaxial cables, twisted pairs, fiber optics, microwave links, laser links, and so on. For the purposes of the simulation it is not necessary to be concerned about these low-level characteristics except as they are represented by a set of channel characteristics: the maximum data rate, delay and error parameters, and directional limitations.

It is also useful to consider setup characteristics if a point-to-point circuit is not always dedicated to a network. These setup characteristics may include the signaling mechanism and delay, circuit setup delay, and the delay for breaking the circuit. In the systems that will be examined later in the chapter, setup characteristics will not be a factor.

Maximum data rates vary from 50 Kbps (twisted pair) up to 150 Mbps (optical cables). This rate represents the raw transmission capability of the line and is not the same as the net rate at which information is transferred. There is always an overhead. Various factors, such as logic failures, electronic interference, and physical damage, give rise to transmission degradations ranging from single-bit errors to total line failure. Depending on the type of line used, typical error rates vary from 1 in 10,000 to 1 in 10,000,000 bits transmitted.

### Interconnection structures

Various network aspects, such as scheduling, message routing, and reconfiguration, are fundamentally related to a network's physical interconnection structure. For example, eligibility for bus control may be dependent on position, the time for a message transfer may be dependent on the location of the processors involved, or a network's continued functioning may be contingent upon the existence of a redundant link. This structure may be represented by a topological organization of the three hardware archetypes—nodes, paths, and switches—that are involved in the transfer of information between processes at different nodes.

These transfers are called message transmissions and do not distinguish between instances of messages, such as data blocks, service requests, semaphores, and so on. Likewise, in restricting consideration to structural issues it is unnecessary to distinguish between a computing element and its interface. They are lumped together as the entity node. The switching elements affect the routing or the destination in some way.

Figure 15.14 shows a general model of an interconnected system. For simplicity, the class of systems with only one switch is represented.

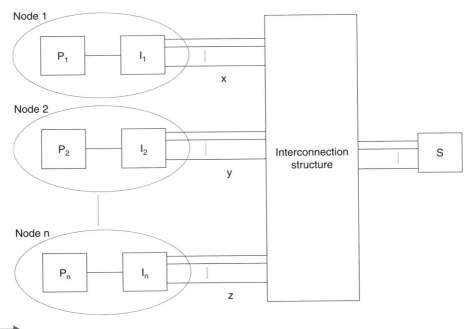

**Figure 15.14**    *General interconnection model.*

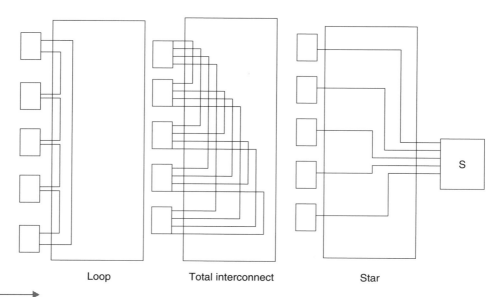

Loop            Total interconnect            Star

**Figure 15.15**    *Examples of interconnection structures.*

Associated with each node and switch are a number of paths or links. Each node can connect to the rest of the network through one, two, or multiple links corresponding, respectively, to a bus system, a ring or loop structure, or a fully interconnected network with direct links between each pair of nodes. Figure 15.15 shows specific examples of interconnection structures.

These diagrams suggest that the interconnection structure can be represented by or implied in tables and/or algorithms that will enable the determination of such things as the next eligible node for resource utilization, internodal lengths, reconfiguration parameters, and optimal paths. A complete representation might be underutilized in the present simulation effort but would provide for increased sophistication in the future.

If the node is resolved into its components (i.e., the computing element and IU), it can be seen that the model can represent the interconnection aspects of the various control schemes possible for distributed networks. Since no assumption is made about the nature of the components of a node or of its communications with the rest of the network, it is possible for a particular node to represent a centralized controller dedicated solely to network management instead of a host processor in the usual sense.

## 15.3.2  Protocols

Network activities occur in a potentially hostile environment because of such factors as nonhomogeneous components, limited bandwidth, delay, unreliable transmissions, and competition for resources. In order to provide for the orderly coordination and control of activities, formal communication conventions or protocols have been developed that encompass the electrical, mechanical, and functional characteristics of networks.

These protocols are almost always complex, multilayered structures corresponding to the layered physical and functional structure of networks. Each lower layer is functionally independent and entirely transparent to all higher-level layers. However, in order to function, all higher-level layers depend on the correct operation of the lower levels.

Every time one protocol communicates by means of a protocol at a lower level, the lower-level protocol accepts all the data and control information of the higher-level protocol and then performs a number of functions upon it. In most cases, the lower-level protocol takes all the data and control information, treats it uniformly as data, and adds on its own envelope of control information. It is in the format of messages flowing through a network that the concept of a protocol hierarchy is most evident. The format of transmitted messages shows clearly the layering of functions, just as a nesting of parentheses in a mathematical expression or in a programming language statement does.

Among the functions provided by protocols are circuit establishment and maintenance, resource management, message control, and error detection and correction. Performance of these functions provided by protocols are circuit establishment and maintenance, resource management, message control, and error detection and correction.

Performance of these functions introduces delays in data transmission and requires adding headers and other housekeeping data fields to messages as well as requiring acknowledgment of correct reception or retransmission in case of errors. This reduces the useful data rate of a network. These overhead aspects of message transfer transmission are taken into account in a measure of the efficiency of the protocols. In general, a protocol is simply the set of mutually agreed upon conventions for handling the exchange of information between computing elements. Although these elements could be circuits, modems, terminals, concentrators, hosts, processors, or people, the view taken in this section is restricted to hosts and processors embedded within other equipment.

The crux of maintaining a viable distributed environment lies in accepting the inherent unreliability of the message mechanism and to design processes to cope with it. In earlier systems, protocols were designed in ad hoc fashion. Typically, these protocols were application specific and implemented as such. All recent protocol work has been moving in the direction of a hierarchical, multilayered structure, with the implementation details of each layer transparent to all other layers and hierarchies.

Although there is no universal agreement on the names and numbers of protocol layers, a widely accepted standard is the International Organization for Standardization, (ISO), Open System Interconnect (OSI) model, which is shown in Figure 15.16. Using this organization, level 1 (physical layer) protocols include RS-232 and X.21 line-control standards, Manchester II encoding, encryption, link utilization time monitoring and control, transmission rate control, and synchronization.

Level 2 (data link) provides for the reliable interchange of data between nodes connected by a physical data link. Functions include provision of data transparency (i.e., providing means to distinguish between data and control bits in a transmission); contention monitoring and resolution; the establishment, maintenance, and termination of interactions (transactions); error detection and correction; and nodal failure recovery.

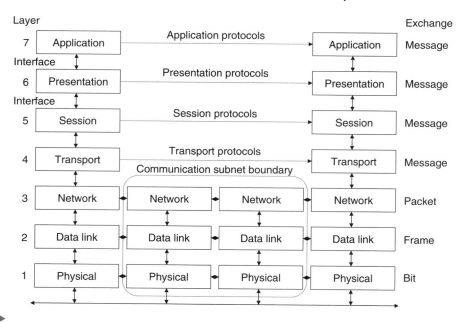

**Figure 15.16**   *ISO OSI model.*

A description of the operational aspects of the general network is best presented in the context of the previously defined protocol structure, since all possible network events and activities, intentional and otherwise, must be managed under this structure. The protocol structure also implies the underlying structures and functional mechanisms that support network operation.

Before any control or data communications can be conducted, the actual means of signaling and bit transmission across a physical medium must be provided. Physical links must be established in accordance with the specified network topology and line parameters.

Frequently, an encoding scheme such as Manchester II is used on this level to provide for synchronization and error detection. In the Manchester II scheme each of the original data bits is transformed into two transmission bits in such a way that it is impossible to get three consecutive identical bits in the encoded message. This implies that the message receiver can detect errors by watching for this occurrence. Also, this encoding can be selectively disabled to provide unique, invalid waveforms that can be used as synchronization signals.

Given the physical layer service capability to exchange signals across the physical medium, the data link layer is implemented to provide the capability of reliably exchanging a logical sequence of messages across the physical link. The fundamental functions of the layer include the provision of data transparency, message handling, line management, and error control. Since, in the original case, data and control information pass along the same line during a transmission, certain techniques must be provided to distinguish between the two. This is done by assigning control meanings to certain bit patterns that are prevented from occurring in the data stream through the use of such techniques as bit and byte stuffing and the previously described Manchester scheme. In this way, control sequences can be used to delimit the beginning and end of asynchronously transmitted, variable-length messages. Common expressions for such sequences include BOM, EOM, and flag.

The elementary unit of data transmission is usually the word. The number of data words in a message is generally variable up to some maximum message length (MML), and a parity bit is usually appended to data and control words. Each message must include addressing information whenever the sender and receiver are not directly connected. Addresses may be physical, in which case each node has a unique address, or they may be logical, in which case each node has associated with it one or more coded sequences representing functional entities. A particular logical address may be associated with an arbitrary number of physical nodes, thus providing for single, multiple, or broadcast addressing. Address information may be contained in the data portion of a message or it may be part of the control information.

Each transaction may be considered to be either a bilateral or a unilateral process, depending upon whether or not the sending process requires a response from the destination concerning the success of the transmission. In the systems in which a choice can be made between these alternatives, the message must contain information about this choice. Response types include but are not limited to the following:

- NO REPLY REQUESTED—In the case of a message being sent to a process where multiple copies exist, the issuance of an acknowledgment is undesirable because collisions would result.

- STATUS REQUESTED—Information regarding the success or failure of the transmission is requested.

- LOOPBACK REQUESTED—Loopback is the situation in which a destination node is also the source node.

## 15.3.3   Transmission error detection

In order to ensure that a transmission is occurring without error, it is necessary for the link control level to include a set of conventions between the sender and receiver for detecting and correcting errors.

There are many possible methods for error control over a transmission link. Two general types of error control are forward error control and feedback error control. The most practical and prevalent method is feedback control.

The simplest form of detection is a parity check on each transmitted character. This is often called a vertical redundancy check, and it is used to provide protection against single bit errors within characters. A horizontal or longitudinal redundancy check (LRC) provides for a check across an entire message. This is done by computing a parity bit for each bit position of all the characters in the message. The most powerful form of check is the cyclic redundancy code check (CRC), which is a more comprehensive algebraic process capable of detecting large numbers of bits with errors.

There is a possibility that a message or response does not even arrive at its destination, irrespective of whether the information is good or bad. This can result from either a physical failure, such as the failure of the link or of the destination node, or a logical failure, such as the use of an incorrect destination name.

These possibilities can be detected by providing a time-out mechanism, which will cause a message to be retransmitted if, after an agreed upon delay (the response time-out), an acknowledgment has not been received. Many systems rely solely on the positive acknowledgment and time-out convention and do not employ a negative acknowledgment.

When multiple devices are sharing a bus, there must be some method by which a particular unit requests and obtains control of the bus and is allowed to transmit data over it. The major problem in this area is the resolution of inevitable bus request conflicts through the use of arbitration and scheduling schemes so that only one unit obtains the bus at a given time. Mechanisms must also be provided for system reinitialization and adjustment in the cases of system startup, nodal addition and removal, line failures, and spurious transmissions in the system.

In all systems collisions can occur when more than one control or data transmission simultaneously occurs. This may be caused by the use of random number techniques to generate allocation sequence numbers upon a node entering the system at startup or some later time, or it may be caused by a message with multiple destinations improperly asking for acknowledgment. Collisions are usually handled by the temporary or permanent removal of involved nodes or the retransmission of legitimate messages.

A limit is often imposed on line use time to prevent a node from monopolizing the bus, either intentionally or because of nodal failure. This condition may be prevented by placing a limit on the maximum message size and/or monitoring line use to determine when a node is maintaining an active transmission state beyond that required to send the largest allowed message.

This monitoring capability is achieved through the use of a loud-mouth timer, which is activated upon nodal allocation and provides an interrupt signal (or causes a collision) if allowed to run out. The usual outcome is the removal of power from the transmitter circuitry, either temporarily or permanently, and the informing of the host processor, when possible, of this condition.

When talking about control, it is important to keep in mind that this is not usually associated with a specific physical device or location but is rather a functional entity distributed (replicated) throughout the network.

## 15.3.4   Events

In order to precisely simulate the operational behavior of networks a more formal and quantitative analytical approach must be taken. In order to do this, the following concepts must be introduced. All actions and activities, intentional and otherwise, that can occur in system operation can be classified as events. An event is defined as any occurrence, regardless of its duration. Events have a number of characteristics, including the following:

- An event has a beginning, an end, and a duration.

- An event can be simple or complex. A simple event is one that cannot or, for the purposes of the simulation, need not be reduced into a simpler sequence of occurrences. Conversely, a complex event is one that consists of simpler events.

- An event may be a random occurrence or of a stochastic nature, or it may be the deterministic result (effect) of an identifiable cause.

- An event has a certain pattern of occurrence (e.g., periodic, aperiodic, synchronous, asynchronous, etc.).

- Events belong to classes. The significance of an event class is that each member has the same effect as each other in a particular context. For example, in certain systems the corruption of a message by noise is equivalent in effect to the incorrect specification of a destination name—both will result in a response time-out and a retransmission. Thus, these two events would be of the same class.

- Events may be concurrent or disjointed (sequential). Events that coincide or overlap in time are concurrent; otherwise, they are disjointed. The concept of effective concurrency is introduced here. Sequential program structures are considered effectively concurrent if they can successfully represent or model events that are actually concurrent.

An example would be the action of processors requesting services. While this is an asynchronous, unpredictable event(s) concurrent with channel utilization by a particular node, these two aspects of system behavior utilization and contention can be effectively separated, since (except in the case of interrupts) the request will not be acted upon until utilization is complete. As long as a record of the duration of utilization is available, an effective history of nodal requests can be generated just prior to contention resolution by the control module of the simulation program.

Following is a list of basic events that may be found to occur in the operation of various LCNs. All system behavior can be ultimately reduced to sequences of these simple events. Events are listed under the component in which they occur.

### Processor

- Production. This is the generation of a message by a host computing element. Parameters associated with this event are production time, message size, destination(s).

- Queue inquiry. The determination by the processor of the state of an input or output queue before reading from or writing to it, respectively.

- Output message disposition. Depending upon the buffer availability strategy, a generated message may be queued normally, it may be written over exiting queued data, it may be held by the processor until it can be queued, or it may be dumped.

- Consumption (read message). This is the reading of a message in the input queue by the host computing element. Assuming a message is available in the input queue, it can be immediately consumed. Consumption with respect to a queue is similar to production.

- Node. It is convenient to associate the following events with the entity node rather than either the computing element or the IU.

- Addition. A node is considered added to the circuit when it informs the network that it wishes to be integrated into the system. This may occur upon initial power-up of the node or upon failure recovery.

- Integration. This is when the node actually becomes a functional part of the network.

- Failure. This is the failure of a node as a functional member of the network.

### Interface unit

- Queue inquiry. This is analogous to the processor event.

- Read message. The IU obtains message from an output queue.

- Preprocess message. This is the formatting or packing of a message for transmission. It is to be distinguished from the formatting that is done by the processor.

- Request. The IU notifies the network that it wishes to use the bus. This may or may not involve the transmission of a control signal.

- Connection. This is the actual acquisition of the channel for utilization.

- (Re)transmission. This is the moment when the first word of a message is placed on the bus or, in the event of a message train, as in a ring structure, the first word of the first message.

- Response time-out activation. In systems in which a response to a message transmission is required within a certain amount of time, a response timer is activated at some point during transmission.

- Detection (identification). This is the detection by an IU of a message addressed to it.

- Reception. This is the moment when the complete message has been received, processing on it has been completed, and it is ready to be queued. This may also be considered queue inquiry time as well as response transmission time.

- Write message. This is when a received message is placed in the input queue.

- Response reception. This is when the message source receives information from the destination regarding the transmission.

- Delete message. This is the deletion of a message from an output queue following a successful transmission.

- Relinquish. Upon completion of utilization, the IU signals that reallocation is to occur.

Using these concepts, overall system activity or flow can be represented by the following sequence of complex events:

NODAL ACTIVITY → CONTROL/ARBITRATION →
UTILIZATION

This simple structure is possible because the concept of effective concurrency is valid in the case of global bus systems.

### Nodal Activity

Nodal activity simulates the behavior of all nodes and interface units during the utilization period of a particular node. During this period nodal activity includes the following:

- The production and consumption of messages

- Queue activity
- IU background processing
- Addition and removal of nodes from the network

### Control

Control may be a number of possible sequences depending on circumstances in which control is activated.

### Utilization

The utilization event encompasses all activity associated with a node's utilization of the bus for the transmission of a message. Utilization begins with being connected to the bus and it terminates either gracefully, in the case of a successful transaction followed by a control output, or unintentionally, as the result of intervention by control because of a protocol violation (message too long, no reallocation signal transmitted, etc.).

## 15.3.5 The LAN simulator model structure

Based on the previous discussion of LAN structure and events, we can typify a LAN as consisting of three major hardware classes: host machines, interface units, and communications links. Additionally, these hardware classes possess varying levels of software and functionality.

The link level is concerned with the management and performance of bit-level physical transfers. This includes timing and control as well as mechanical and electrical interface. The interface units provide the main services to bring the simple communications media and protocols up to a true network. This component and its services must provide for node-to-node, host-to-node, and end-to-end protocols. This includes error detection and correction, media acquisition and control, routing, flow control, message formatting, network transparency, maintenance of connections, and other services. The host class of device provides the LAN with end-user sites that require remote services from other hosts. The services provided at this level are host-to-node interface, host-to-host protocols, and resource-sharing protocols. Implemented at this level of a LAN would be user-visible services, such as a distributed operating system, a distributed database management system, mail services, and many others. A model of this structure implies a minimum of a component for each of these items. Therefore, the simulator must have components of sufficient generality and flexibility to model these components and provide for analysis. Figure 15.17 depicts these basic components and the necessary simulation components to mea-

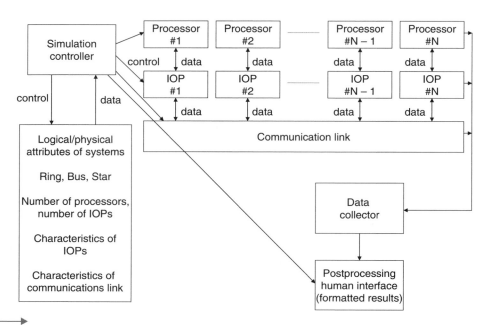

**Figure 15.17**   *Basic components of a simulation model.*

sure the performance and operations of a simulation. Using this structure, it can be seen that the simulator consists of a modular structure with components that can be turned to the modeling of specific LAN nuances. The physical and logical characteristics peculiar to each system design are contained in independent software routines and/or data tables. The high-level design of the LAN model shows the need for the following functions:

- A simulation controller, which will be responsible for the coordination and timely operation of the remaining software modules. This function will initialize the system architecture and distributed computing techniques in accordance with user input data, schedule events, calculate system state, maintain the common timetables, and initiate the processing of the other software routines as dictated by the particular logical and physical configuration.

- A system processor routine, which will be capable of simulating the time-dependent activity (data in, data out, processing time) of each proposed computing mode.

- An interface processing routine, which will be capable of simulating the activity (time delays, message handling, priority determination, addressing technique, resource allocation, etc.) of each proposed front-end processor as required by the particular logical and physical characteristics.

- A communications link routine, which will be capable of simulating the timing delays and the data and control transfer characteristics of the proposed transmission medium.

- A data collection routine, which will be responsible for collecting, formatting, and collating the requisite system evaluation parameters.

Data items collected will include, but will not be limited to, a minimum, maximum, and average of the following:

- Time to transmit message from A to B

- Message wait time

- Number of messages in the queue or system

- Message size

- Bus utilization

- Interface unit timing (as previously presented)

It will also include a postprocessing routine, which will be responsible for presenting the data in human-readable forms (graphs, plots, tables, etc.).

## 15.3.6    **LAN simulator overview**

This simulator was developed to provide a flexible research, development, and analysis tool for local area network architectures. The tool has been used to aid in the selection, development, and evaluation of local area network architectures that support large, distributed, real-time command control and communications (C3) environments.

The simulator was designed with the intention of comparing a wide range of possible distributed C3 configurations. This capability was achieved by providing the following:

1.    A modular structure, which allows the model to be adapted to suit a variety of system specifications

2.    A standard driving routine, which mimics the communications within a C3 system

3.    A standard routine, which analyzes the distributed system on the basis of detailed evaluation criteria

Such a design allows for the implementation, testing, and evaluation of new strategies for improving system performance with little effort.

### 15.3.7   Next event simulation

The modeling technique used in the LAN software simulation is called next event simulation. Next event simulation views the world as a sequence of events rather than a continuum. If a department store checkout line is simulated in next event simulation, the process of checking out would be viewed as the following sequence: (1) a customer enters the checkout line, (2) the customer starts checkout, (3) the customer completes checkout. Between these events the customer is performing other activities, but these are unimportant if we are simply interested in the length of the waiting time.

The view of time taken by next event simulation is important in understanding the design and implementation of the LAN simulation. Time in next event simulation is viewed as a means of sequencing events and calculating time-related statistics. Events one hour or one second in the future are treated identically. Simulation is achieved by creating a file that contains future events along with the time of their occurrence. A simple loop program scans this file and selects the event with the lowest time. At that time, an internal memory location, which contains the simulated time, is updated to the occurrence time of the event. After the event occurs, mathematical calculations or logical operations can be performed to schedule other dependent events. In the checkout line example, this means that when checkout begins, the end of the checkout event is scheduled. In this way, the simulation proceeds from event to event and time constantly progresses.

The random or stochastic nature of scheduled events gives the simulation the characteristics of a real system. In the checkout line example, the time taken to serve a customer is not a constant; it may be one minute or ten minutes. The service time is also randomly distributed. That is to say, the service time of previous customers does not have any effect on future customers. The service times usually fall into a pattern; that is, it may be highly likely that a service time is 5 minutes but relatively unlikely to be 20 minutes. The likelihood of certain service times can be described by theoretical patterns called distributions. These distributions can be used to generate service times or arrival patterns that resemble those occurring in real systems.

### 15.3.8   LAN model implementation

The LAN simulator is a general-purpose simulation package used for modeling a wide range of local area network architectures. Its basic structure is shown in Figure 15.18 and consists of the following five major components:

1.    Arrival module. The arrival module is concerned with generating the messages to be communicated and places them in an interface unit queue. It must also handle the queue overflow problem and the possibility of a processor being unavailable.

2.    Arbitrator module. The arbitrator module is concerned with the determination of which interface unit will communicate over the link next, based on the policy of the communications link control in place.

3.    Use module. The use module is concerned with the modeling of the passage of messages from source to sink nodes over the communications link.

4.    Analysis module. The analysis module performs statistical analysis on the messages within the system.

5.    Interface module. The interface module handles overall control of the characteristics of the simulation.

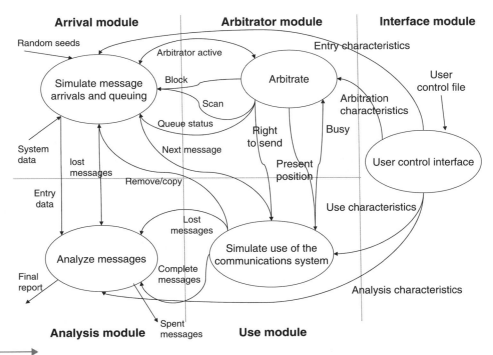

**Figure 15.18**    *Basic structure of LAN simulator.*

One of the critical modules of MALAN in terms of general characteristics modeling is the use module. Its major components are as follows:

1.    ADD NEXT MESSAGE TO THE FILE. This process takes the next message from the processor that has the right to send and stores it in a file until it arrives at its destination.

2.    SIMULATE TOPOLOGY. This routes the message through the simulation topology.

3.    SIMULATE TRANSACTION DELAY. It simulates the passage of a message over a physical transmission line (link), including messages retransmitted.

4.    SIMULATE MESSAGE ERRORS. This determines the number of retransmits and lost messages from information on the physical transmission line.

5.    UNFILE MESSAGE. This process removes messages from the message file upon completion of message transmission.

6.    SIMULATE STATUS CHANGE. This simulates the loss of a link or node.

Table 15.3 describes the composition of entities represented in this model. Each of the items in the table is an attribute of the model's entities. Attribute 1 is the event time; it contains the time at which the message will arrive. Attribute 2 is the event type, which distinguishes this event as an arrival, since there are other events that occur in the system. Attribute 3 is the source IU number or the designated IU that generated the message. Attribute 4 is the destination IU number and describes the ultimate destination of the message. Attribute 7 is the message size expressed in words. Attributes 17 and 18 are used when a message is too large to be sent in one packet. In this case, the message must be divided into a number of smaller messages, each with the same source, destination, and generation time. Attribute 17 is used to identify the sequence number of any multipacket message. Attribute 18 is used to identify the total number of packets in the entire message. With attributes 17 and 18, it can be determined when the complete message is received.

As with interarrival times, message size and message destination must be generated by the system. Here again, the data could be generated by measurements within the real system or by using theoretical distributions. Thus, part of the arrival module is devoted to drawing from distributions of message size and message destination and initializing the appropriate attributes. The only remaining function performed by this submode is to divide mes-

**Table 15.3**   *Entries in the LAN Simulator Model*

| Attribute | Data Name | Data Type | Abbreviation |
|---|---|---|---|
| 1 | Event time | real | ETIM |
| 2 | Event type | real | ETYP |
| 3 | Source interface unit (IU) number | integer | SP |
| 4 | Destination interface unit (IU) number | integer | DP |
| 5 | Present interface unit (IU) number | integer | PP |
| 6 | Generation time | real | GT |
| 7 | Message size (words) | integer | MS |
| 8 | Message overhead length (bits) | integer | MO |
| 9 | Message wait time $\Delta t\,1$ (in processor queue) | real | WT1 |
| 10 | Message wait time $\Delta t\,2$ (transit from queue to IU) | real | WT2 |
| 11 | Message wait time $\Delta t\,3$ (within IU) | real | WT3 |
| 12 | Message transfer time | real | TT |
| 13 | Message transfer time | real | XFER |
| 14 | Number of stops | integer | NS |
| 15 | Number of retransmits | integer | RT |
| 16 | Messages lost | integer | ML |
| 17 | Sequence number of multipacketed messages | integer | NMES |
| 18 | Number of parts to a packetized message | integer | PARTS |
| 19 | Message time to complete | integer | MTTC |
| 20 | Message priority | integer | MP |
| 21 | Message identification (ID) number | integer | MI |

sages that exceed the maximum message size into a sequence of smaller messages. The total number of messages generated is placed in attribute 18 of each message. Each message receives a sequence number, attribute 17.

Once messages enter the system, they must be held in a waiting line or queue until the IU can transmit them. To facilitate this, a FIFO queue is formed to contain the waiting messages. In a real system, this queue would consume some real memory, which normally would be limited. In the simulated system, this limit must be taken into consideration. When queue memory is exceeded, appropriate action should be taken.

Appropriate action consists of: (1) waiting until sufficient memory is free to accommodate the message, (2) throwing away the message, and (3) overwriting an older message. Any of these can be selected in this submode.

### Topology module description

The topology module consists mainly of a group of subroutines that facilitate the retrieval and modification of the data that physically describe the local computer network. These routines reside within the body of the simulation program with the exception of the initialization program, which is a separate entity.

## 15.3.9   Analysis module

The goal of the analysis module is to provide quantitative measures, which establish the effectiveness of distributed processing systems, and to provide statistical measures, which can be used to compare distributed processing systems having divergent design philosophies. To meet these goals, it is necessary to identify constant factors that unify distributed processing systems and derive statistical measures by which these factors can be compared. That is to say, a common language of analysis must be established by which a wide range of distributed systems can be described.

### Establishing analysis criteria

In order to develop wide-ranging analysis criteria, it is necessary to identify those characteristics that are common among distributed processing systems. These common characteristics will be developed into statistical measures that analyze the relative merits of the underlying system. In developing common characteristics, three areas will be explored: (1) the basic physical structure of distributed processing networks, (2) the basic sequence of events, and (3) the overall function of distributed processing networks.

To provide flexibility and simplicity, most distributed processing systems have adopted a modular design philosophy. Modularity has resulted in a common physical structure, which allows the distributed processing systems to be divided into several functional components. These component parts can be examined and evaluated separately. Dividing the evaluation of a system into functional components allows more accurate analysis of the intermediate factors that contribute to the strengths and weaknesses of a system.

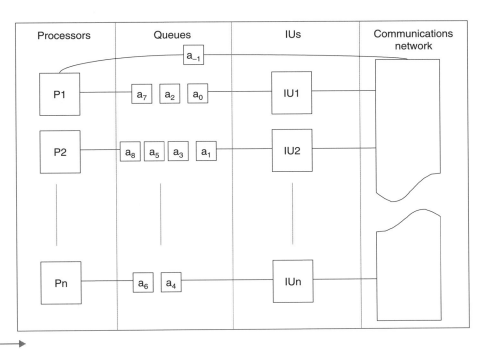

**Figure 15.19**   *Functional components of a distributed processing system.*

The basic functional components that form the physical structure of a typical distributed processing system are shown in Figure 15.19. This figure illustrates each distributed processing system in terms of the following components: (1) a number of processors that generate and consume messages, (2) a waiting line or queue containing messages that cannot be serviced immediately, (3) an interface unit that prepares messages for transmission, and (4) a communications network that performs the actual physical transmission of data. The physical implementation of these component parts differs widely from system to system. The outline presented in Figure 15.19 represents an accurate, generalized picture of distributed processing systems. The physical mapping presented in Figure 15.19 allows the identification of certain common features and checkpoints, which are discussed in subsequent paragraphs.

The primary structural feature of quantitative interest in Figure 15.19 is the queue, or waiting line. The length of these queues gives some quantitative information concerning the effectiveness of the underlying communications system. Exceptionally long or unbalanced queues could indicate the presence of system bottlenecks. Queues that grow and retreat wildly could suggest poor responsiveness to peak loads.

**Figure 15.20**
*LAN evaluation
metrics.*

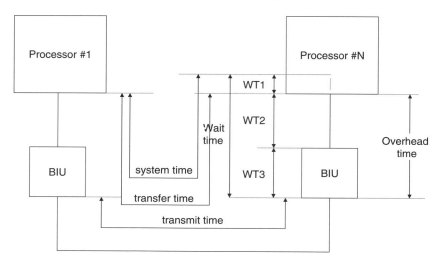

The basic components, which form the functional event structure in the typical distributed processing network, are shown in Figure 15.20. This figure reproduces the same general physical layout presented in Figure 15.19 but divides the passage of messages through the physical system into specific steps, or phases. The major events of interest along the message path of Figure 15.20 are: (1) a message arrives, (2) a message enters the queue, (3) a message leaves the queue, (4) a message becomes available to the interface unit, (5) a message starts transmission, (6) a message ends transmission, and (7) a message becomes available to the receiving processor.

These common checkpoints are significant, because they allow time measurements that chart the passage of the message through the system. As long as a particular system accurately implements communication, timing becomes a most critical factor. That is, the speed at which accurately transmitted messages are completed is of primary interest. This series of checkpoints allows analysis of overall as well as intermediate delays imposed on the communications process.

The time between basic checkpoints and combinations of checkpoints gives rise to specific descriptive quantities, shown by the arrows in Figure 15.20. These quantities will be compiled for each simulation run on specific distributed processing networks. These are described in more detail, as follows:

1.     System time is the time between message generation at the source processor and message reception by the sink processor. System

time quantifies the total delay the distributed processing system imposes on a message.

2.  Transfer time is the time that elapses between a message leaving the queue and its reception at the sink. Transfer time indicates the time required for the system to effect communications, disregarding the time spent waiting to commence the transfer process.

3.  Transmit time is the time a message spends in the process of physical information transmission. This quantity indicates the actual timeliness of the low-level protocol and the speed of the physical transmission.

4.  Wait time is the time that must be expended before a message begins transmission. This quantity is divided into four smaller quantities: wt1, wt2, wt3, and wt4, described as follows:

    ■ wt1 is the time a message spends in the queue.

    ■ wt2 is the interval between removing the message from the queue to the point at which the IU begins preparing the message for transmission.

    ■ wt3 accounts for the time required to prepare a message for transmission.

    ■ wt4 includes the time required to make the message available to the sink processor once the transmission is complete.

5.  Overhead time equals the sum of wt2, wt3, and wt4. The overhead time is considered the time that must be yielded to the IU as the price of message transmission.

Analysis criteria can also be approached from a functional point of view. Functional criteria allow evaluation and comparison of the performance of distributed processing systems. These criteria fall into the following categories: (1) the amount of information carried by the communications system in unit time (i.e., throughput), (2) the amount of useful information transferred in unit time excluding overhead (i.e., information throughput), (3) the information lost in the communications process, (4) the amount of information overhead, and (5) the proportion of data that arrives late.

The throughput statistics quantify the total volume of information carried by a distributed processing system in unit time. This value is an overall indicator of the capacity and utilization of a distributed processing system. Unfortunately, the volume of real information transferred is reduced by the portion of overhead appended to the message. The overhead information is the part of a message that is attached by the distributed processing system to facilitate communication. The measurement of throughput that disregards overhead is called information throughput.

In addition to the overall flow of information through the system, we are interested in the loss of information. This loss can be the result of three conditions: (1) message loss because of a full queue, (2) message loss because of a bit(s) in error during transmission, and (3) message loss because of the casualty of a system component. These quantities will be computed as a percent of the total number of messages transmitted. A statistic relating total messages lost will also be computed.

Also of interest is the amount of overhead that is attached to each message. This quantity allows analysis of the degradation of system performance caused by overhead. This statistic expresses overhead as a percentage of the total information transferred.

A more sophisticated functional evaluation criterion is the data late statistics. This statistic evaluates the proportion of messages that arrives past the time of expiration. In a very practical sense, this measure is one that is of ultimate concern in real-time environments. If all messages arrive in their allotted time, the system is working within capacity and responds to the peak requirements demanded of it.

In summary, the criteria used for analysis are generated by three characteristics of distributed processing systems, as follows:

1.  Basic physical structure. This characteristic yields criteria such as queue length, which results from the physical link between the processor and interface unit.

2.  The event structure. This characteristic yields analysis criteria such as transmit time, which is the result of the requirement to physically transmit the data during some point in the communications cycle.

3.  The overall function. This characteristic yields analysis criteria such as throughput, which results from the overall function of the system (i.e., to communicate).

### Analysis criteria and simulation

From the point of view of statistical analysis, Figure 15.21 illustrates the essential nature of the model. The block on the left shows simulation messages arriving to the communications network from the real-time system.

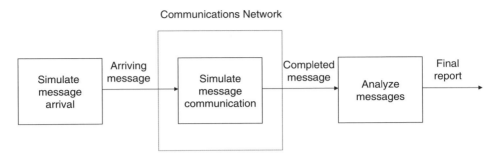

**Figure 15.21**    *Simulated message flow graph.*

Messages in the simulation are not real system messages but are buffers of computer memory that contain information regarding the nature and history of the message. The central block shows simulation of messages passing through the communications network. During this passage, data, which capture the history of the message, are added to the simulated message. When the message is either complete (reaches its destination) or lost (failed to reach its destination), the message is analyzed by the analysis module shown as the block on the right.

During a simulation, many messages will take the path illustrated in Figure 15.22. A large number of messages are required in order to build up what is called statistical significance. This refers to the fact that a large sample of occurrences must be taken into consideration in order to eliminate any bias that may be produced by taking too small a random sample.

The structure of the software for collecting statistics and formatting the final report is also shown in Figure 15.22. During a simulation run, information from large numbers of completed messages will be accumulated and stored, and the memory occupied by these messages will be released. At the end of a simulation run, these accumulated data will be used in statistical calculations, which will be formatted and presented in the form of a final report.

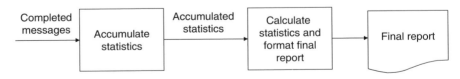

**Figure 15.22**    *Analysis module functional diagram.*

### Statistical output

The statistics generated by the system can be divided into three main groups: (1) time independent, (2) time persistent, and (3) periodic.

The time-independent statistics are from independent observations. The traditional mean and standard deviation can be calculated for this group. These data, which are accumulated during the simulation run, are as follows: (1) the sum of each observed piece of data, (2) the sum of each piece of data squared, (3) the number of observations, and (4) the maximum value observed. From the accumulated data, the mean, standard deviation, and maximum observed value will be calculated and formatted for the final report. These statistics will be provided for all the time-independent data points.

Time-persistent statistics are important when the time over which a parameter retains its value becomes critical. An example of this is a waiting line. If the line has ten members in it for 20 minutes and one member for 1 minute, the average is not $(1 + 10)/2$, or 5.5. This quantity would indicate that there were approximately five members present in the line for a 21-minute period. The true average is more like $20/21 \times 10 + 1/20 \times 1$, or 9.57, or approximately 10. This is the time-persistent average. As can be

**Figure 15.23**
*Example performance evaluation plots.*

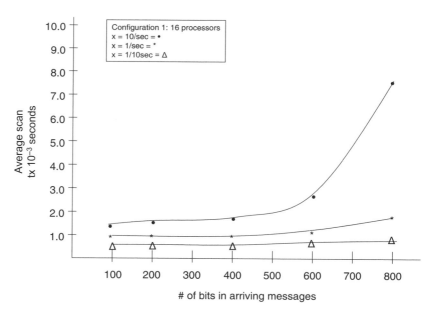

seen in this case, the average is weighted by the time period over which the value persisted. There is a similar argument that can be made for the time-persistent standard deviation. These data, which are accumulated during a simulation for the time-persistent case, are as follows: (1) the sum of the observed value times the period over which it retained that value, (2) the sum of the observed value squared times the period over which it retained its value, (3) the maximum observed value, and (4) the total period of observation. From these accumulated data, the time-persistent mean, the time-persistent standard deviation, and the maximum observed value will be calculated and formatted for the final report. These statistics will be provided for all the time-persistent data points.

Periodic statistics are designed to yield a plot of observations as a function of time. This group of statistics affords a view of the system as it operates in time. Data are accumulated as in the previous two examples, except, rather than sums of statistics, an individual data point graph of time versus the value of the data points will be plotted. These plots will be produced for all groups of periodic statistics. Some example plots for evaluations performed on the HXDP and token ring networks are shown in Figure 15.23.

## 15.4  Summary

This chapter illustrated the usefulness of analytical and simulation modeling for studying a component of a local area network, in this case the control scan time for the queuing model and throughput for the simulation. These models provide a fairly easy means to extract such information. They have been applied to a variety of other LAN problems. The reader interested in more details of such modeling is directed to the references cited in this chapter.

# *References*

[1]  P. J. Fortier, ed. *Database Systems Handbook* (New York: McGraw-Hill, 1997).

[2]  K. Trivedi, *Probability and Statistics with Reliability, Queuing, and Computer Science Applications* (Englewood Cliffs, NJ: Prentice Hall, 1982).

[3]  A. D. Allen, *Probability, Statistics, and Queuing Theory with Computer Science Applications*, 2d ed. (New York: Academic Press, 1990).

[4]  A. Papoulis, *Probability, Random Variables, and Stochastic Processes* (New York: McGraw-Hill, 1984).

[5]  R. E. Walpole, *Probability and Statistics for Engineers and Scientists* (New York: Macmillan, 1978).

[6]  L. Kleinrock, *Theory*, vol.1 of *Queuing Systems* (New York: John Wiley & Sons, 1975).

[7]  L. Kleinrock, *Computer Applications*, vol. 2 of *Queuing Systems* (New York: John Wiley & Sons, 1975).

[8]  J. R. Jackson "Networks of Waiting Lines," *Operations Research* (August 1957).

[9]  J. P. Buzen, "Computational Algorithms for Closed Queuing Networks with Exponential Servers," *Communications of the ACM* (September 1973).

[10]  J. P. Buzen and P. J. Denning, "The Operational Analysis of Queuing Network Models," *ACM Computing Surveys* (September 1978).

[11]  M. Reiser and S. S. Lavenberg, "Mean-Value Analysis of Closed Multichain Queuing Networks," *Journal of the ACM* (April 1980).

[12]  J. P. Buzen, "Fundamental Operational Laws of Computer System Performance," *Acta Informatica* 7 (1976).

[13]  S. S. Lavenberg, ed., *Computer Performance Modeling Handbook* (New York: Academic Press, 1983).

[14]  A. Pritsker, *The Gasp IV Simulation Language* (New York: John Wiley & Sons, 1974).

[15]  A. Schriber, *Simulation Using GPSS* (New York: John Wiley & Sons, 1974).

[16]  J. Krivait, *Simscript II Programming Language* (Englewood Cliffs, NJ: Prentice Hall, 1969).

[17]  A. Pritsker et al., *Slam II: Network Models for Decision Support* (New York: John Wiley & Sons, 1989).

[18]  K. Jensen, *Coloured Petri Nets. Basic Concepts, Analysis Methods, and Practical Use*. Vol. 1, Basic Concepts. Monographs in Theoretical Computer Science (Springer-Verlag, 1997).

[19]  K. Jensen, *Coloured Petri Nets. Basic Concepts, Analysis Methods, and Practical Use*. Vol. 2, Analysis Methods. Monographs in Theoretical Computer Science (Springer-Verlag, 1997).

[20]  K. Jensen, *Coloured Petri Nets. Basic Concepts, Analysis Methods, and Practical Use*. Vol. 3, Practical Use. Monographs in Theroetical Computer Science (Springer-Verlag, 1997).

[21]  G. Nutt. "A Case Study of Simulation as a Computer Design Tool," *IEEE Computer* (October 1978): 31–36.

[22]  M. Yuen, "Traffic Flow in a Distributed Loop Switching System," in *Proceedings of Symposium on Computer Communications Networks and Teletraffic* (Brooklyn, NY: Polytechnic Institute of Brooklyn, April 4–6, 1972).

## Additional reading

Abiteboul, S., R. Hull, and V. Vianu. *Foundations of Databases*. Reading, MA: Addison-Wesley, 1995.

Balakrishnan, V. "A Framework for Performance Evaluation of Parallel Discrete Event Simulators." Master's thesis, University of Cincinnati, Cincinnati, OH, 1997.

Bancilhon, F., C. Delobel, and P. Kanellakis. *Building an Object-Oriented Database System: The Story of O2.* San Mateo, CA: Morgan Kaufmann, 1992.

Banks, J., and J. S. Carson. *Discrete Event System Simulation.* Englewood Cliffs, NJ: Prentice Hall, 1984.

Banks, J., ed., J. Carson, B. Nelson, and D. Nicoles. *Discrete Event System Simulation.* 3d ed. Englewood Cliffs, NJ: Prentice Hall, 2000.

Barquin, R., and H. Edelstein. *Building, Using, and Managing the Data Warehouse.* Englewood Cliffs, NJ: Prentice Hall, 1997.

Bause, F., and P. Kritzinger. *Stochastic Petri Nets—An Introduction to the Theory.* Wiesbaden, Germany: Advanced Studies in Computer Science, 1996.

Berenson, H., P. Bernstein, J. Gray, J. Melton, E. O'Neil, and P. O'Neil. "A Critique of ANSI Isolation Levels." In *Proceedings of ACM SIGMOD International Conference on Management of Data* (1995).

Bernstein, P., V. Hadzilacos, and N. Goodman. *Concurrency Control and Recovery in Database Systems.* New York: Addison-Wesley, 1987.

Bertino, E., and L. Martino. *Object-Oriented Database Systems: Concepts and Architectures.* Reading, MA: Addison-Wesley, 1993.

Bhuyan, L., and X. Zhang. *Multiprocessor Performance Measurement and Evaluation.* IEEE Computer Society Press, 1995.

Blaha, M., and W. Premerlani. *Object-Oriented Modeling and Design for Database Applications.* Englewood Cliffs, NJ: Prentice Hall, 1998.

Blau, R. "Performance Evaluation for Computer Image Synthesis Systems." Ph.D. diss., Department of Computer Science, University of California, Berkeley, 1992.

Bobrowski, S. *Oracle 8 Architecture.* Berkley, CA: Osborne/McGraw-Hill, 1998.

Bolch, G., S. Greiner, H. de Meer, and K. S. Trivedi. *Queuing Networks and Markov Chains.* New York: John Wiley & Sons, 1998.

Boyse, J. W., and D. R. Warn. "A Straightforward Model for Computer Performance Prediction." *ACM Computing Surveys* (June 1975): 73–93.

Bowman, J., S. Emerson, and M. Darnovsky. *The Practical SQL Handbook.* 3rd ed. Reading, MA: Addison-Wesley, 1996.

Brown, A., and M. Seltzer. "Operating System Benchmarking in the Wake of Lmbench: A Case Study of the Performance of NetBSD on the Intel x86 Architecture." In *Proceedings of the 1997 ACM SIGMETRICS Conference on Measurement and Modeling of Computer Systems*. Seattle, WA. (June 1997): 214–224.

Buzen, J. P. "Computational Algorithms for Closed Networks with Exponential Servers." *Communications of the ACM* 16 (1978): 527–531.

Cattell, R., ed. *The Object Database Standard: ODMG-93, Release 1.2*. San Mateo, CA: Morgan Kaufmann, 1996.

Celko, J. *SQL for Smarties*. San Mateo, CA: Morgan Kaufmann, 1995.

———. *Instant SQL Programming*. WROX Press, 1995.

Chamberlin, D. *Understanding the New DB2, IDM's Object-Relational Database System*. San Mateo, CA: Morgan Kaufmann, 1996.

Chichester, E. *Multiprocessor Performance*. West Sussex, England, and New York: John Wiley & Sons, 1989.

Codd, E. F. "A Relational Model of Data for Large Shared Data Banks." In *Readings in Database Systems*. 2d ed. San Mateo, CA: Morgan Kaufmann, 1994.

———. "Extending the Database Relational Model to Capture More Meaning." *ACM Transactions on Database Systems*. (December 1979).

———. *The Relational Model for Database Management*. Reading, MA: Addison-Wesley, 1990.

Coronel, R. *Database Systems Design, Implementation, and Management*. 3d ed. International Thompson Publishing, 1997.

Date, C. *An Introduction to Database Systems*. 5th ed. Reading, MA: Addison-Wesley, 1990.

Date, C., and H. Darwin. *A Guide to the SQL Standard*. Reading, MA: Addison-Wesley, 1993.

Delis, A., and N. Roussopoulos. "Performance Comparison of Three Modern DBMS Architectures." *IEEE Transactions on Software Engineering* 19 (February 1993): 120–138.

Eisenberg, A. *A Brief Description of the SQL3 Data Model*. Redwood City, CA: Oracle Corporation, 1995.

Elmasri, R., and S. Navathe. *Fundamentals of Database Systems*. Menlo Park, CA: Benjamin/Cummings, 1994.

Farber, D. J. "A Ring Network." *Datamation* (February 1975): 44–46.

Feverstein, S., and B. Pribyl. *Oracle PL/SQL Programming.* 2d ed. Sebastopol, CA: O'Reilly and Associates, 1997.

Finkelstein, S., N. Mattos, I. Mumick, and H. Pirahesh. "Expressing Recursive Queries in SQL." ISO WG3 Report X3H2-96-075 (March 1996).

Fishwick, P. *Simulation Model Design and Execution.* Englewood Cliffs, NJ: Prentice Hall, 1995.

Fortier, P. J. *Handbook of LAN Technology.* 2d ed. New York: McGraw-Hill, 1991.

———. "A Communications Environment for Real-Time Distributed Control Systems." In *Proceedings of ACM Northeast Regional Conference* (1984).

———. *Design and Analysis of Distributed Real-Time Systems.* New York: McGraw-Hill, 1986.

———. *Design of Distributed Operating Systems.* New York: McGraw-Hill, 1986.

———. *Handbook of LAN Technology.* New York: McGraw-Hill, 1989.

Fortier, P. J., and P. Turner. "A Simulation Program for Analysis of Distributed Database Processing Concept." Nineteenth Annual Simulation Symposium (1986).

Gallagher, L. "Object SQL: Language Extentions for Object Data Management." International Society for Mini, and Microcomputers CIKM-92 (1992).

German, R. *Performance Analysis of Communication Systems: Modeling with Non-Markovian Stochastic Petri Nets.* New York: John Wiley & Sons, 2000.

Gray, J., and A. Reuter. *Transaction Processing: Concepts and Techniques.* San Mateo, CA: Morgan Kaufmann, 1993.

Gross, D., and C. M. Harris. *Fundamentals of Queuing Theory.* 3d ed. Wiley Series in Probability and Mathematical Statistics. New York: Wiley-Interscience, 1997.

Groth, R. *Hands on SQL.* Englewood Cliffs, NJ: Prentice Hall, 1997.

Haring, G., C. Lindemann, and M. Reiser, eds. *Performance Evaluation: Origins and Directions, Lecture Notes in Computer Science.* Springer-Verlag, 2000.

Hoover, S., and R. F. Perry. *Simulation—A Problem Solving Approach.* Reading, MA: Addison-Wesley, 1989.

Jain, R. *The Art of Computer Systems Performance Analysis.* New York: John Wiley & Sons, 1991.

Kant, K. *Introduction to Computer System Performance Evaluation.* New York: McGraw-Hill, 1992.

Karian, Z. *Modern Statistical, Systems, and GPSS Simulation.* 2d ed. Boca Raton, FL: CRC Press, 1998.

Kim, W. "UniSQL/X Unified Relational and Object-Oriented Database System." In *Proceedings of the ACM-SIGMOD International Conference on Management of Data. SIGMOD Record* 23 (June 1994).

————, ed. *Modern Database Systems, The Object Model Interoperability and Beyond.* New York: ACM Press, 1994.

Kreutzer, W. *System Simulation—Programming Styles and Languages.* Reading, MA: Addison-Wesley, 1986.

Kulkarni, K. "Object-Orientation and the SQL Standard." *Journal of Computer Standards and Interfaces* 15 (1993).

Kulkarni, K., M. Carey, L. DeMichiel, N. Mattos, W. Hong, and M. Ubell. "Introducing Reference Types and Cleaning up SQL3's Object Model." ISO WG3 Report X3H2-95-456 (November 1995).

Law, A., and W. D. Kelton. *Simulation Modeling and Analysis.* New York: McGraw-Hill, 1982.

————. *Simulation Modeling and Analysis.* 3d ed. New York: McGraw-Hill 1999.

Lazowska, E. D., J. Zahorjan, G. S. Graham, and K. C. Sevcik. *Quantitative System Performance.* Englewood Cliffs, NJ: Prentice Hall, 1984.

Lilja, D. *Measuring Computer Performance: A Practitioner's Guide.* New York: Cambridge University Press, 2000.

Lindemann, C. *Performance Modeling with Deterministic and Stochastic Petri Nets.* New York: John Wiley & Sons, 1998.

Little, J. D. "A Proof of the Queuing Formula: L = l[W]." *Operations Research* 9 (1961).

Marsan, M., G. Balbo, G. Conte, S. Donatelli, and G. Franceschinis. *Modeling with Generalized Stochastic Petri Nets.* Wiley Series in Parallel Computing. New York: John Wiley & Sons, 1994.

Marti, J. *Object-Oriented Modeling and Simulation with MODSIM III.* CACI Products Company, 1999.

Melton, J., and A. Simon. *Understanding the New SQL: A Complete Guide.* San Mateo, CA: Morgan Kaufmann, 1992.

Melton, J., J. Baur, and K. Kulkarni. "Object ADTs (with Improvements for Value ADTs)." ISO WG3 Report X3H2-91-083 (April 1991).

Melton, J., ed. ISO-ANSI Working Draft. Framework for SQL (SQL/Framework). X3H2-98-518. American National Standards Institute, Technical Committee X3H2 Database (September 1998).

———, ed. ISO-ANSI Working Draft. Database Language SQL—Part 2: Foundation (SQL/Foundation). X3H2-98-519. American National Standards Institute, Technical Committee X3H2 Database (September 1998).

———, ed. ISO-ANSI Working Draft. Call-Level Interface (SQL/CLI). X3H2-98-515. American National Standards Institute, Technical Committee X3H2 Database (September 1998).

———, ed. ISO-ANSI Working Draft. Persistent Stored Modules (SQL/PSM). X3H2-98-520. American National Standards Institute, Technical Committee X3H2 Database (September 1998).

———, ed. ISO-ANSI Working Draft. SQL Host Language Bindings. (SQL/Bindings). X3H2-98-521. American National Standards Institute, Technical Committee X3H2 Database (September 1998).

———, ed. ISO-ANSI Working Draft. SQL Global Transactions Interface (SQL/Transaction). X3H2-98-529. American National Standards Institute, Technical Committee X3H2 Database (September 1998).

———, ed. ISO-ANSI Working Draft. SQL Temporal (SQL/Temporal). X3H2-98-530. American National Standards Institute, Technical Committee X3H2 Database (September 1998).

———, ed. ISO-ANSI Working Draft. SQL Object (SQL/MED). X3H2-98-523. American National Standards Institute, Technical Committee X3H2 Database (September 1998).

———, ed. ISO-ANSI Working Draft. SQL Object Language Bindings (SQL/OLB). X3H2-98-522. American National Standards Institute, Technical Committee X3H2 Database (September 1998).

———, ed. ISO-ANSI Working Draft. SQL Multimedia (SQL/MM) X3H2-98-535. American National Standards Institute, Technical Committee X3H2 Database (September 1998).

————, ed. Accomodating SQL3 and ODMG. X3H2-95-161. American National Standards Institute, Technical Committee X3H2 Database (April 15, 1995).

Menasce, D., and V. Almeida. *Capacity Planning for Web Performance.* Englewood Cliffs, NJ: Prentice Hall, 1998.

————. *Capacity Planning for Web Services—Metrics, Models, and Methods.* Englewood Cliffs, NJ: Prentice Hall, 2001.

Nutt, G. "Operating Systems: A Modern Perspective." 2d ed. Lab Update. Department of Computer Science, University of Colorado, 2002.

O'Neil, P. *Database Principles—Programming and Performance.* San Mateo, CA: Morgan Kaufmann, 1995.

Payne, J. A. *Introduction to Simulation.* New York: McGraw-Hill, 1982.

Peterson, J. *Petri Net Theory and the Modeling of Systems.* Englewood Cliffs, NJ: Prentice Hall, 1981.

Pooch, U. W., and J. A. Wall. *Discrete Event Simulation—A Practical Approach.* Boca Raton, FL: CRC Press, 1993.

Pradhan, D. *Fault-Tolerant Computer Systems Design.* Englewood Cliffs, NJ: Prentice Hall, 1996.

Pritsker, A., and J. O'Reilly. *Simulation with Visual Slam and Awesim.* New York: John Wiley & Sons, 1999.

Ramakrishnan, R. *Database Management Systems.* New York: WCB/McGraw-Hill, 1998.

Richey, J. "Condition Handling in SQL Persistent Stored Modules." *SIGMOD Record* 24 (September 1995).

Robertazzi, T. *Computer Networks and Systems: Queuing Theory and Performance Evaluation.* Springer-Verlag, 1994.

Russell, E. C. "Building Simulation Models with SIMSCRIPT II.5." *CACI* (1983).

Sahner, R., K. Trivedi, and A. Puliafito. *Performance and Reliability Analysis of Computer Systems.* Boston: Kluwer Academic Publishers, 1996.

Schwartz, M. *Computer Communication Network Design and Analysis.* Englewood Cliffs, NJ: Prentice Hall, 1977.

Sessions, R. *Object Persistence: Beyond Object-Oriented Databases.* Englewood Cliffs, NJ: Prentice Hall, 1996.

Sheldon, R. *A First Course in Probability.* Englewood Cliffs, NJ: Prentice Hall, 1998.

Silberschatz, A., P. Galvin, and G. Gagne. *Operating System Concepts.* 6th ed. New York: John Wiley & Sons, 2001.

Stallings, W. *Operating Systems: Internals and Design Principles.* 4th ed. Englewood Cliffs, NJ: Prentice Hall, 2001.

Stone, H. S. *Introduction to Computer Architecture.* SRA, 1980.

Stonebraker, M., ed. *Readings in Database Systems.* 2d ed. San Mateo, CA: Morgan Kaufmann, 1994.

Tanenbaum, A. *Modern Operating Systems.* 2d ed. Englewood Cliffs, NJ: Prentice Hall, 2000.

Trivedi, K. *Probability and Statistics with Reliability, Queuing, and Computer Science Applications.* 2d ed. New York: John Wiley & Sons, 2001.

Ullman, J., and J. Widom. *A First Course in Database Systems.* Englewood Cliffs, NJ: Prentice Hall, 1997.

Wang, J. *Timed Petri Nets, Theory and Application.* Boston: Kluwer Academic Publishers, 1998.

Watson, H. J., and J. H. Blackstone. *Computer Simulation.* New York: John Wiley & Sons, 1989.

Widom, J., and S. Ceri. *Active Database Systems.* San Mateo, CA: Morgan Kaufmann, 1996.

Zeigler, B., H. Praehofer, and T. Kim. *Theory of Modeling and Simulation: Integrating Discrete Event and Continuous Complex Dynamic Systems.* 2d ed. New York: Academic Press, 2000.

# *Index*